The publisher gratefully acknowledges the generous contribution to this book provided by the Ahmanson Foundation Humanities Endowment Fund of the University of California Press Foundation.

TRAVELS AND JOURNAL

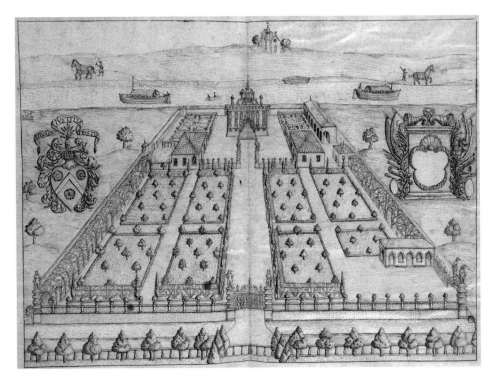

FRONTISPIECE. Bembo villa in the Republic of Venice.

THE TRAVELS AND JOURNAL OF
AMBROSIO BEMBO

Translated from the Italian by Clara Bargellini
Edited and Annotated and with an Introduction
by Anthony Welch

WITH ORIGINAL ILLUSTRATIONS BY G.J. GRÉLOT

UNIVERSITY OF CALIFORNIA PRESS
BERKELEY   LOS ANGELES   LONDON

University of California Press gratefully acknowledges the
support and assistance of the James Ford Bell Library of
the University of Minnesota.

University of California Press, one of the most
distinguished university presses in the United States,
enriches lives around the world by advancing scholarship
in the humanities, social sciences, and natural sciences. Its
activities are supported by the UC Press Foundation and
by philanthropic contributions from individuals and
institutions. For more information, visit www.ucpress.edu.

University of California Press
Berkeley and Los Angeles, California

University of California Press, Ltd.
London, England

Library of Congress Cataloging-in-Publication Data

Bembo, Ambrosio.
    [Viaggio e giornale per parte dell'Asia di quattro anni
incirca fatto da ma Ambrosio Bembo Nobile Veneto
(1671–1675). English.]
    The travels and journal of Ambrosio Bembo /
translated from the Italian by Clara Bargellini ;
edited and annotated and with an introduction
by Anthony Welch.
        p.   cm.
    Includes bibliographical references and index.
    ISBN: 978-0-520-24938-7 (cloth : alk. paper)
    ISBN: 978-0-520-24939-4 (pbk. : alk. paper)
    1. Middle East—Description and travel—Early works
to 1800.   2. Goa, Daman, and Diu (India)—Description
and travel—Early works to 1800.   I. Bargellini, Clara.
II. Welch, Anthony.   III. Title.
DS47.2.B46   2007
915.04'3—dc22   2007000206

Manufactured in the United States of America
15 14 13 12 11 10 09 08 07
11 10 9 8 7 6 5 4 3 2 1
This book is printed on New Leaf EcoBook 50, a 100%
recycled fiber of which 50% is de-inked postconsumer
waste, processed chlorine free. EcoBook 50 is acid free and
meets the minimum requirements of ANSI/ASTM D5634-01
(*Permanence of Paper*).

To HyeSoon Kim
ANTHONY WELCH

To Gabriel Cámara
CLARA BARGELLINI

CONTENTS

ILLUSTRATIONS

PREFACE AND ACKNOWLEDGMENTS

IN 1964, THE JAMES FORD BELL LIBRARY at the University of Minnesota acquired an Italian manuscript with a very long title: *Travels and Journal through Part of Asia during about Four Years Undertaken by Me, Ambrosio Bembo, Venetian Noble.* Written in an elegant hand by a professional scribe and provided with fifty-two line drawings, the manuscript described a four-year trip from Venice to Goa and back again during the seventeenth century. (The manuscript's provenance is briefly presented in the Introduction.) The *Travels and Journal of Ambrosio Bembo* remained nearly unknown until 1973, however, when a single drawing, which had been produced for Bembo's manuscript by the French artist G. J. Grélot, was examined in a book by Anthony Welch published by the Asia Society.[1] In the following year, Grélot's drawings of the great seventeenth-century plaza, the Naqsh-i Jahan (Image of the World) in Isfahan, Iran, were shown in a film commissioned by the National Endowment for the Humanities and the Harvard University Museums. At that time, Clara Bargellini and Anthony Welch, believing that Bembo's story deserved to be well known, began a collaborative effort to publish an English-language translation of the text in a fully annotated and illustrated edition that would make Bembo's text available to an international audience.

A few words about transliteration are in order. Bembo tried carefully to render words and names in his native Italian. Rather than convert his transliterations from Spanish, Portuguese, Turkish, or other languages into

---

1. Anthony Welch, *Shah 'Abbas and the Arts of Isfahan* (New York: Asia Society, 1973).

xi

modern Italian, we have generally chosen to leave them as they are, except for place names for which contemporary toponyms are widely in use.

Both Anthony Welch and Clara Bargellini wish to acknowledge the patient enthusiasm for this project from Jack Parker and Carol Unger of the Bell Library. Likewise, we are grateful for support from our respective academic institutions: Anthony Welch from the University of Victoria, Canada, and Clara Bargellini from the National Autonomous University of Mexico.

We are very pleased to acknowledge the early sharp-eyed attention to this project from Stanley Holwitz of the University of California Press, who immediately understood the significance of Bembo's work and its implications for a greater understanding of the relationship between western Europe and the Islamic world in the seventeenth century. More recently, we were fortunate to have skilled editorial attention from Randy Heyman, Suzanne Knott, and Suzanne Copenhagen.

Huge gratitude goes to Professor Howard Crane at Ohio State University for his exacting perusal of Bembo's travels through the Ottoman Empire and for his catching errors both large and small: thanks to his generous gift of time and expertise, this is a better book.

Most of all we thank our spouses, HyeSoon and Gabriel, to whom we dedicate this book. As we worked on the project, they learned more about Bembo than they ever dreamed they would. Fortunately, they seem to have appreciated him as much as we have.

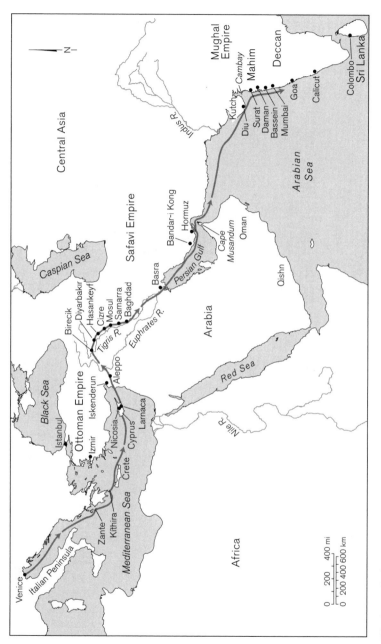

Venice to India.

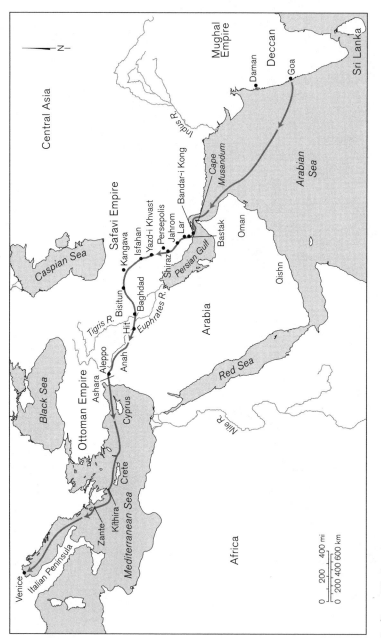

India to Venice.

INTRODUCTION

IT WAS RELATIVELY RARE FOR EUROPEANS in the Middle Ages and Renaissance to travel to the Middle East, Iran, and India, but a few individuals who journeyed to these distant regions, different from their own homelands in language, faith, and customs, wrote accounts that number among our most valuable historical documents. Without the books of the thirteenth-century Venetian Marco Polo or his seventeenth-century compatriot Pietro della Valle, our knowledge of historic West and South Asia would be far poorer. Even in the seventeenth century, extended travel outside one's own linguistic and cultural milieu was far from commonplace, although knowledge gained from travel was increasingly recognized as a valuable commodity. Travelers such as Sir John Chardin or Jean-Baptiste Tavernier were primarily merchants trying to expand commercial ties with Iran and India; they were also keen and critical observers who took the time to write lengthy and detailed accounts of their travels after they returned home.[1] Emissaries such as English diplomats Sir Thomas Herbert and Thomas Roe wrote memoirs that recorded their observations and some of their official dealings,[2] whereas members of Christian religious orders such as the learned Capuchin father Raphaël du Mans in Iran

---

1. John Chardin, *Voyages en Perse* (Amsterdam, 1711), partially translated into English in Sir John Chardin, *Travels in Persia* (London, 1927); J.-B. Tavernier, *The Six Voyages of John Baptiste Tavernier . . . through Turkey and Persia to the Indies* (London, 1678).

2. Thomas Herbert, *Travels in Persia,* ed. William Foster (London: Argonaut, 1928); Thomas Roe, *The Embassy of Sir T. Roe,* ed. William Foster (London: Hakluyt Society, 1922).

composed careful scholarly accounts, in this particular instance on the commission of the government of French king Louis XIV.[3] Du Mans's work was destined for the French government rather than for a wide public and remained in the French national archives unpublished until the nineteenth century; other travelers, however, expected that their books, particularly if such works were illustrated, would earn them royalties. The literate public in contemporary Europe appears to have had a pronounced interest in the great Islamic monarchies to the east.[4] A few individuals also appear to have traveled solely for personal edification. Pietro della Valle left Venice in June 1614 on a journey that would take him across the eastern Mediterranean to the Syrian coast, overland to Iraq, by sea to the western coast of India, and then back again, although on his return journey he chose to travel overland through Iran to Baghdad. He spent some seven years in Iran and did not reach home again until April 1626. His *Viaggi,* a voluminous account of his journey written in the form of letters to a learned friend, was published in Italian between 1650 and 1658 and subsequently translated into French, Dutch, and German. Despite its verbosity, both Goethe and Gibbon praised it.[5] It also awakened the interest of Ambrosio Bembo, a young Venetian who decided to broaden his own knowledge of the world through travel. On August 8, 1671, Bembo set out on a trip that almost exactly followed della Valle's route but brought him home sooner, some three years, eight months, and a week later, on April 15, 1675.

Not too long after his return, Bembo used notes, drawings, and memory to compose an account of his travels, but it was never published, despite

3. Raphaël du Mans, *Estat de la Perse en 1660* (Paris: Leroux, 1890).

4. For a study of travelers to Iran, see Roger Stevens, "European Visitors to the Safavid Court," in *Studies on Isfahan, Iranian Studies,* ed. R. Holod (Boston: Society for Iranian Studies, 1974), vol. 7, 421–57.

5. The *Viaggi* has never been completely translated into English. Della Valle's travels in India were published in 1892 by the Hakluyt Society. A highly readable account of his travels is Wilfrid Blunt, *Pietro's Pilgrimage* (London: James Barrie, 1953). A recent edition and study of part of his travels is Antonio Invernizzi, ed., "Pietro della Valle," in *Viaggio per l'Oriente* (Torino: Edizioni dell' Orso, 2001). For a presentation of key documents for the study of relations between Iran and Venice, see Maria Francesca Tiepolo, ed., *La Persia e la Repubblica di Venezia, Mostra di Documenti dell'Archivio de Stato e della Biblioteca Marciana di Venezia* (Tehran: Central Library of the University of Tehran, 1973).

the fact that it is illustrated with fifty-two line drawings by G. J. Grélot, a French artist and Bembo's traveling companion on his return voyage from Iran to Venice in 1674. As a result, the *Travels and Journal through Part of Asia during about Four Years, Undertaken by Me, Ambrosio Bembo, Venetian Noble,* is a new document of European perceptions of western and southern Asia that is now fortunately emerging from three centuries of obscurity.[6] Bembo realized that his journal could not compete with the travel memoirs of other Venetians such as Marco Polo and della Valle, and he recognized his own and his journal's deficiencies with honest humility: "One should realize, too, that this account might be as boring (if not more so), because it is less distinguished than others. In addition, my youth and inexperience did not permit me to weave an ornamented and ordered story of so many kingdoms and of such great countries. Nevertheless, this diary will be the truthful account of the voyage."

Bembo was born on March 10, 1652, in Venice. He belonged to one of Venice's most distinguished families and was connected to several other powerful families. The great Renaissance scholar and cardinal Pietro Bembo (1470–1547) was the most famous family member, but other Bembos were also highly placed.[7] His uncle Marco, a distinguished military commander, was Venetian consul in Aleppo, the great commercial center of northern Syria, and Orazio Bembo was consul in Cairo. His father was Francesco, and his mother, Caterina, was from the Cornaro family, whose relation had been queen of Cyprus from 1474 to 1489, when she was advised by a previous Marco Bembo. Ambrosio was also related to the Morosini family, who likewise supplied admirals and consuls to the Venetian state. Bembos, Cornaros, and Morosinis, like other leading families in Venice, were deeply involved in the politics and commerce of the eastern Mediterranean and were no strangers to the power and prestige of the Ottoman sultanate, on whose trade much of their own prosperity depended. Although Ambrosio

6. See Anthony Welch, "Safavi Iran as Seen through Venetian Eyes," in *Society and Culture in the Early Modern Middle East, Studies on Iran in the Safavid Period,* ed. Andrew Newman (Leiden, Boston: Brill, 2003), 97–121; and Anthony Welch, *Shah 'Abbas and the Arts of Isfahan* (New York: Asia Society, 1973), 104, 117.

7. The widely used Bembo typeface bears the family name. It was designed about 1495 by the celebrated goldsmith and engraver Francesco Griffo for the Venetian publisher and printer Aldus Manutius.

Bembo was proud of his family, his *Travels and Journal* seldom refers to them. He seems to have been an open and polite young man, conscious of his social position and its responsibilities but not particularly given to haughtiness. He speaks only once of his upbringing and education, when, near the end of his book, he refers to the new Venetian consul in Aleppo, who succeeded his uncle in 1675: Francesco Foscari, "my friend, fellow student, and older companion in the School of the Somaschi Fathers."[8] Otherwise, his aristocratic family and friends are mentioned only in the final pages, when he carefully lists the people who welcomed him on his homecoming.

Bembo was enrolled in the Venetian navy when he was very young. At the age of seventeen he took part in the Venetian republic's conflict with the Ottoman sultanate in the last year of the 1648–1669 War of Candia; he was steersman on a galley, the *Fontana d'Oro,* in the service of a squadron commander. He was young but evidently anxious to distinguish himself in a military post of this sort, and his appointment suggests that he was talented in addition to being well connected. The naval forces were under the command of Taddeo Morosini, whom he calls "the lord of our house and Captain of the Navy." The Venetian army in Crete was led by Francesco Morosini. During this initial period of service to the republic, Venice suffered defeat in 1669 when it withdrew its forces from Crete. Ambrosio's Morosini relatives continued to assist him during and after his travels. The Venetian ship *Confidenza,* captained by Taddeo Morosini, took him on the first leg of his journey east, and after his return he served under Francesco Morosini in the republic's 1686–1687 Peloponnesian campaign. But in 1671, with the War of Candia behind him, Ambrosio Bembo was clearly bored. He was too young to enter the Grand Council of Venice, the assembly of the nobility, and he did not want to wait until he was twenty-five, when he could assume his rightful place there. When his uncle Marco was appointed consul in Aleppo, he invited Ambrosio to accompany him, aware of his nephew's frustration. They left Venice on August 8, 1671. For Ambrosio it was the beginning of a voyage far longer than he anticipated, and even though his introduction to the *Travels and Journal* glowingly asserts that

8. A charitable religious organization principally dedicated to education, the Order of the Somaschi Fathers was founded in the sixteenth century by St. Jerome Edmiliani. Prior to the French Revolution, it operated 119 colleges in Rome, Lombardy, Venice, and France.

travel is edifying and broadening, it seems likely that his original intent was to stay in Aleppo: "The world is a great book, which, when perused attentively, proffers teachings and delights with its variety. True, one must tolerate expense, discomfort, and danger, but the effort, if blessed by fortune, brings its reward. Idleness eats away at all virtue and is the worst companion for youth."

BEMBO'S JOURNEY

They arrived in the Levantine port of Tripoli on September 21 and proceeded to Aleppo, which they reached on October 29. Ambrosio remained in Aleppo for fifteen months, until January 1673, and studied the city and its society well enough that his account of these months is a very valuable source of information about the ancient city. Among the illustrations to his book are a splendid panorama of Aleppo and a drawing of the city's Great Mosque. Bembo provided the names, titles, and responsibilities of the Ottoman officials, and he obviously found amusing the struggles over precedence and protocol that occupied the lives of the diplomatic corps. He paid particular attention to architecture, carefully describing the city's gates, walls, doors, bathhouses, and bazaars and reporting that the city had about three hundred mosques.

But Bembo grew bored once more, and, excited by the stories about India told him by a visiting Portuguese Franciscan traveling back to Goa, the capital of Portuguese India, he decided to set out for points farther east. Well supplied with money, equipment, letters of credit to merchants and to Capuchin and Carmelite missionaries along the way, Ambrosio left the security of his uncle's residence in Aleppo for what he knew would be a dangerous journey. "Thus I courageously left the sight of Aleppo and began my trip." He had good reason to be apprehensive.

On January 3, 1673, he set out with a large caravan from Aleppo through southern Turkey to Diyarbakır. From there, he descended the Tigris on a river raft, called a *kalak,* to Baghdad. Bembo, an experienced sailor, was fascinated by its construction. The wooden frame rested on three goatskins filled with air; it floated effectively, if somewhat precariously, on the fast-moving river. In Baghdad the raft was taken apart and sold for its wood. Bembo reported that the famous metropolis of Baghdad had five city gates and that it took about two and a half hours to walk around the outer walls. He found the streets to be narrow and dirty but praised the large, solidly built bazaars. He was also very impressed with the city's mosques and their colorful glazed tiles. He resided at the Capuchin mission, and his reliance on the Christian orders and their mission houses continued throughout his trip; in Iraq, Iran, and India he mostly stayed with Capuchins, Augustinians, Theatines, Franciscans, Dominicans, or Carmelites, who were sustaining a Catholic presence and laying the groundwork for subsequent European colonial expansion.

After a few days in the city he hired another river raft to take him south to Basra on the Persian/Arabian Gulf. He was very impressed with the high level of commercial activity and with Basra's diverse population: Arabs, Turks, Indians, Jews, Armenians, Jacobites, and European merchants (Italians, French, English, Dutch, and Portuguese) who came to Basra with spices and jewels from ports in South and Southeast Asia. In Basra he booked passage on a ship that took him to the port of Bandar-i Kong in southeastern Iran, where he was able to find another ship that took him to western India, which he reached in April 1673. With the exception of a brief visit to Mumbai (Bombay), he spent more than a year in the various Portuguese colonies on India's west coast and resided most of the time in Christian mission houses in Daman, Surat, Mumbai, and Goa.

He was intrigued by the European strongholds in or adjacent to Gujarat, and he presented an encapsulated history of Gujarat and the great commercial center of Cambai. His source must have been one of the Christian fathers who knew the 1611–1612 *Mir'at Sikandar ibn Muhammad,* one of the key histories of the region. Like della Valle before him, Bembo chose not to visit the great cities of the Mughal Empire. He was well aware of the military struggle between the emperor Awrangzeb and Shivaji, the brilliant leader of the western India Maratha rebellion against the Mughals; and he may have concluded that inland travel was unsafe. On May 11 in Daman he witnessed the arrival of an ambassador from the Mughal emperor, and on May 12 a rival envoy from Shivaji, the great opponent of Awrangzeb, also came there. The Portuguese were anxious to keep their distance from the conflict. So, too, was Bembo, and on May 13 he left for the major commercial entrepôt of Surat, the richest city in India and one of the world's most active commercial centers. He was keenly interested in the organization of the French, English, and Dutch trading companies and noted that they maintained large fortified houses for their goods and their citizens. The city's diversity fascinated him, and he remarked on people who came from several European countries, the Middle East, Central Asia, South Asia, and Africa. He was deeply curious about religious doctrines, and he outlined the Hindu caste system and described *sadhus* and their practices. Everywhere in the city he saw Parsees: "When the Arabs conquered Iran in the seventh century, they fled to India. They worship fire, the sun, and the moon and maintain a constantly burning fire." Elephants he saw for the first time and noted their importance in daily life and in warfare.

After a brief stay in Bassein, Bembo went to Mumbai, only recently established by the English East India Company. The port's size, security, and beauty impressed him enormously, and he correctly assumed that Mumbai and the English would soon become a threat to the Portuguese control of trade with India. After a few days in Mumbai he proceeded to Goa. The Portuguese colony's Christian missions were rich and powerful, but, he noted, the missionaries were conspicuously inattentive to the poverty of the people and the run-down condition of the city. He stayed in Goa for a number of months, and his book provides detailed information on customs, produce, religious sects, and the activities of the Inquisition. Bembo generally disliked the Portuguese, and he faulted them for racism and intolerance. He seems to have had no regrets when in February 1674 he sailed back across the Arabian Sea and the Persian Gulf to Bandar-i Kong, which he reached on May 19. The trip across the Arabian Sea was overlong and filled with apprehension about naval attacks from Oman.

Although he knew it would take longer and would be more dangerous, he chose not to return to Basra by ship but to follow della Valle's example and travel overland from Bandar-i Kong in southern Iran to Shiraz and Isfahan, the capital of the Safavi Empire. His observations on Iran and the Iranians are among the most interesting and important in his book.

In Shiraz he remarked on the beauty of the principal mosque but described the appearance of houses and of the main bazaar at greater length:

> Most of the bazaars are large, beautiful, and majestic, covered by vaults of baked bricks. The houses are low, and from the outside they seem to be poor, because they have earthen walls and no windows along the road. But inside they are of baked bricks and are similar in structure to those of Turkey and Europe. In addition, they are decorated and ornamented with various works in low relief on colored and gilt plaster. The beams, too, are sculptured and painted with much gold. Some also have the walls covered with porcelains.

He particularly noted the kilometer-long avenue that extended from the city center to the Royal Garden *(Bagh-i Shah)*.

One of the traditional centers of Iranian culture, the city had about

40,000 Muslim households, but Bembo noted that there were also households of other persuasions, notably Armenians, Jews, Nestorians, and other Christians. He praised Shirazis for their love of learning and the arts, and he even commented that their knowledge of the sciences was based upon ancient authors rather than contemporary ones. The city's steel mirrors and glassware pleased him, and he liked Shirazi perfume so much that he took some back with him to Venice. He also appreciated the good food available in the city:

> Among all the bazaars the best organized was the bazaar of sweets. They make many of these, and they are of good quality, the equal of our Italian ones. I walked through the bazaar of foods, where they sell all sorts of cooked foods. . . . The bread is rather good and white. They make it in large flat cakes with fennel. The wine is the best in all of Persia. They make a lot of it. Even the present king drinks a lot of it, although it is strictly forbidden to his subjects. All the countries provide themselves with wine for their armies here. They ship it to India. Thus the French, Dutch, English, and Portuguese have a license to buy what they need, as well as an agent who keeps it, and every country has a house where he lives; they keep it well furnished so that it also serves for the lodging of [members of] their company when they happen to be in that city. The Armenian Giovanni Belli had the commission for the Portuguese. At the proper time he takes the wine to Kong at his expense in cases of ten flasks, each one of which contains a pound and a quarter of wine. The superintendent pays him twenty-five 'abbasi per case. He then sells it for double that price to the fleet, and the earnings are for him. However, when the Armenian brings him more, the superintendent is obliged to sell it at fifty 'abbasi to anyone, and the earnings from that go to the Armenians.

On July 3, after a week and a half, he left Shiraz and traveled north toward Isfahan with several companions. On the second day they turned off the Isfahan road to visit the great Achaemenid site of Persepolis, which he described in detail and which Grélot drew.

> In the façade are two stairways to go up, one from the south and one from the north. They end on a small square level area which is the width of the same stairs. At that point both stairways continue to climb in the opposite direction. . . . In the mountain face abutting the plain and in the middle of the natural crevices there are two structures at some distance from one another. . . . carved in low relief in the mountain itself, . . . various tombs that are commonly called the tombs of Darius.

He also visited the nearby Achaemenid and Sasanian site of Naqsh-i Rustam.

His journey north from Persepolis was difficult. On July 14 he and his companions stopped for the day at the mountain town of Yazd-i Khvast: "because of the narrowness of the place [it] has houses one on top of the other." Two days later they reached the extensive ruins of Qumisheh, and his account is particularly valuable since scarcely any of the ancient city is extant today:

> It was, in effect, a city in ancient times. There are vestiges of many tombs in the form of towers, where one sees many stone lions. There are also remains of many bazaars and caravanserais, of which ten still stand. I went to most of them. . . . I found many kinds of fruit, particularly some very good melons. I saw many ruins of ancient houses and buildings.

He reached the capital city of Isfahan on July 18 and was immensely impressed by the appearance and wealth of the metropolis early in the reign of Shah Sulayman.

> I entered a very great plain and saw Isfahan at a distance. It seems rather a delightful wood because of the multitude of trees that obstruct the view of the buildings . . . Before entering the city, I passed a large and very long street, similar to that of Shiraz . . . Along its sides, however, are the walls of the orchards, and along the road itself many trees are distributed in an orderly manner. Water flows on both sides and makes that passage delightful. At the end of this street I crossed a bridge that the Europeans called the Bridge of Shiraz . . . It is all made of fine bricks with twenty-seven small arches. . . . Above the arches there is a very beautiful cornice of porcelain of various design in very fine work.

He went immediately to the Carmelite mission, which he described as "rather comfortable, with a lower cloister with twelve rooms and with a good dormitory above." And like other travelers, he referred to Shah 'Abbas I's interest in printed books that the Carmelites tried to encourage: "There is a room that served as a printing shop. It was unique in those parts and had been introduced to please the Shah 'Abbas, who had wanted it. They gave him a printed book of the Four Gospels and an Arabic alphabet, but at present the press is all ruined."

Shortly afterward, he met the affable scholar and Capuchin father Raphaël du Mans, whom Bembo, like the Isfahanis, admired for his knowledge of mathematics and of the Persian language. Apparently Bembo did not know that only fourteen years earlier du Mans had been commissioned by the French government to undertake an encyclopedic study of Iran, *Estat de la Perse en 1660*. In addition to du Mans, there were many other Europeans in the city, among them merchants and artisans. Bembo met some French goldsmiths and watchmakers working for Shah Sulayman:

> They have their shops near the royal palace. They are much esteemed by the king and well treated. Besides giving them houses and money, he provides them with monthly provisions of every sort of food of the country. The provisions are very abundant, and he also gives them more for every new piece of work that they do. They are at liberty to work for other individuals, whom they charge considerably, when they are not working for the king.

He also met and took an instant dislike to the merchant and diplomat Jean Chardin, whose manners and deviousness held no appeal for him. Bembo noted that Chardin was well supplied with cash and had already published a book on the coronation of Shah Sulayman. Chardin made no attempt to conceal his maltreatment of G. J. Grélot, a modestly talented French artist whom he had hired to illustrate his own voyages. Because Chardin refused to pay him, Grélot was penniless and could not leave his service and return to Europe. Bembo, who saw the utility of acquiring both a traveling companion who could cook and an artist who could document his journey, offered him a job. Grélot jumped at the chance and joined Bembo with his drawings and talent, leaving Chardin, who was not at all pleased. As a result, only seven of Grélot's drawings illustrate the Anglo-French traveler's *Voyages*, those Chardin presumably held onto after the artist abandoned him. Bembo's book contains fifty-one Grélot illustrations, including those printed by Chardin.

Bembo was enormously impressed with Isfahan's size, diversity, and architecture.

> This city is large in itself and also very big due to the three citadels, or suburbs, that are about a mile from the city and can really be called contiguous and united, because they continue the gardens of the city itself. . . . Besides the Persian natives of the city, there are many from subject countries, and there are 12,000 Indians, partly Muslims and partly Gentiles, all rich merchants. . . . In addition to these, Arabs and Turks from many places are engaged in business there. Also from Europe there are Muscovites, Poles, French, English, Portuguese, and Dutch. . . .

There are, however, many buildings of good architecture, among which are the caravanserais, which are many, and three hundred baths and quantities of bazaars with large stone arches, arranged in good order. . . . Their main streets are long and beautiful to look at, but the other streets are terrible, since they are not only narrow but also full of refuse and sewage. . . .

Another day I went to see the maydan of the Shah . . . This maydan is the King's Plaza, and it is the principal one in the whole city. For size and beauty it surpasses many of the most beautiful in Europe . . . All around, it is surrounded by a building of equal arches in a double order, one above the other. The arches of the upper level have very beautiful openings with imaginative ornaments of the same material. The [upper] arches serve as dwelling places for merchants, and the lower arches as porticoes under which are bazaars with shops on one side and the other. . . . Near these porticoes runs a stream of water that surrounds the entire plaza. . . . About two-thirds of the way along one of the long sides there is a façade with a gate to the palace of the king, which is not too big in its perimeter, being a little more than a mile. . . . On top of the whole construction there is a very large hall or loggia, open on three sides . . . in it the king gives public audiences to ambassadors and other people, and he banquets there publicly. . . . On the other side of the plaza and facing the palace of the king there is a mosque with dome and façade in fine polychrome porcelain. At both ends of the Square there is a beautiful fountain, and at the side that is closest to the palace there is the royal mosque . . . On the other side there is a large and majestic arch through which one passes to other bazaars. . . . A very beautiful apartment of the king's that is called Bab-i Bulbul is . . . open on three sides with arches and colonnades that are covered with sheets of Venetian mirrors. . . . The broad road called Ciahar Bagh ends in a beautiful bridge, commonly called the Bridge of Julfa.

Bembo described goods, customs, and clothing, and he was fascinated by the doctrinal differences among the Muslim and Christian populations of Isfahan. He also provided an abridged history of the Safavi dynasty that he presumably learned from du Mans.

After more than two months in Isfahan, Bembo, accompanied by Grélot, joined a large caravan and left the city on September 22, traveling toward northwestern Iran. On October 7 they stayed in Kangavar and spent a day wandering around the second- and third-century ruins, which Bembo compared favorably with Persepolis. On October 10 his group lingered at Bisitun, where Bembo admired the rock relief of Darius's victory over Gaumata. Grélot drew the whole pictorial scene as well as a copy of some of the trilingual inscriptions. On the following day they reached the great Sasanian site of Taq-i Bustan. Bembo was fascinated by the friezes cut into the stone of the two rock grottoes, described them at great length, and helped Grélot produce five drawings. His detailed account is the earliest illustrated European record of the artistic remains there.

Bembo and Grélot were able to join a caravan heading toward Hamadan and Baghdad, and they spent enough time in Baghdad for Grélot to produce a panoramic view of the city. But they were anxious to get back to Aleppo. Marco Bembo's term as consul was all but over, and Ambrosio did not want to miss the opportunity of traveling home with his uncle. Despite the very real danger of Bedouin attack, Bembo, Grélot, and a single guide decided to ride overland from Baghdad, for the most part along the Euphrates River. They reached Aleppo without incident on November 22, where they were gratefully welcomed by Marco Bembo. They need not have proceeded in such haste after all, however, for the new consul had not yet arrived. Some two months later, once more a member of his uncle's entourage, Ambrosio left Aleppo on January 30, 1675. The land and sea journey, much of which Grélot rendered in drawings, lasted two and a half months, and they arrived in Venice on April 15, 1674. Bembo changed out of his Turkish clothes, shaved his beard, and was joyfully welcomed home by family and friends. He was twenty-three years old and a world traveler like few others.

Two years later he entered the Grand Council of State and subsequently served as a naval officer in the republic's military campaigns against the Ottomans. On July 4, 1680, he was appointed commander of a ship, and in 1683 he was promoted to governor of the Adriatic Sea, with the primary charge of keeping out the Barbary pirates. In May 1685 he led a convoy of twenty-two ships to Corfu in support of an army under the command of his relative Francesco Morosini, and in 1686 he was appointed commander in Corfu. It was not a happy post, for in April 1687 he had to defend himself against a charge of abuse of power. Ten years later he was elected superintendent of arms in Venice, and in 1703 superintendent of the arsenal. His health may have suffered from these many naval campaigns, for he died in 1705 at the age of fifty-three. He was buried in the Church of San Salvador. His journal is the primary source of information about his life and allows us to glimpse the personality that supported this distinguished, although not atypical, Venetian aristocratic career. His passion for archaeology continued after his journey to the

Middle East and India and was recognized by Bartolomeo Dotti in a sonnet that he dedicated to Bembo.[9]

The *Travels and Journal* was composed not long after his return, although he gives no clear indication of exactly when he wrote down his impressions. But after leaving Bembo's service, Grélot traveled to Constantinople and prepared text and drawings for his own important book on the great city, *Relation nouvelle d'un voyage de Constantinople,* published in Paris in 1680.[10] In discussing the successes of the Venetians against the Ottomans he offers some remarks about the Bembo family:

> I am the more obliged to make the *Relation,* as being engag'd in my acknowledgments to those two illustrious Persons to whose kindnesses and company in my Travels I was so peculiarly bound, as being highly honoured in their affection. These were the Lords *Mark* and *Ambrose Bembo,* both Gentlemen of *Venice,* who have always performed great Exploits, and daily add to the Fame and Splendour of the noble and ancient Family of the Bembos.
>
> The first of these two noble *Venetians* was General of the Gallies[11] of the Commonwealth of *Venice* in this Expedition. The second is a young Gentleman his Nephew, who at the Age of eighteen years, perceiving that the leisure of the Republic in Peace could not afford him matter sufficient to exercise his active Courage, generously quitted the pleasures of a sedentary Life, and betook himself to five or six years travel over the Eastern World. And in these perils and dangers he the more readily engag'd himself, to the end, that upon his return to his Country with mature Age and well-purchas'd Experience, he might render himself the fitter for such Employments which the Senate might deem worthy his merit. I had the happiness to meet him at *Hispahan,* returning from the *Indies,* whence I also had the honour to enjoy his Company all the way into *Europe.* In pursuance of which Journey, we came first into *Syria* to his most illustrious Uncle *Mark Bembo's* Residence, then Embassadour for the Republic, and so at length ariv'd at Venice, where I was shew'd in the Palace of the Bembos the whole Expedition of the

9. For greater detail on Bembo's naval career, see *Dizionario Biografico degli Italiani* (Rome: Instituto Giovanni Treccani, 1966), vol. 8, 101–2.

10. Published in Dutch in the Netherlands in 1681 and in English (London: J. Playford) in 1683 under the title *A Late Voyage to Constantinople.*

11. Galleys.

Dardanels, set forth in a large piece of Painting, and rarely well done; and so from those who were there present, I had this account.[12]

Since Grélot made a drawing (frontispiece) of the Bembo villa for inclusion as a frontispiece to the *Travels and Journal*,[13] it seems reasonable to assume that Ambrosio composed the book soon after his return in 1675, while Grélot was still in his service to supply illustrations, even of scenes and events, such as those in western India, where the artist had not been present. From his own remarks it seems that Ambrosio reread the *Viaggi* of Pietro della Valle before he even started writing his own account, and he modestly indicated that he was writing for the edification of those who might some day want to make a similar trip; for that reason he even appended a detailed expense account so that future travelers would be aware of how much money and what equipment they would need. Knowing that other travel memoirs had been published, he probably had the intention of seeing his own book in print, but he evidently did not pursue this ambition, even though his family's wealth and status would surely have made it easily within his reach. His book remained in manuscript form, copied in an excellent hand by an unidentified scribe (fig. 1); some marginal notes, as well as the expense account, in less accomplished penmanship, were presumably Bembo's own additions.

There appear to have been two manuscript copies of Bembo's book. One passed into the possession of the Gradenigo family in Venice, where it was studied by Iacopo Morelli, who privately printed some remarks about it in 1820.[14] In his remarks Morelli noted that there were two copies of Bembo's manuscript, the one that he examined, which belonged to Joseph Gradenigo,

12. *A Late Voyage*, 11–12.

13. The Palladian mansion sits at the end of a formal garden. On the left is shown the Bembo family arms with the words *Redolent Iustitiae Fructus* and on the right a group of military trophies with the words *Gratitudinis Aeternae Monumentum Ponebat G. I. Grélot.*

14. Iacopo Morelli, *Operette ora insieme raccolte con opuscoli di antichi scrittori* (Venice: Alvisopoli, 1820), vol. 2, 85–123. Morelli published some passages from the manuscript that related to the pre-Islamic Iranian antiquities of Bisitun and Kermanshah. For a brief discussion of Morelli's remarks on Bembo's book, see Maria Francesca Tiepolo, *La Persia e la Repubblica di Venezia,* no. 134, 59. The Gradenigo copy of Bembo's book is referred to in the

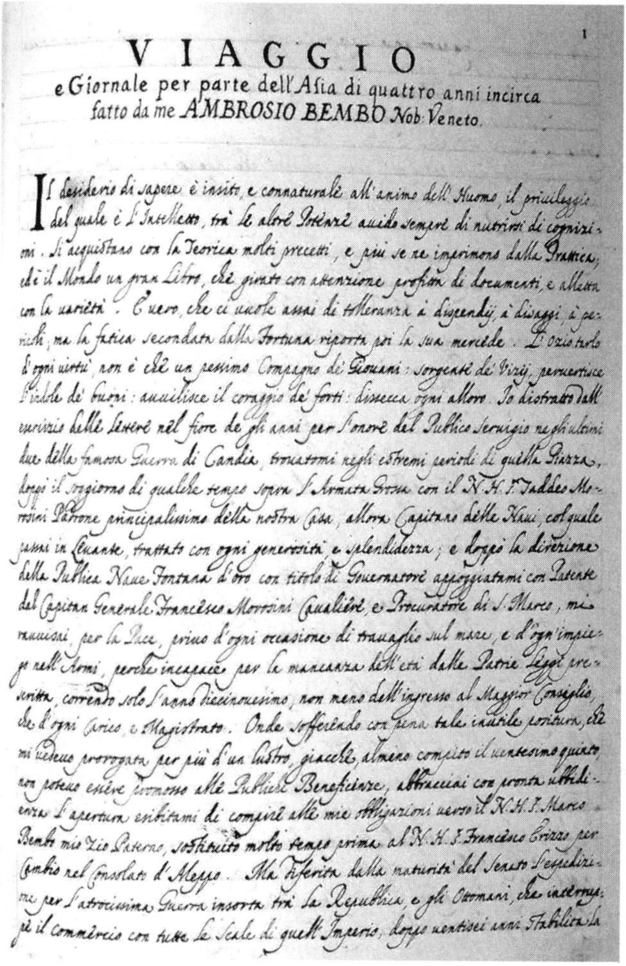

VIAGGIO
e Giornale per parte dell'Asia di quattro anni incirca
fatto da me AMBROSIO BEMBO Nob. Veneto.

FIGURE 1. Folio 1 of text.

and a second, apparently abridged, version in the possession of Abbé Celotti. The Gradenigo manuscript with its fifty-two line drawings was examined by M. A. Langlès, whose praise in a letter addressed to the abbé is now bound with the volume. Langlès regretted that he had not been able

entry on Ambrosio Bembo in the *Enciclopedia Italiana* (Rome: Instituto Giovanni Treccani, 1930) and is clearly to be identified with our volume.

to consult it when he was preparing his own edition of Chardin's travels.[15] The Gradenigo manuscript left Paris in the late nineteenth or early twentieth century, for its ornate, gold-stamped brown morocco binding is English of that date and bears the inscription "Drawings by Grélot" on the spine. The manuscript's 316 pages are gilt edged, ruled, and margined; they measure 38 centimeters by 27.5 centimeters. The text is written thirty-two lines to the page, and the paper is fine and heavy, lightly brown in color. Marginal notes include dates of entries and subject indicators to aid the reader. The volume was purchased in 1964 by the James Ford Bell Library of the University of Minnesota from Frank Hammond, Bookseller, Sutton Coldfield near Birmingham, England.

The second copy, which belonged to Abbé Celotti, has only recently been rediscovered.

HISTORY

The Venice that Ambrosio Bembo knew was a major Mediterranean power, struggling with the Ottomans for empire and control of trade. Its history during the seventeenth century is marked by notable failures, such as the War of Candia, and by equally notable successes, such as the campaigns in Dalmatia and in the Peloponnesos. If war characterized one part of the relationship between Venice and the Ottomans, peace, prosperity, and mutually beneficial commerce defined another. With its Mediterranean maritime presence and its commercial links to western Europe, Venice was dependent upon the Ottoman Empire's domination of the western terminus of overland trade routes from eastern and southern Asia and from eastern Africa. Ottoman armies or their surrogates controlled Anatolia, Syria, the Levant, Iraq, Arabia, and Egypt, and fleets of the Ottomans or their Arab allies in Oman patrolled the Red Sea, the Persian/Arabian Gulf, and the Arabian Sea. But the days of Ottoman and Arab supremacy over this vital and valuable trade link were numbered. Although Vasco da Gama's navigation around Africa in 1498 did not engender an immediate commercial revolution, it did lead to the establishment of a string of Portuguese forts and trading settlements on the eastern coast of Africa, and Portuguese colonies such as Sofala, Mozambique,

15. This ten-volume publication (Paris, 1811) was the first complete edition of Chardin's travels and included a volume of plates.

Mombasa, and Malinde challenged long-established Arab mercantile communities in Lamu and Kilwa. It also quickly led to the development of equally valuable Portuguese settlements, such as Diu, Daman, and Goa, along the west coast of India. During the second half of the seventeenth century, this Portuguese expansion was contested by the sultans of Oman, who, supported by the Ottomans, also tried to dominate politics and commerce on the east African coast, for across the Arabian Sea was the west coast of India and, via the Maldive Islands and Sri Lanka, the more-distant routes to eastern India, Southeast Asia, and China. The prize was control over the immensely lucrative spice trade, as well as commerce in many other resources and manufactures, such as ceramics, silk, and textiles. The possible loss of Arab power over this trade was a direct and potentially devastating threat to the Ottomans, whose economy significantly depended upon the maritime route that made their lands the transit routes for goods. Thus Ottoman and Arab fleets operated in the Persian/Arabian Gulf, the Arabian Sea, and even the Indian Ocean to counter the expansion and consolidation of Portuguese power.

Bembo was well aware of this conflict, as well as newer ones with other European powers anxious to take over what the Portuguese had seized. Portugal's maritime success and its immediate cultural rewards aroused envy and competition. The Dutch were among the most active, but in 1672, shortly before Bembo's visit, the English East India Company established a permanent military and commercial presence in Mumbai. Although Venice was still an important Mediterranean naval power, it was not an active player in this wider game; it did not have the resources or the population to support a significant role beyond the Mediterranean. The young Venetian traveler was therefore recording a period of great political change with long-range implications, but during a time of transition in which Venice now played a lesser part. Bembo was an educated observer, but we cannot reasonably expect someone so young to be a profound or incisive thinker about politics on a grand scale, and like most individuals in a time of change, he did not perceive that it was going on. He did not seem personally affected by or even aware of the enormous long-term damage to Venice's wealth and to its position as middleman that was occasioned by the western European takeover of commerce and shipping in the Indian Ocean from Ottoman, Arab, and Indian merchants. Although he knew that the Ottomans viewed the erosion of their role in the Indian Ocean as a major threat, he did not realize the impact that this loss to the Ottoman Empire would have on Venice, culturally tied to western Europe but economically linked with the Ottomans. What Ambrosio Bembo recorded was the aftermath of earlier European victories and European consolidation and expansion of power in India and farther east to the detriment not just of the Ottomans but also of Venice. In this sense he did not recognize that an era had ended and that, as Venice's role in world trade and politics rapidly drew to a close, he was one of the last of the great Venetian travelers.

From the vantage point of the early twenty-first century, it is also clear that it was a period of imminent decline for all three great Islamic empires, as well as for Venice. Western and central Europe indulged in a notably romantic mystique about Safavi Iran and Mughal India in the seventeenth century. They were less inclined to do so with the Ottomans, who were more familiar, too close for comfort, and an ongoing military threat. Carpets, ceramics, and luxury textiles were imported from Iran; spices, jewels, and textiles were favored goods from India. Both the Safavi and Mughal empires were perceived in Europe in terms of wealth and absolute power, images that appealed to European royalty. August the Strong of Saxony (1694–1733), for instance, commissioned, at very great expense, a miniature procession of his contemporary, the emperor Awrangzeb (r. 1658–1707), complete with courtiers, soldiers, and elephants, numbering many dozens of enameled and bejeweled figurines. Mughal miniatures were used to decorate the walls of a gallery in the Viennese palace of Schönbrunn; Rembrandt was fascinated by Mughal drawings and paintings; and European aristocracy commissioned from Iran so-called Polonaise carpets with their own coats of arms in the center.

Christian missionaries and Christian merchants expanded their activities in the Safavi and Mughal states. Bembo accompanied Franciscans who were traveling to India, stayed with Capuchins, Franciscans, Augustinians, Theatines, Dominicans, and Discalced Carmelites in Iran and India, and observed the power of the Jesuits in Portuguese India. Shah 'Abbas in Iran (1587–1629) was notably friendly toward emissaries of Christian states whose aid he sought against the Ottomans, and he encouraged the indigenous Christian Armenian community of Iran to serve as commercial intermediaries with European merchants. Prints by European artists including Albrecht Dürer were admired in Iran and India, and illustrated Bibles were shown to both the Safavi shah 'Abbas and the Mughal emperor Akbar (1556–1605), who discussed religious issues with visiting Jesuits and accepted a copy of the illustrated *Royal Polyglot Bible* of 1568–1573, printed by Christopher Plantin in Antwerp. These illustrations, along with others by European artists, exerted a substantial influence on the work of Safavi and Mughal artists. Christian missions also served other important roles. Some of their residents, such as Father Raphaël du Mans, were trusted sources of information for governments at home and were instrumental in the development of European academic expertise about Islamic societies. Mission houses served as post offices for traveling Europeans, and it was through their good offices that Bembo was sometimes able to use his letters of credit to get funds on his journey. They were also hostels where visitors could find safe and somewhat familiar accommodation, speak their own language, pick up mail and news from home, get locally useful advice, and meet other Europeans. Without them it would not have been possible for so many adventurous Europeans to travel in Turkey, Iran, and India. Bembo's bitterly critical remarks about the Jesuits in Goa indicate that he recognized the missions were also instruments of European colonial expansion and exploitation, and his journal demonstrates in very tangible ways how important they were to colonialism. Bembo described how the networks of the missions provided him with specialized news about the rest of the world while he was in Isfahan.

> I had much other news and was surprised at the differences in the news coming from Europe. The news comes through the Capuchin fathers, the Jesuits, and others, besides through letters of various individuals . . . To the Augustinians and Carmelites comes all the news from the East Indies and from Portugal. The Carmelites also get news from Turkey which arrives from their missions in those parts; they also get the reports and councils of Venice. . . . These things got communicated from one to another, and many of the Persians themselves, curious about happenings in Europe, go to interrogate those fathers in their convents. The fathers explain everything to them in Persian, and in return the Persians tell them what is new in the country. Thus, although late and with some alterations, European accounts reach Isfahan, as does news of all the world.

Seventeenth-century Islam was no more a political or religious unity than was Christendom. The Ottoman Empire (1281–1924) was strongly Sunni and persecuted Shi'i Muslims. It was a huge, highly centralized state that encompassed Turks, Arabs, Kurds, Armenians, Greeks, Albanians, and Slavs, among others, with much of its still very formidable military power dependent upon the janissary corps, soldiers who by the middle of the seventeenth century were recruited from free-born Muslims and were often unruly and sometimes unreliable.

The Ottomans' great opponent to the east was the Safavi Empire (1501–1722). With Sunni states to the west, north, and east, Iran was stridently Shi'i, and its shah was recognized as head of the Safavi mystical Shi'i religious order. As centralized as the Ottoman state, Safavi Iran was a land-based empire with no significant naval forces. Safavi commercial policy favored traditional overland trade routes, and enormous sums were spent on building impressive caravan inns (caravanserais), which Bembo much admired, to protect merchants and their goods and to serve as entrepôts where they could sell their goods. Iran therefore posed no threat to Europe's maritime expansion, and it offered the possibility of military alliances against the Ottomans. The Safavis needed to cooperate with European powers. Thus, despite occasional friction, the Portuguese maintained small trading settlements along Iran's southern coast, such as Bandar-i Kong, where Bembo stayed before embarking for India. Bembo enjoyed Iran far more than he did Turkey, perhaps because they had a common enemy. He also admired the safety of Iranian roads and the official protection given to travelers.

Muslim invaders founded the first Islamic sultanate in northern India in 1192, and although Muslims remained a minority in predominantly Hindu India, rulers in the Delhi sultanate and in other sultanates in northern and central India expanded Islam's role and power in India over more than three centuries. Like their predecessors, the Mughal dynasty (1526–1858) fostered a system of cooperation between the Hindu and Muslim aristocracies; this system was most efficacious under the emperors Akbar and Jahangir (1605–1627), who encouraged toleration between the various religious communities and supported a centralized and expansionist state. Under Awrangzeb the system broke down, and major rebellions broke out in central and western India, particularly in Maharastra, where the Maratha leader Shivaji contested Mughal authority and occasionally threatened European interests. Because the Portuguese settlements occupied only a thin strip of coastal lands otherwise surrounded by Shivaji's domains, these political and military uncertainties may have been behind Bembo's cautious visit to India. Like Pietro della Valle before him, he remained in the Portuguese settlements on the western coast and had no direct contact with either the Marathas or the Mughals. He chose not to travel inland to the great Mughal cities of Agra and Delhi, though many of his contemporaries, such as Tavernier, did. Perhaps he was exhausted or had seen enough of the world and wished to remain in somewhat familiar surroundings.

PERSONALITY

Ambrosio Bembo was a keen traveler whose excellent powers of observation became more developed as he traveled. He carefully described landscape, cities, architecture, food, shipping, officialdom, coinage, costumes, and customs, and he must have kept notes, for he recorded exact dates and times of day when certain events took place. He was proud of the knowledge gained from his arduous travels. In discussing earlier views about India, its heat, and its summer monsoon he observed: "But the conclusions reached through theories by those seated at their desks who travel only in their thoughts, which seem at first sight self-evident and necessary, are discovered false in practice. Those who personally travel to those countries discover the opposite to be true." He also had a very retentive memory and relied on the observations of others to supplement what he recalled. Thus in Surat on May 17, 1673, he recorded: "Since there are many idolaters in this city and in the kingdom of Cambay or Gujarat, it seems to me appropriate to tell here with some clarity what I can about the various rites and superstitions that they have, without obliging myself to put them in order, however, but only putting down what I remember of what I saw or of what I was told by those who stayed a long time in those parts and who observed more carefully." Unlike many other travelers, then as now, he was careful to cite his sources, particularly referring on several occasions to his Venetian predecessor della Valle. Only occasionally did he refer to his own journey in the past tense. On his return trip through Baghdad, he mentioned a future event: "However, sometime after I left they built a new bazaar for dealing in textiles imported from India."

He was proud of his aristocratic family connections, and he instructed Grélot to show the family coat of arms in several of the drawings in his *Journal and Travels*. He surely found this assertion of status to be fitting and instructive rather than obtrusive.[16] Grélot also included what must be portraits of Bembo in a number of drawings, as well as some representations of himself.[17]

Bembo's trip took him out of cosmopolitan Catholic Venice into a world of much greater religious diversity, and he was fascinated by it. Though he makes obligatory remarks about Muslims being schismatics and followers

16. The frontispiece, folios 8–9, 10–11, 222–223, and the final drawing of a ship breaking up in a storm.

17. It is likely that Bembo appears in folios 10–11, 94–95, 220–221, 260–261, and 312 #3. Grélot appears to have represented himself in folios 10–11 and 260; in both drawings he also includes his tools.

of "their false prophet" Muhammad, he was obviously and genuinely fascinated by Islam. He set out the months of the Muslim year and discussed the times of daily prayer, the yearly fast of Ramadan, the major festivals, and the pilgrimage to Mecca and Medina. That Muslims venerate Mary and Jesus was, of course, appealing to him. He was well aware that Shi'i Iranians followed a different kind of Islam, that they held Muhammad's son-in-law 'Ali in special veneration, that their chief martyrs' shrines were in Kerbala and Najaf, and that they believed in a messiah, the Mahdi.

He was also intrigued by the varieties of Christian belief he found, though he also dismissed them as "schismatics." Adherents of the Syrian Catholic Church he mistakenly referred to as Nestorians. But he also mentioned on several occasions actual followers of Nestorian doctrine, particularly when he discussed the Chaldeans of Anatolia and of the island of Socotra. Their patriarch resided in Baghdad and, according to Bembo, there were seven Nestorian archdioceses and seven dioceses. In the city of Diyarbakır in southeastern Anatolia he found "ten different rites, five of infidels and five of baptized persons. These latter are Armenians, Greeks, Nestorians, Jacobites, and Shiamsi, who were, and still are, worshippers of the sun." In India he found the Christians of St. Thomas and asserted that they had been converted by St. Thomas after the saint had left Anatolia. Their tortuous internal politics fascinated him. He found Jews in Syria, Iraq, and Iran, and he described their costume, customs, and occupations. In India he made no distinction between Jains and the different types of Hindus, and he referred to all non-Muslim and non-Christian Indians as Gentiles, to whose clothing he paid more attention than to their religious beliefs. In the Portuguese Indian city of Daman he saw Parsees and identified them as Iranians who had "fled from Persia at the time when that kingdom became Moslem. They adore fire, the sun, and the moon. They keep a fire lit all the time as the Vestals did in Rome."

Bembo was a remarkably open-minded and decent person. He respected those missionaries who were fine human beings, and he did not conceal his dislike of those he considered untrustworthy, overbearing, or obnoxious. He could be sarcastic about their pretensions: before leaving the southern Iranian port of Bandar-i Kong for India he noted that "the Carmelites . . . , like all religious, were at the best hostel." Bembo intensely disliked Father Giovanni Seabra, the Franciscan who had initially enticed him to travel from Aleppo to India, and he took real pleasure in seeing the difficulties that befell him. For the Jesuits in Goa he had no general affection, and he identified their prevalent racism with obvious distaste: "Since, as is often true of the Portuguese, some [Jesuits] were too rigid and not fond of those people [the Indians of Goa], because of their dark color, and since they despised them and maltreated them, the [Indians] could not support their dominion, even if only spiritual." The actions of the Inquisition in Goa appalled him, not only by its famous brutalities but also by its inequities, and he noted that erring Portuguese "rarely reach such extremes" of punishment as the indigenous Indians. His active social conscience is reflected in other observations. In Goa he remarked that the Christian missionary communities lived very well in the midst of general squalor:

> The Augustinians have [a school] attached to the monastery and thus occupy a good part of that hill, which is the best location in the city for air. At the foot of that hill there is a convent of nuns, unique in the city, subordinate to the archbishop, but administered in temporal and spiritual affairs by the Augustinians, since it is of the same order. It is quite rich and ample. Usually there are about eighty nuns of the most noble families. They are served by many native women and Moorish women from Africa, who stay there with them. All the monasteries are big and magnificent, and they continue to grow. The clergy buy ruined places near them, or they receive property in inheritance, since the Portuguese want to give much to monasteries when they die. These latter get bigger, and the clerics live splendidly without reflecting about the rest of the city, which is deteriorating, nor about the poor beggars who die of hunger.

To his credit, this cultured, worldly, urbane, and generally tolerant young man was not himself given to such self-indulgent excesses and was sensitive to the plight of those less fortunate. He was also aware that his own cultural and religious background was not necessarily the only valid one. With an appealing mixture of humor and objectivity, he acknowledged that the Indians "make fun of our ceremonies as much as we do of theirs."

He was interested in languages and in Diyarbakır worked to learn Turkish. There is some evidence in his text that at some point he studied Arabic, and during his stay in Isfahan he learned some Persian. He wore Turkish clothing for much of his trip, but in Iran he dressed as a Persian. He contrasted Turks and Turkish manners and customs most unfavorably with those of Iranians, whose kindliness and courtliness he much admired. About the Arabs of Syria and Iraq he had almost nothing good to say.

Like a good Venetian, he paid careful attention to every kind of ship on which he journeyed; whether river raft or ocean-going vessel, he noted how it was made, how much it could hold, how well it handled. He was proud of his own rational approach and coolly dismissed the habit he observed among the Portuguese of hanging saints' images upside down when they were seeking a favor. He had a good sense of humor that must have served him well during his difficult travels. On his arrival in Baghdad after a difficult journey down the Tigris, he was warmly welcomed by the Capuchins, who put him up in their mission house. "Since I was very tired," he wrote, "I went immediately to rest. I did not want to use the sheets, though, so as not to lose the habit of difficulty and suffering all at once." He reported on his experiences with masseuses in Goa with a mixture of detached commentary and wry personal involvement:

[T]hey have themselves massaged to make it easier for them to sleep. The men do the same. It is impossible for them to sleep without these things. Not all do it in the same way. Some have their whole bodies rubbed, others have their joints moved, others have their bodies pinched; and others have themselves tickled and slightly scratched all over. Still others have their feet scratched. Since this is women's work, they pass easily from these to other, greater confidences and freedom. I tried this custom of theirs because they insisted. At first, it kept me from sleeping and bothered me, but after a few times I enjoyed it.

He enjoyed bathhouse massages in Bandar-i Kong considerably less, for his modesty was offended. After the bath, "they have one lie down on the floor, and the employees of the bathhouse wash one in a very improper way. They climb on one and rub the whole body indiscreetly; as a result, during the whole time I was in Persia, I did not want to go into their baths anymore."

Food was important, particularly when it was awful or impressive. He was a normal twenty-year-old in this regard, and perhaps in later life he may have been something of a gourmand. He recorded remarkably few instances of food poisoning or of ill health (in one instance a persistent headache lasting for several days; in another, a fever that did not abate for several weeks), and he seemed to have sustained himself well during his travels. He was a person of generosity and courage and was only occasionally discouraged, and then as much by the foibles of fellow travelers as by the rigors of travel. That he attracted loyalty and affection from most of those with whom he was associated suggests that he was a good-natured, decent, and appealing individual.

Bembo had a well-developed aesthetic sense that expressed itself in his admiration, sometimes of landscape but more often of architecture, both monumental and utilitarian. He was also attentive to detail, whether in food, wine, commerce, architecture, or the arts. He admired Shirazi arts, architecture, and urban design, though he noted failed upkeep and maintenance. The palace in the Royal Garden was half in ruins, and its gardens were rented out by the king. Outside the city was the Bagh-i Firdaus, its buildings run down but its garden still productive. Bembo was keenly interested in technical achievements, whether in the ships he traveled on or in buildings or utilitarian structures, such as the great cisterns of Lar in southern Iran and of the Portuguese colonies in western India. And he greatly esteemed the many solid and secure caravanserais available for travelers along Iran's main trade routes and compared them favorably to their meager counterparts in Ottoman Mesopotamia.

Bembo was not haughty, but he was conscious of his noble antecedents and upbringing and expected to be received with appropriate protocol. Thus he was extraordinarily pleased by the attention granted to him by the president of the English East India Company in Mumbai:

> I saw at the end of the hall a majestic chair from which rose the President. He came toward me and greeted me with kindness. He had me sit at his right on a chair different from all the others with a green velvet cushion, like the one that he had on his own chair. With his good manners he kept me in conversation about my trip as well as about several things to do with Venice. He then passed to talk of India and told me that his company was no longer finding there the earnings that it had at first, when they were earning fifteen and twenty for one. Now the Dutch had taken some of the profit. His name was Gerard Aungier, a rather civil man of good height. He wore a wig and black clothing and had velvet slippers embroidered in gold on his feet and a sword at his belt.

Bembo was very attentive to material culture, particularly when it reflected rank and privilege. After seeing the tableware of the Portuguese governor of Goa, he could not help noting in his journal that there was nothing extraordinary about it: "In one of the rooms there was a window that looked into a smaller room that had the silverware of the viceroy on display. This consisted of a good set for the table and some bowls. I did not stop to comment about them for fear that they should think I had not seen things like them in our country, where, in fact, such items would have been ordinary." Despite his laudable open-mindedness, he rarely missed an opportunity to draw a favorable comparison between Venice and other European states. Though he was acutely aware of his own personal expenses, he reflected only obliquely on the physical impediments the Portuguese faced in India. He did not seem to take into account the fact that they operated under difficult circumstances, far from home, and that maintaining the culture of the homeland was costly and imperfect at such a distance and in the midst of a vibrant and attractive south Indian culture.

GRÉLOT AND HIS DRAWINGS

Fifty-one of the fifty-two line drawings that illustrate *The Travels and Journal* are the work of Guillaume Joseph Grélot, a French artist, who was born about 1630. Twenty-five of these drawings bear the artist's signature,[18] and sixteen are dated. He lived in Constantinople for six years, from 1665 to 1671, where he met the Anglo-French jeweler and traveler Jean Chardin. Nothing if not shrewd in his business relations, Chardin planned to write and publish an account of his travels in Iran, and he knew that attractive illustrations would significantly increase his sales. Grélot must have fallen on hard times, for he accepted the highly disadvantageous contract that Chardin offered him: all of his drawings were to belong to Chardin, who would not pay him until they returned together to Paris, where the jeweler might also give Grélot a bonus if he chose. Were Grélot to leave Chardin's company at any point along the way or to produce a single drawing for anyone else he would forfeit all of his pay. Grélot essentially put himself at Chardin's mercy and was to suffer for this unwise agreement.

The two men set out together for Iran on July 17, 1671, and remained there until September 1674, when Bembo, staying at the Carmelite mission in Isfahan, was introduced to Grélot by the Carmelite father Giacomo. Grélot was desperate to leave Chardin's employ but had no funds for the expensive trip back to Europe. Bembo seems to have seen at once that here was a great opportunity: "Advised of this and thinking that through him I would be able to make a good number of drawings of the curious things

18. The signed drawings are folios 10–11, 60–61, 94, 220, 230, 234, 238, 240 (# 1, 2, 3, 4,), 244, 246, 260, 263, 263 (#2), 266, 266 (#2), 272, 274, 310, 312, 312 (#2), 312 (#3), and 314. Folios 234, 238, 240 #1, 240 #2, 244, 263 #1, 263 #2, 266 #1, 266 #2, 272, and 274 are dated 1674. Folios 10–11, 60–61 (initially dated 1674 and subsequently corrected to 1675), 310, 312 #1, and 312 #2 are dated 1675.

that I had seen and that I would see (which I had always wanted to do, since it is very appropriate for an itinerary to be illustrated), I proposed my companionship to him with the promise to take him to Europe with me." They apparently took to each other and quickly came to an agreement about their travel together. Before they left the city, they worked together, using Bembo's memory and Grélot's sketches, to prepare drawings of Isfahan and of other places, such as Persepolis, that they both had seen. Grélot also drew three illustrations for Bembo's entries on India, even though he had never been there. On September 21, 1674, they set out from Isfahan, and during the ensuing eight months Grélot drew dozens of sites, buildings, and landscapes for Bembo, who presumably looked on and offered suggestions. With Bembo's advice, Grélot produced startlingly accurate renderings of the Sasanian rock reliefs at Taq-i Bustan and the great Achaemenid relief.

Perhaps because of his higher social status, the twenty-two-year-old Bembo describes Grélot as a youth, even though the artist was twice his age:

> Yet this Grélot was a very discreet young man of great goodness and modesty. In addition to his own French, he also understood many languages, such as Latin, Spanish, literary Greek, Arabic, and Persian, if not perfectly, then at least well enough to be able to get along. During the trip he applied himself to everything with great amiability and without ulterior motives. Often he would have us enjoy very good food that he had prepared. Since he and I had still fresh in our memories some of the things we had seen, he made various drawings before we left Isfahan with the help of some sketches that he had, most particularly of the city and important places in it.

After their return to Venice, Grélot stayed for some time with the Bembo family and visited the family estate, which he drew as a frontispiece for the manuscript. It seems that another artist drew the picture of a storm-tossed ship that concludes the book. Grélot may have subsequently gone to Paris, where in 1680 his other major documentary study, *Relation nouvelle d'un voyage de Constantinople,* was published. This book was much admired by François Bernier, a French physician who was at the Mughal court from 1656 to 1668 and who in 1709–1710 published his account of the Mughal Empire as he saw it. Bernier's praise is recorded in the preface to Grélot's book:

> It were to be wished that all who had travelled into foreign countries had made as good use of their time as Monsieur Grélot, the designs which he has made publick in this book and others which he has shewed me of other parts

where I have been, sufficiently demonstrate what an exact observer he has been of things most worthy [of] remark; such as are the platforms and delineations of those places to which it is no easy thing to get access. And therefore, believing myself obliged to do him that justice which he deserves, I do assure the world, that all the representations of the draughts which he has made are all exactly conformable to what I remember of the places themselves.[19]

The fifty-two drawings are not works of great artistic finish or merit. Only the dramatic final drawing of a storm-battered naval vessel is reasonably well turned out, and it bears no direct relationship to Bembo's text. It is also unlikely that it is Grélot's work. Bembo was educated enough to know that, and Grélot seems to have been both modest and talented enough to share that view. His illustrations in Chardin's *Voyages* and in his own *Relation nouvelle* are far more distinctive and polished. They reveal an artist who was thoroughly skilled in perspective, capable of excellent, detailed renderings of architecture, and accustomed to close observation of people and their dress. One presumes that his fifty-one illustrations to Bembo's *Travels and Journal* are more in the nature of preparatory sketches that would have been corrected and more deliberately worked as they were made into copper plates for publication. But he clearly responded to the interests of his patron, who rarely devoted any of the written text to descriptions of plant or animal life, so Grélot's illustrations accordingly focus almost entirely on landscape, buildings, ships and rafts, rock reliefs, ruins, and costume. In concluding his observations of the Sasanian rock reliefs at Taq-i Bustan, Bembo indicated that he closely supervised the drawing process.

Some, though by no means all of them, bear signature and date, such as *G. I. Grélot delineavit 1674*. They are of diverse size. The majority are single sheets, but a number are double pages; and a few, notably the views of the cities of Aleppo, Baghdad, and Isfahan and the archaeological site of

19. W. J. Grélot, "Attestations to the Reader," in *A Late Voyage to Constantinople* (London: John Playford, 1683), pp. 13–14. In his *Voyages de Corneille Le Brun par la Móscovie, en Perse, et aux Indes Orientales* (Amsterdam, 1718), vol. 2, 437–452, the French traveler Corneille Le Brun criticizes the accuracy of some of Grélot's drawings published in Chardin's *Voyages*. L. Langlès's 1811 edition of Chardin's *Voyages* rejects this criticism and also repeats the account that Grélot left Chardin's service to work for Bembo.

Persepolis, are panoramas spread as foldouts over several pages. Most are rendered in brown ink, though Grélot sometimes combines brown with black ink on the same page. A few sketches are wholly in black (view of Taq-i Bustan). There are several explicit references to Bembo's identity through the inclusion of the family coat of arms and, in particular, the frontispiece, which depicts the Bembo villa outside Venice. The device appears in the picture of the entry of the consuls into Aleppo, the subsequent view of the city itself, the panorama of Persepolis, and the upper right of a Persepolis tomb. Bembo seemed proud to show how far he had carried the family name. Grélot also drew at least three portraits of Bembo. We can safely assume that we see Bembo's face as the bearded bust in the lower right of the rendering of Persepolis. His portrait sits on top of the family coat of arms and sports a Turkish turban. We also see him sitting next to Grélot in the view of the city of Canea. In fig. 16 Bembo is shown in European clothing being carried on his palanquin in India.

Grélot also incorporated four self-portraits into the drawings, presumably with Bembo's approval. In all of them we see him from the back. In the view of Aleppo on folios 10–11 he is dressed in Italian clothing, and next to him rest the perspective box, compass, and rulers that demonstrate he is a skilled and well-trained artist. Folios 200 and 312 show him in Turkish attire, and folio 260 shows him in Iranian dress outside the Iranian town of Respè.

Not all of the drawings record sober details of the trip. In a view of the fine caravanserai at Missian (fols. 258–259), we see a rider who is being abruptly thrown from his horse. Bembo does not mention such an incident in his text, and we should probably assume that Grélot included it to add some liveliness to the drawing. Likewise, Grélot included a number of passing riders in the representation of Bisitun (fol. 260), and he took pains to show us details of the campsite at the ferry station of Beherus, where he and Bembo crossed the Diyala River (fols. 274–275). Bembo was not shy about giving Grélot specific instructions. The caravanserai at Maidast (fol. 268), for instance, was to show the interior, and he worked with Grélot the whole day of October 13, 1674, to successfully finish the drawings of Taq-i Bustan. His description of the rock reliefs is full and exacting, and, according to his own remarks, he supervised Grélot's drawings carefully: "On the 13th I was able to finish the drawings as I liked."

Given this close involvement, it is simply astounding to look at the renderings of Isfahan, a city that both Grélot and Bembo knew well. When Bembo hired him, Grélot had already lived in the city for many months.

Apart from three bridges, none of the structures in the foldout panorama is clearly identifiable, with the possible exception of the early seventeenth-century Mosque of the Imam across the river from the middle bridge. Neither the medieval jami' mosque nor the central quadrangle (the maydan) is evident. Instead, the drawing gives an overall impression of woods and palaces, very much in keeping with Bembo's verbal description. Surprisingly, all of the minarets and domes are Ottoman in style, though both Bembo and Grélot must have been thoroughly familiar with the distinctive Safavi minarets and domes that are so much a part of the glory of the city. In the great maydan the minarets of the Shaykh Lotfallah mosque on the east side and the Mosque of the Imam on the south side have been transformed from Safavi to Ottoman style, and the ogive arches of the arcades that enclose the quadrangle have been transformed and made round. These mistakes are extremely puzzling, particularly when other drawings, such as the interior of the Ayineh Khaneh (fols. 246–247) and the caravanserai at Missian (fols. 258–259), are drawn correctly with pointed arches. According to Bembo, the two men worked together in Isfahan on drawings of the notable monuments, and each was a practiced observer. Did Grélot rework the drawings after their return to Venice and fall prey to his memories of Constantinople? And did Bembo, who prided himself on his memory, unaccountably forget what the *minars* and arches of Isfahan really looked like? Were these drawings, in fact, only sketches that the two men intended to correct once they prepared the book for publication?[20] The latter seems likely, particularly when we compare Grélot's drawings for Bembo's memoirs with his far more finished illustrations in his own book on Constantinople, which are accurate and suitably professional. Presumably, the illustrations to Bembo's *Journal* would have been much more polished had the book been published. In any case, the errors and discrepancies indicate that we must proceed with appropriate caution in using the drawings as historical evidence.

Another instance in which we are faced with the mystery that Bembo's text is sometimes more accurate than the drawings involves Bembo's visit to the

20. Note that the illustrations to Chardin's 1711 edition are more accurate: the minars are Safavi, the arches are ogive. Chardin uses the same format of foldouts to show the maydan in Isfahan. Although Grélot worked for him for some time, the pictures in Chardin's book bear various other names and later dates—Fonbonne, 1701; Fonbonne, 1710; and L. Sur, n.d.

Royal Zoo in Isfahan, where he was suitably impressed, particularly with the Indian rhinoceros that had been presented to the shah by the Uzbek khan.

> I went one morning to see the enclosure of the lions and the dogs, which are very fierce and of extraordinary size. They serve as night guards for the king, as is the custom here. In another half-destroyed place I saw two elephants, rather old and very tame. While I was present, I had the pleasure of seeing them take food with their trunks with which they also defend themselves and eat everything. In the same place there was a rhinoceros tied with a heavy chain on his feet. It is a very fierce and ugly animal, as can be seen in the drawing [fig. 29, page 347]. It is taller than a buffalo and twice as broad, and it has short, thick legs with three nails on each foot. In the head it is little different from a buffalo, but on its nose it has a horn similar to a sugar cake, with which it fights, particularly with elephants, toward which it has great antipathy. It vanquishes them when it can wound them in their lower parts with its horn. Its skin is very thick and resists the shots from arquebusses. It is scaly and bumpy, and in some places it is doubled, so that the head and the feet seem to come out of it like a turtle's. It was given to the king by the Great Khan of the Tartars.

Grélot's picture of this Indian rhinoceros is signed and bears the notation that it was "drawn from life" *(ad vivum)* in 1674. The animal is represented in profile and facing to the right. It stands in a landscape that is barren except for two plants in the foreground and, in the far right, a distant village with a distinctly Ottoman single-domed mosque and minaret. One presumes that Grélot was so assertive about his drawing being "from life" to emphasize that he did not copy Dürer's well-known drawing of a rhinoceros, which was, of course, exactly what he did.[21] (In his introduction to his own book on Constantinople, Grélot pronounced his personal abhorrence of plagiarism.) But the inclusion of an Ottoman building as a set piece in a scene from Iran once again calls into question Grélot's accuracy, as well as the thoroughness of Bembo's supervision. It is intriguing that all of these odd and egregious mistakes are centered on architectural representations.

21. For his 1515 woodcut of an Indian rhinoceros, Dürer relied entirely on written descriptions of the animal. See K. A. Schröder and M. L. Sternath, *Albrecht Dürer,* catalog of an exhibition at the Albertina, Vienna, 2003, figure 3, pp. 51–52.

Other drawings by Grélot are of great historical interest. The Safavi palace of the Ayineh Khaneh (Palace of Mirrors, fols. 246–247) was destroyed in the nineteenth century, and Grélot presents us with the only known view of its interior. The caravanserai at Maidast (Mahidasht, fols. 268–269) that impressed Bembo is now a police station, and the drawings of Bisitun (fol. 260) and Taq-i Bustan (fols. 264–265) are the earliest known European renderings of these major archaeological sites. Though Chardin only cursorily refers to Persepolis, Grélot's drawings of the great Achaemenid site are detailed and informative. Despite their errors, the drawings convey a sense of immediacy and offer personal impressions, such as the portraits of the author and the artist.

Bembo did not claim to be a scholar or describe himself as a seasoned traveler with a wealth of experience and information. He never claimed to be other than a young man with an abiding interest in other peoples and other cultures. He traveled not to proselytize, spy, or sell but simply to see and learn as much as he could. Because he was not representing Venice in any official capacity, he did not associate with royal courts, or fill his book with the gossip and intrigues that make those of Chardin and Tavernier such fascinating reading. Instead, Bembo informs us about a humbler way of travel, and we are presented with the sorts of obstacles and frustrations that an unofficial traveler faced. He struggled with the importunities of petty officials and complained about their injustices; he suffered cold, wet weather and meager or very bad food. His detailed expense account makes abundantly clear how closely he had to watch his costs. Like all travelers, he was sometimes ill, and he was grateful for small and large kindnesses. He spent much of his time in European circles, doubtless for a greater sense of security so far from home and with so few resources. Already experienced in war, he had a high sense of adventure and curiosity, but when he set out on his long and risky journey, he must have known that his odds for surviving it were not overwhelming. His book is as valuable a view of the network of Christian mission houses in the Near East and India as it is of the countries themselves, but most of all it is an appealing self-portrait of a bright, decent, remarkably tolerant, and thoroughly likable traveler who was a good observer and a lively writer. His trip obviously affected him deeply and probably filled his conversation with anecdotes for the rest of his life. We are in his debt that he took the trouble to leave us this record of it.

TRAVELS AND JOURNAL

THROUGH PART OF ASIA

DURING ABOUT FOUR YEARS

UNDERTAKEN BY ME,

AMBROSIO BEMBO,

VENETIAN NOBLE

PROLOGUE

THE DESIRE TO KNOW IS innate and natural to the spirit of mankind, whose special gift is the intellect, the sense that is always most eager to feed itself with knowledge. Many things are learned through theory, and more through practice. The world is a great book, which, when perused attentively, proffers teachings and delights with its variety. True, one must tolerate expense, discomfort, and danger, but the effort, if blessed by fortune, brings its reward. Idleness eats away at all virtue and is the worst companion for youth; a source of vices, it perverts the inclination of the good, weakens the courage of the strong, and withers every laurel of glory.

In the flower of my youth I was taken from the study of letters for the honor of public service during the last two years of the famous War of Candia.[1] At the end of that struggle, after having spent some time with the

---

1. A Muslim Arab force invaded Crete in A.D. 827 and established an initial base at Candia on the site of ancient Heraklion, from which Arab authority spread rapidly over the whole island. Cretan Arabs were a major maritime force in the eastern Mediterranean until the recapture of Crete by the Byzantine Empire between 960 and 972. Taken by the Crusaders in 1204, the island came under Venetian control in 1207. In 1645 Maltese corsairs based in Crete captured an Ottoman fleet on the way to Mecca with pilgrims, including several of Sultan Ibrahim's wives, and the ensuing war lasted twenty-five years. Under Ottoman siege from 1648 to 1669, the port city of Candia was well supplied by the Venetian fleet and supported in part by seven thousand French troops sent by Louis XIV. When the French force was withdrawn in 1669, the Venetian general Francesco Morosini surrendered, and Crete came under Ottoman control. Bembo was later to accompany Francesco Morosini in his 1686–1687 Peloponnesian campaign.

Great Fleet with the nobleman Taddeo Morosini,[2] the lord of our house and Captain of the Navy and with whom I had gone to the Levant and been treated with all generosity and splendor, and after having directed the Public Ship, the *Fontana d'Oro*, with the title of Governor (under the authorization of the General Captain Francesco Morosini, Cavalier and Procurator of S. Marco), I found myself after the peace without opportunity to work at sea or in arms.

At nineteen I was too young, according to the laws of the country, to enter the Grand Council[3] or to take up any other position or public office. Since I would be unable to ascend to public service until my twenty-fifth year and unhappy at the prospect of having to spend more than five years in a position of uselessness, I embraced with ready obedience the opportunity given me to fulfill my obligations toward the nobleman Marco Bembo, my paternal uncle. A long time previously, he had been assigned as the replacement for the nobleman Francesco Erizzo in the consulate of Aleppo. The deliberations of the Senate, however, had delayed his voyage due to the fierce war that had arisen between the Republic and the Ottomans, which had resulted in the interruption of commerce with all the ports of that Empire. When peace with free passage was established after twenty-five years, and former traffic was reestablished, my uncle was once again confirmed as consul of Aleppo. In the meantime he had served in many capacities, among them that of Captain of Ships and General Provider of the armed forces in Candia. Wishing to travel in various foreign countries, I accompanied him.[4]

2. The Morosinis had been one of Venice's major families since the twelfth century, and this statement indicates that they were closely related to the aristocratic Bembos. Several generations of a family might live together in the same palace.

3. Maggior Consiglio.

4. It was a common practice for a senior Venetian official to take a young son or nephew with him to a new post so that he could begin to learn how to represent Venice effectively.

ONE

From Venice to Aleppo

[AUGUST 1671]

WE EMBARKED ON AUGUST 8, 1671, on the ship *Confidenza,* leased with cargo but a large vessel furnished with many cannons that had already served the public in the preceding years of war. That which transpired from my leaving the port until my return to my country—a period of almost four years—I have wanted to set down in these pages in a smooth and easy narrative so that the bother that I suffered alone during long wanderings, attempted by few and to few granted, may bring pleasure to all those who, during the leisure of domestic tranquility, may want to spend only a little time in reading them. I have described all that I thought worthwhile and sufficient to give an idea of the places I saw. As for the material part of this work, I took advantage as best I could and at no little expense of the services of an ingenious Frenchman who traveled with me and provided many drawings of towns, costumes, and other famous memorabilia or rarities. Thus I am able to provide more pleasure.[1]

It is unfortunate if this sort of itinerary should seem a bit dry for the delicate tastes of modern minds, since it is the same that was undertaken by Marco Polo, also one of us Venetians, and by almost all the others who underwent similar troubles. One should realize, too, that this account might be as boring (if not more so), because it is less distinguished than oth-

---

1. Guillaume Joseph Grélot was born about 1630 and lived in Constantinople, where he met the Anglo-French jeweler and traveler Jean Chardin. They set out together for Iran on July 17, 1671. After his return to Paris Grélot published in 1680 an important illustrated study of Constantinople, *Relation nouvelle d'un voyage de Constantinople.*

ers. In addition, my youth and inexperience did not permit me to weave an ornamented and ordered story of so many kingdoms and of such great countries. Nevertheless, this diary will be the truthful account of the voyage that began under the auspices of the Virgin Mother of God on the 15th of August at dawn, which was also a Saturday.[2]

We left Malamocco with four other merchant vessels, on one of which was the nobleman Alvise Cornaro who was also going as a consul, but to Cairo.[3] Since much of the voyage the ships would be together, the command of the group of vessels was given to my uncle. As captain of our ship itself was Pietro Melle, whom I had known well while in the armed forces and who had served in the same office and on the same ship then. The voyage was troubled not only by contrary winds but also by many periods of calm. The resulting tedium was relieved by the varied company. On the ship were the nobleman Giovanni Antonio Soderini, who was on his way to the Holy Land and surrounding areas, merchants going to Aleppo, and many ministers necessary for the operations of the consulate.[4] Besides these, the consul of Cyprus, Giovanni Antonio Santonini, was also on board with many merchants going to that island.[5] My uncle was honored by the presence of the consul and of the noble Soderini at his table. Many members of religious orders had also taken advantage of the voyage. Among them were four Discalced Carmelites going to Goa. One of these was a Visitatore by the name of Father Valerio, from whom I was to receive many favors while in India.[6] Without him I would have found myself in many troubles, as I will recount at the appropriate time.

2. Bembo refers to their setting out a week earlier, on August 8, the date that they left the city of Venice itself to proceed to the port of Malamocco on the lagoon.

3. Alvise Cornaro was presumably a relative, as Bembo's mother was a member of the Cornaro family.

4. Syria and Palestine had been under Ottoman authority since the defeat of the Mamluk sultanate in 1517. The Aleppo consulate was of central importance to Venetian trade with the Ottoman Empire, and it was accordingly amply staffed.

5. Cyprus was under direct Venetian control from 1489 until 1570, when it became part of the Ottoman Empire. The Venetian merchant community on the Ottoman island remained large and influential.

6. Discalced (or "unshod") Carmelites were a religious order that wore sandals with or without stockings. A *visitatore* was a church official engaged upon an official inspection of an area under his jurisdiction.

FIGURE 2. Zante.

At midday on September 1 we dropped anchor at the beach of Zante, where Alvise Pasqualigo was the Captain of Ships.[7] He attended us. In the same port were twelve French warships commanded by M. d'Almere. Since he was my uncle's friend, the groups of ships greeted one another with full artillery salutes. I also enjoyed that meeting because I had already met M. d'Almere in Candia when he arrived there with the convoy of the Duke of Beaufort. The French ships had captured a small Berber vessel loaded with lumber for constructing a galley.[8]

7. The Ionian island of Zakinthos (Zante) was under Venetian control. The beach is in its southeast, immediately opposite the Peloponnesos, at the time part of the Ottoman Empire. Bembo also mentions below that they saw the island of Cerigo (Kíthira) south of the Peloponnesos.

8. The Berber ship may have come from a North African port under Ottoman control.

We stayed in that port several days to stock provisions, and on Saturday, September 5, we lifted anchor from Zante with the Captain of the Ships. Immediately afterward, we saw the island of Cerigo, a drawing of which is provided here. Since the wind was favorable, we proceeded on our voyage with only one escort vessel, called the *San' Antonio,* which was going to Acre. The *Europa,* which was going to Izmir, had already left us, and on Tuesday night we lost the Captain of the Ships and also [the ship] of consul Cornara, which had headed toward Candia with provisions of biscuits for the fortresses there. Since the wind continued to be rather favorable, we arrived in two days within sight of the island of Rhodes.[9] In those waters we discovered a vessel that made us hurry on and put us on our guard, since we thought that it was a pirate ship: they are frequent in that place. As it approached, it unfolded the flag of Livorno. In order not to waste time, we continued on our way without even exchanging words.

On the 13th we arrived at Saline, the beach of Larnaca on the island of Cyprus. There is a small castle there with four cannons, as can be seen in the drawing.[10] Around the castle are ten or twelve houses made of clay dried in the sun, some dwelled in by Turks and others by Greeks, some warehouses of stone and a good house of the aga of the customs house, whose officials are all Greeks. There is a coffee house,[11] a place where the Turks meet to drink coffee, and a mosque. In addition, there is an ancient church of the Greeks with a convent where several nuns live. It is called S. Lazaro, for they say that that saint is buried there. The tomb is behind the altar, but the body is no longer there, because it was taken to Constantinople by the Emperor Leo. It is now said to be in Marseille. It is impossible to enter the

9. Acre became part of the Ottoman Empire in 1516. Rhodes had been under the command of the Knights of St. John until 1522, when it was conquered by the Ottomans.

10. Grélot's drawing identifies the harbor as Saline, the name for the port area of Larnaca. For a study of Bembo's information about Cyprus, see Michael D. Willis, "A New Document of Cypriote History: The Journal of Ambrosio Bembo," in *ΚΥΠΡΙΑΚΑΙ ΣΠΟΥΔΑΙ* (Cypriot Studies), 42 (1978): 35–46.

11. Bembo obviously means "coffee house," but his transcription here *(cafegi)* is from the Turkish word *kahveci* for coffee seller. The first coffee house opened in Istanbul in 1554, and coffee drinking rapidly became very popular, despite occasional fierce religious and official opposition to the beverage. The Turkish word for coffee house is either *kahvehane* or, more simply, *kahve.*

FIGURE 3. Cerigo.

tomb because it is full of water. A mile away is Larnaca; although it cannot
be termed a city, it can be called a large center. There reside a lieutenant of
the pasha[12] of Nicosia and a qadi (or minister of law).[13] In that center our
consul has his residence, as well as those of France and England. This man
is not of the aristocracy but of the citizenry. He is selected by the magistrate
of the Five Savii alla Mercanzia[14] and is subordinate only to the Bailo of

12. A *pasha* was an official title given to high-ranking Ottoman military
officers and administrators of the rank of *beylerebeyi* (governor general of a
province) or vizier.

13. A *qadi* was a specialist in *shari'a* (Islamic canon law) and other components of Islamic jurisprudence, particularly *kanun* (secular law decreed by the
sultan). He functioned as a judge in legal disputes, both within the Muslim
community and between Muslims and non-Muslims, and as chief administrator of a judicial district.

14. The Venetian Board of Trade.

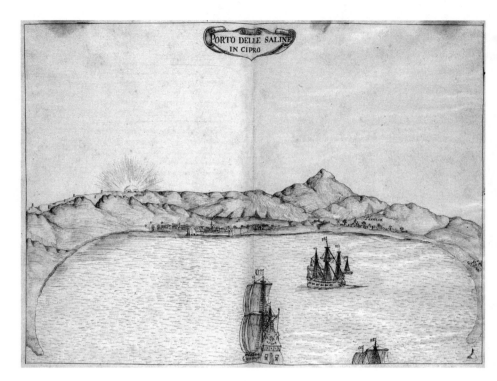

FIGURE 4. Larnaca.

Constantinople.[15] In the territory there is a Franciscan church that serves the Venetians. It is called S. Maria. Capuchin fathers officiate at the Chapel of the French.

We stayed in that place to let off the consul, along with some merchants and goods. Soderini, who was a relative of the consul, remained there. I took advantage of the time to visit parts of that kingdom, particularly the metropolis of Nicosia, twenty-four miles distant from the sea. It is governed by a pasha sent from Constantinople, who has dominion over all the island with the exception of the Fortress of Famagusta (the ancient and famous Salamina): a bey,[16] also sent from Constantinople, resides at that fortress and guards it without depending upon the pasha. He lets no European enter it.

15. The *bailo* was the Venetian ambassador to Constantinople. There was a bailo in Aleppo and also one in Alexandria. It was an enormously lucrative post.

16. Bey was the title of a district commander.

Wishing to know that country that had once been owned by the Republic, I went around the city even though the excessive heat of that season prohibited one's leaving the house at certain hours. Among the ruins and broken walls I observed many traces of Venetian work, though no longer splendid, while barbarism has left nothing at all. The city is surrounded by walls. On them, as well as on the ground, I saw several cannons with the seal of S. Marco. In various places I saw many winged lions that had been decapitated by the Turks. There are three gates: that of Famagusta, the second of Baffo, and the third of Cirene.[17] Most of the houses are made of clay, except for some remains of ancient palaces, many of which have been made into mosques. Among the ruins one can still see vestiges of the Palace of Queen Cornara.[18] Inside the city are Capuchin and Franciscan fathers with their missions to serve the Greek Catholics. The mission of the Capuchins is called S. Giacomo and that of the Franciscans, the Holy Cross.

The kingdom is almost entirely destroyed and with few inhabitants. The majority of these are Greeks (about 20,000), while the Turks are about 6,000. Most of the latter are of Greek blood, and Greek is spoken by all. The Greeks have maintained their Venetian hearts, so they wear Venetian dress, both men and women, as can be seen in the drawing. The women do not cover their faces, and the men keep their hair and wear hats and Italian dress. They treat even the Turks with much liberty. The rulers and the majority of the janissaries[19] come from Constantinople. They tend rather to destroy than to build and look upon foreigners only as a source of possible gain. The consul and the merchants have much freedom in this kingdom. They can even entertain themselves with Greek women. Our Venetians enjoy the privilege of not being judged by [local] Turkish officials

17. The three gates formed part of the Venetian artillery fortifications designed by Giulio Savorgnano in 1567.

18. The Venetian noblewoman (and ancestor of Ambrosio's mother) Caterina Cornaro married James II of Cyprus in 1472. He died two years later, allegedly due to poison administered by the queen's uncle Andrea Cornaro and her cousin Marco Bembo. She ruled Cyprus in an uneasy relationship with the Venetian state until 1489, when she abdicated.

19. The *yeniçeri,* or "new troops," were professional infantrymen of the Ottoman Empire. In Istanbul they constituted the sultan's elite infantry corps, paid out of the state treasury. By the middle of the seventeenth century the term was also used to describe local infantry under the authority of a provincial governor. It is these local troops to whom Bembo is referring here.

FIGURE 5. Costume of the people of Cyprus.

in any case involving more than 5000 *aspri*, a coin of little value, corresponding to one of our *soldi*.[20] Cases involving more are submitted to Constantinople.

The country abounds in food, particularly in excellent wines, much fowl and pork. This latter is not permitted in other places by the Turks because of the prohibition of such food imposed on them by their false prophet. Four miles distant from Larnaca is a wonderful garden, which I went to see. They call it Chiti.[21] There are some very beautiful fountains and many ruins of a sumptuous building that served as a pleasure house to the ancient queens.

On Saturday, the 19th of the month, we left Cyprus, and on the 21st we

20. A *soldo* was a coin of small value, similar to a penny or farthing. An *aspri*, known in English as an *asper*, was a small silver coin, in Turkish called an *akçe* because of its silver or white color.

21. Chiti, or Citium, was to the south of the city and may be identified with the modern site of Hala Sultan Tekke.

reached the port of Tripoli, which is very exposed to the winds. Tripoli is a large city situated at the foot of Mount Lebanon, half a league from the port. It is governed by a pasha sent from Constantinople and by several other officials, about whom I will say more when I describe Aleppo. This city does commerce in silks and in ashes to make glass: thus there are vice-consuls from every country there. They are subject to and appointed by the consuls of Aleppo. There are several clergy who have their chapels located within their houses. In addition, there are the chapels in the houses of the consuls. The clergy are Franciscans, Jesuits, Capuchins, and Discalced Carmelites. These latter also have a mission on Mount Lebanon. They travel in the mountain area, where there are many Christians without clergy. When necessary, they have the privilege of celebrating Mass twice in one day, but in two different towns.

We stayed here several days to unload some merchandise, and I went to see a little of the country. Not far from the city I saw a large bridge supported on three arches. Over it passes water from one mountain to another. It is called the Bridge of Goffredo,[22] and on the central arch one can see a cross. I also went to see a fountain with fish that was rather beautiful. Not far from the marina were some rather good fig orchards that had been left to the city by a Turk to benefit cats. The proceeds of the orchards were to go to feed the cats of the city. Since the character of the people and the costumes of all of Turkey are the same, I will give an account of them only once when describing Aleppo.

In Tripoli in addition to the native Turks there are many Christians of different sects, most of them schismatics.[23] There are also many Drusi,[24] a

22. Bembo is referring to the *Qanatir al-Brins* (Arches of the Prince), a Crusade-period aqueduct that takes water from the Rashin River to Tripoli. The coastal area of present-day Lebanon came under the authority of the pasha of Tripoli in the north and the pasha of Sidon in the south: both reported to the pasha of Damascus.

23. The Christian communities of Lebanon were diverse, and Bembo's term *schismatics* presumably excludes the largest community, the Maronites, as well as the Melkites, both of whom acknowledged the authority of the pope in Rome.

24. The Druze, in the seventeenth century as today largely concentrated in greater Syria, owe their origin as a religious community not to French Crusaders but to the Isma'ili Fatimids and particularly to the Fatimid caliph Hakim (A.D. 996–1021), whom they consider to be the last Imam. Bembo here apparently

people whose origins are French. They are the descendants of those who with so many pious desires carried arms to recover the Holy Places. Attacked by the plague and by the fury of the Berbers,[25] they mixed their seed with circumcised people and lost their faith. Thus, having put out that first holy light, they attached themselves to a new prophet, hateful even to the Turkish superstition. This prophet, called Isman, was known only to them and only by them held in esteem. The true Drusi are not circumcised; lacking all sense of respect, they think it lawful to take even their daughters as wives. Unlike the Turks, they do not despise wine. Living as they do separated by customs from the Ottomans, they have also tried to render themselves independent in government and laws. They have always obeyed their native princes, who govern through ancient lineage. Never have they wanted to admit the jurisdiction of any Ottoman chiefs or governors. They inhabit the part of the country that is between the confines of Jaffa[26] and the Orontes and Jordan Rivers. Their territory extends as far as the plain of Damascus, even though in recent years they have lost much of their lands. All that is left to them are the most mountainous regions where they can defend themselves with more facility. They are a very warlike people, strong, intrepid, bold, and respectful of their laws. They fight with harquebus, saber, bow and arrow, and lance. They wear a long robe and a turban in Turkish fashion. They are a people used to coarse food as is found in mountain areas.

[OCTOBER 1671–NOVEMBER 1672]

On October 12 we left Tripoli, and not until the 18th did we arrive in Iskenderun.[27] The port is a rather good one at the farthest reach of the Mediterranean and a famous stopover for all European merchant vessels going on to Aleppo, a distance of three days' travel overland. Not far from

------

reflects Ottoman hostility and popular prejudice in his account of the origins and beliefs of the Druze but also shows appropriate Venetian respect for a people who had successfully resisted the Ottomans for many decades.

25. Following Venetian custom based on the Republic's maritime contacts, competition, and warfare with the states of western North Africa, Bembo regularly uses the term *Berber* to mean Arab Muslim.

26. Bembo spells it as "Gioppe." His description of Druze territory is accurate.

27. Bembo calls this city in southern Turkey "Alessandretta" or "Scanderona."

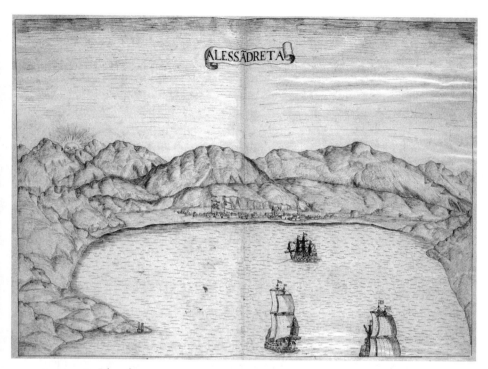

FIGURE 6. Iskenderun.

Iskenderun is Payas, a large city with a good port for caiques,[28] which go there to load rice, lemons, and other goods. On the shore between Payas and Iskenderun can be found two pilasters, as can be seen in [the lower left of] the drawing. These once supported an arch said to have been erected by St. Helena to commemorate the place where Jonah was cast up by the whale. Near these pilasters is a little castle or fort where lives an old aga with several people.[29]

Iskenderun is a very small town with few houses. In times past it had

28. Bembo calls it a *saiche* (in Turkish, *kayık*), a skiff with one or two oars and/or a lateen rig used in the eastern Mediterranean. He uses the name Bagaisso for modern Payas (16 km north of Iskenderun), where there is a sixteenth-century mosque, as well as a small fort built by the Genoese or Venetians in the fourteenth century. Six kilometers to the south on the road to Iskenderun is the fort of Kız Kalesi, to which Bembo refers. Two kilometers farther is a white limestone wall still known as Jonas' Pillar, probably the remains of a Roman monumental gate.

29. The term *aga* literally translates as chief, master, or lord and could be

been abandoned because of the foul air there, but when it became a stopover point on the way to Aleppo, several Turks and Greeks settled there. An aga resides there, sent by the Great Aga of the customs house of Aleppo. His duty is to make note of the merchandise that is put ashore there so that no one will be able to defraud the tax office. There are the houses of the vice-consuls of all the nations, which are quite good. Each flies the flag of its prince over the roof. These vice-consuls are those of Venice, France, and England, all appointed by the consuls of Aleppo. As for clergy, there are Franciscan fathers sent from the Holy Land who officiate in the chapel that is located in the house of the French vice-consul. All the Europeans who disembark here to travel into the interior pay to the aga a fee of twenty-one *piasters,* that is, *reales.* This is done every time one arrives there, except if one has already paid and is just returning there from Tripoli, Cyprus, or other nearby places. But if one is arriving from Europe, one must always pay the fee. The ships also must pay for the right to anchor there.

When we arrived in Iskenderun, all the stuffs were unloaded and sent on their way on a caravan of camels. They use camels during the summer instead of mules, which do not bear the heat and are thus kept in the higher areas. We remained aboard ship because of the foul air of that place. It is produced by vapors of several lagoons and swamps nearby, and it causes the death of many people. Those who survive retain a yellow coloring on their faces.[30] Thus, when we did disembark, we immediately mounted horses. We were accompanied by all our retinue as well as by several Turks who came to meet my uncle and to enter into service in his house. The English vice-consul, Martin Loe, also came to accompany us. That same evening he conducted us to Belen, a rather large town about two hours' travel by road from Iskenderun. It is situated on a mountain, also named Belen, that divides Syria from Cilicia. There we took lodging in a house belonging to the British vice-consul, who used it in the summers because of the very good air in the place. Near the house was a most perfect spring whose waters then flowed down the mountain with a sweet murmur. The houses of the place are one above the other because of their locations on the mountainside. There is also a covered public area roofed not with tiles but

------

used to refer to an official, an important landowner, or a tribal chief. Here, however, it is probably used in the sense of a person employed in government service, often of a military or nonbureaucratic character.

30. Bembo is describing yellow fever.

rather with lead forming several domes.[31] We stayed only two days and returned to our voyage. My uncle had himself carried in a litter borne along by mules that traveled with very great skill in those rather difficult mountains. We stopped for a day along the River Orontes at a site that was quite narrow. They say it has its source on Mount Lebanon. Its first name was Tifone, and then it took the name Orontes from one who built a bridge over it. Today it is also known as Farfaro. During an entire night we traveled along its banks to avoid the hours of heat. We passed not far from Antioch, which is along the banks of this river. Antioch is now a ruin and preserves only the ancient nobility of its name because it was the Seat of St. Peter and the place where the name "Christian" was first used.

The day we arrived in Aleppo, we were met in the following manner, while still a few miles distant from the city. At a place called the "broken-down khan"[32] we found everyone of our nation. It is the custom that the first greetings should be given by those of the same nationality as the consul who arrives. It is true that the group that met us hardly deserved the title of nation, because it consisted of only one merchant, Antonio Caminada, with his attendants, and of some Italians who were married to natives of the country. Even before the war they had come under the protection of our consuls. Among them were some who claimed to have been elected first and second interpreters and four janissaries. These, as is usual, were to remain always in assistance at the door of the consul. We also were met by a *çavuş*[33] sent by

31. Bembo could be describing either a *sabil* (public fountain) or a *hamam* (public bath).

32. *Han* is a Turkish word from the Persian *khan* (caravanserai). Bembo renders it as *cham*. (I will use the Persian word.) It could be used to denote two types of buildings: (1) a stage and relay post for travelers on a main road; (2) a warehouse where merchants could temporarily lodge and conduct business. The "broken-down khan" to which Bembo refers might have been called Kırık Han in Turkish. The great mid-seventeenth-century Ottoman traveler Evliya Çelebi does not refer to any *khans* in Aleppo in his *Seyahatname,* and the twentieth-century German scholar Ernst Herzfeld does not mention a "Broken Khan" in his discussion of Aleppo in *Matériaux pour un corpus inscriptionum arabicarum, Deuxième partie: Syrie du Nord.*

33. *Çavuş* is a word with several meanings. It could denote an attendant, footman, or soldier of relatively low rank, as it apparently does in the first instance here, where Bembo equates it with the Italian word *fante.* A çavuş could also be an official in a palace department, particularly a herald or mes-

the Turkish officials. Their office corresponds to that of *fante* (attendant or footman). They were playing some drums, which were attached to the saddles of their horses. With these were several richly outfitted horses, sent by the officials and commanders of the city as a sign of honor. They were led by another man, also on horseback. In fact, this honor implies a considerable expense, because it corresponds to a donation of several reales for each horse. The consul mounted one of the horses after having received the homage of our national representatives. It is a custom that the consul mounts the horses of the first officials as a sign of esteem. Shortly after having remounted, we met the French representatives on a low hill. This group was composed of its two interpreters and four janissaries and the official dressed in red who is by us called *zago*. His office corresponds to that of the Turkish *çavuş*. When we had approached and dismounted, the secretary and chancellor of the French expressed the usual compliments in the name of his consul. These compliments are sometimes presented personally at these meetings when all the consuls are present. Then, each merchant made a bow, and we remounted, the consul on another of the horses that had been presented to him. After a brief distance we met on another hill the English delegation, which was made up of the same members as the others and with which the same courtesies were exchanged. We then remounted, this time the consul on the horse of the pasha who was to take him to his house. With the entire group we proceeded to the city: first the *çavuş*, as can be seen in the drawing; then the three chief interpreters followed by second interpreters; after them the *zaghi;* then the outfitted horses followed by the twelve janissaries with their long caps; then more interpreters; then the consul, dressed in red and with four staff bearers or pages dressed in the Turkish fashion: two of them walked by the horse's head and the other two by its flanks. On the consul's right rode the French chancellor and at his left the English. The various foreign officials followed: the deputies, as the French call them. (The English have only one, called a treasurer; our two are called *tansadori*.) Behind them followed the French and then the English delegations. That of the newly arrived consul always goes last.

---

senger for the state council, and might form part of the sultan's ceremonial escort. He could also be responsible for conveying the orders of the sultan or the grand vizier to provincial authorities. It is apparently this higher function that Bembo describes below and interprets as the Italian *zago* (pl., *zaghi*).

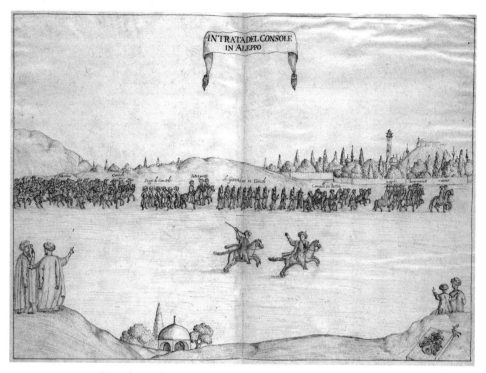

FIGURE 7. Consuls in Aleppo.

Before we arrived in the city, there was some confusion among the representatives because an Englishman had struck a Frenchman with a rod. Everyone's hand went to his sword. Nothing worse happened, however, because the Italians intervened as well as the soldiers. All quieted down with the thought that the Turks would profit from any bloodshed among the foreigners. Outside the city as well as inside along the street, there was an infinite number of people, men and women, who had come to see the entry of the consul, which was through the gate called Bab al-Faraj.[34] Once at the house, the consul stood on the threshold and received the greetings of all the members of the various delegations as they passed by on horseback one by one.

Aleppo is a large city, as can be seen in the drawing. It is called *Aleb* or *Alib*

34. The Bab al-Faraj, or the Gate of Deliverance , is a city gate in the northwest part of Aleppo.

by the Arabs and Turks, which means "milk." Giovio calls it *Alapia;* Bellonio, *Hieropolis;* and others, *Heliopolis.* The Jews called it *Aram Soba* and consider it to go back to the time of David, and some to the time of Abraham, who ruled there.[35] Now it is under the Ottoman Empire, having been taken from the Sultan of Babylon by Sultan Selim in the year 1515.[36] He found much wealth there. The city is situated in a low place and is surrounded by some mountains and hills. Within it, too, there are four or five hills. It is about eight to ten miles in circumference: its form is round rather than elongated, as I had occasion to see while traveling around it many times on horseback. It is surrounded by a wall made of rough-hewn stone. The wall is not very high and in some places is in ruins. It has ten gates, one of which is never opened. The names of the gates are [as follows]: the first is called *Bab al-Feraj* in Arabic and *Kapı-yı Feraj* in Turkish, which means the Gate of Deliverance; the second is *Bab al-Jinan* in Arabic and *Kapı-yı Cinen* in Turkish, which means the Gate of Ginen, a man's proper name;[37] the third is *Bab al-Antakya* in Arabic and *Kapı-yı Antakya* in Turkish, that is, the Antioch Gate; the fourth in Arabic is *Bab al-Qinnasrin* and *Kireç Kapısı* in Turkish, that is, the Gate of Mortar, also known as Gate of the Prisons, because in it are the debtors' prisons; the fifth is *Bab al-Maqam* in Arabic and *Şam Kapısı* in Turkish, that is, the Damascus Gate; the sixth is *Bab al-Nirab* in Arabic and *Kapı-yı Nerab* in Turkish, that is, the Nairab Gate; the seventh is *Bab al-Qanat*

35. The Arabic name for the city is Halab; the Turkish is Halep. The Ottoman sultan Selim I defeated the Mamluk sultanate, based in Egypt and the Levant, at the battle of Marj Dabik near Aleppo on August 24, 1516; the city was occupied by the Ottomans four days later. Aleppo and Izmir were the most important commercial centers in the Levant in the seventeenth century. Caravans set out from Aleppo to travel to Gilan on the Caspian coast for silk to be sold to Venetian merchants in exchange for Italian textiles. The Venetians had established a consulate and business headquarters in Aleppo in 1548; consulates were subsequently established by the French (1562), the English (1583), and the Dutch (1613). The basic study of the city of Aleppo is Jean Sauvaget, *Alep: Essai sur le développement d'une grande ville syrienne des origines au milieu du XIXe siècle* (Paris: Librarie Orientaliste P. Geuthner, 1941).

36. From medieval times many European Christian writers, following Coptic Christian practice, referred to Egypt as Babylon, though the name actually denoted simply a town in the vicinity of Cairo. The Ottoman sultan Selim ruled from 1512 to 1520.

37. Bembo was misinformed: the *Bab al-Jinan* is the Garden Gate.

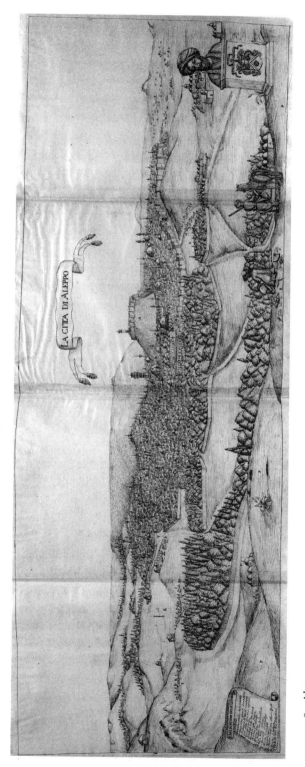

LA CITTA DI ALEPPO

FIGURE 8. Aleppo panorama.

(or *Bab al-Hadid*) in Arabic and in Turkish *Demir Kapı,* that is, the Gate of Iron, which leads to the suburb called Bancussa, inhabited by Turks; the eighth in Arabic is *Bab al-Zalam* and *Karanlık Kapı* in Turkish, that is, the Dark Gate, which they keep always closed because its darkness was the cause of many robberies and murders; the ninth in Arabic is *Bab al-Ahmar* and in Turkish *Kızıl Kapı,* that is, the Red Gate; the tenth is *Bab al-Nasr* in Arabic and *Kapı-yı Cengi* in Turkish, that is, the Victory Gate, called by the Christians the Gate of St. George.[38]

Near the walls are several suburbs that surround most of the city. Where there are no houses near the walls there is a moat, that is, from the Gate of the Prisons to the Gate of Damascus. One of the principal suburbs is called Jedeideh,[39] where all the Christians live, and it is near the Bab al-Feraj. The buildings in the city are for the most part of stone. They are the best in all of Turkey and more like European buildings. Instead of tiles on their roofs, there are terraces where one sleeps at night, since the air is perfect. Most of the streets are paved in stone, and the walls of the houses are high and without windows on the street, not displaying from the outside what they are

38. Bembo proceeds counterclockwise from the Christian quarter of Jedeideh (Giudaita) in the northwest in his list of the city's gates, many of whose names are, remarkably, still more or less the same. His transcription of their Arabic and Turkish names is as follows: "The names of the gates are [as follows]: the first is called *Bab Ferg* in Arabic and *Cappi Ferag* in Turkish, which means Gate of Deliverance; the second is *Bab Ginen* in Arabic and *Cappi Ginen* in Turkish, which means the Gate of Ginen, a man's proper name; the third is *Bab Antachie* in Arabic and *Cappi Antachie* in Turkish, that is, the Antioch Gate; the fourth in Arabic is *Bab Chienisserin* and *Chires Cappi* in Turkish, that is, Gate of Mortar, also known as Gate of the Prisons, because in it are the debtors' prisons; the fifth is *Bab Macan* in Arabic and *Sciam Cappi* in Turkish, that is, Damascus Gate; the sixth is *Bab Neram* in Arabic and *Cappi Neram* in Turkish, that is, Neram Gate; the seventh is *Bab Bancussa* in Arabic and in Turkish *Demir Cappi,* that is, Gate of Iron, which leads to the suburb called Bancussa, inhabited by Turks; the eighth in Arabic is *Bab Etem* and *Caram Cappi* in Turkish, that is, the Dark Gate, which they keep always closed because its darkness was the cause of many robberies and murders; the ninth in Arabic is *Bab Almar* and in Turkish *Chesil Cappi,* that is, Red Gate; the tenth is *Bab Enars* in Arabic and *Cappi Jengti* in Turkish, that is, Victory Gate, called by the Christians the Gate of St. George."

39. Bembo renders it as "Giudaita."

like inside. There are three hundred mosques, seven of which—the principal ones—have great domes covered with lead. There are also several well-constructed baths and bazaars, which are covered streets with shops on either side.

In the center of the city is a castle built on a rather high, round, and craggy hill. The castle is encrusted on all sides with stones, all of the same shape, and surrounded by a deep moat full of water in which live many aquatic birds, such as ducks, coots, and the like. The Jews say that the castle was built by Joab, the captain of King David; [some of them also] say it is [even] older, saying that inside a stone was found on which was written "I, Joab, took the castle for King David." The date was also written on it and from whom it was taken. One enters this castle through a single gate on a very beautiful stone bridge that goes from the plain of the city to the top of the mountain. Inside the castle in the mosque there is a room that the Turks call *khalili,* which means "room of Ibrahim Khalil," which is how they call Abraham.[40] Some Jews affirm that the city was not built by Abraham, but rather that he lived there with his family on the mountain where this room is that now bears his name. There is also another place that served as the mint in ancient times. They now call it *khazana,* which means "treasury," and there they keep whatever money there is.[41] There are also the prisons in the form of towers in the mountain. One enters them through the castle. One of these is terrible and is called the Prison of Blood.

This city is very populous. Besides European merchants, an infinite number of Greeks, Armenians, Arabs, and Persians go there with merchandise. There are more than 300,000 Turks and Arabs and 50,000 Christians—some Greek, Armenian, Syrian or Jacobite, Nestorian, and Maronite schismatics, who number 6,000 souls.[42] The Maronites are Catholics, since their prelates render obedience to the Roman Pontiff.[43] There are also one thousand Jewish families that live all together in one

40. The Prophet Abraham is known to Muslims as *Khalil Allah,* or Friend of God.

41. Bembo writes it as "casnà." The Arabic word is *khazana;* the Turkish is *hazine.*

42. Bembo's estimation of the population exceeds those of other sources, which record 14,000 households in Aleppo at the end of the seventeenth century.

43. The Maronites were reunited with the Roman Catholic Church at the 1445 Council of Florence: they were permitted to elect their own patriarch and to retain their own liturgical practices.

place in the city. The city is governed by a pasha who is a vizier. In his absence there is an official called a *müsellim*.[44] There is a qadi who is minister of the law and of justice, and a mufti who is like a bishop, an aga of the taxes called a *muhassil,* an aga of the janissaries and an aga of the *sipahi,* another aga of native janissaries, inferior in rank to the first, a *sabandar* or chief of the merchants, a chief of the *sheriffi* or relatives of the Prophet, and a *subaşı* who corresponds to a constable.[45] There are other less important posts. The castle is governed by an aga sent from Constantinople who cannot leave the castle without the permission of the pasha. There is also an aga of janissaries there. These number about five hundred. The territory or jurisdiction of the pasha of Aleppo is all around for two or three days' travel. On one side it borders with Bagaisso, a city I have already named; on another with Birecik and Urfa; on another with Gaziantep; and on the other with the castle of Thaibba in the desert. Some days were spent in receiving the visits of [Venetian] merchants and clergy before going to pay respects to the Turkish commander and before receiving the visits of other nationalities. The house was only furnished after the things had been sent from the customs house, and it was furnished in our fashion, as all the consuls do and also the merchants.

The residence of our consul is the best and the most ordered of all [the consular houses]. Up until the war it was cared for by the consuls themselves, who have always lived in it. They have purchased the house without the land, since Europeans are not permitted to buy land. The purchase is made by paying a sum stipulated by the Turkish owner and by taking on the obligation of paying to the same an annual fee that serves as rent or lease. The Turkish owner cannot take back the property without paying back the first sum, and the European, when he leaves or when he no longer wishes to live in the house, can sell it to another, who receives the obligation of paying the rent. The above-mentioned house is in the most noble quarter of the town and around it live almost all the "Franks," as the Europeans are called. It is near the customs house, the principal bazaars, and the residences of the most important commanders. A Jew had been chosen

44. Bembo writes it as "mussalem," the head civil service official and chief administrator of a district.

45. Bembo subsequently defines all of these terms, which he renders as follows: *muassil, spahini, sabandar, sheriffi,* and *surbassi.* He uses the term *bargello* for "constable."

as dragoman,[46] since Jews are usually also the dragomans of the other nations. This one had been recommended by the aga of the Customs, where he was serving as *Titabanno*,[47] which is an official. For household and daily affairs a Maronite Christian of Aleppo was chosen as second dragoman. He had spent many years in Venice, and his name was Attala,[48] which means Diodato [God given], and he knew the Arabic tongue as well as the Turkish. These two were sent with the usual entry gift to the qadi to set up an appointment. People go to him in the absence of the pasha, who was at that time engaged in the war with Poland. One never gets an audience with a Turkish official without first having sent a gift, and without an appointment it is difficult to settle even a private affair.

On the appointed morning came the small escort that was to accompany us to the residence of the qadi, which was not very far. First went the four janissaries with their large caps on their heads and their staffs in their hands, next [came] the two dragomans and livery servants, then the consul, followed by the rest of us. When we arrived, we were led to an open place where the qadi appeared, accompanied by several agas and youths. He had the consul sit in front of him, and the dragoman expressed the consul's greeting, which the qadi seemed to appreciate greatly. The youths brought coffee, sherbet, and then perfume, and the qadi gave the consul a golden robe. Having dealt a little with several questions, the consul took leave. The qadi remained standing in the same place until the consul stepped out of that place, and in the same order in which we came, we returned home.

It seems necessary not to delay the explanation of the offices of the qadi and the other officials. I will only say that the pasha of this city is always a vizier, whose government usually lasts a year, unless he is made *ma'zul*, that is, removed from office, as often happens.[49] Pashas are changed two or three times in a year, but sometimes they are confirmed for more than a year on paying a fee of 500,000 reales to the great lord (the Ottoman sultan) for

46. The dragoman (from the Arabic *turjuman*) was an official, functioning as guide and translator, who was responsible for assisting foreign merchants, diplomats, and travelers.

47. Presumably an Italian term.

48. 'Ata' Allah.

49. There were far more qualified individuals than available judicial posts, so that appointment to high office was limited to a year, after which time the officeholder would be relieved of office, and his name would be placed at the bottom of the list of the *ma'zul* (the "dismissed"). This rotation of officials also

a year of government. Besides, they make a large gift of money to the Grand Vizier[50] so as to receive the appointment, since the distribution of all government offices depends upon him. The pasha has supreme authority over the city and its territory; from the official posts he assigns in the towns and places of his government he gains for himself more than 100,000 reales, besides which he receives every day in the city a certain portion of meat, bread, oil, coffee, tobacco, rice, and other similar foodstuffs, all without payment. He also gets funds from judicial proceedings, and from taxes,[51] which give more or less profit depending on the pasha's tyranny. He has, in addition, the gifts of the consuls and other things of little importance. Not unlike the earnings, however, are the expenses. Besides the expense to get his office [that I have] mentioned above, he also has to maintain his court, which is numerous and sometimes numbers more than 3,000 people. When the pashas are obliged to go to war, they leave their lieutenants, called müsellim, whom they can change at will according to how they comport themselves. In the year 1672 three had been changed in one month. This official is usually an aga of his court and receives as his pay 10% of all that he collects on the pasha's behalf in tributes, judgments, condemnations, and every other affair having to do with the pasha, to whom he renders a minute account. Some, however, do steal beyond their right in the judgments, which they secretly sell. The city gives to them, too, that portion of foodstuffs that I mentioned above.

The qadi is the second official and has much authority. He is selected by the Grand Mufti of Constantinople, to whom he donates a substantial gift to have his job. His government lasts a year, during which he has the right to 40,000 reales, in addition to what he gets from his judgments and taxes. He, too, receives a limited contribution of foodstuffs, like the pasha. His job is to see to it that the city has abundant food and to set the prices for bread, fruit, and every other food, and to see that the weights and measures of all these things are just. He is called minister of laws and justice because his office is to administer justice in all that happens in the city and to pass sen-

---

prevented any one individual from building up a significant local power base, always a major Ottoman concern. While among the ma'zul, the former office-holder would still receive a pension.

50. Bembo uses the term "First Vizier." The Turkish is *sadrazam*.

51. Bembo uses the term "avania." There was an Ottoman extraordinary levy called *avariz,* to which he may be referring.

tences, referring death penalties to the pasha, who then has them executed. But when the pashas are proud and violent men, they do what they want with absolute power without the consent of the qadis. The dress of this minister is that common to all Turks; it is different only in the knotting of the turban, which is rather larger than those of others, not unlike the Persian in size, and made of white material pointed at the top with graticulated binding, like all the 'ulema wear, that is, the Doctors.[52] All the qadis have a profession, like doctors in law; most of them descend from 'ulema, which is a family of doctors; and, before taking over an office, each member must have spent several years in Constantinople in a certain place, like a seminary, where there are some old men who teach the law and precepts of the *Qur'an,* which is the most sacred book of the sect of Muhammad. Having finished these appointed years, they are sent as qadis in various parts of the Empire. They are distinguished in various ranks according to the pay in aspri assigned to each one. Those of highest rank are called qadi of 500 aspri a day, and they go to the principal cities. Others have 300 aspri, and still others less; the lowest rank is of 150 aspri. Those of the top rank do not take their pay, but the title gives them honor; they hold no other office besides the one of principal qadi.

The mufti is like a bishop or patriarch chosen by the [Sublime] Porte.[53] It is an entirely honorary post: he makes no donation and receives no benefit for himself. Usually it lasts one year, but when the mufti is of the locality, it lasts for life. His office is to judge and decide points of laws and the difficulties that arise in trials and similar things.

The muhassil (or aga of the Customs House) is an official whose office it is to collect the earnings, taxes, and duties of the country for a year, paying to the Great Lord 225,000 reales, in addition to the donation of another 125,000 reales that he makes to the Grand Vizier so as to receive his office, which often is confirmed for two or three years.[54] In this way the Great Lord collects his income throughout the entire state without disturbance and without fraud on the part of the ministers. Their earnings depend upon

52. The term 'ulema designated those learned in Islam who constituted the religious hierarchy in the Ottoman Empire. The Grand Mufti of Constantinople was the head of the 'ulema.

53. In this Ottoman context the mufti was an officially appointed interpreter of religious law *(shari'a).*

54. In other words, he was a tax farmer on royal land.

Fortune, more or less, according to the quantity of merchandise and on the abundance of duties.

The aga of the *sipahi* is like a colonel of the cavalry and is appointed by the Great Aga of Constantinople, to whom he makes a small donation. He has no rights other than what he receives from the trials of his own *sipahi,* who, like the janissaries, cannot be judged by the pasha or other officials, but only by their aga. The Great Aga of Constantinople also appoints the aga of the janissaries, or colonel of the foot militia, but without a donation and without rights other than those over his soldiers, that is, the true janissaries noted in the book of Constantinople.[55] Since the War of Candia, however, they are very few, and many are called *oturak* [or housebound persons].[56] They are paid sixty aspri and are unfit or invalid officers. This aga has the keys of the city. However, during the day the gates are guarded by the janissaries of the country, whose aga is called *aga delcul.*[57] He is appointed by the Porte and is of inferior rank. Nor does he make a donation or have any rights other than over his janissaries, who are 200 people of the area, recorded only in the book of Aleppo. They are paid from five to eight aspri a day and in time of war are obliged to leave the city whose gates they guard. Their aga auctions the gates to the highest bidder, and they get part of the fees exacted on all the goods that enter the gates. The aga has a further source of income from these janissaries, who are shopkeepers and who take their titles only for the honor and authority and leave their pay to the aga, who in turn exempts them from military duty.

The chief of the sheriffi (or relatives of their Prophet) is elected in Constantinople by the Great Chief of the sheriffi without a donation.[58] It is his office to judge all the sheriffi of the city, who, when they commit any crime, are sent to their Chief for punishment. The *sabandar* is a chief of merchants created by the Porte without donation and without significant rights; his office lasts many years. The subaşı is like a constable,[59] placed in

55. The phrase "aga of the janissaries" here refers to the local commander of a provincial garrison. The military rank would have been *yayabaşı,* and this officer would have been in command of either a hundred or a thousand soldiers.

56. Bembo's *oturach* was an official retired on a pension.

57. The meaning of *aga delcul* is unclear.

58. This reference must be to the *nakibü'l-eşraf,* the marshal of the local descendants of the Prophet's family. The local *nakib* had to report to the chief *nakib* in the capital.

59. In Istanbul a *subaşı* was one of the principal police officers responsible

office by the pasha, who confirms him every three months, for which he donates 2,000 reales. He receives many fees from the taverns of the Christians, from the public prostitutes, who must be 1,000 [in number] and who must pay a fee every month (of eight reales each). He also receives fees from men he finds with prostitutes if they are not soldiers (who alone have the right to frequent such women), from drunks, from anyone walking in the city at night, which is forbidden after one o'clock when the doors of the quarters and bazaars are closed. He also gets some donations from the foreigners who want permission to walk at night from one of their residences to another, but only in carnival months. The aga of the citadel is appointed in Constantinople, and this appointment is for a lifetime. He can never leave the citadel without the permission of the pasha. He keeps the keys of the citadel, in which are two hundred pieces of large and small artillery. He is paid a sum a day and also has fees from the justice rendered in the castle, which has an aga of janissaries, also appointed in Constantinople, who has about five hundred soldiers.

After the visit with the qadi we received [the visits] of the consuls. The first was that of the consul of France, who came on the appointed day at the 24th hour. He wore shoes and robe all in red (except for his hat), which is the way the other consuls also dress. He was accompanied by all his countrymen, dragomans, and janissaries. He was met by our consul with all his countrymen at the gate of the street, and the consul of France took up a position to the right of our consul and went with him up into the audience hall accompanied only by the dragomans who serve as masters of ceremonies not only during encounters among consuls but also at meetings with the Ottomans. All the nationals remained in the portico where, as was the custom, a great, long table was spread with a breakfast that can well be called a dinner, even if it was made up of cold foods, cakes, pastry, sweetmeats, and similar things. Much glass was broken without regard during the meal [in toasts] to the health of the rulers and officials. In the gaiety full bottles of wine were thrown to the ground and, without exaggeration, a lake of wine was formed in the entire portico. The consuls ate separately in the hall with the door closed, and thus they passed more than two hours in continual festivities and amidst applause. The Frenchman was accompanied by our consul to the gate of the street once again and by our countrymen to

---

for general obedience to police ordinances. In the provinces they held military fiefs *(zeamet)* and commanded a detachment of cavalry.

his residence; I also went along to attend him. Ahead of us along the street went eight torches borne by staff bearers in uniform, four from our consul and four from the French. For this occasion permission had been obtained from the *subaşı* to walk at night. When we arrived at the house of the French consul, we found set out in the portico another breakfast, this time rather modest, and the same revelries and toasts were repeated with infinite destruction of goblets and bottles. In the heat of the drinking they over-turned the table with all the food almost on top of their consul, who was little loved by them, even though he was a fine person of modest height and a Knight of Marseilles, named Monsieur Josef du Pont. He has been a con-sul for more than three years, through the bounty of the king an hereditary office in three families of the Knights of Marseilles. Since the three families are related, they arrange things among themselves, sometimes taking the office themselves and sometimes renting it. When this second recreation was finished, the consul insisted on accompanying me to the gate, where, having taken leave, I returned home with the rest of my countrymen.

Several days later in the same form and with the same ceremonies, we received the visit of the English consul, with less confusion although his del-egation was more numerous.[60] The consul is a merchant elected by the Company of Merchants of the Levant in London. There were some Dutch-men, who in other times had had their consul, who held fourth place, but through lack of commerce their consulate has been suspended, and they are now under the protection of the consul of France, as are some Flemish. They pay the French consul a fee like those of his own nationality, and he has the obligation of maintaining them and protecting them with the officials and from taxes, as if they were of his own nation. Afterward we went to return the visits, first to the French consul and then to the English, by whom we were treated in the same fashion. Both these consuls and the other merchants have their houses above the Grand Khan (Great Caravan-serai),[61] which is a square area with houses all around it and beneath them many warehouses and the customs house, the officials of which are called *titabanni*[62] and are all Jews, atrocious thieves, through whose hands pass all

60. Benjamin Lannoy was the English consul in Aleppo from 1659 to 1672.
61. Bembo is apparently referring to the Khan al-Gumruk (the Customs Khan), built in 1574, which contained a total of 344 shops, both on the inside of the building and along its exterior façade.
62. *Titabanni* is the plural of *titabanno*, used previously.

business concerning the duties on the Franks, from whom, as from the aga himself, they rob what they want with very great industriousness. This plaza is closed at night and the keys are kept by the *bawwab*,[63] who is the gatekeeper and who pays a sum to the owner of the plaza and receives a limited payment from everything that goes out of that gate: [this is] a custom practiced in every khan, as also in individual houses, where the tips are given to the servants. In the houses of the consuls it [receiving tips] is the right of the janissaries who attend them and who receive a salary of forty and a half reales every three months. In this plaza and in the adjoining bazaar the Frankish merchants gather in the mornings to stroll and to do their business, since that place serves as the public square. Throughout the city there are many other khans of good construction made in the manner of cloisters. These belong to individual Turks who live there themselves; parts of [these khans] serve as warehouses for foreign merchandise, while other parts are set aside for the lodging of subject and foreign peoples.

There are five curious things in that city and in almost all of Turkey: iron gates, wooden keys, iron-shod men, women in trousers, and bells that speak. The first two are self-explanatory. All the doors of bazaars and of khans are completely covered by sheets of iron, and they are closed by a lock made of two pieces of wood and are opened with another piece of wood. They are as secure and strong as those of iron. The next two can be understood in the costumes. Beneath the heels of their shoes[64] men wear a small piece of iron in the form of a horseshoe; and the women wear trousers like the men, and the rest of their dress is also similar to that of men. The only difference is in the turban, instead of which they wear on their heads an *'araqiyya*,[65] which is shaped like a bowl and is of gold, silver, tin, or cardboard covered with silk, depending on the rank and wealth of the wearer. They keep these *'araqiyya* on their heads bound in their hair, which they wear in one or more plaits down their backs. The plaits have ribbons that reach their feet, and some attach to the ribbons silver bells that they call *sarpagi*.[66] All the women go out of their houses with their faces covered.

---

63. Turkish *bevvab*. In Bembo's transcription it is "baobo."

64. Bembo uses the Italian word *papuccie*. The Persian word is *papush*, and the Turkish is *pabuç*. Bembo was presumably struck by these similarities.

65. A soft felt cap, often embroidered, worn by both men and women, it is called *'araqiyya* in Arabic and *arakıye* in Turkish.

66. This is apparently derived from the Turkish word *serpuşe*, Persian *sarpush*, for "headdress."

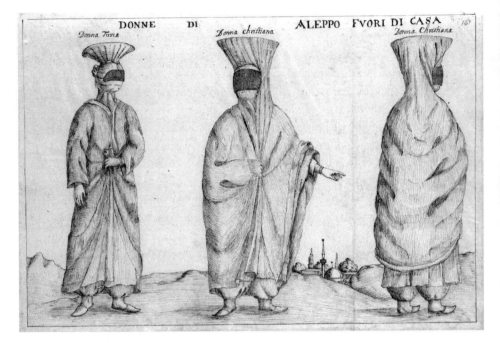

FIGURE 9. Women of Aleppo #1.

They cover their chins and part of their cheeks with a white linen tied to the bottom of their 'araqiyya. The rest of the face, that is, the forehead and the eyes, is covered with a transparent black veil, made of horse hair, through which they see very well without being seen or recognized even by their own relatives. The Christian women wear the same dress, and, in addition, they wear a great white linen cloth that covers them entirely. They put it over the 'araqiyya, and it falls behind them almost to the ground; and in front they hold it under their arms, as can be seen in the drawing. This costume is also used by many Turkish women, since it is more graceful and more majestic with the linen cloth than without. The women of Tripoli have a similar dress, except for the 'araqiyya, which, instead of being of the shape described, is a long and pointed cone. The Bedouin women, who are the peasants, do not cover their faces and dress simply, as can be seen in the drawing. They have the custom of decorating their arms and abdomen with flowers and figures drawn with a certain mixture that lasts forever, as do the pilgrims of Jerusalem.

At this opportunity I will say that the dress of the men is long, as is the

FIGURE 10. Women of Aleppo #2.

custom everywhere in the Orient, and they wear long beards and shave their heads. The Christians, too, dress this way, not differently from the Turks, except only in the turban, which is not white but has stripes of various colors. Soldiers and travelers wear one other color on their turbans besides white, such as red, yellow, or some other color, or green, but [this latter color is] with silk because only the sherifs can wear green, which is a color dedicated to their prophet, so that it is forbidden to Christians to use it in anything. The Jews, too, are different. They wear instead of a turban a tall, round, and violet cap, as is seen in the drawing. It very much resembles the form of an old-fashioned hat without the brim. Some of the Jews, however, pay a fee so as to be able to wear a turban like the Christians. They may not ever wear yellow shoes, but only violet ones to distinguish them from the Turks and the Christians. The large cap, or *gibellini*,[67] is permitted only to the dragomans, as is seen in the drawing. The doctors, who are called

67. Presumably the Italian word *zibellino*, "sable fur or skin."

FIGURE II. Men of Aleppo.

'ulema, have a turban different from the other Turks in the way that it is bound; theirs is graticulated, like that of the qadi. The Franks wear hats and dress in their own costumes, but the majority wear an outer robe, as is the custom in that country, so as to accommodate to that nation and so as to avoid the insolence of the people for whom our costumes are a folly. The insolences, however, come only from the youth, soldiers, and women and consist in a few insulting words. The most common are *Fringe Coco*[68] and similar things, by which they believe to be giving great insult. Sometimes they even throw small stones.

The last of the five things over which we have dwelt considerably is that of the bells that speak. To explain them I will say that all the mosques, which are very many, have their minaret, which is like a tower in the shape of our bell towers but round. They are called minaret because that means the place of the lamp,[69] and they light many lamps on top of these for their feasts. They

68. "Franks are cuckoo."
69. Bembo's definition of the Arabic *minar* is correct.

are rather high and not very wide. On the top is a crescent moon, and at a height above two-thirds of the minor there is a little terrace all around to which one accedes by internal stairs. This serves to call the people to prayer. Depending on its wealth, each mosque pays four or more persons a large salary. Their office is to take turns going up to the terrace at the appointed hours to invite the people to prayer six times during the day and night.[70] The first, which is at the break of day, is called in Arabic *salat al-subh* and in Turkish *sabah namazı;* the second is at midday [and is called] in Arabic *salat al-zuhr* and in Turkish *öğle namazı;* the third, around the time of compline, [is called in] Arabic the *salat al-'asr* and in Turkish *ikindi namazı;* the fourth [is] at the setting of the sun and the appearance of the first star [and is called] in Arabic *salat al-maghrib* and in Turkish *akşam namazı;* the fifth is at the second hour of the night [and is called] in Arabic *salat al-'isha'* and in Turkish *yatsı namazı;* the sixth is at midnight [and is called] in Arabic *salat tahajjud* and in Turkish *teheccüd.* On every one of the minarets they make these calls at the same instant, which makes no little noise; and for this office are chosen those who demonstrate a vigorous voice. There was one while I was there who shouted so loudly that with the help of the wind he could be heard many miles distant; and these men are called *mulla.*[71] The words which they say in their language are the following in ours: "God is great. God is great. I affirm that Muhammad is the apostle of God. The hour of prayer has come. God is great. A prayer and a greeting to you, O my Lord and Apostle of God. A

70. Common Muslim practice is limited to five daily *salats* (ritual prayers) at specific times: the *maghrib* at sunset, the *'isha'* at nightfall, the *subh* or *fajr* at daybreak, the *zuhr* shortly after midday, and the *'asr* at midafternoon. Bembo's reference to six prayers includes the nonobligatory *tahajjud* (or *lail*) at midnight. His rendering of the Arabic is less than precise, and sometimes badly garbled: "The first, which is at the break of day, is called in Arabic *ctenialam* and in Turkish *sabach namati;* the second is at midday [and is called] in Arabic *zar* and in Turkish *oiele zamani;* the third, around the time of compline, [is called in] Arabic the *assera* and in Turkish *ichindi;* the fourth [is] at the setting of the sun and the appearance of the first star [and is called] in Arabic *mapel* and in Turkish *axian namasi;* the fifth is at the second hour of the night [and is called] in Arabic *esshe* and in Turkish *iazi;* the sixth is at midnight [and is called] in Arabic *annuel* or the *moro* and in Turkish *tengiti.*"

71. The more common term in English is *muezzin* (in Arabic, *mu'adhdhin;* and in Turkish, *müezzin*). Bembo's word "mualla" is perhaps a confusion with *mulla.* (*Mualla* in Turkish means "exalted, transcendent, sublime.")

prayer and a greeting to you, O my intercessor to God, O Seal of the apostles of God. A prayer and a greeting to you, O Prophet of God. I affirm that there is only one God." The above words they shout as loudly as possible in each of the four directions—east, west, south, and north—always making the first call in the direction that looks toward where the tomb of the Prophet is, where 3,000 gold and silver lamps are lit. It is in Arabia in the city called Medina al-Nabi, which means "city" of the Prophet.[72] In addition to the six calls just described, they make another [one] two hours before midday, which in Turkish is called *salat-i duha*.[73] This is a long call with many prayers that six or more persons make shouting all together like a choir. It is made only from the minaret of the Great Mosque on Fridays, which is the weekly holy day among the Turks, as Sunday is among us Christians. However, on that day they are not obliged to abstain from work, although the majority and the most zealous close their shops. On Thursday night, besides the ordinary prayer at the second hour of the night, they make another immediately following. It is long, and many make it together, and in Arabic it is called the *salat al-lail*.[74] Early Thursday evening they light many lamps around the minaret of the Great Mosque, which is justly so named. It was made by the Christians in a square shape, as can be seen in the drawing, tall and of good architecture, and it was of the church of St. John Damascene, which with its convent they have converted into the Great Mosque.[75] In the wall is still preserved a stone pulpit, where the said saint is supposed to have

72. Bembo writes "Medina Talnati." He must have taken this spelling from written Arabic, since in spoken Arabic or Turkish the pronunciation would be *Madinat an-nabi*. It suggests that Bembo may have used his months in Aleppo to learn at least some written Arabic.

73. Bembo uses the word *sella* for this supererogatory prayer, *salat al-duha* in Arabic (and in Turkish *salat-i duha*).

74. Bembo refers to it as a prayer named *mulleta*.

75. Bembo's account seems to be composed of several elements. The pre-Muslim Christian basilica of Damascus was founded by the Emperor Theodosius and subsequently placed under the name of St. John the Baptist. In 708 the 'Umayyad Caliph al-Walid appropriated the site to build the Great Mosque of Damascus. The Great Mosque of Aleppo was probably founded by his brother, the Caliph Sulayman (r. 715–717). A thirteenth-century Arab source states that the site of the Great Mosque was acquired from the Christians of Aleppo by treaty; during the Byzantine period the site had been occupied by the cathedral's cemetery and garden. See K. A. C. Creswell, *Early Muslim*

FIGURE 12. Great Mosque of Aleppo.

preached; and the chapel, where mass used to be celebrated and which is kept closed, has a wall in common with the house of the consul of Venice. Another ceremony is held on the minaret on the occasion of the death of an important person. Various prayers of many people together are recited, usually on the minaret of the Great Mosque, since there are people who leave good sums of money at their deaths so that such prayers can be said there. These prayers are also recited on public occasions, such as at times of great need or of victories and other happy events.

All the mosques have a plaza enclosed by a wall in front of their doors.[76]

―――――

Architecture, revised 2nd ed. (Oxford University Press, 1969, 2 vols.), vol. I, p. 483.

76. Bembo is describing a classic Ottoman mosque with a domed sanctuary preceded by an atrium-like forecourt containing a facility for ablutions known as a *şadırvan.*

In the middle is a fountain that serves the Turks for washing before entering the mosque. Nor is it permitted to Christians to set foot into these spaces except in the Bab al-Hadid Mosque and the Bayramiye Mosque, since their builders wanted to permit free passage to all.[77] Mosques have two doors. Inside the mosques there is nothing other than a niche on the side that looks toward the burial place of the Prophet, toward which they face in making their prayers. There are also many small glass lamps hung on strings. It is not permitted to women to enter mosques, since they say that their prayers are not acceptable to God. After death their souls go to a certain separate place until the Day of Judgment, when Muhammad will intercede with God for their ascension to Paradise. I do not want to omit one observation that I made of a truly unimportant thing, but which in my opinion merits some reflection, and that is that in the crowds that go to each mosque there is never a case of anyone taking someone else's shoes on going out (they leave them at the gate when they enter), even if they are three or four hundred. They never change them for those of a comrade, either through error or through malice.

Near the Antioch Gate,[78] close by, is a bridge under which passes a small river that comes through underwater aqueducts from Ailan Villa, two miles away.[79] Near the bridge there is a waterwheel, and around it are many houses that look out on the water, and for pleasure the Great Turks often go to eat and enjoy themselves. Toward evening many people of all nationalities go out from the city to stroll in this place. This water supplies the entire city. It is brought to many fountains through great underground pipes. Some of these are in the public streets, and others are in private houses. There are paid specialized workers in each quarter who renew the water in the fountains several times a week and continually in the houses of the great and of the commanders. For pleasure in private houses they keep the fountains running all day for a small fee. They are kept busy because, besides maintaining the public fountains and those of the mosques,

77. Although Bembo's mention of the mosques of Bad Adelie and Veramie does not specify location, he is presumably referring to two extant mosques: the Bad Adelie mosque (*masjid Bab al-Hadid,* the Iron Gate Mosque), probably built around 1500 by the Mamluk sultan Qansu al-Ghori, who built the Iron Gate; and the Veramie mosque (*Bayramiye* mosque), a large, Ottoman-style mosque founded by Bayram Pasha, the Ottoman vizier from 1637 to 1638.

78. Bembo terms it redundantly the "Gate Bab Antachie."

79. The Quweiq River provided water for Aleppo.

they are obliged to provide water in abundance for the baths, which are more than one hundred and to which a great number of people of both sexes go continually. They go immediately after having committed any sin, since they think that water will wipe it away. The great have baths in their own houses for greater convenience and more privacy and usually also pray inside their houses.

The frequency of these baths is believed to be the reason that the Turks are free of syphilis. In the house of the Venetian consul is a fountain that can be turned on whenever one wishes, as well as two wells of spring water, which, however, is not good and is used for ordinary things. For drinking water there is a great cistern that holds enough for five months' use by the entire court. Whenever it is refilled, it is allowed to rest for about twenty days, after which the water is perfect. Thus, many people have in their houses similar cisterns.

Not far from the bridge mentioned above there is a great stretch of very beautiful sandy plain that they call [the] *maydan*,[80] where every Friday the pasha and his people go to play the game of *jerida* on horseback after dinner. On one side there is a covered loggia where the pasha rests to watch the game, which consists of chasing after one another on horseback and throwing staffs at one another.[81]

Not too far outside the Gate of the Prisons there is a small hill under which are several grottoes, or caverns. They are very long and made by chiseling, since the stone is soft and almost like chalk. There they make ropes. The prisons of said Gate are very weak, and with little effort one could escape from them, since it is easy to remove the stones. But inside it are only

80. A large open plaza *(maydan)* that could serve as a playing field, parade ground, festival center, and occasional commercial area was a central feature of many Middle Eastern cities.

81. Bembo renders it as "gerida." His "staff" was the *jarid* (Arabic, *jarid*; Turkish, *cerid*), a blunt javelin used in the game of the same name, one of the most popular of all Ottoman sports, particularly in the second half of the seventeenth century, when the *cerid oyunu* was one of the chief equestrian games at the Ottoman court in Istanbul and in the provinces. The javelin could range in size from 75 to 150 centimeters in length and was hurled from horseback at one's mounted opponent. Like polo, the game required formidable equestrian skills; it also demanded courage, since players frequently suffered injury or even death. Rival players were divided into two mock armies, and the role of pursuer and pursued alternated between them.

those who are held for debts which they were not able to pay, and after forty days they are released, and the creditor has the right to remove the clothes from their backs or to take other things as he sees fit. Public debts are extracted by force of the stick, especially from Jews and poor Christians, who, without distinction, pay a tax of six reales apiece each year.[82] Some who are poorer pay four and others three. Yet although 50,000 Christians are counted, they receive taxes for only 40,000, for it does not include children under fourteen years of age, who are not obligated to pay taxes. While collecting this money, the agents of the muhassil walk through the city and suburbs with a Christian and with a Jew, [each of] whom has a book with the names of those who are debtors, and finding them, they force them to pay, if not everything, then a part. And when they resist, they use the stick, and they also put them in prison. The Christians or Jews who are foreigners and who remain in the city only one day pay a tax of 3½ piasters when they are found by the agents of the same muhassil. This sum is often stolen from those officials, since the names of these people are not included in the tax book. There are other taxes also that are paid equally by foreigners and Turks. They are collected by the heads of the quarters, which are seventy-two between the city and the suburbs, forty-seven in the suburbs, and twenty-five in the city. One of these quarters is occupied by the Jews, who live all together, and that is between the Gate of Bab Ferag and the Gate Bab al-Nasr,[83] near the wall that is called *Basita,* that is, the first.[84] Many Christians live in the city, but the majority in the suburb Jedeideh, not far from the gate known as Bab al-Faraj, where they have good houses and several churches, since they are of different rites, among whom our missionaries work with great success.[85] They are Capuchins, Franciscans, Discalced Carmelites, and Jesuits. They instruct them and remove them from schism, and on the occasion of confessions and sermons they are much venerated and

82. The *jizya* was a head tax on non-Muslims that had been in use since the earliest days of Islam.

83. Since *bab* means "gate," the combination of the two terms is redundant.

84. Bembo is incorrect. The Arabic word for "first" is *awwali,* and the Turkish is *birinci.* I suggest that Bembo's "Basita" is a misunderstanding of the Arabic *wasta,* meaning "middle." The wall is in the middle of the two gates.

85. Bembo is referring to the Jedeideh quarter to the north of the Bab al-Faraj, one of the best-preserved areas of the city. Catholic missions were especially active in Aleppo in the seventeenth century, so that by the early eighteenth century the city had a significant Catholic population.

esteemed by the people, who find them useful. All these clergy live in the city and use their own habits. Only the Jesuit fathers have adjusted theirs to the costume of the country, and they wear black shoes and a black aba instead of a cloak and underneath it their long robe. What most attracts attention is that they wear a black turban with a white band instead of a hat, as do the religious of those Christians. All these missionaries have in their houses secret chapels with their vestments, which they keep hidden, celebrating mass at dawn because it is permitted by the Turks only in the chapels of the consuls and officiated by the Franciscan Fathers of the Holy Land, who were under the protection of the Venetians before the war and who were supported by them.[86] After the public church that they first had was closed, they used to celebrate solemnly the offices, masses, sermons, and other ecclesiastical functions in the Venetian chapel, and now they do it in the chapel of the French. The Venetians have the services of only one chaplain, a Franciscan of the Osservanza, who at my visit was named Fra Giacomo da Venezia and who celebrated mass every day.[87]

Not far from the suburb of the Christians just described are the burial places of the Turks, which are also located in two or three other places. The tombs have nothing more than a stone set upright at the head and another at the feet of the deceased. When they bring the dead to be buried, they close them in a casket in which, however, they do not bury the body, since it serves only as a catafalque,[88] and to distinguish the men from the women, they place at the head of the casket a turban for a man and a *rakiya* for a woman. They are accompanied to the burial by many people, relatives and doctors ('ulema), singing various prayers, and I was told that they close the mouths, noses, ears and other body openings of all the dead with cotton wool so that the devil will not enter into them when they are buried. It is the custom that all the women go twice a week, on Mondays and Thursdays, to weep over the tombs of their dead, and on some occasions I saw from six

86. The Franciscans had been active in the Middle East since the thirteenth century, and they had frequently accompanied Italian merchants as they established commercial establishments. In the fourteenth century Franciscans were granted residence in Palestine in order to serve as caretakers of Christian holy sites.

87. The Friars Minor of the Observance were one of the major reformist divisions within the Franciscan order.

88. In Islamic practice the deceased is wrapped in pilgrim's garb and interred without a coffin, with the body resting on its side facing Mecca.

to seven thousand together. With the pretext of piety they rest a little and sometimes do some smuggling. Not far from the same suburb are also the burial places of the Franks, which are of large marble stones with inscriptions, partly in Latin and partly in the native tongue of the individual.

Since the Turks are not easy to deal with or to converse with, the Franks have little familiarity with them outside of business matters. The entertainment of the Europeans thus consists of exchanging frequent meal invitations by day and by night. Many of the houses adjoin one another and communicate by way of terraces. In the summer they serve as pleasant walking places where people can eat in the open air, which is perfect and healthy. Like the local people, the Europeans also sleep there, many totally uncovered, and many with pavilions of black cloth, certain that from the beginning of summer until the next winter not one drop of water will fall from the sky, nor will any clouds be seen. If one is there when the sun sets, one can enjoy the sight of millions of crows that pass over the city as they go at night to places near water. And in the morning one can see many Turkish women arising from their sleep, but to avoid accidents and fines, one doesn't pay much attention to them. Another available pastime is to go on horseback out of the city to the gardens and on through the very attractive countryside. The horses are beautiful and high-spirited: the finest of them are found in Aleppo, and from there they are then sent to Constantinople and to Persia. The very best are Arabic, very swift and well formed.

In the house of some merchant or other, one can play cards, but the greatest entertainment that is open to everyone is in some taverns run by Frenchmen and by Englishmen that serve as inns and resort places, and there many merchants go to play and to dine. In one of these taverns that belongs to some Frenchmen there was a table tennis game where I would spend several hours at a time.

At this point I will tell how wine is made in those parts, for by law it is forbidden to the Turks. To have permission for winemaking, foreigners apply to the pasha every year and give him a sum of money, as do the native Christians themselves to whom some years it is even denied. Once permission has been obtained, one buys grapes on the farms and brings them to the city in sacks, paying for them so much a *qintar*, which is a weight of _____ pounds.[89] They put them, once pressed, into large containers with the must and only the skins, and instead of letting it boil, they beat it with a stick con-

89. Bembo calls it a *cantaro* and omits the equivalent measure here but

tinually for many days, after which they strain it, and a yellow, almost golden-colored wine remains, since most of the grapes are white. The taste is not very delicate, and it is rather strong and able to take much water. It is also not too healthful, because it has some small stones, since the vines grow low and close to the earth when planted in the fields.

As for foodstuffs, one is rather well off—that is, for bread, meats, poultry, and game birds, of which there is a great quantity, especially partridges, woodcocks, and warblers, at very good prices, whereas the Turks eat little of these things. There are few fruits, but they are healthy and rather beautiful, without worms growing inside them, as they do in ours, which is the result of that beautiful climate. Nevertheless, the city is troubled a little by some sort of contagious disease almost every five years. Preceding it, there appears a great abundance of white truffles, which are sold very cheaply in the bazaars. The Turks, however, pay little attention to the plague, not bothered by it, and staying in their houses without caring at all if they come into contact with an infected person. They always say that if they have to die, they will die. The Franks and many of the subject Christians close themselves in their own houses on these occasions, and many go to live in the villages in the mountains, where they stay until the disease has passed.

In the month of September begins the most delightful recreation that the Franks have over there, which is the hunting of hares practiced by the English. They have a most flourishing business there and thus [can] pay for a horse for each of their youths, who are many for this purpose. Since they are a rather numerous group, the Turks permit them to hunt only with falcons. They hunt twice a week, on Wednesday and Saturday, and also invite other foreigners as well as some Turks. They also have excellent dogs. So that the recreation will be more pleasurable and without disorder, they elect a captain of the hunt and other officials, who arrange everything and stay in office for a year, during which are held two general hunts and two sumptuous banquets. One is held on the occasion of the election of the new officials, and the second at the time of the first hunt after the election of the officials. These two dinners take place on a hill two hours' distance from the city, and the expenses are paid in different measures by the officials themselves. They receive only the fines of those who break the laws of the hunt, to which, however, only their countrymen are subject. These are some of the

defines it in his account of his travels from Isfahan to Aleppo as "a weight of 120 pounds." A *qintar* equals 53.9 kg in present-day Syria.

fines: going on horseback too near the dog, leaving the horse to chase the hare, bumping into another horseman while galloping, eating hares not caught in the hunt or killed by the gun, and similar things. To each [of these rules] is attached a particular punishment that results in the game's being more fun. I went very many times, the first of which was a few days after my arrival in that city. The captains of the hunt came to the house to invite me, and on the appointed morning they came to accompany me. Having gone out of the Iron Gate (Bab al-Hadid)[90] to find all our countrymen with the consul, we waited there for the French consul, who also had been invited and who arrived soon afterward. Thus together we passed the pistachio gardens, a known fruit, the tree of which resembles the fig in size. The fruit matures in the month of August, and it is sweet when fresh and similar to the broad bean in texture. Then it is placed to dry on the terraces before being sent to our parts. Having passed the gardens, one enters a great open country without trees and without dips, where the horses, the dogs, and the hares have freedom to run as much as they like without obstacles. As soon as we arrived there, numbering about 150 persons on horseback, everyone began to search [for hares]. The aga of the Customs was also with us along with some of his court. The hunt was splendid, since we found many hares. Even for ordinary hunts, they always let loose about twenty. Whoever catches one immediately cuts its tail and puts [the tail] on his hat, carrying the hare home or making a present of it to some guest by throwing it at the feet of his horse, as is the custom during the hunt. The fun continued until dinnertime. Then, on the customary hill, under a great pavilion with rugs and cushions, was set out the table for the entire party, except for the aga, for whom there was a separate pavilion. The meal was generous and abundant but of coarse food, which is the food of [the English] country. There were chicken pies, many of them with abundant leavening, many boiled chickens and roast ones, and entire quarters of beef, much liked by the English, also boiled and roasted. Everything was cold. On the days of the ordinary hunts they usually return to the city for a heavier meal, taking with them a small portion of the food to eat at various parties. Without doubt this is the greatest entertainment that there is in that country.

However, even in those large numbers, one never goes there unarmed, [since one has to be able] to defend oneself from the Arab thieves that over-

90. Bembo calls it the *Bab Bancussa*. It is also known as the *Bab al-Qanat*, or Canal Gate.

run the countryside, robbing passersby and even the caravans. They are the remainders of the Saracens who once dominated that whole country.[91] Put to flight by the Ottomans, they retired into the deserted countryside under various chiefs and princes called emirs. They divided themselves and spread throughout those provinces. Through necessity, being a lazy people without [other] occupation in that sterile land, they gave themselves over to robbing. To live, they overrun the countryside even near the cities, despoiling everyone they meet without distinction and imposing fees on the caravans, many of which they sack, without, however, being cruel to the people, other than robbing them without provocation. And even though they are not many in numbers, they almost hold the cities under siege, since the caravans cannot go far from [the cities], nor pass from one city to another, except in great numbers. It has never been possible for the pashas to hold them in check, since [the bandits] do not have permanent settlements, but are to be found now here, now there, under pavilions in the open countryside. Besides, their horses are accustomed to hardship and are tireless, take little food, and are so fast that it is impossible to catch them. As Tasso says: "Asciutti anno i cavalli, al corso usati, alla fatica pronti, al cibo parchi."[92]

Some of these emirs render obedience as feudatories to the Great Lord by whom they are confirmed. Among these was the Amir 'Abd al-'Aziz,[93] whose jurisdiction extended from Baghdad or Babylon to Damascus. But he incurred the hate of his people because he administered justice and punished thieves, so they deposed him, putting in his place Mehemed Shadid,[94] a relative, an easygoing man who let assassins go unpunished. He took over on September 20, 1672, while I was in Aleppo.[95] 'Abd al-'Aziz had therefore taken refuge under the walls of the city with five hundred of his men, pavilions, and baggage to implore help from the commanders against the usurper, who had halted not far away in a town. Since the pasha was not

91. Bembo's reference to "Saracens" probably refers to local Bedouin.

92. "Wiry are their horses, used to running, ready for hardship, and in feeding sparing."

93. Bembo writes his name as "Abdelassii."

94. "Chiedie" is Bembo's transliteration of his name, Mehmet Shadid, that is, "Mehmet the Strong." Later, on his return trip through the Syrian desert to Aleppo, Bembo describes him as "Lord of the desert and nearby places."

95. According to his journal, Bembo arrived in Aleppo in October 1671. Therefore, he remained in the city for over a year.

FIGURE 13. Arab and janissary.

in residence, nor the militia, the müsellim sent his first minister to Mehemed Shadid to ask him to give up his position and not to pursue 'Abd al-'Aziz, who was a dependent of the Great Lord. [Mehemed] Shadid was scornful and angry at the message and wanted to have the ears and nose of the ambassador cut off, but, due to the urgings of his attendants, he let him go free with the order to tell the müsellim that he [Mehemed Shadid] did not want to recognize him [the müsellim] at all and that he had no authority at all over him. Desperate, 'Abd al-'Aziz resolved to assault the enemy at nighttime and to try his luck, trusting in the valor of his five hundred followers and hoping to surprise the enemy in their sleep and thus achieve victory. However, the [enemy] were warned by the neighing of the horses that were approaching and took to arms, and after a brief battle 'Abd al-'Aziz was routed and put to flight by the superior forces that numbered about four thousand. Some of his men gave themselves up to the victorious enemy. Others with baggage and the family of the Emir took shelter in the city, while the victors came up to the walls, devastating many gardens and pleasant places, taking spoils of all that they found and impeding the passage of foodstuffs to the city, which began to feel the scarcity. That obliged the müsellim and the other commanders to recognize the Emir as the victor until other orders might arrive from the Porte, which was immediately informed of the events. Meanwhile, 'Abd al-'Aziz had hid; he was finally restored to part of his power, and the [Mehemed] Shadid went over to obedience to the Ottomans as well.

There is also another kind of very famous thief. They go well armed on horseback and attack travelers in a [disciplined military] order. They are called Turcomans, and they are shepherds that live in the mountains near Antioch and Aleppo. Like the Arabs, they have movable houses that are pavilions of cloth and felt. In the summer they live in some small castles in the mountains, and in the winter they come down to the plain with their families and rather large herds, mostly of camels. During the passage that they made in 1672 they stopped a mile from the city, where they stayed for three days, selling many animals in the city and making many provisions for their needs.

I had the chance to see the *Zina*, which are festivities of joy that they held for the taking of Caminiecz in Poland, which lasted four nights and three days since the news arrived toward the evening of October 2. Immediately the order was given to discharge the cannons throughout the whole castle and also many muskets, something that was repeated several times. They also offered many prayers on the minarets in the manner I described above, and celebration was ordered throughout the whole city and was soon obeyed. Business was suspended, shops were closed, except those of the principal bazaars, that is, those of the Goldsmiths and of Merchandise. All the shops were decorated, not with their wares, as is the custom in Venice, but with rugs, tapestries, velvets, and gold silk cloths. The citadel, too, was decorated all around its walls with an immense number of cuirasses, helmets, shields and other arms, and very old instruments of war that were found in the same castle when it was taken by the sultan already cited. All the parts of the city were richly decorated, particularly the Khan Gate, which was the most important for the Turks, who had rushed to outdo one another in decorating it.[96] In each khan there was a great platform raised above the ground and furnished with rugs and cushions where the notables sat to see the ceremonies here and there, stopping a while at each place,

96. This is the first and only mention of a "Khan Gate" (Caravanserai Gate), and the reference is unclear.

where they were regaled with tobacco, coffee, and sherbet and entertained by various companies of male dancers and players who went around the entire city, celebrating now in a bazaar and then in a khan, to their profit. For this occasion all the guilds went to the house of the müsellim. They went in order, all dressed in ridiculous costumes that resemble our carnival disguises, but with their faces uncovered. Each guild carried a float on which there was someone actually doing the work of the guild: the goldsmith was setting a gem; the tailor was finishing a robe; and so all the others in their profession.[97] At night, too, there were the same entertainments of music and dancing, and two gates of the city were left always open so that the people of the suburbs could also participate in the festivities. Everyone was permitted to go throughout the entire city, since all the minarets, streets, and principal bazaars were lit by an infinite number of oil lamps. The foreigners, too, made a show of gaiety and decorated the entrances of their houses, where they usually [display] several paintings of women. Many Turks and Christians of those parts came to see these [pictures] and stopped astonished at seeing those clothes and fashions that seemed to them rather more graceful and to their liking than the clothes of their own women.

Available in abundance to all who came into the houses of the consuls were candies, tobacco, sherbet, coffee, bread, and even wine for some, especially for commanders, who are [incidentally] required to punish drinkers. They got even more drunk than the others! At our consul's, among the many who came, the aga of the janissaries stopped by one evening for more than two hours with a glass always to his lips, eating olives and cheese from Piacenza, which he liked very much. All the companies of dancers and players also came to the houses of the consuls, and to everyone was given some trifle. Dressed like a Turk, I also went to see the city, and I went to the *kahveji*,[98] where there were many people, and then on throughout the whole city. The subaşı also went all around the city, punishing those he found sleeping and not making merry.[99] Only the women were forbidden to leave their houses at night. They could come out only during the day and

97. The parade was a provincial version of processions before the Ottoman sultan, as recorded in Ottoman manuscripts such as the *Sürname*.

98. Coffee house. Bembo writes "cafgi."

99. Bembo's subaşı were assigned military fiefs with an annual revenue and commanded a detachment of soldiers who were responsible for the maintenance of order in a district.

[had to be] veiled as usual. Many had parties together, celebrating day and night in merry conversation. The thing that is most noteworthy is that in such a multitude of people there was not one homicide or wounding, [events] that do not happen at other times either, since they never resort to arms, even though almost everyone carries knives and sabers. But when they quarrel among themselves, they insult one another with words said in such resentment that it would seem impossible to avoid reaching for arms. Still, they never put their hands to [their weapons]; at the most they use their fists or staffs.

[NOVEMBER 1672]

On November 26 came the news of the peace established between the Porte and Poland, with conditions most advantageous for them. I gained the confidence of many of the Christians of the country and of some Jews and was taken to their houses many times. [Their houses] are very comfortable and well furnished in their manner with rugs and silk and golden cushions. I also observed the women of those Jews, even though they are kept in separate apartments where they usually also eat, as is the custom also among the Turks. They are dressed not very differently from the Christian women, except that, perhaps because they were in the house, they had their faces uncovered and wore a great velvet cap on their heads instead of the rakiya, as is seen in the drawing. I observed very beautiful complexions on all of them, a good height and not a little spirit, so that if they had freedom they would be no less charming than ours; and they showed not a little inclination for Franks. They wear for whimsy a little ring or pendant in their nose, which is pierced, as are the ears of our women. Others pierce their upper lip on one side, where they put a gold rosette that looks like a mole and gives them great charm. As is the custom in the greater part of the Orient, they also paint their eyebrows and eyelids with a black line that lasts for a while. With another mixture they paint half of all their fingernails red, also making on their hands and face several marks with similar colors, and among them these [marks] are considered to be ornaments of beauty, but in truth they little satisfy the eye and seem less civil. Similar dyes are used also by many men in their beards, which they make of many colors, and also their eyes and their fingernails in imitation of the women. Neither the Christian nor Turkish women give a dowry when they marry. In fact, it is the husband who, to have them, makes a gift to the relatives, and the wife brings many household goods with her, depending on her wealth. The Turks, who take as many women as they can support, promise in writing when they get married that the qadi has in trust a certain dowry for each wife, because in the case of divorce, which occurs for many reasons that are permitted and recognized as legitimate by the qadi, he remains obliged to give the promised dowry, thereby annulling the written contract and leaving the woman free to marry others.[100]

If the income of the cats in Tripoli seemed to me worthy of laughter, I was no less surprised by the alms that are given in Aleppo to dogs and cats, who get the interior parts of all animals, since people are not permitted to eat them. And many buy entrails and bread out of devotion and distribute them on the public streets [to these animals] that come around in great numbers. This practice is considered by them to be of such piety that much money is left for this purpose, for the feeding of the dogs and cats of the city. The dogs usually live in the bazaars, where they sleep outside the shops, and each one goes to his accustomed place at night, and if by chance one [dog] remains closed in a bazaar not his own, all the dogs of that bazaar attack him and make such a mad and loud attack on it all night that it is impossible for the neighbors to sleep. Besides not being able to shut an eye the first night that this confusion occurred in the bazaar near our house, I was worried that some great disorder had happened in the city, until the next morning, when I understood the real reason for all the commotion.

A curious entertainment that is practiced by many Turks is that they like keeping doves. The doves are accustomed to several signs that the owner makes to them with a white cloth, and they go and return with great obedience. Around the 23rd hour they make them go out of the dovecote, and these [doves] fly, trying to stay together and not to go too far from the owner, who is on the terrace observing them, because if he sees that they separate too much one from the other, he immediately recalls them so that they will not be taken by other doves and made prisoners. In fact, when [other doves] see up in the air one or two doves flying alone and far from a numerous company, they keep them so tightly surrounded within their group, like prisoners, that they cannot escape. Instead, they bring the stranger to their cote at a signal from their master. He takes the bird as a

100. Bembo seems to have an appreciative understanding of the fact that women in Islam possessed more substantial rights and protections than their counterparts in Christian Europe.

hunting prize and enjoys it in glory and usefulness, since he eats it or sells it to its own previous owner or to others. This is a great contest, and they spend many hours a day setting up tricks to steal one another's doves and watching out to recall their own at the opportune moment.

There is also another species of pigeon, no less scarce and unusual than the first, [and it is] called "of Baghdad" or "of Babylon." They are larger than the others, [and they have] around the eyes and beak a kind of hard substance nearly half a finger thick that is red and whitish in color and featherless. They are of the type that used to carry letters in ancient times from Baghdad to Aleppo, and from Aleppo to Baghdad, [but they have now] lost the instinct of that journey. But some Franks have some of them, which they use to obtain the earliest information about the arrival of vessels at Iskenderun. These pigeons are kept in Aleppo, and some days after they have laid and hatched their eggs, they are placed in a basket or cage and forwarded to Iskenderun, where they are kept until the arrival of some ships, when [their owners] tie under their wings a small note containing the name of the vessel, the day of its arrival, and the quantity and quality of its cargo. Then [the pigeons] are set free, and, drawn by love for their young ones, they soar above the neighboring mountains and, perceiving Aleppo, they arrive there in three hours, and the notes are immediately taken from them.

By means of one of these pigeons that belonged to the Frenchman Monsieur Forestier, we had news of the arrival in Iskenderun (which up to now we have referred to by its Turkish name of Scanderona)[101] of the English ship *Girasole,* which had left from Livorno. On the ship was a Portuguese Franciscan who was going to the East Indies with the title of Custodian of the Province of Goa. When he arrived in Aleppo, he made the customary visits to the consuls, and he was often the guest of my uncle. His name was Friar Giovanni Seabra of the Trinity, [and he was] tall and of dignified and somewhat pretentious appearance, as are many of his nationality, given to exaggeration and boasting, although we did not discover it until later. In many conversations he presented a trip to India as interesting and fruitful, not very expensive, and not even as difficult as is believed. Thus he aroused in me the desire to travel in those parts and to leave the boredom that I was feeling in Aleppo. The fact followed the idea, since my uncle not only gave me permission but also affectionately and generously gave me assistance for all I might need and want. Besides, this said friar

101. The modern Iskenderun.

assured him that he would never abandon me and that he would provide me with money once in India, since the principal knights and merchants of the place were obligated to him. All this turned out to be entirely false; he had no object other than to provide himself with company for greater security during his trip.

Once having decided to leave, I let my beard grow in order to be better accepted in those countries. We inquired in the city and found that the earliest occasion would be a caravan of horses that was preparing to travel to the metropolis of Mesopotamia.[102] We arranged with the *mukarin*,[103] called Seffer Cristiano, who owned many horses, for those that I needed, giving him a deposit with the obligation to settle with him entirely on our arrival at our destination. I bought saddles since the horses were accustomed to them and immediately began to make the necessary provisions for the long trip. First I bought eating utensils of the Turkish kind, which they call *tingerie*,[104] some large leather vases for holding oil and broth, other small ones also of pleasant-smelling leather made in Constantinople, which are called *matara*,[105] for carrying water and wine to drink. I took some rugs and coverlets to serve as a bed that could be used anywhere we might stop. I provided myself with many biscuits (since it often happened that one could not find bread), dried fruit, salt meat (among it [was] even some pork meat but [I did not let] the Turks know about it),[106] goatskin bottles of wine and *araq*, which is quite necessary for such trips,[107] caviar, cheese, rice, vegetables, candles, coffee, spices, coal, wood, and all that I might need. All was placed in large, thick sacks that are made for this purpose. As for clothes and underclothes, I limited myself as much as possible, putting them in *sepetti*,[108] which are large baskets covered with leather, very strong and made for trav-

102. That is, traveling to Baghdad.

103. A *mukarin* (Turkish *mükari*) was a muleteer or camel driver who hired out horses, donkeys, or mules or who used them to transport goods. Bembo transcribes it as *muccaro*.

104. Presumably from the Turkish *tencere* (saucepan).

105. Bembo's word is *mattara*, derived from the Turkish *matara* (from the Arabic *matara*), a leather flask.

106. Bembo's caution is due to the Muslim injunction against eating pork.

107. Bembo seems less concerned about the Muslim prohibition of alcohol. The *araq* to which he refers is Turkish *raki*, or aquavit. Syria and Lebanon were centers for its distillation.

108. Arabic *sabat;* Turkish *sepet*, "basket."

eling. Finally, I took a tent for [those times] when we would stop in the open countryside. My uncle procured letters for me from the Capuchin and Carmelite fathers in every locality where they had a mission with the order that I should be given any money I might need. From the Capuchin father Valerio, who had come from Venice on our ship, he got a most efficacious letter with ample orders that I should be given all the money I might need from any merchant with the assurance that he would pay it back promptly in Aleppo. This was done because it was too risky to carry much money with one on such a long trip because of the Arabs and robbers. Even so, I took with me a belt that held one hundred *ongari* and thirty *zecchini*,[109] which I wore under my clothes without having told anyone, besides which I had about one hundred silver reales, all of which was spent considerably before arriving in Goa, where I had the greatest need and where I had to work hard to provide myself with the necessary funds for my return after the friar had abandoned me. I also took two letters of recommendation from the Turkish commanders, which I still have, since I never presented them for the reasons I will tell in their place. They were directed, one to the *voyvoda*,[110] or aga of the customs house, in Diyarbakır and the other to the qadi of Mosul. They are written in their fashion on heavy smooth paper and made in a roll and placed in a silk container made for that purpose; some use velvet or gold cloth. They were tied with a string, and the knot was bound in wax with their seal, which usually contains the name of the writer or other words. So that this would not be broken, the seals were covered with an ivory cap that was tied on with a small cord: that is the way they send letters. I took another from the aga of the city of Birecik, who was in Aleppo at the time, to his lieutenant who was living [in Birecik], with the assurance that the aga had already been paid the fee that is exacted of all Franks passing through there without permission of the Porte, but it is a practice established by the Franks themselves to save themselves from the insolence of those ministers. We thought it best to deal directly with the aga himself, to whose house we sent the dragoman, accompanied by the second servant of the müsellim. He decided to please us and asked for seven reales per person and with effort was persuaded to take twenty-two reales for six

109. Italian coinage.

110. A *voyvoda*, which Bembo renders as "vaiuoda," was the administrator of a tax farm *(mukataa)*; here the term is used loosely to refer to the aga of the customs house.

persons. He acted as if he had done us a most unusual favor, although he cheated us and got more than he usually would have received, as will be understood later.

A few days before my departure I went to take my leave of some merchants who were friends of mine and of the consuls, who gave me some letters directed to their merchants in Persia and India, by means of which I was recognized by them and treated with great respect. In those very days there arrived from Constantinople Signore Giulio Patton, a native of Trento, who had been living in Venice for many years and who liked to travel around the world, since he had means and was still young and strong. When he heard of my intentions, he decided to accompany me, which was much appreciated by my uncle, who was glad that I would be with a good-natured and amiable person. I also took in my company the Franciscan father Giacomo of Venice, who was my uncle's chaplain and who had been convinced by the promises of Father Giovanni, too.

TWO

From Aleppo to Basra

[JANUARY 1673]

ON JANUARY 3, 1673, THE DAY OF OUR DEPARTURE, we all dressed in Turkish fashion in ordinary clothes to attract less attention and to spend less. We all pretended to be clergy since these [local] people are more accustomed to see religious persons traveling to their missions and because one travels more safely in this way in Turkey. After having said good-bye to those of the house, I left the city at midnight in the company of the two Franciscans, Father Giuliano, a servant, and a dragoman named 'Ata' Allah, that is Diodato, who had been the second dragoman of my uncle. We were all on horseback, and there were two [additional] horses with our provisions and luggage. Just before they were to close the gates, we went out of the city by [the gate] the Turks call *Kapı-yı Cengi,* the Arabs [call] *Bab al-Nasr,* and the Christians [call] Gate of St. George. That night we took shelter in a grotto only a mile from the city where the caravan was gathered. It turned out to be a large one with many people joined to it. We spent the night there, and the morning of the 4th before the day broke there was much noise of people packing and getting ready to leave. But when all was in order and I thought that it was to be our caravan, the group disbanded, and three different caravans were formed that were going to different places. It had been a trick of the muleteer to make us leave quickly: we had been told that there would be more than 150 armed men with the caravan in addition to the merchants. And to give the appearance of truth to that story he had led us to that grotto, where there were people from two other caravans: he had used the same stratagem with them, saying that there were going to be many Franks in the caravan with their firearms. Among the thieving Arabs, who are absolutely ignorant of military discipline, [the Franks] are well known [for their firearms] as well as for their good order in fighting so that the Turks feel themselves very secure when they have Franks in their company, and the thieves are very reluctant to make an assault. When the caravan was in motion and all were counted, there were no more than twenty knights with arms, some merchants, 160 horses and loaded mules, and about twenty men on foot, who were muleteers for these animals and who do not carry any arms other than a staff, which they don't use even when the occasion arises in order not to anger the Arabs from whom they later recover their animals at the cost of a few soldi. When I saw such a small company, I was alarmed and, in view of the risk to which I was exposing myself, almost abandoned my decision to leave. But reflecting then that I had already begun a trip that I had always known would be arduous and dangerous, I did not want to regret my decision at the first appearance of difficulty.

Thus I courageously left the sight of Aleppo and began my trip, which was slow, as one can believe it would be with packhorses continually in motion. After two hours of travel we passed close to the town of Haylan, not far from which we saw the beginning of the small river (the Quweiq) that passes through Aleppo and is all that provides water to that great city. The journey of that day was of twelve continuous hours, mostly in the countryside, where we saw many other towns from a distance. Around 10 o'clock in the evening we stopped at a town called Actaria, where we found nothing to eat. It is inhabited by a few very poor people, and our lodging was in a very small house, but one of the best of the place, and we gave to the owner more than what the lodging was worth. The others also accommodated themselves in other houses; but when one sleeps in the countryside, one places all the luggage of the caravan in a circle inside of which all the people stay, each one taking his share of the watch for fear of thieves. Otherwise, one hires at the expense of the caravan some foot soldiers,[1] who, circling round, watch all night. A caravan is nothing but a group of many people with their luggage or merchandise who pass from one place to another to secure themselves against Arabs and other robbers who own and infest the countryside and steal from travelers, as I have explained. To avoid confusion in the crowd of people one elects a chief of the caravan, called the caravan pasha, who is usually one of the more esteemed and creditable Turks. In Persia, however, they don't mind electing even a Christian

1. Bembo uses the word *chiaus*.

if he is known to them. This chief orders the stops, being careful to give appropriate rest to the men and the animals. Thus, some days are rather long and others of a few hours; sometimes one stays for even two days in one place, since they try to stop in places that they believe to be safe from robbers; thus, one often sleeps in mountains. It is also his responsibility to take care of any differences that may arise in the group and to tax persons and merchandise for any costs that must be incurred for the caravan. Whenever there is danger from robbers, he places guards where there is greatest need. The usual order in a caravan is to send some armed men ahead as a vanguard, and the rest of the armed men walk, some ahead and some at the flanks. When robbers in great numbers are discovered, the caravan pasha stops the caravan and unloads the animals and places them inside the circle of luggage from which all defend themselves.

On the morning of the 5th two hours before daylight we were on our way, and, after six hours of travel through almost entirely barren countryside (since we had left the towns behind), we stopped at the foot of a mountain in several small grottoes, most of which were naturally formed and the others artificial. Only four or five people fit in each one, and there we spent the rest of the day and part of the night. In order to be charitable and to lighten the burden of the servant, who could thus be saved for the most important things, I took as a cook a poor Armenian who was following the caravan on foot. I found myself satisfied with that poor man, who served me quite well until Diyarbakır.

On the 6th the caravan set out six hours before day, still through countryside, and at dawn, while all of us were sleepy and cold, there was much confusion when we heard the vanguard shouting, "Arabs, Arabs!" At the shouting we immediately stopped, and the more frightened among us said that they saw many Arab flags in the semidarkness, and they wanted to unload the animals and put themselves on the defensive. But some horsemen went ahead and saw only twenty Arabs on horseback, who, when the sun came up, realized that the caravan was able to defend itself and took another road. After an hour of daylight we arrived at a small branch of the Euphrates River, whose water was about one meter deep and four meters wide.[2] Shortly thereafter we passed a similar branch, after which we began to travel through mountainous territory. It was rather steep terrain but not

2. Bembo writes "two cubits deep and two picche wide." A *cubit* is about half a meter; a *picca* is approximately two meters.

uncomfortable by road. After six hours of such travel we arrived at Messar, a rather beautiful but not very large town at the foot of which is a stream of water. The houses are all of sunbaked mud, and all the inhabitants are peasants. We lodged in one of those poor houses, from whence we left on the 7th, four hours before daylight. We crossed the stream, which reached halfway up the horses' legs and was more than two meters wide. After two hours of mountain road we passed through a river called Nizip in Turkish,[3] which means "running water." It was about one and a half meters deep. In five hours, also by mountain road, we arrived at the Euphrates, called Muratsu by the Turks, which means "water of Murat."[4] It flows to Basra and with the Tigris goes into the Persian Gulf. It is seven and a half to eight meters deep and [its width varies] from six to seven meters to twelve to fourteen meters. It flows very quickly, and it can be crossed with some boats, and on the other side is the city of Birecik.[5] The boats are roughly made of oak. Their sides are rather high, and their prows even higher, while the stern is open like those Brenta river boats that are called "*passi.*" They use long and narrow pieces of wood as oars, since they cannot provide themselves with anything better. Each boat can hold six or seven horses, and since there are many, they go one after the other and do better than our Venetian ferries *(traghetti).* They do not go along the river because for large stretches it is not navigable. In rocky places it becomes very broad [and shallow], but afterward it is navigable to the sea. The whole caravan passed [over to the other side] on the boats. The Turks paid four *saie* (which corresponds to two of our Venetian pounds) per horse, and the Franks double. Here the jurisdiction of the pasha of Aleppo ends.

This city of Birecik (called Birre or Esbir or by some Birtha), which means ancient well of Syria, is located on two or three hills, whose bases reach the river, and looks somewhat like Zante. Most of the houses are made in the hills, since there are many grottoes, and they are all of stone, but rough, because they are cut into the mountain. The city is surrounded by

---

3. Bembo transcribes it as *Nessispsui.* They probably reached the Nizip River, a tributary of the Euphrates, at the town of the same name in southern Turkey. Bembo translates the Turkish word *su* as "water," but it also means "stream."

4. Bembo incorrectly identifies the Murat River (Murat Su) with the Euphrates, the Turkish (and Arabic) name of which is Firat. The Murat River joins with the Kara Su 160 km north of Birecik to form the Euphrates.

5. Bembo calls it "Birre." It is on the left bank of the Euphrates.

a small wall with six gates; the streets are narrow, and most of them have water from the hills running along them, which makes them muddy. There is also a castle with the same name of Birecik on a mountain, one of whose sides faces the city and the other the countryside on the other side of the river. It is rather strong because of its site, and [it is] of ancient construction, but they do not allow Franks to enter it.

The city is governed by an aga, a qadi, and an aga of janissaries, who are rather few. The inhabitants are not very civilized, nor is there much abundance of foodstuffs except for fish from the Euphrates, which gives a plentiful supply, and it is rather good. No lodging is given to caravans in the city but instead in a caravanserai about a pistol shot away on a stony mountain. Here, as soon as we arrived, we received the visit of agents of the aga, who came to ask for a zecchino apiece.[6] In answer, I presented the letter of the aga himself, which they read and read again several times but continued to insist on the fee of the zecchini. I had the dragoman tell them that their request was not just and that if they did not go away I would send a courier on horseback to Aleppo to their aga. They quieted down somewhat and stopped trying to get as much as they could, and they had some Maronite Christians tell me to give them something. Advised by them, I gave them a half piaster, which they did not want to accept, because it was too little, and they renewed their demands for the zecchini. Finally the aga of the janissaries intervened, and they accepted my offer. But when I thought that their insolence was finished, the aga himself started up, asking me for a gift for having adjusted things. This second scene did not end until I had handed over another one-half piaster. I understood on that occasion that Franks usually pay one zecchino apiece, and I had paid three and a half reales through the offices of the müsellim of Aleppo, as I have already told. Thus it is an infallible rule in Turkey never to use Turkish intermediaries for any business that one can handle oneself by paying money, because, besides being certain of not saving any money but rather of ending up paying more than one would have done by oneself, one must also give a generous gift to the person who has cheated one, no matter what rank he is; and this is something that they do even among themselves. Half a piaster may seem a small reward to the aga of the janissaries, but in those parts, even if the titles are the same, the persons are not, nor are the jurisdictions.

The caravanserai where we were lodged was a grotto carved out by chisel,

6. A *zecchino* was a gold coin of the Venetian Republic.

rather large and [in appearance] like a caravanserai, but covered and not higher than ten feet. In cutting it, they had left eighteen pilasters of the same stone of the mountain; all around the upper part are carved arched grottoes that serve as rooms for travelers, but they are so dark that at noon I found it necessary to light a lamp, since there was no light other than that which entered through the door, because the whole place was within the mountain. The principal door is well adjusted, with an inscription above it that says that the construction of the entire place cost only three aspri, that is, three of our soldi. This seemed to me impossible, so I sought out with much curiosity the real meaning of that inscription. I was told that, in truth, it had not cost more than that, plus what had been got for the stones that had been cut out of the place. We spent the entire night there and the day of the eighth and the next night, so that the caravan could rest.

On the morning of the 9th, after the sun was up, we set out on our way divided into two groups. One took the way of Urfa (formerly Edessa), the land of Abraham, a city not far distant. The other, in which I was, passed through the city of Birecik. Many travelers joined us and increased the number of armed persons; in all we were 150 with merchandise and other luggage. The journey was through mountains and hills, in which I saw several towns made up of grottoes. After five hours of travel we stopped in some mountain grottoes, so small that one could barely stand up inside them. There we stayed the whole night in great danger of being robbed. Robbers do not usually attack openly but rather remain hidden and steal what they can without being seen; they are the people of that country themselves. Around three o'clock at night [a man] came to our grotto with a bow and arrows to ask to borrow a leather pail, leaving us the bow and arrows as security. He was a robber, and with that pretence he had come to spy where the luggage was, in order to be able to return later to steal it if he could. But having seen the firearms, he dared not risk it. Nor did we neglect to keep a diligent watch, first one, then another. We were excellently guarded by a dog of the muleteer's that did not let anyone come close. He would bark furiously at any small noise. Meanwhile the pail was returned, and our diligence had proved worthwhile. It was not sufficient for the whole caravan, however. Around midnight a load of soap and a horse saddle were taken from a poor Armenian. Because of this incident, we arose five hours before daylight on the day of the 10th. Along the road I observed the remains of ancient structures of good architecture with the vestiges of arches. They seemed to have been important buildings, but I was not able to obtain any information about them from those ignorant people. We traveled thirteen continuous hours that day, partly through mountains and partly through fertile plains [in which were] abundant [domesticated] animals. We stopped at the town of Saf on a hill,[7] and I lodged in the house of one of the peasants, in a room where we barely fit. We spent the night, and we found poultry there, which we had been without ever since leaving Aleppo.

The morning of the 11th we continued the journey through hills two hours before daylight. When the sun came up, we found a stream two palms deep and about four arm's lengths wide.[8] After three hours we found two other small streams as we proceeded two hours down to a plain. We went up the hills again and stopped in a town called Mullasarai.[9] First, however, we had met ten horsemen in the open country who had come to reconnoiter the caravan. A tax on all the merchandise was paid to the aga of that village. He, in turn, is obliged to keep the countryside free of robbers. In the town we accommodated ourselves in a small house. As soon as we arrived, we were visited by the officials of that aga, who is subordinated to the pasha of Urfa. They came to see our luggage and to check carefully whether we had any merchandise, in the process of which they stole several trifles from our trunks. When they saw that there was no merchandise, we were given to understand that the aga wanted a zecchino apiece from us. I told the dragoman to tell them that it was not customary to pay anything for passage through that place. But it was useless. In fact, the agent became angry and began to threaten the dragoman. To appease him, I gave him three piasters on the advice of an aga of janissaries who was traveling with us and was friendly with me. Our lodging was in a stable, rather than in a bedroom, since we had animals for company. Nothing to eat was found in the town. I saw that the people were so poor that their children went naked even in January.

The morning of the 12th we started traveling three hours before sunrise, and after six hours in a plain we climbed into mountains and hills, and after two hours we passed a stream about a meter deep and five meters wide, called Abdisacgi, that is, River of the Deer. About an hour from there we found another, [called] Aslansacgi, that is, River of the Lion.[10] After a little

7. A town east of Urfa on the road to Diyarbakır.
8. Bembo writes "two *palmi* deep and about four *braccia* wide."
9. Molla Saray was a town east of Urfa on the road to Diyarbakır.
10. Abdi Sakci and Aslan Sakci.

more than an hour we stopped on a hill called Deyèmagarosi, which means Mountain of the Camels.[11] There we set up the tent, since there was no town, nor grottoes, and we had some Turks under it with us who had demonstrated friendliness toward me.

From there we left on the morning of the 13th, five hours before daybreak. It was so cold that we could barely stay on horseback; and the road was terrible, not because it was mountainous but because it was rocky countryside that was more difficult than even mountain roads. After six hours of such a road we passed a stream called Chialtucsui,[12] which means River Water. Two hours from there over very rough road we stopped at Scuerech,[13] a place that is called a city, although it doesn't deserve the name, since it is not surrounded by walls. It is also a small place, with few inhabitants and lacking in foodstuffs, except for wine, which is good and resembles that of Provence. A pistol shot away is a little man-made hill, which was encrusted with stones all around in ancient times, as can be seen from a part that is preserved intact. On the top of it is an uninhabited castle that is mostly ruined. Almost all the houses of the city are of stone, but roughly worked. In one of these we lodged. The aga of the city, subordinate to the pasha of Diyarbakır, sent for our dragoman and demanded five reales. When the dragoman tried to tell him that it was not the custom to pay anything, the aga became angry and insisted. The dragoman, who was full of wine, replied insolently, and he was charged with insubordination and threatened that he would be kicked in the stomach, and orders were given to put him in jail. But all was taken care of by giving a piaster and a half to the aga.

On the morning of the 14th, an hour before daylight, we took up our journey again, almost frozen because of the cold and because of a wind that sent the rain directly into our faces and hampered our breathing. The janissaries, who had their own good horses, went faster and ahead of the caravan to Diyarbakır, since there was no danger of robbers. But our journey with the caravan took twelve hours on bad road, during which we passed several streams. I became annoyed at the discomfort, and so I left the main part of the caravan about halfway through the journey and joined some

11. Probably Bembo's rendering of the Turkish *Deve Mağarası,* or Cave of the Camel.

12. Kialtuk Suyu.

13. In his financial statement at the end of the book Bembo spells it "Severec."

Armenians and Turks to arrive at the city more quickly the following day. At sunset we stopped close to a spring at the foot of a mountain, where we slept under the tent. The morning of the 15th, four hours before daylight, we continued over impossible roads, across which flow many streams. Two hours before our arrival, we saw the city from the top of a mountain, after which there was a good road. It seemed to be a strong city. We entered through the gate they call "of the Greeks," and many people asked us where we came from, because they thought we were [their] countrymen, since we were not many. Since the dragoman had remained behind, and we could not answer, we aroused their curiosity even more. We had not realized that we were alone as we entered the city on horseback and without knowledge of the language. Most of our company belonged to the place and had dispersed to their houses through various streets, and the merchandise had gone to the Customs House. With great difficulty we made ourselves understood to one of the people, and he led us to the Messaterà caravanserai across from the Customs, where foreigners usually go. From there I immediately sent to advise the Capuchin fathers of our arrival. They came right away and led me with a very great deal of courtesy to their hospice. There they served us an abundant supper, which was provided by some Christian friends of theirs, some bringing one thing and others another. They gave us good rooms that had floors covered with rugs, with good beds placed on the floor, as is the custom of the country. Mine consisted of a mattress stuffed with plant fibers, not very wide, covered with a thin red cloth embroidered with white and other colors; a pillow of the same materials; a heavy stuffed quilt, lined with red cloth below and with fine white material above embroidered with wine-colored silk. I slept there with my clothes on and without sheets.

The following day, the 16th, I ordered the dragoman to procure food for us and for those fathers during our entire stay there, so that we might enjoy the company of those good missionaries by whom I had been so lovingly received. There were only four, a layman and three priests, who took care of the mission in that city with much zeal. They were all Frenchmen. The superior was named Father Giuseppe de Polué, one [priest] Father Giorgia, the other, Father Antonio, and the layman, Friar Daniele, who also knew medicine and surgery. He was thus held in much esteem and affection by the Turks, who, contrary to their usual custom, are very friendly to all those fathers. They tired themselves out in my service and to my advantage, taking me through the city and showing me the more curious things and providing me with all that I needed. They recovered all my luggage, which had gone to the customs, with the expense of only sixteen saie (that is, two-thirds of a real), the usual fee to be given to the janissaries of the gate through which we had entered. I was given this treatment because of the friendliness between those fathers and the müsellim, since the pasha had gone to war, and the agents of the aga in the Customs House released my luggage to the fathers without even looking at it. Of little avail would have been the letter of recommendation that I had from the governor without the help of those fathers. He had been killed two or three days before, when he had gone with 500 horsemen to collect taxes through the towns of Kurdi.[14] These had withheld their tribute and persisted in armed resistance and disobedience. But when the aga came with so many men they resolved to adjust the matter by paying half of their debt. The aga was satisfied, considering how difficult it would have been to punish them, since they are warlike people and in secure places. He had remained in one of those towns where he was to receive the payment. However, since there was not sufficient food for all his people, they divided themselves up, and most went to neighboring towns, while he remained there with only twelve or fourteen of his court. The night following this separation—it is not known whether they had planned it all ahead of time or whether they had decided only that day—the Kurds came in great numbers in the deepest night to the house of that unhappy aga, who was asleep. The few who were with him were awakened by the noise made by the assassins and gave generous resistance to the death, but the greater number of the Kurds finally made them victorious, and they furiously entered, cruelly slaughtered the aga and a small son that he had with him, and stole all that they could find. Then the soldiers who were here and there in other settlements nearby, when they heard of the death of their master, returned to the city. The müsellim immediately sent the news to the Porte in order to receive from it the orders to execute a deserved punishment.

This city, where the sun rises with two and a quarter hour's difference from Venice, is called in Turkish Kara Amid; by Giovio[15] and by Sacred

14. That is, Kurdistan. Much of the population of eastern Turkey was and still is Kurdish.

15. Paolo Giovio, an Italian historian, was born in Como in 1483 and died in Florence in 1552. His *Commentari delle cose dei Turchi* was written in 1531 and covers military, cultural, and political events from the reign of Osman I (1281–c. 1324) to that of Sulaiman II (1520–1566). Bembo's rendering of Kara Amid is "Caráemit."

Scripture it is called Amida; and commonly it is known as Diyarbakır, Metropolis of Mesopotamia, that part of the earth contained between the two rivers Tigris and Euphrates. The whole province is called Diyarbakır or Kama Amid. The city is not very extensive, but it is surrounded by beautiful, strong walls with seventy-six round and square towers, seventy paces distant from each other. It has five gates, named the Urfa Kapısı or Rum Kapısı (Bab al-Rum, or Gate of the Greeks) on the west, the Mardin Kapı (Bab al-Tell, or Mardin Gate) on the south, the Yeni Kapısı (New Gate) on the east, the Harput Kapısı (Gate of the Mountain) on the north, and the Aslan Kapısı (Gate of the Lions) on the east, which is always kept closed.[16] There is a fort or castle on one side of the city, inside of which there is a seraglio of the pasha, lodgings for the janissaries of his guard, and some other houses. It is governed by a pasha who is vizier, by a qadi, a müsellim, an aga of janissaries, and other ordinary officials, as has been explained on other occasions. Its population is of 200,000 people, among whom are 20,000 Christians. There are ten different rites, five of infidels and five of baptized persons. These latter are Armenians, Greeks, Nestorians, Jacobites, and Shamsi, who were, and still are, worshippers of the sun.[17] At one point

16. The imposing black basalt city walls of modern Diyarbakır are well preserved and still retain five gates, which Bembo names as follows: "[the Gate] of the Greeks, [the Gate] of Merdin, the New Gate, the Gate of the Mountains, and the Gate of the Lions, a postern gate that Evliya Çelebi calls the Ogrun Kapısı, or Sneaking Gate, on the east." The pre-Roman town was known as Amida, and the town continued to be known as Amid or Amida until the end of the sixteenth century, when the name Diyarbakır came into use. In 394 the Emperor Constantine began construction of its walls, and they were extensively repaired under the Byzantine emperor Justinian in the sixth century. Diyarbakır was captured by the Arabs in 638, and it served as a major center for assaults on the Byzantine state. It was a formidable military stronghold in the eleventh century and was captured by the Mongols in the middle of the thirteenth century. Subsequently seized by Timur (Tamerlane) at the end of the fourteenth century, it was a focus of contention between the fifteenth-century Qaraquyunlu (Black Sheep) and Aqquyunlu (White Sheep) Turcomans. In 1517, during the reign of Sultan Selim I, it became part of the Ottoman Empire. It prospered under Ottoman rule: it was the focal point for military campaigns against Safavi Iran and was an important commercial and cultural center.

17. The Christian world of the Near East was complex. The widespread and powerful Nestorian communities of the Near East were largely destroyed by

they were forced to receive baptism when one of the Ottoman emperors passed through there and saw those people living as Gentiles,[18] which the Turks abhor, and also without paying taxes. He called their chiefs and obliged them all to receive baptism and to pay the usual taxes paid by all subject Christians, or to profess Islam before his departure. After having tried even with gold, the normal intercessor to whom nothing is refused, to have such an order lifted, they resolved, after cautious if not holy deliberation, to put themselves under the Nestorian patriarch. They saw that if they did not elect one of the two parties, they would all be miserably massacred. The infidels are Turks, Arabs, and Kurds, who live in the mountains above the Tigris. Although they are all of the sect of Muhammad, they all disagree and hold various opinions. The others are Jews and Yazidi, who adore the devil and make sacrifices so that he will not do them harm, since they believe he dispenses evil; and they adore God so that he will do them good, which they say comes from his hands.[19] These latter mostly inhabit Mount Taurus,[20] from which they are also called Taurussiti. Those that now inhabit the neighborhood of the mountain are people of the forest (i.e., uncivilized people) who are warlike and live by robbing. It is told of them that in ancient times they had the custom of cutting off the heads of their enemies and impaling them on long sticks, which they would set up on the roofs and chimneys of their houses, saying, perhaps in jest, that those were their guards.

Timur's conquests. The largest surviving group was located in northwestern Iran and eastern Turkey. In 1551 a significant part of the Nestorian community elected to reunite with the Roman Catholic Church; since then, they have been known as Chaldeans. The Chaldean patriarch resided in Baghdad. Those who remained separate were known as Assyrian Christians. Adherents of the Syrian Orthodox Church, with its patriarch in Antioch, were known as Jacobites. Bembo's last group is *shamsi* in Arabic, a word derived from the word *al-shams* (sun).

18. Bembo uses this category to refer to those who are neither Muslim, Christian, nor Jew. As "people of the Book," Christians and Jews are protected but must pay a tax known as the *jizya*.

19. The Yazidi, followers of a distinct religion in Kurdistan, were sometimes vilified as "devil worshippers," though they in fact deny the existence of sin, evil, and the devil. Their chief pilgrimage site is the shrine of Shaykh 'Adi in northern Iraq.

20. The Taurus mountain range to the north of Diyarbakır.

The houses of the city are usually of earth or of wood with earth above. Those of the wealthy are of stone, with terraces instead of tile roofs, like those of Aleppo. There are also some well-built mosques. The house of those Capuchin fathers is rather well made, with many conveniences for travelers. The rooms are not very large. They all have places under the floor where a fire can be built, because the winters are very cold. Most of the houses have the same convenience. The dress of both men and women is the same as in Aleppo, except that few women wear the raqiya, which is also rather smaller. Also, they wear a white linen cloth tied across their faces like our masks. Their noses are pierced, and they wear there a large gold ring, while the poor ones [wear] a silver one. There is an abundance of foodstuffs [that are] also cheap, such as meat and excellent fish from the Tigris. The wine is rather strong, and only the bread is not very good, not because of the quality of the flour but because of the foolish way of cooking it. They make it in thin pancake form, and they extend it on stones placed in the fire, so that it is burned in some parts and in others it remains uncooked. It is sold by weight, as are also wood, oil, wine, and similar things. Fruit is also abundant in season, and even in winter I ate very tasty melons, since they are especially careful to conserve them for the winter. As for coins, they use zecchini, ongari, reales, abuchelb, in addition to the local coins, which are of silver—saye and aspri—and gold sultani.[21] I also saw that there were fake French louis d'or, which have a value of 32 per real and which are forbidden in other cities.

After lunch on the 16th I went out of the city through the Mardin Gate accompanied by the Father Superior. There one sees the Tigris in the distance, a rifle shot away from the city, which on that side is on a mountain, at the foot of which are some sandy stretches. The river forms there, when it is low. At that time it was as wide as a musket shot. Sometimes one can even wade across it. On the other side there are many hills full of settlements that make a fine sight. Walking along the bank I found my fellow travelers, who had come out of the city to avoid the watchful eye and insolence of the Turks. There on the sand I ate with them. Observing the city, I saw it to be unassailable from that side. We went back home by the New Gate and, seated around a small table under which was a charcoal fire in a hole in the

21. The first three coins are European; *abuchelb* and *saye* may be Ottoman; *aspri (akçe)* and the gold *sultani* are Ottoman. In the following sentence Bembo refers to *luigini* (louis d'or), a French gold coin.

floor of the room, spent the evening with those religious in talking of travels. The table was covered with a rug, under which everyone put his feet and hands, and thus keeping warm we spent hours of rest.[22]

On the 17th, also after eating, I went with the same fathers through the city to see the principal bazaars, which are higher and more beautiful than those of Aleppo. I saw that water runs along almost all the streets. I went to see the caravanserai where slaves are sold, which is made in the shape of a fortress, all of stone. In the middle of it is a very beautiful fountain, and it is [enclosed on all sides by] arches like a cloister, with the same arrangement on the upper level, which is covered with an iron roof. Here men and women are sold into slavery. Most of them are Georgians, Russians, Poles, and Moors. Those who want to buy go to look at them. Women are sold according to their beauty; some buy them as servants, and others to enjoy them; thus they are worth more if they are young and virgins. I went to see the convent, which was once of St. Basil, whose church is now the Great Mosque of the Turks.[23] Its architecture demonstrates great antiquity, and in the middle of the courtyard is a fountain where they wash themselves before entering to pray. In many places in the city one sees quantities of broken columns and vestiges of ancient buildings, since this city was once held by the Romans. In the walls one can see many imperial eagles, lions, leopards, and some hieroglyphics.[24] I went to see a Turkish-built mosque that was rather beautiful. It was covered with a lead roof and had a façade in the shape of a loggia with many columns of very fine marble.[25] I also saw the Church of the Jacobites, which used to be of the Greeks and is named for the Madonna. It is an ancient, half-destroyed building, inside of which there are two hundred lamps that they light on holidays. Outside the city from the Gate of the Greeks to that of the Mountain are many ditches of stone where water sits and freezes in the winter: [the ice] is then put into store-

22. Bembo is being warmed by what is known in Iran as a *kursi*.

23. Legend, but no evidence, ascribes a Christian origin to Diyarbakır's Ulu Cami (Great Mosque), which resembles the great Umayyad mosque of Damascus. See A. Gabriel, *Voyages archéologiques dans la Turquie orientale*, 2 vols. (Paris: E. de Bocard, 1940), vol. 1: 184–194.

24. Bembo is probably recording his observations of Seljuq Turkish stone carving of the eleventh to thirteenth centuries, rather than Roman.

25. He is probably describing the largest mosque in Diyarbakır, the 1572 Mosque of Bayram Pasha, a classic Ottoman mosque with an arcaded forecourt and a single-domed prayer hall.

rooms for the summer, not far from the city. I saw ordinary people running on the ice as they are said to do in Germany. Before entering these ditches, the water passes through tubes cut through stone pilasters, by which it is divided into various parts. Inside the Gate of the Mountain I went to see the house of a wealthy man who had been pasha. The beams were gilt and painted in many colors, and the fireplaces were decorated in low relief. The house was of two stories, an unusual practice in those parts.

The day of the 18th I went to see the citadel, which is small and surrounded by walls. Inside is a well-constructed mosque, recently founded by a pasha. Next to it is a public place with many holes for the natural needs of the Turks, and through each hole runs water that they use to wash themselves. They do not use, nor does anyone in the Orient, rags or paper, but only water to clean themselves. In the absence of water in the countryside they use a stone. For this act they never sit down but always squat to do their necessities. There is also a church in the castle with an ancient convent that was once Christian. I went with the Fathers to see the seraglio of the pasha when they were curing the müsellim and the qadi who were sick. They are thus very well liked by those leaders, especially since they do not charge. Sometimes, however, they give [the missionaries] lamb, rice, puddings, and similar things.

In the middle of the castle is a small destroyed tower with two very large arches, and around the walls are other relics of famous antiquities. I went outside the city through the Gate of the Mountain, on top of which they say a church had been built by the Emperor Constantine. Soldiers prayed there before leaving the city. This church, like all ancient Christian ones, has three windows of equal size in the façade in commemoration of the most holy Trinity. This custom began with the miracle that was seen in Constantinople at the time of Constantine himself. Over that Gate of the Mountain are inscribed in a stone the names of Valentinian and Gratian, Roman emperors, with many words that I could not read because of the height, however. And I did not want to stop to attract the attention of the Turks. It is general opinion that that stone was placed there when the walls were remade and that it was taken from the ruins of the Greek church. On that side the city is located on a beautiful plain, and the walls are joined to those of the castle, and a part of them are of the convent just mentioned. Between this Gate and the New [Gate] there is the Gate of the Lions, which they say was walled up because through it the city was suddenly surprised by Turks when it belonged to the Armenians: it was summer, and the people were in the countryside getting away from the summer heat along the banks of the river. Not far from the Gate of the Lions a stream comes down from the mountain, and it passes swiftly through various little canals and easily turns ten wheat mills placed one lower than the other and a pistol shot away from each other. Outside the New Gate are the burial places of the Nestorians, who put up large stones with various hieroglyphics cut into them that tell of the occupation, age, sex, marital status, etc., of the dead person.

On the 19th, having gone out of the city through the Gate of the Greeks, I saw a great number of women who were going to weep over the graves of their dead, since it was Thursday. They were so many that I did not remember having seen such a great number even in Aleppo, which is bigger and more populated. On this side of the city there are also many water deposits and many mills turned by a single stream, like those I described above. That evening several cannons were set off in the castle to signal the coming of the new moon and the beginning of the feast called Ramadan Bayram, which ends their fast, about which I will tell at length in its place.[26]

On the morning of the 20th I went to the church of the Armenians, where I was shown a piece of nail from the cross of Our Lord by their archbishop. They had lit many oil lamps on that occasion, which they usually light on holidays and during the celebration of Mass. They preserve this relic in the wall to the left of the main altar behind two small iron doors. Before taking it out, the clergy dress in priestly robes, and [the dress] of the archbishop is similar to that in which St. Anthony Abbot is painted, but of a violet color. The iron was in a silver box inside a glass, as the relics of our saints are kept. The foot of the glass, which was of silver, was of triangular form with Latin words that on one side were the following: *Ecce Clavus Christi;* on the other, *Hoc Signum Simonis a Sancto Andrea Strenuissimi Equitis Famagustani.* And on the other instead of words, there is a coat of arms with two crossed beams in the shape of a St. Andrew's cross on an azure field, and the beams [are] of silver. They told me that from tradition they know that this piece of nail was given by Godfrey of Bouillon to the said Simon of S. Andrea, a Knight of St. John, as a reward for his valor in the conquest of the Holy Land. When the Christians were chased from Syria, he went to live in Cyprus, bringing his relic with him to Famagusta.

26. In Turkish the feast at the end of Ramadan is called the *Küçük Bayram* or *Şeker Bayram;* in Arabic it is called *'Id al-Fitr.* Bembo renders the Turkish as "Ramasan Beirani."

When Cyprus was taken by the Turks, the Holy Nail fell into the hands of a Turk during the sacking of Famagusta, who, not knowing what it was, sold it for a small amount of money to an Armenian, who placed it in his church. Thence it was taken to this city for fear that it would be seized by the Catholics. Others say that he actually brought it there to the church where it is now preserved, and since he kept it a secret, the memory of it was lost for eighty years, and that it was found only twenty years ago in making an inventory of the things of the church. Since they did not understand those letters, they were read and explained by some of our clergy, who, on seeing the relic, fell on their knees to adore it. Therefore, the Armenians began to hold it in much esteem and refused to give it to the Catholics when a great sum of money was offered to them. Every year they get about two hundred scudi for the two times they display it, which is a lot for those poor Christians. I, too, left an offering of an ongaro. There were two Frenchmen who, on passing by there, offered 2,000 reales for that relic, but the Armenian archbishop did not accept it. When the service was over, he insisted on taking me to his house, where he treated me most kindly and had me eat some things made according to their customs. When I left, I gave him an ongaro, since those priests and prelates are very poor. They have no income and keep themselves only through alms and their own work. That day winter began in that city with a heavy rainfall.

On the 23rd I went to the river to see if I could stop a *kielek,* or *kalak,*[27] which are barges that go to Baghdad by the river. I had already decided to travel by river since there were no caravans preparing to go to that city. Besides, the overland trip is long and tiring; although the trip by river is more dangerous, it is much faster and easier and can be undertaken when one wants. By land it is necessary to wait two or three months before getting together a caravan for those parts. In addition, since it was winter, the river was full, and the river trip would be faster and less dangerous; whereas, on land there would be mud, and one would have to stop for months in some village if the roads were impassable. In the summer, however, the overland trip is more practical, since the days are long and the ground is dry; and at that time the river has little water and cannot be traveled. When I arrived at the bank, I saw that the river was swollen and swift from the rains,

27. *Kalak,* an Arabic term for a raft of inflated animal skins (Turkish *kelek* or *kalek*). Bembo offers two transcriptions, perhaps evidence of his interest in different pronunciations.

but I was sorry not to find any barges getting ready to leave and thus to find myself held up in my journey.

On the 24th a poor aga who had been in my company in the caravan from Birecik came to visit me. He had always been friendly to me, and I had given him some foodstuffs during the trip, so he came to see me in friendship. He asked me for some wine, and since I knew him to be discreet, I gave him as much as he wanted. He got drunk very quickly without my realizing it. Under the influence of the wine he began to ask me for a present, saying that I had promised him one during the trip and adding other insolences. I answered everything in the manner that seemed best through the dragoman. Meanwhile, a shoemaker appeared with many pairs of boots that he wanted to sell me for my trip. The aga took a pair, gave it to his servant, and sent it to his house without saying anything. But he was not happy even with that, and I could not get rid of him. Instead, he continued to make more insistent and outrageous demands. I thus decided to leave him alone in that room with the dragoman. He kept on protesting that he did not want to leave and that he wanted to eat with us. Finally, when it was late, he decided to leave; I don't know how, because he could hardly stand up. In the following days he was ashamed to let himself be seen. I thank God that he was a good man, for if he had been ill intentioned, he could have got me fined heavily.

On the 25th, while coming back to the city through the New Gate after having walked along the river, we met with a group of Turks. Besides insulting us, they also became directly offensive and threw a piece of wood after us. One must put up with all this so as not to be treated even worse.

On the 26th and 27th I did not go out of the house due to the heavy rain that was falling. I passed the time learning something of the Turkish language from the Father Superior. I learned more from him through grammar rules than I did during the whole rest of the trip.[28]

On the 28th, while walking through the city, about one hundred steps to the right of the New Gate, I saw inside the walls a small ruined tower in which are some stones with Latin letters that were corroded by time and illegible.

On the 29th I also stayed in the house because of the bad weather.

On the 30th, after supper, arrived a son of Monsieur Caron, a Dutchman

28. Presumably Bembo also studied Arabic during the year that he resided in Aleppo.

who is one of the directors of the French Company in the East Indies.[29] He was coming from Persia, and for seven years he had been traveling around the world. He had already been to America, part of Africa, the East Indies, and was passing [from Diyarbakır] through Aleppo to go from there to Venice and then home. He said that in Persia he had been made prisoner twice and that his freedom had cost 150 reales. But his servant told me that this had happened to him for having tried to violate a Persian woman and that he could thank God that this had happened in Persia, for in the Ottoman state such a folly would have cost him much more. That evening the Fathers asked me if I would mind having this foreigner dine with me and [said] that he would also contribute to the expenses. I received him gladly but did not allow him to spend anything either for himself or for his servant.

On the morning of the 31st we heard Mass before daylight, which is when the fathers must say it because they are not able to use the Armenian church during daytime on holy days. On other days they say it in hiding in a room. They also hid all the sacred implements immediately afterward. When the foreigner did not show up, we found out that he was a Lutheran. When I saw that our departure was being held up because there was no *kalak*, I decided to buy a small one so as to be able to leave with two large *kalaks* that were going to depart in two days' time.

[FEBRUARY 1673]

On the 1st of February, after a heavy snowfall, we saw a lunar eclipse. The Turks behaved crazily. They all got on the roof terraces and made a great noise beating with dishes and copper vessels and other things. They believe that the moon is fighting with the earth and that that noise defends her.

On the 2nd I finished bargaining for the small kalak and put a deposit on it. On the 3rd I finished getting provisions, and the *kalakgi,* that is, the skipper of the kalak, put all the things on board on the 4th. I took in my company an Armenian whose name in Arabic was Jibrail, which means Gabriel, a relative of my dragoman who had been recommended to me by

---

29. The French traveler Abbé Carré also met Monsieur Caron and gives substantial information about his career.

the Fathers. He was going to Surat on business. He was a man of spirit and courage whose company I enjoyed a lot on that trip, although he knew no Italian.

At around the 22nd hour I took some letters from the Fathers who insisted on accompanying me to the kalak. I gave them a donation that was commensurate with all the kindnesses that they had shown me. I also took a letter from the foreigner for his father in Surat and gave him one to my uncle in Aleppo, although he never presented it, since he left there immediately after arriving. When I got on the kalak, I bade good-bye to the fathers with a glass in my hand as is the custom there. We then began the journey in a convoy of three kalaks, which are, as has been said and as can be seen in the drawing, barges held afloat by air-filled goatskins, tied with the heads up out of the water so that they could be easily inflated every evening. The sides of the kalak are of wood and are as high as one's waist. Also of wood is a big shed in the aft part, where all the luggage is placed. On top of it sit the crewmen, who row backward as on galliots, with two oars, one across from the other. The oars are held in place by a small piece of wood and are themselves long, unworked pieces of wood to which are tied small pieces of wood four fingers wide and half an arm long that serve as the wide part of the oar. They row little, however, due to the swiftness of the river; they rather use the oars to keep the kalak on its course, far from land, sandbars, and stones, and to go to that part of the river that they want. In the middle of the kalak a carpet is spread out to sit on. Kalaks can be large or small (according to one's need, from 50 to 1,000 goatskins) and can hold sixty or more people and sixty *cantaros* of goods (there are 120 of our *libre* for each cantaro). To rent them, one pays a sum per *qintar,* that is, per weight, not per trunk of luggage.[30] These kalaks go as far as Babylon and no farther. There they take them apart and sell the wood, which is expensive there. The goatskins are deflated and taken back to Diyarbakır to make new kalaks. They cannot take the kalaks back up the river because the water runs too quickly. From Baghdad, that is, Babylon, then to Basra, one goes with other ships of that country. Some Turks wanted to board our kalak, paying their portion. In all we were thus eighteen people, seven of my

30. A *cantaro,* or *qintar,* consists of 100 *ratl,* but its weight varies according to geography. Bembo noted that it was the equivalent of 120 Venetian pounds. Obviously, a large kalak could carry sixty persons as well as an impressive amount of cargo.

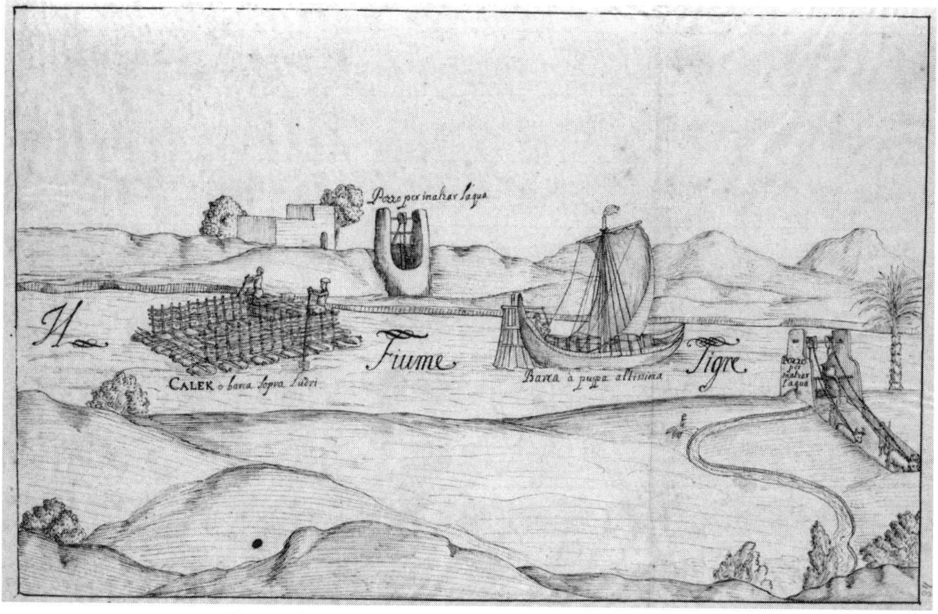

FIGURE 14. Kalaks crossing the Tigris.

company, three Armenians, a Jew, and seven Turks, including the two that were rowing and a janissary. Around the 23rd hour we began the trip leaving behind Mount Taurus, which was then covered with snow. After two miles we passed underneath a stone bridge with ten arches, over which caravans pass when the river is high. It was built when the city was under the control of Armenian Christians. On the banks of the river one could see many towns, but almost all destroyed. After five hours we stopped on the left side of the river, where we found three other kalaks that had left three hours before us and that were full of janissaries with the luggage of the Great Aga of the janissaries of Babylon. On the first of these kalaks was the son of the aga with the luggage of his father and two *odabaşı,* who are captains of one hundred janissaries—the real ones from Constantinople who have their quarters there. In another there were two other odabaşı with their people and servants and families. On the third was a subaşı, which is a commander a rank higher than the odabaşı. During the night some of the passengers slept in the kalaks, and the rest on the banks of the river.

On the morning of the 5th we left all together an hour before day. First went the kalak of the son of the aga, which had an unfurled flag; behind went the two odabaşı; then the subaşı, who also had a flag; we followed last.

We found on the way three swift streams that entered the Tigris, and along the banks were many towns of Kurds. I saw many eagles and other raptors among the mountains, and also on the river there were many aquatic birds. Half an hour before night we stopped at the foot of a little hill on the left side, even though on the right there was a town of grottoes situated in a hill, which seemed like a great house of many floors. The houses communicated with one another by means of ladders formed in the same hill. That night we slept under the stars because we would have to rise before day and did not have time to set up the tent, since the Turks did not want to wait for us. None of them had a tent, not even the aga. Our rule for eating on that trip was to have a little breakfast in the morning before leaving, and something cold at lunch, which we carried in the *sufra*,[31] a round piece of leather with a cord strung along its edge, which can be laid out as a tablecloth, and the leftovers can be kept in it afterward. We would also heat something in a small stove that [held] coal and kept the fire on the kalak. In the evening, on land, we would go look for wood to cook our provisions, or we would cut fresh wood. We always had a great pilaf, which is a soup of dry rice, with much sauce, which makes a good meal. That night we also slept in the open.

Before daybreak on the morning of the 6th we got on the kalak. The trip was tortuous, with many turns of the river through mountains. There were several towns all made of grottoes, and the terrain was so rough that it seemed impossible to get to them. There was some danger there too, because it was a convenient place for robber Kurds and very frequented by them. But by the grace of God we did not run into any danger. Around the 20th hour we arrived in a very ancient city named Hasankeyf,[32] situated on

31. Arabic for tablecloth (Turkish *sofra*).

32. Bembo renders it as "Assanchef" (Arabic *Hisn Kayra;* Turkish *Hasankeyf*) The former Roman fort of Cephe, Hasankeyf guarded the border between the Roman and Sasanian empires. It was taken by Arab forces in A.D. 640 and remained an important town until the Mongol conquest of 1260. Restored in 1116 under the name of Hasankeyf by the Urtuqid dynasty, the great bridge over the Tigris was much admired by the eleventh-century Arab geographer Yaqut, who described it as having a single great arch rising over two smaller arches. Bembo describes four arches: their remains can be found now on either side of the river. The ruins of an Urtuqid palace can also be seen on top of the citadel, there are remnants of several mosques in the town itself, and on the left bank of the Tigris are the remains of a convent. Bembo's description of the site is detailed and informative.

the right side of the river. It has many towers and is mostly destroyed. There is also a rather strong castle on top of a mountain in which one sees an ancient building that seems to have been a church. In the façade it has three equal windows like those of the ancient churches of Diyarbakır. Over the river there is a broken stone bridge of four arches, one of which has fallen and has been remade in wood.[33] In the middle of the bridge there is a covered place that serves as a guardhouse. The entire bridge used to be covered in ancient times. All around, it has several figures in relief, but I was not able to get any information about it from those ignorant people. On the left side one sees a large destroyed structure that was a church or a mosque with the remains and vestiges of many other buildings around it. Since we stopped there to buy something, the aga of the castle sent for our boatman. The other three *kalaks* had already left, and he had not been able to get anything from them because they were janissaries, so he wanted twelve reales from us. After some argument he was satisfied with five, of which I had to pay three and a quarter, and the rest was divided among the other passengers. This delayed us until after the 23rd hour, after which we found the river was narrower and swifter, and the current carried us along to where it would be making many meanders, or, as our people say, many *bovoli*.[34] For two whole hours we were in constant danger of thieves, since we were passing through mountains inhabited by Kurds, and the river was not wider than the Brenta. It was a good thing we passed through that part by night and in great silence, moving the oars only slightly so as not to be heard onshore. However, some Turks told me later that those thieves never fight, but rather attack at night, which I do not really believe. I gave thanks to God that I had passed through there so easily. At 3:00 at night we stopped at the foot of a mountain on the left side of the river where there were the other kalaks, and we got off to look for wood because of the great cold, but we did not cook anything that night. My bed that night was the bare earth, and my pillow a stone.

Three hours before daybreak on the morning of the 7th we went on our way, going for five hours through mountains that were very dangerous because of thieves and because of the river being rather narrow. Thus we always remained ready with our arms at hand. In the third hour of the day we saw to the left a destroyed settlement and the Garzan River, which unites

33. The bridge built by the Urtuqid ruler Qara Arslan in A.H. 519 (1125–1126).
34. Winding stairs are called a *bouolo* in Italian.

with the Tigris and is almost as large as the Tigris.[35] Then the Tigris becomes wider and faster. After a quarter of an hour we saw to the right a ruined castle on a small mountain. I was told that in ancient times one had to pay a toll passing through here.[36] Shortly afterward, we saw two caravanserais, a new one and an old destroyed one. On the left we saw a bath with naturally warm water. An hour after noon, when we had a brief meal as usual, we found a boulder in the middle of the river, and a stream that enters the Tigris. After another hour we passed two other small boulders. To avoid them, it was necessary to keep to our right. As soon as the first two kalaks had passed, twelve Kurdish robbers armed with arquebusses came out of the mountain and began to shoot at the third kalak. They hit one of the oars. Since we were the last, we did not realize what was happening until after many shots had been fired, and we answered with shots from our own arms, although these were wet from the rain of the past days. The Turks who were with us did the same, and I observed that when the Portuguese father who was with us shot with the arquebus, which was loaded with several balls, two of them ran away, perhaps wounded. Over our kalak passed five or six shots and, without a doubt, if they had realized that we were behind, they could have killed us all, since they could shoot at us easily all the time we passed around that mountain. But they did not realize we were coming until we turned the bend, since they were intent on giving chase to the first three kalaks, which were well ahead of us. Assisted by the hand of God and carried away by the very swift current of the river, we soon escaped that grave danger, and those barbarians were disappointed in their cruel hopes. They usually shoot first at the rowers, because if those are lost, the kalaks are carried ashore by the current, where the robbers fight until they kill all the passengers and seize all the cargo. And they are so inhuman that they do not take it without having taken the lives of the people, even if one promises them ransom. In those mountains there is not even a peasant without an arquebus or sword or bow and arrows, and no one goes unarmed even to work the earth. These people do not render obedience to Turks or Persians and govern themselves in the villages, as do the people of the Islands of the Archipelago,[37] and [they get] together [only] for great occasions. It is impos-

---

35. Bembo says that this tributary of the Tigris "is called in Arabic *Moiè Cert*, in Turkish *Cer Suì*, which means 'contrary water.'"

36. Bembo uses the word *caffaro* for "toll."

37. That is, the Greek islands.

sible to dominate them because, in addition to knowing how to bear arms, they are defended by the location and inaccessibility of those mountains.

I was also told that the women give as a dowry to their husbands an arquebus, twenty pounds of powder, two hundred balls, a sword, a bow, and arrows. That entire day we were bothered by continual rain, since we were traveling without shelter. At around the 23rd hour we passed a place that is dangerous for its rapids, which destroy many kalaks. In those mountains there are many man-made grottoes. The inhabitants join eight or more goatskins to make small kalaks so as to be able to cross the river and go from one bank to the other. To the right we saw a half-destroyed place, called for unknown reasons the Serail of the Whore by those people. When the sun went down, we stopped by the left bank at the foot of a mountain. Immediately each of us, like soldiers, went to gather wood to cook supper. I usually invited the Turks of our kalak without increasing the quantity of food, as is the practice of wealthy Turks. It is not convenient, however, if the Turks accept the invitation, for they ask for a gift then, and besides, they consider it our duty to invite them. Thus it is good to invite a few each time we eat, so as to avoid some insolence and sometimes to gain some good. That night I lay on the earth wrapped in my coat and with my head on a stone. But that which was most bothersome was the incessant rain that obliged us to dry ourselves time and again by the fire as best we could. We left the fire burning, since we had found no cover where we could shelter ourselves.

On the morning of the 8th we left the bank before daylight. The river soon got wider, and after three hours of daylight we saw to the left on a mountain an ancient castle, half destroyed, called Chilich, well protected by the harshness of its location.[38] At the foot of that mountain there is a large town with many gardens and water mills not far from the river. Not very far from the castle and also on a hill one sees the remains of another, and farther inland many remains of ruined towns, all of which lead one to believe that this was once a place of importance. The inhabitants of the town are country people, and the castle is without soldiers.

At midday we arrived at the city of Cizre, located by the river to the right and bathed by two streams of water that then enter the Tigris and leave the city on an island, as its name signifies, since *Cizre* means "island" in their

38. The Buhtan River joins the Tigris where it bends south toward Iraq. Bembo has noted the hill site now known as Tall Fafan, which was a flourishing community in the tenth century.

language.[39] This city is very ancient and not very large. It has many remains of ancient palaces, among which is a building with a rather high wall and three windows in the façade. It is governed by a pasha not elected by the Porte but only confirmed by the Great Lord to whom he pays a yearly fee. He is a Kurd. He is a prince rather than a pasha, since the dominion passes to his family descendants. The city has 15,000 people and is rather well provided with food, especially with most beautiful pomegranates better than anywhere and in great quantity. It has a bridge over the river that begins at both extremes with two stone arches, and the rest is formed by twenty-one pontoons joined together by two great chains. In the center is a small construction where a guard stays day and night so that the pontoons will not be burned and so as to advise of the arrival of all kalaks. As soon as we arrived at the bridge, we were stopped by order of the pasha, who wanted a heavy fee from us Franks, so that it was convenient to send Gabriel to treat with him. He managed to arrange things for five and a half reales. They asked for another one-half real to open the bridge. The Jew remained there as well as a Turk from our kalak. We left at the 23rd hour and found the river wider as we went. After a short while we saw a half-destroyed bridge on five very tall arches. At the 24th hour we stopped on the left bank at the foot of a mountain. We were all wet from the rain that had fallen all day. I suffered much because of it and had the tent set up, since [the rain] continued throughout the night.

On the morning of the 9th at an early hour we continued traveling. Until midday I saw nothing but very rough mountains. Then a plain began to be seen. It was full of towns, built partly of earth and partly of straw and extended on both sides of the river. We found five torrents that emptied into the Tigris. Since we were bothered by the rain, which had not let up all day, we tied up at dusk at the foot of a mountain to our left. On the other bank there was a rather beautiful plain, but there was also danger from the *Carachers,* who are thieves.[40] They try to take things by stealth and flee and do not carry arms. I entertained myself there by fishing with a net that I had

---

39. Bembo renders Cizre (in Arabic *Jazirat ibn 'Umar*) on the eastern border between Syria and Turkey as "Giesire." The city is built at a bend in the Tigris, the two ends of which are linked by what was originally a canal, reputedly built by ibn 'Umar, so that the city is on an island *(jazira).*

40. The word *carachers* may come from the Turkish *karakçi,* an obsolete word meaning "plunderer."

bought for the purpose in Diyarbakır. I used it often on the trip to pass the time and often caught many fish. That night I set up the tent because of the cold and wind, which bothered us a lot. Some Turks from the kalak made themselves at home there. Most of them used to eat with me, and one of them would drink wine in secret.

When the day of the 10th broke, we boarded the kalak. After an hour's journey we saw an ancient castle on a little hill. Its name was Kafir Kalesi, that is, Castle of the Christians.[41] Near the river at that point there are many houses made partly of stone and partly of straw. After this castle one sees many towns on both banks of the river. To cross the river, the inhabitants of these towns, both men and women, disrobe from the waist down, and, with their clothes on top of their heads, they enter the water mounted on an air-filled goatskin, as if on a horse, and pass to the other side. They take advantage of the current and hold on with their feet. When they want to carry across something heavy, they make a kalak with however many goatskins are necessary. At midday we saw a castle on the right side on top of a mountain. Only a few remains of walls are left, and inside, it is full of grass, which shows that it is very ancient. It is called *Cah' Carà*, which means Castle of the Woman.[42] We left behind many towns inhabited by Yazidi people, who adore the devil, as I noted above. The three kalaks of the janissaries stopped at the foot of a mountain on our right side an hour before night came. Our kalakgi did not want to stop there. He was an old man who knew that journey and said that the place was not good, not secure and without wood. Thus we continued traveling until the fourth hour of the night. However, since it had got dark, we inadvertently got stuck in a sandbar. So as not to run further risks, we stopped on the left on a plain. Since it was inhabited, we decided to sleep on the *kalak* and keep guard all night with our arms ready and without making noise so that the inhabitants would not hear us, since they are almost all thieves. Thus we did not light any torches or make fire. It was Fat Friday [before Lent], and I had only biscuits and garlic and suffered from the fierce cold. I slept without being able to stretch out or barely move.

41. Bembo writes the site's name as "Chaffer Calassi," but his translation (Castle of the Christians) is incorrect. The Turkish name of the ancient fortress must have been *Kafir Kalesi*, or Castle of the Infidels.

42. "Cah' Carà" is Bembo's transcription. "Cah" may be the beginning of the word *qasr* (castle), and Carà is presumably the Turkish word for "qara" or "black."

There we waited for the other kalaks, which passed on the morning of the 11th as day was breaking. Together we continued the journey accompanied by continuous rain. To shelter ourselves, we set up the tent, which did not do much good, so that we arrived in Nineveh half-drowned. I would have been much worse off if I hadn't had a large coat that protected me rather well. Before arriving at that city, one sees many waterwheels that raise the water to be distributed to many gardens and rice fields. At the 20th hour we arrived at the bridge, which is made of twenty-seven pontoons, but before arriving there one sees the walls of the city for a mile. The city is on the right. The walls are so ruined that they are only vestiges. Near the gate that corresponds to the bridge there is a fort and an ancient castle. It has been repaired and almost rebuilt. It is on an island formed by the river that goes around it, and one passes to the city from it by a bridge with two arches of ordinary size. Before arriving at the gate, we had great difficulty because the water made a countercurrent and came against us with great impetus as it went between the castle and the city. When one is not quick enough to tie up, one goes backward and is in danger of colliding with the other kalaks. Since we had tied up in a good spot, the two odabaşı struck our boatman with poles because he did not want to give up the spot.

As soon as I debarked, I went to the house of the Capuchin fathers, who welcomed me with every courtesy. They were only three, all Frenchmen and priests. They have a beautiful and clean house, newly built with a large yard. They are esteemed by the Turks, but they live a rather restricted life, since there are few Christians there.

This city, where the sun rises three hours earlier than in Venice, is called Mussol or Mossul and by many Nineveh.[43] Its walls are very extensive, but full of breaks. In ancient times it was so vast that it was united with old Mosul, a half day's journey away. It, too, is situated on the river, but I did not see it, because we passed there during the night. Most of the houses are of earth, but rather beautiful inside. All have terraces instead of tiles on the roofs. The streets are dirty and muddy, and throughout the city there are piles of refuse and ruins. It is governed by a pasha, a qadi, an aga (com-

43. The modern Mosul in northern Iraq is on the west, or right, bank of the Tigris; ancient Nineveh, first surveyed and mapped in 1820 by Claudius Rich, is across the river from it on the east, or left, bank. Mosul had come under Ottoman control in 1535. Bembo uses the two names, Mosul and Nineveh, almost interchangeably.

mander) of the castle, an aga of the janissaries, a muhassil, and other lower officials. It has five gates, four of which are always open and the other rarely. There are not more than 30,000 Turks and 3,000 Christians counting Jacobites, Armenians, and Nestorians. I was told by the Capuchins, who had been in that mission for many years, that this city was not the ancient Nineveh, but that it was much older still. They said that that land was the first seen by Noah after the flood. He built the city. Mosul in their language means, "It happened."[44] And they say that [the other] Nineveh was on the left of the river in Chaldea and was destroyed by Arbaza, King of the Medes. It took three days to travel around it and had been built by Nino, first king of the Assyrians, who had called it from his name Nineveh.[45] He had built it in the Assyrian countryside in Anno Mundi 1950 [the year 1950 after the Creation]. It had 1,500 towers around the walls, which were one hundred feet high and so wide that three chariots side by side could go on them, and [they were] greater in extent than those of Babylon. In those parts where that city was, they say that there is the tomb of the prophet Jonah in a large town on a hill at the top of which is a mosque where they believe that tomb is.[46] They let Christians only see the place out of spite and do not let them enter. Sacred Scripture makes no mention of this; it is known only from some Jewish stories that tell that he died there and was buried and that not far distant was the city of Nineveh, of which no vestiges remain. One can see that

44. Bembo has been misinformed. Derived from the Arabic verb *wasala*, meaning "to connect, to combine," the city's name means "place of joining," presumably referring to the fact that several branches of the Tigris, including the Khawsar, meet there to form a single stream and a rich agricultural area.

45. The first-century B.C. historian Diodorus Siculus, basing his work on Ctesias (405–359 B.C.), reported that King Ninos (a name probably derived from the Assyrian king Tukulti-Ninurta, who ruled from 1244 to 1208 B.C.) founded the city of Nineveh. He also recounted the city's capture and destruction by Medean King Arbakes (in 612 B.C.), who may be identifiable with Herodotus's Harpagos and Bembo's Arbaza.

46. Two mounds mark the west wall of Nineveh, founded by the Neo-Assyrian ruler Sennacherib around 690 B.C. Nineveh's palace and temple quarter are located at the northern mound. The village of Nabi Yunus (the prophet Jonah) occupies the southern mound. After his travels in the belly of the whale, the Prophet Jonah was said to have preached in Nineveh, and the *'Ayn Yunus*, or Jonah's spring, located a kilometer from Nineveh, was credited with healing powers; there was a mosque beside it.

place from the terraces of Mosul, whose walls are not the ancient ones, since they have been destroyed twice by the Persians down to the foundations. The walls that are there now and that are half destroyed were rebuilt about three hundred years ago.

On the morning of the 12th I heard mass in the most hidden room of the house at the break of day, as do all the missionaries, so as not to be observed. In this city I began not to find wine, since making it is not allowed. That which they use to celebrate mass is sent to them from Diyarbakır. Because of the continuous rain I couldn't go to any of the strange things that are in many places in that city. Around midday I boarded the kalak, and as I left the city I observed that the walls were so destroyed that one could have entered in many places without going through the gates. Around the 22nd hour the sun let itself be seen as we were leaving the shores of Mesopotamia. We had changed our boatman for an Arab, as had the other kalaks, which had left before us, since the Arabs are more familiar with the way to Baghdad. Before leaving, we paid the aga of the Customs three piasters. After an hour and a half of journey we found the other kalaks on the right side in a plain where there was much wood. This was very useful for keeping us from the cold, which was making itself strongly felt. We did not set up the tent since that place was very dangerous because of Arab thieves, and we slept aboard the kalaks. At around midnight, however, came a wind with rain so terrible that I was obliged to debark and set up the tent, although I got all wet under it anyhow, even though I was in the best place, in the center near the pole supporting the tent.

In the morning of the 13th we left two hours before daylight because of the great wind, which was getting stronger and made it necessary for us to stop after two and a half hours' journey on the shores of a plain to our left. Not far from there was a town. When the wind stopped around the 19th hour, we continued our trip, even though the rain continued. After three hours we tied up the kalak on the left-hand side by a plain. We found no wood and thus left our clothes on as they dried.

On the morning of the 14th we left at the rising of the sun, and around midday we found a river that enters the Tigris, called *Zarb Su* in Turkish, that is, "Running Water." [47] At a distance one can see the remains of an

47. The Great Zab River joins the Tigris about fifty kilometers south of Mosul. The ruins of the Assyrian city of Nimrud, founded by Ashurnasirpal II, are located a short distance to the north. The area between it and the Lesser Zab

ancient fortress on a mountain. Two hours after midday we found other remains of a castle, and shortly afterward a stream that made the Tigris considerably wider. The whole afternoon we saw plains with towns and ruined palaces that indicate that some city of importance had been in that place. At sunset we stopped on a small flat island in the river, where we were not able to set up the tent because of the many stones there and had to sleep aboard the kalak.

At daybreak on the 15th we arose, and it was the first day of Lent. Before midday we found a half-ruined castle on the right, built into a mountain. Some pieces of wall are preserved, and those people believe that it was built by Nimrud. After midday we saw another ruin of a castle on the right, called the Castle of the Proud One. Quite a ways afterward we found a bridge called *Altın Su* in Turkish, that is, "Gold River," which crosses the Tigris.[48] After having seen several Arab towns of tents, we stopped at sunset on the right on another island, where we set up the tent, which protected us a great deal from the rains that continued night and day. The season was so difficult that two animal furs were not enough to keep me from the cold. Yet the Arabs of those places crossed the river nude mounted on goatskins, as described above.

On the morning of the 16th we left before daylight while the rain continued. Since the wind grew, we stopped nearby on a plain to the right, where we made a fire to dry out, since we were drenched. When the wind improved, we returned to our voyage, and after two hours we were at Tikrit,[49] where once had been a great city and a castle on the top of a hill by the river, of which now nothing can be seen other than a piece of wall and two half-destroyed towers, all in baked brick. Around the castle is a moat in which runs the river. One can also see some remains of a bridge by which one entered the castle. The city is farther inland between two hills, surrounded by a stone wall and inhabited by 10,000 people of Arab nationality. On the shore I saw some boats being made rather roughly, which must

---

had been intensely settled and cultivated for thousands of years before Bembo's trip. *Zarb* does not mean "running" water; more likely it is derived from the Syriac word for "wolf."

48. Bembo transcribes it as "Altum Su."

49. Ruined by Timur's armies in 1394, Tikrit had a large Christian population in medieval times and even a large monastery. It was celebrated for its woolen textiles, the major source of its wealth.

have served to carry people to the city of Basra. We did not spend the night in the city, but near the river in the tent, in order to leave early on the morning of the 17th.

We left before sunrise, and after half an hour's journey we saw another castle similar to the one just described, since the city was between the two of them. After three more hours we saw a large town in a plain called Emandur from the name of a great saint or prophet of theirs who is buried there.[50] After another hour we saw on the left side for twelve continuous miles quantities of ruins, which those people believe to be those of ancient Baghdad or Babylon. This cannot be, because that city had been built of [unbaked] bricks, and those ruins are of baked bricks. Since the ruins are not all together, one can believe that it had been more than one city.[51] After midday we saw a castle on the right and a building which they say, but I do not know with what proof, is the tomb of Pyramus and Thisbe, the lovers. A little farther on the left is a great building supported by three arches.[52] Farther inland from it one can see a large town called Samarra from a prophet of the same name who is buried there in a minaret, which is not high.[53] Near it are two other minarets. One sees this place for more than an hour because of the meandering of the river. From there one can go over-

50. Samarra was a small town when the 'Abbasid caliph Motasim (833–842) moved the capital there from Baghdad in 836 and renamed it *Surra Man Raa* (Happy Is He Who Sees It). Bembo's Emandur comes from the eleventh-century tomb of the Imam Dur in Samarra. It flourished as the capital of the 'Abbasid caliphate from 836 until 892. Bembo's estimation of its size is accurate: the site extends for some 30 km, mostly along the east bank of the Tigris.

51. This is a very astute observation, since Samarra grew additively as each 'Abbasid caliph developed a new urban center.

52. On the right (west) side of the river Bembo probably saw the al-'Ashiq palace and, about 1.2 km south, the tomb known as the Qubbat al-Sulaibiya, constructed over the grave of the caliph al-Muntasir, who died in 862. (Readers should appreciate Bembo's skepticism about its being the tomb of Pyramus and Thisbe.) Here on the east side of the river he may be describing the Bab al-Amma, the Jawsaq al-Khaqani palace's immense three-arched ceremonial entrance that overlooks the Tigris.

53. Bembo is referring to the tomb of the Imam Dur in Samarra, a site that he calls *Assecmassuch*. The two minarets are the spiral minarets of the Great Mosque and, 6 km to the north, the mosque of Abu Dulaf, both built during the reign of Caliph al-Mutawakkil (847–861).

land to Baghdad in half a day. By water the trip is longer because of the already mentioned meandering of the river. That day we found many kalaks loaded with wood for Baghdad. Their oars were made of various pieces of cane. At sunset, although the other three kalaks stopped in a plain on the left, we continued traveling, since the Turks who were with us had not wanted to stop. We slept while traveling that night, which was infinitely uncomfortable.

On the morning of the 18th we began to see immense gardens of palms that give dates. Two hours before daylight (Be warned, however, that one cannot be sure of either hours or days because one travels at the whim of the boatman.) we stopped in a town to the left, where I disembarked to look for horses to get to Baghdad in a few hours. I did not find any, however, and so continued the journey in the kalak. Around midday we were reached by the others, who had stopped the night before. That whole day we saw by the river many towns, gardens, and hydraulic devices, as can be seen in the drawing, where they raise the water to distribute to the gardens by means of wheels.[54] Large leather containers with necks half-an-arm's-length long are tied to the wheels with ropes. The mouth of the containers is held up by another rope that is pulled by oxen, which makes the wheel turn and carries the container full of water up and automatically spills it out in a great stone deposit from which it then goes out through many little canals. When the animals return, the container dips into the well and fills. In this way they water the gardens, which are considerably higher than the river. Around the 22nd hour we saw a mosque with two domes covered with ordinary porcelain tiles and a rather high minaret. One sees this for over an hour. There is another to the left that is similar, and because of the many turns of the river, it seems that the two are only one. At the 23rd hour the kalak of the aga stopped on the left in a town made of bricks. After that there are gardens on one side and, as described, many water deposits on the other side until the city of Baghdad. We saw it as the sun went down to the left. At the beginning of it there is a new castle and behind it the seraglio of the pasha and then the monastery of the Dervishes, Turkish monks who whirl around on Thursdays. Behind this there is a gate, through which we entered just in time. They wanted to close it since it was an hour after sunset. I had myself led immediately to the house of the Capuchins, who had been advised of my travels in those parts and welcomed me with great

54. Bembo is observing the waterwheels known as *nouria* (na'ura).

benevolence and gave me rooms and beds as I needed. Since I was very tired, I went immediately to rest. I did not want to use the sheets, though, so as not to lose the habit of difficulty and suffering all at once.[55]

On the morning of the 19th I recovered all my things through the help of the Capuchins from the Customs for only one real. Babylon, which is called Baghdad by Turks, Persians, and Arabs, is on the left of the river Tigris. Even though many people think so, it is not, however, the ancient Babylon, which was situated on the Euphrates, built of bricks and pitch.[56] This Baghdad, some say, was built by Caliph Mehmet, son of Harun al-Rashid, 24th of the Caliphate in the year A.D. 809.[57] Others say it was al-Mansur, caliph in the year 762;[58] and some Persians say it was the caliph Abu Jafar, who founded it at the advice of a Gentile astrologer called Naubakht, and that it cost eighteen million in gold and that it was finished in four years.[59] However it may be, one sees that it is erected from the ruins of the ancient Babylon, as Pietro della Valle affirms.[60] He recounts that so many ruins were found that an Arab story says that a cock who got lost in Baghdad was found in Basra, where he had gone just by jumping from one house to another through those ruins. It is surrounded by walls nine palms wide and 50 palms high. On the land side it has a moat almost four meters wide and six meters deep. To go around it on the land side I took two and

55. Bembo has a dry sense of humor.

56. Bembo is, of course, correct: ancient Babylon was on the Euphrates, while Baghdad is on the Tigris.

57. The 'Abbasid caliph Harun al-Rashid ruled from 786 to 809 and was succeeded by his son al-Amin. He embellished, but did not found, Baghdad.

58. The original Round City of Baghdad was begun in 762 under Caliph Abu Jafar al-Mansur.

59. "Bugiafar" is Bembo's rendering of Abu Jafar [al-Mansur], so this account tallies with the former. The foundations of Baghdad were laid at a time selected by the Iranian astrologer Naubakht.

60. One of the greatest Italian travelers to the Near East and India, Pietro della Valle (1586–1652) traveled extensively in Turkey, Iran, and India from 1614 to 1626, when he returned to his native Rome. His travels were published in three volumes: Turkey (1650), Persia (1658), and India (1663). Bembo had apparently read della Valle before he left Venice, for soon after his arrival in Shiraz he paid his respects to the sister of della Valle's Iranian wife. I suspect that, back in Venice after 1675, he also reread della Valle before he penned his own journal.

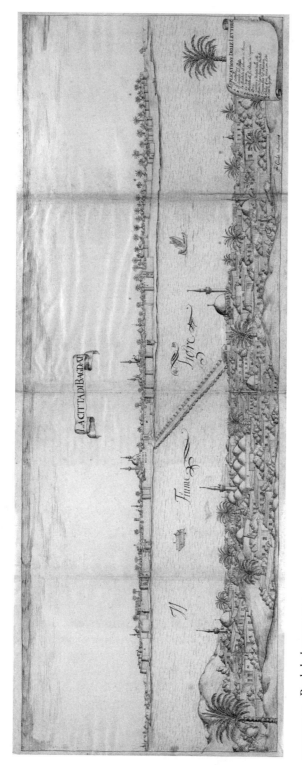

FIGURE 15. Baghdad panorama.

a half hours walking at a normal pace.[61] It has five gates, four of which are on the land side, one of which is closed, and one on the river side that corresponds to the bridge that goes to the suburb called Ras al-Jisr.[62] The bridge is usually of thirty-nine pontoons, but the number decreases or increases according to the size of the river. The pontoons are so distant from one another that one more could fit between them. They are tied together by a large iron chain, and in some parts the bridge opens to give passage to boats. On the side of the river there are two or three other doors that are only for the men who provide the city with water. The walls and many houses are along the river, and the city makes a fine sight from that side. Inside the walls in the part of the city toward Basra there is a large uninhabited section, full of palms, called the desert of Baghdad. In the inhabited part, too, there are many gardens with palms, lemon trees, orange trees, and rather good pomegranates. The houses are almost all below street level, so that soldiers won't enter with their horses and also so that [residents] can protect themselves from the heat. They have no windows but only some small holes and get air from the courtyards and divans, which are all covered on one side like great loggia. All the houses are only one story high, and mostly they live in underground rooms because of the excessive heat. The streets are narrow and dirty, except those of the bazaars, which are many. Some are of wood and some of stone, vaulted and well constructed. There are also well-constructed mosques with minarets that are rather beautiful and covered with majolica tiles. The most beautiful one is near the Capuchins' house, and it was made by the Persians.

These fathers say that there have been three Babylons: the first by the Euphrates and built by Semiramis, of which nothing is known other than the location and a few ruins that the Turks call Babel; the second was where I saw those many ruins the day before, which is called Old Baghdad; the third is this one, which was taken and retaken by the Turks and Persians and is now under the Ottoman Empire, which gave it a new circle of walls. This city is governed by a pasha, who is a vizier, by a qadi, by a mufti, and by a

61. Accounts from other travelers mention a distance of about 11.5 km.

62. The Talisman Gate was closed by the Ottomans after they retook the city from the Safavis of Iran in 1638. The other four gates were the gate at the bridge that led to the suburb of Ras al-Jisr (Bembo calls it "Rachiche"), the northern Bab al-Imam al-A'zam, the eastern Bab al-Wastani, and the southern Bab Kalwadha.

Great Aga of the janissaries, like the one of Constantinople, and he has under him 10,000 paid janissaries, although in effect they are not more than six or seven thousand who are paid. The rest are shopkeepers who let the aga keep their pay so as to be exempted [from military service]. Only 2,000 of these are [imperial janissaries] of Constantinople with their odabaşı.[63] The city is not very populous. The people of that country, although subjugated to the Ottomans, incline rather to the Persian sect, although they pretend the contrary for political reasons.[64] They are all of good race, the Turks as well as the Christians. The clothing of all is the same; the Christians, too, wear turbans with bands of all colors except white and green. The Jews also use the same clothes and are not differentiated from the rest. In the house of the Capuchin fathers there was a Portuguese Dominican who had already been there two months and who was going to Rome after having been for many years in the Indies and in China. He kept to himself in a separate room, and gossip had it that he had many jewels and precious things from those parts. He had with him a Chinese servant who, like all the people of that kingdom, had a rather funny face. The house of those fathers is large with many rooms and lodgings for foreigners. It has a church and a good vegetable garden from which they get lettuce and medicinal herbs. In the middle of it is a well of water that is used only to water the garden. There are four clergy of French nationality. Three are ordained and are called Father Francesco, the Superior; Father Antonio; and Father Raffaele. One is a layman who practices medicine and is named Friar Daniele. They have a school for young Christians to whom they teach reading and writing in Arabic and in Italian. They are esteemed by the Turks and venerated for their practice of medicine. The Christians respect them as if they were popes and entrust all their documents to them. The Superior is a rather learned man who knows Arabic and Turkish. He has written a book in Italian in which he demonstrates the errors contained in the *Qur'an*. I met one Venetian who had given up his faith twenty-five years before when he was taken as a slave during the War of Candia when he was a soldier. His name is Lorenzo da Sesto or Cinto. Before being a soldier, he had worked making mirrors at S. Canziano. Now he is called Hasan Pasha[65]

63. The others, therefore, are local.

64. In other words, the populace is largely Shi'i Muslim, Shi'a being the state faith in Iran, whereas the Ottomans were Sunni.

65. Bembo's transcription is "Assan Bassa."

and is a janissary with a pay of eight aspri a day. He is very friendly with the fathers and does many services for them, and, when strangers come, he helps take care of them. He shows some sorrow for his error, conserves his native faith in his heart, and would like to return to Venice. But he has constructed a house that cost him 1,000 piasters, which he earned carrying water in goatskins throughout the city. He was made a chief of the water carriers also. He would like to sell the house without loss and return to his country with the money and take with him his thirteen-year-old son, born of a Turkish mother, who has not yet been circumcised. He loves Christians and continuously reads the Gospels. The son, too, shows the desire to pass to Christianity, although they do not confide their common desire to each other for fear of being betrayed one by the other. Those good fathers try to find them passage, and I promised to conduct them. However, whether through a hidden judgment of God or through fear of being discovered before their escape, or being in doubt that they might not be able to sell the house well and then have to live as beggars in a Christian land—something the father would never want—or for some other reason, they could not resolve themselves [in the end]. They continually lose excellent opportunities and will do so until the day, God forbid, that they lose their souls.

After supper I went with that ex-Christian to see the city and especially the Bazaar of the Goldsmiths, Shoemakers, and Merchants of Silk Cloth, who are very rich. Going out of the city through the River Gate, I crossed the bridge and arrived in the [old] town[66] from where one can see the great length of the city. I saw many boats that go to Basra, which on their return upstream not only use oars but are also pulled by men. Behind the old town there is a great plain in which one sees in the distance the remains of a tower that they say is the ancient Babel, although others believe the contrary and say it is the relic of another, less ancient tower. However, its nearness to the river, its great size, and the way it is constructed, with a layer of palm leaves and pitch every two or three courses of brick, are rather strong arguments to make one believe that it is the Tower of Nimrud.[67] I was sorry not to be able to go close to it because of thieving Arabs who infest that plain.

66. Bembo uses the term *borgo,* which probably refers to the original site of the city on the western bank of the Tigris.

67. Travelers often identified the ruined c. 1390 B.C. Kassite ziggurat at Aqar Quf (Dur-Kurigalzu), a short distance to the west of Baghdad, as the Tower of Babel, built by Nimrud. Bembo's description of its construction method, par-

On the day of the 20th the Artillery Commander came to visit me, that is, the chief cannoneer, a Greek from Canea, well regarded by the Turks.[68] He was present when Sultan Murad took that city from the Persians.[69] It is said that it took him thirty-nine days. Having behaved valorously, he received as a gift from the same Sultan Murad a villa for himself and his descendants that he inhabits and that is under the jurisdiction of Damascus. He works making mines and is obligated to go every year to Baghdad to check the cannons and to stay there for a certain time during which there is always the danger of some surprise from the Persians. He is about seventy-five years old but energetic and bold. They wanted him to go to the War of Candia and [to the war] against the Poles, but he got out of it because of an agreement that he had made with the then Sultan Murad that he would not engage himself against Christians, so he was not pressed any further. In those days while I was there, something rather difficult happened to him. He had bought a female Georgian slave. When the owner of the caravanserai asked him for the fee of two piasters, which was what one paid for both merchandise and slaves on leaving the caravanserai, the Artillery Commander covered him with insults for having asked such a thing. The owner of the caravanserai put up with it because the Artillery Commander was highly regarded and asked him to at least tell him who had sold him the slave so that he could ask the latter for the fee. But not even in this [regard] did he want to oblige him and answered [with] even more and worse insults. The owner, angry, went to the pasha, gave him a present, and told him that the Artillery Commander had bought a Turkish woman. As soon as [the owner] left, the pasha immediately sent for [the Artillery Commander], who presented himself to the pasha with the slave woman who claimed she was Christian and kissed the cross in the presence of everyone to prove it. The pasha nevertheless gave him a strict reprimand

---

ticularly of the horizontal courses, is accurate: the building still rises some fifty-seven meters above the plain.

68. Bembo describes him as the Toppagi Bassi, from the Turkish Topçubaşı. The Turkish *top* means "cannon" or "gun"; *başi* means "head" or "chief." This official was in charge of the Ottoman artillery in Baghdad.

69. Baghdad had been conquered by the Safavi ruler of Iran, Shah 'Abbas I (1587–1629), in 1623. Bembo uses the name *Amurat* to refer to the Ottoman sultan Murad IV (1623–1640), who personally led the forces that recovered the city in 1637–1638. The sultan's grand vizier repaired the castle.

because he had mistreated a faithful [Muslim], as the Turks call themselves. The Artilllery Commander answered with such boldness that the furious pasha gave him two or three blows on the head with his hand. These [blows] were so bitter to the Artillery Commander that he put his hand to his khanjar,[70] that is, his knife, and held it in front of him and would have killed himself, knowing for certain that the pasha would have paid for his blood with his head, since he (the Artillery Commander) was so esteemed by the Great One of the Porte. But the pasha prudently kept him under arrest in the house of an aga who found himself in a lot of trouble with the fear that the Artillery Commander would kill himself and that he would have to give an account of it. The aga met with the Father Superior of the Capuchins and laid out to the pasha the disorders that could take place, and they persuaded him to let the Artillery Commander free and to give him back his slave, although he tried first to get some money out of him, but did not succeed. As soon as he was freed, he left that same evening for Damascus. In leaving me, he told me that he hoped to repair the affront to himself with the heads of more than one person. When he travels, he always takes with him the flag unfurled and a falconet, as a sign that he is the Artillery Commander of the Great Lord.

On the morning of the 21st, before daylight, I heard the Armenians singing in the church of the [Capuchin] Fathers, since, except for [the church] of the Nestorians, the Christians have no other church. All the others use that of the Fathers, which is allowed by the Turks. All those Christians, Catholics, and schismatics are not quite 3,000 people. The Jews, who are numerous, have two synagogues. The church of those [Capuchin] Fathers is in an underground place, but beautiful and large. It has a separate section for women. There is only one altar, well kept, where on feast days the Syrians[71] celebrate masses early in the morning, then the Fathers, then the Armenians at midday. There are also Greeks and Maronites who use the church of the Fathers; the Armenians say prayers two times a day

70. Bembo calls it a *gangiaro*. In Turkish it is a *hancar*.

71. Since Bembo uses the term *Nestorians* for members of the Syrian Orthodox Church, he must be referring here to the Syrian Catholic Church, which has its own patriarchs and its own liturgical languages (Syriac and Arabic) but which has been in communion with the pope in Rome since the seventeenth century, when the church was converted to Catholicism by Capuchin and Jesuit missionaries.

in the church. The masses are celebrated by the priests, each one according to his rite, with differences in song and ceremony. As an instrument to signal the elevation of the sacrament, they use a round thing, like a cymbal, to which are attached small bells all around. The Fathers celebrate feast days with liturgical singing, as in the churches of priests in Christian lands and in the churches of some orders, although not theirs. Before mass they chant the Office. As deacon there is a Catholic Armenian, who, after the priest has said the epistle and the gospel in Latin, reads them in Arabic. The Father Superior preaches in Arabic in the middle of the mass on points of doctrine. All this makes the mass itself rather brief so as to fit the tastes of those Christians who sing many prayers before the sacrifice. The Fathers take care to fit themselves to the character and customs of the people in their fasts also. They are very observant of them and believe that abstinence alone is sufficient to merit Paradise. They eat only once on fast days and also during all of Lent. They also abstain from fish that has blood. They do all this to attract the people with greater ease to the Catholic rite. Since they thought they might give scandal to those people, since it was Lent and I wanted to eat with them, I used to have a light breakfast in the morning, and in the evenings I would eat with them delicious and very cheap fish from the river. The bread is not good, since they make it in flat, thin cakes, although the flour is of good quality. We did not find wine. [Wine] for the mass comes from Diyarbakır in goatskins. Thus I drank water that they take from the river. They put it through large filters of earth.[72] As it passes from one to the next, it becomes clear and purifies itself so as to be left clean and healthful. Those Christians drink a brandy made from dates, but I did not like it.

On the day of the 22nd I arranged for a boat and passage to Basra. So that it would be only for me, I gave [the boatman] thirty reales and made a written contract so that on our arrival in that city he would not want more money, since those people are untrustworthy and think of nothing else but to empty the pockets of Franks.

On the day of the 23rd the Armenians celebrated the vigil of the Madonna of the Candles [the Purification]. In the evening they celebrated the Holy Fire in the church of the Fathers, in imitation of the celebration of the Greeks in Jerusalem. They form a small pile of thin wood, easy to light, near the door of the church. First they bless the candles and distrib-

---

72. Probably low-fired earthenware filters.

ute them. Each person who takes one gives an offering of three aspri. Having then lit the candles, which are of wax and rather small, they form a circle with their priests around that small pile of wood, which they bless. Since everyone would like to be the first to light the fire with his candle, the priests assign that function to that person who offers most. The largest offering that time was to keep the lamp of the church supplied with oil for a year. After the first person all can add their fire to the wood. They say many prayers and finally everyone takes a small piece of wood from that fire, takes it home, and preserves it out of devotion. Going out of the church, they kiss a cross and a book of the Gospels held by a priest. They also leave some offerings that are for the priests themselves.

On the day of the 24th I was obliged to complain to the qadi because the owner of the boat wanted to increase the price we had established in the contract. When he heard my just demands, which the fathers presented to him, he ordered that either the man would return my money or that he should take me to Basra for the sum agreed upon. This judgment of his did not cost me anything, which is no small thing, since those officials always sell all their decrees.

On the day of the 25th I assisted at the baptism of an Armenian baby in the church of the Fathers.

On the day of the 26th the qadi sent a message asking me if I would permit the son of the one of his officials to go on the boat with me. I accepted willingly, hoping that he would help in seeing to it that the owner of the boat would respect me. [The owner] was a most insolent Arab and had been forbidden to receive any passenger on the boat without my orders. Before leaving, I went to change some of the money I had from Aleppo. I was asked for 10% and was even given some coins that would not be useful to me later on, and to change them to gold I would have to lose 5%. Some Jews, relatives of Zitton, a Jew of Aleppo, who had met me in Aleppo, wanted to make the exchange. However, when they received the money, they wanted more than that upon which we had agreed, so I left that place, which is where all the coins used in other parts of Turkey are available. The ongari and the zecchini are worth a little more here than in Aleppo. There are some copper coins called "fulli" among which one can find some medals, but not good ones.[73] They also use them as weights in the shops. We prepared the

73. Since Constantine's time Byzantine coinage had been based on the nomisma (then worth $1/72$ of one pound of gold), subdivided into twelve miliaressia,

provisions for the trip, especially fish, which we put in oil and vinegar to continue the observance of Lent.

On the morning of the 27th I had things loaded on the boat at an early hour and departed from the Fathers, to whom I had given all the money necessary for everything they had spent on me during my stay. I left the city through a small gate that is used only by the water carriers and that is a pistol shot's distance from the bridge. I found the boat near the house of the qadi, and I saw that the owner was missing and that it was almost full of the belongings of other people. Five Turks had boarded without my knowledge. I did not complain so as not to argue. The aga of the janissaries sent to ask that I permit the boarding of two of his soldiers. Thus I was not able to leave until four hours after sunrise. That lapsed Christian helped me all this time, and I left him an appropriate tip, which he tells other foreigners about when they come.[74]

The ship follows the river's current. It has oars several wood lengths long with boards at the ends. Each oar is managed by three people. There were six sailors and a cabin boy who also took care of the sail. The sail, however, is not of much use because of the river's tortuous course, which doesn't allow for favorable winds for great stretches at a time. At the 20th hour we stopped on the left side of the river where the Turk who had been recommended by the qadi boarded. At around the 22nd hour we found on our left a large river that enters the Tigris [and is called] the Diyala.[75] The land that was ahead was Shinar, mentioned in Sacred Scripture where ancient Babylon was built.[76] We traveled all night, and on the morning of the 28th, with the wind against us, we went against first one bank, then the other, since the sailors were not very skillful. Thus it was decided to go near the land and to pull the boat with a rope, as is done by horses on the Brenta.[77]

<hr />

each further divided into twelve pholles, the Greek for Bembo's "fulli." A copper coin known as a *fulus* (pl., *fulis*) was also minted in contemporary Safavi Iran.

74. This is an interesting remark, indicating that after his return to Venice Bembo was in touch with other travelers who had made the trip to Baghdad.

75. The Diyala joins the Tigris a short distance below Baghdad. Bembo gives two transcriptions of the river's name: *Dialà Sui* in Turkish and *Frison* in Arabic.

76. Presumably, Bembo is referring to the plain of Shinar (Genesis 11:1–9), where the Tower of Babel was built.

77. River that comes from the area near Trento and descends to Padua and on to the Adriatic at Venice.

Due to the turns of the river, we continued sometimes using the sail and sometimes being pulled by men. Since to the right there was the desert, we saw toward evening wolves and other animals coming to drink at the river; and during the day we saw *coccali, grotti,* and other water birds.[78]

[MARCH 1673]

After continuing the journey all night, two hours after sunrise on the morning of the first of March I saw a boat bigger than ours. This [boat] was used so that the Arabs of those towns could cross the river. They also use some baskets made of palm leaf rope, which are round and covered with pitch and with which they cross the river. They use these baskets also as containers in boats like ours or larger, with which they carry merchandise from Baghdad to Basra, since there are no caravans that go from one city to the other because of the Arabs. These boats, large and small, are called *dainech.*[79] They are usually pointed and high in the prow and low in the bow. They are covered with such a thick layer of pitch that it seems to be a board. Inside they have a layer of boards without oakum. They are rather well made to take the continuous blows against the banks of the river. As protection against the rain, I set up a *felce,* or covering, under which, besides all the things, also fit all my company. The boat has a mast toward the prow and a very large rudder made of many boards tied together with palm leaf ropes and without any nails. Two hours before midday, we stopped to get provisions of wood so that we could cook aboard. There was an earthen hearth to cook the flat breads, and all around it there is room for many pots. We met many boats that were going to Baghdad loaded with wood. They were being pulled up the river by many men. On both sides of the river one could see many Arab towns of tents. I saw that instead of oxen they use buffaloes that allow themselves to be mounted by those villagers. At the end of the day I saw a lion that came to drink at the river. We traveled all night, passing a large town called Al-'Amarah, where a toll is paid that the boat's owner had to cover according to our agreement that I was not to have any expenses from Baghdad to Basra and would provide him with food.[80]

78. A *coccali* was a waterfowl. A *grotto* was a bird resembling a swan.

79. Bembo may be describing a large boat *(safina)* that plied the lower Tigris and the Shatt al-'Arab.

80. Al-'Amarah is about 150 km north of Basra.

On the morning of the 2nd at daybreak we saw on our left the mountains of Armenia, which were covered with snow.[81] Two hours after sunrise we met three boats. One large one, loaded with goods, was being pulled by more than twenty men. Two small ones, rather well made, with a covered place at the bow were somewhat like our *copani* but with rather badly made oars.[82] Boarded on them was a *kapıcı*[83] sent by the Great Lord to get the goods of the pasha of Basra, a very rich man who had only recently died. Two hours before midday we saw a large town to the left. At the distance of two pistol shots the river divides in two, and after two days' journey reunites.[84] We took the narrower fork, which was the shortest and least costly but the more dangerous. The other is longer and safer but more costly. The owner of the boat took the more dangerous one to save time. Almost immediately after our entering that fork we found an Arab town made of mats,[85] and shortly afterward on the left a large town called al-Azair, made of bricks. At the beginning of it there is a marble mosque and the tomb of one of their prophets.[86] It is governed by a bey who has thirty janissaries under him, and the town has 6,000 armed people of Arab nationality who united themselves with those of Basra when that city was taken from the Turks who recovered it five years ago.[87] Since this city was formerly

81. He is seeing the Kabir Mountains in western Luristan.

82. A *copano* was a small boat.

83. A *kapıcı,* or gatekeeper, was an Ottoman official responsible for guarding the gates of the sultan's palace, conveying orders, and carrying out the sultan's decisions.

84. The Tigris forks some 25 km south of al-'Amarah; the two parts rejoin at al-Qurnah.

85. The Marsh Arabs of southern Iraq build dwellings of reed mats.

86. Probably the tomb of the prophet Ezra, just south of the town of al-Azair, which Bembo transcribes as "Giabaser."

87. Control of Basra was vital for the Ottomans, who sought to match their suzerainty over the Red Sea by gaining control of the Gulf. Basra had recognized Ottoman authority in 1539, but the local Arab dynasty on its own initiative vigorously furthered commercial relationships with European powers. Basra did not come under direct Ottoman rule until 1547, and the city's relationship with the Ottoman Empire remained unsteady thereafter. Portuguese opposition to Ottoman power in the Gulf was intense, and after the 1554 defeat of the Ottoman Gulf fleet by the Portuguese, the Gulf became essentially closed to Ottoman shipping.

Persian, many of the inhabitants preserve ancient habits. I observed that the river is destroying this town, even though they have put up many dikes to defend themselves. We left there at the 22nd hour, the owner of the boat having paid seven reales of toll. A little farther than a mile [downstream], we saw a destroyed town called Mil. That day we began to feel the heat, accompanied by the annoyance of most insolent flies, which doubled the annoyance of the slow journey we were making due to the many turns in the river. Besides, at night we were obliged to keep our arms ready because of the danger of the Arabs who live in some straw houses in the middle of the wood, and all of them there use arquebusses. Around two at night we arrived at the town of Vasset or Vasser. The guards had seen us from a distance with our arms ready and called to us to stop. So that they would take little toll, one of the Turks pretended to be an aga and the Christian Gabriel [pretended to be] a janissary, and they went to the aga of the town pretending to have been sent by the aga of the boat. But when the officials came to the boat and recognized from his accent that the aga was not from Constantinople, they asked for a toll of six reales. All of this took us two hours, after which we continued our journey with our arms always ready, since the river was narrow and [there were] Arab towns on all sides.

After sunrise on the morning of the 3rd we stopped to gather wood. Continuing our journey we saw several Arabs on the banks and shot some rounds in the air after them. They fled immediately, although they weren't bad people. We did not meet any boats. It was not possible to pull them there because of the quantity of trees. At the 22nd hour on the right we reached a large stream that unites itself with the Tigris and enlarges it considerably. All through the night we traveled by sail.

At daybreak on the 4th we passed in front of the town Al-'Uzayr,[88] where ordinarily one has to pay a toll. The owner of the boat was exempted because it was an overcast day. The town is inhabited by Arabs who bear great hate for the Turks of Constantinople and who easily rebel against the Great Lord. We traveled a lot with favorable wind and stopped a little while on the right bank to gather wood. Around midday I saw in a great plain a town built of reeds, called Imam 'Abdullah[89] from the name of one

88. Bembo transcribes it as "Abusederre."

89. Bembo's *Imon Abdalà* implies a Shi'i community, though 'Abdullah does not figure among the twelve imams of Ithna 'Ashara Shi'ism.

of their prophets. Before sunset we found on the left the 'Ajam River,[90] that is, water of Persia, which unites itself with the Tigris. A little afterward, on the same side, we saw a reed town near the remains of a castle called al-Qadir.[91] Shortly thereafter we stopped on the right by a town surrounded by walls with towers, called Isaacia,[92] where we paid a toll of four reales and two pairs of slippers. Gabriel pretended to be an aga, which served as pleasant amusement for us, since he was accepted as such. When we left there, we saw a town called Mahmudiyyah,[93] shortly after which the river feels the tides of the sea every six hours. At sunset we saw the town of Jisair and then many swamps formed by the *met* (thus is called the coming in and going out of the water). At midnight we stopped on the right at the castle called al-Qurnah,[94] and we remained there in the boat until the morning of the 5th. I saw that the castle was located in the middle of the city, also called al-Qurnah, surrounded by walls with some bastions. It is located between the two rivers, Tigris and Euphrates. A branch of the Tigris enters the Euphrates some miles upstream. The customs house is about a pistol shot's distance from the city at the point where the two great rivers meet. In Sacred Scripture they are called brothers born of the same father, that is, the sacred fountain of the earthly paradise. They run their courses close to one another and race toward Syria. United in that place the Tigris loses its name, called in Arabic *Dijla* but *Tigris* in Turkish.[95] It is born at the foot of Mount Taurus. Although it begins small, it is often swelled, particularly by melting snow, and then rises out of its bed and runs close to cities. It receives several rivers and streams from the side of Armenia. Throughout its entire course it has clear water, which is pleasant to drink but not very healthy. It causes diarrhea because of its fineness. It has tasty fish, and its banks are more fertile than those of the Euphrates. It irrigates many gardens and fields

90. What Bembo identifies as the *Agiam Sui* is probably the Karkheh Kur River, which flows from the region of Ahwaz into the marshes midway between the cities of al-'Amarah and Basra.

91. Bembo's "Codaire."

92. Bembo's "Ezachia."

93. Bembo's "Mamudie."

94. Al-Qurnah is about 30 km north of Basra and is the point where the Tigris and Euphrates unite to form the Shatt al-'Arab. Bembo has spelled it in the text and also in the margin as "Cornà."

95. Bembo's rendering is "Dagiella."

of palm trees, which receive its water through the force of waterwheels. It bathes many illustrious cities in its course. Diyarbakır is the first. Passing then the plains of Mesopotamia, it bathes the city of Mardin,[96] Mosul or Nineveh, then the ruins of Old Baghdad, then the walls of Baghdad where it divides Persia from Chaldea, and finally many towns and castles at the beginning of Arabia Felix. At the said castle of al-Qurnah it unites with the Euphrates, which alone keeps its name to the sea. By the Arabs it is called *Ferat* and by the Turks *Morat*.[97] This river, too, has its origin at the foot of Mount Taurus, not far from the Tigris. Its course is slow and tranquil. It is not very deep when it is not swollen by the snows. It rather spreads out in some places and floods many fields. Its waters are good to drink, and if one lets the mud settle, they are pleasant and healthy. Thus the Arabs think they can be healed from any disease or pestilence [by] drinking of these waters. It has many fish, the best of which are the large ones called by the name *Frati*. It sets out at first toward the south and passes through the middle of Armenia, Syria, and Arabia and divides them from Mesopotamia and Chaldea. It bathes various cities and castles. On first flowing out of Armenia, it bathes Birecik and then several castles; after which it bathes 'Anah, a rather famous city in past years, and many other castles, [such as] Karbala, a city much praised by Muslims for the tombs of some of their prophets, [and] Aria, a city where it slows its course and feels the tides of the Persian Gulf, thirty leagues distant. It then joins the Tigris at al-Qurnah and flows out with it into the Persian Gulf. It feels the sea for one hundred miles. It unites with other waters twenty miles above Basra and is called an Arab river by the Arabs.

That city of al-Qurnah, which is the defense of Baghdad, as armed ships can reach it, is guarded by 1,800 janissaries and by another 1,000 soldiers under the command of an aga dependent on the pasha of Basra. In addition, there is a qadi, an aga of janissaries, and an aga of the Customs. The second in command of the customs house came aboard around midday to see whether there was merchandise. Gabriel made him believe that he was the nephew of Monsieur Baron, his friend, as he called me. I gave him some candies and peach conserves that I had kept from Venice. I also gave him

96. Bembo is mistaken. The Tigris does not flow by Mardin.

97. In Arabic *al-Furat*. Bembo is confused and repeats his earlier assertion that the Turkish name for the Euphrates is the Murat Suyu. The Murat Suyu is, in fact, one of the northern tributaries of the Euphrates.

some coffee and sherbet. In return, he sent me some fresh fish and made the search of the ship with every courtesy, since merchandise has to pay taxes when it passes through there.

We left on the 5th at the fourth hour of sunlight. On the right we saw several fishing boats made of reeds where fish are kept. After an hour, on the left we saw a river called Agiam Sui, by which one can go into Persia.[98] At its mouth is a castle called *Suep,* half ruined, where a brother of the official of the qadi of Baghdad who was with us was commander. The river was deep with clear waters and wider than a mile. At sunset we saw to the right a place called "the Convent." The river was slow and had become about two miles wide. We traveled all night by sail, and at daybreak of the 6th we arrived at Basra, a city that is situated on a small body of water that the river makes to the right. It passes inland four or five miles, and it is about two spear-lengths[99] wide and grows and recedes and sometimes goes dry. We entered this body of water at daybreak, and soon afterward the officials of the customs house came to search for merchandise. We gave them a real, and thus they did not look in our things.

When the Discalced Carmelites heard that some Franks had arrived, they immediately came to meet us with a little boat. They knew of my trip to those parts thorough a letter written to them by the English consul of Aleppo. They insisted that I should go to their house, not far from the river, and treated me with infinite courtesy.

98. Bembo has already identified an 'Ajam River; here he must be referring to either the Karun River or the Nas Sabilah River.

99. Bembo uses the word *pica.*

THREE

Basra, the Gulf, the Arabian Sea, India

[MARCH 1672–MAY 1674]

BASRA IS SITUATED HALF ON ONE SIDE and half on the other of the body of
water [I mentioned]. It was three times the length of Baghdad, but now
it is half destroyed. Near the river there are many date palm trees and earth
houses that were included in the city in ancient times. It was built two
hundred years ago, fifty leagues distant from the Persian Gulf and eight
leagues distant from ancient Basra, or *Balséra,* which was built at the time
of 'Ali by Attabud, son of Garuan.¹ In ancient times this city had its own
kings under whose dominion was part of desert Arabia, but in 1547 during the reign of Mehemet Assenam it was taken by the Turks.² It was retaken by the same Arabs with the help of the Portuguese. They no longer
called themselves kings, but absolute pashas passing their command to
their sons and recognizing themselves as feudatories to the Great Lord so
as to avoid troubles from Baghdad. Their guards were janissaries who had
escaped from Baghdad, attracted by the good pay that they received from
these pashas who had 10,000 horses and 40,000 foot soldiers. From the

---

1. The second caliph, 'Umar (634–644), ordered the construction of a military camp city in southern Iraq, and the site for this settlement, Basra, was
selected by his general 'Utba ibn Ghazwan in A.D. 638. Bembo renders *Ghazwan*
as "Garuan," and it has been suggested to me that Bembo had some knowledge
of the Arabic alphabet but in this instance read the Arabic "r" instead of the
Arabic "z."

2. Basra had been taken by the Ottomans in 1534; two punitive expeditions
were dispatched in 1546 to put down rebellions. The Ottoman sultan at the
time was Sulayman the Magnificent (1520–1566); Bembo's "Mehemet
Assenam" may be the Ottoman governor in Baghdad.

customs house they received 250,000 reales, and they were so loved by their subjects that it was believed of these pashas that they had the keys of Paradise and that they could give of the good of heaven by their will. There were people so ignorant and credulous that they left all their goods to the pasha when they died so that he would give them the equivalent happiness in the next world. And they did this in writing and in public documents. The rule of these pashas continued for a long time until at last the Great Lord sent many people to remove his head. Not having sufficient forces to defend himself, [the pasha] abandoned the city and fled to the Great Mughal.[3] When the city was taken by the Ottomans, they sent from the Porte a pasha and other ministers to that government such as there are in the other subject cities. But since the nature of the Arabs is contrary to the Turks of Constantinople, the city was taken and retaken by one and then the other. The last retaking that the Ottomans made occurred only five years ago. Because of this war, the city is little inhabited and has no more than 30,000 people established there of many nationalities: Arabs, Turks, Persians, Indians, Jews, Armenians, Jacobites, and Christians of St. John, called *Sabis*,[4] thus called from St. John Evangelist, from whom they claim to be descended when he went in these parts. But others claim that they come from St. John the Baptist. The ceremonies of their rite recall this saint, since they baptize one another in the river and pronounce these words: "I baptize you thus, in the form used by the Holy Christ our Lord." They have no sacrifice,[5] which is unknown in any other kind of Christians converted by the Apostles. They have many Jewish ceremonies that indicate that they are descendants of those whom the said saint converted on the banks of the Jordan. When their divine preceptor was gone, they went to the banks of the Euphrates and in the kingdom of Bombarecha and Basra, forgetting the precepts of the faith that the saint had taught them. They do not eat any meat that has not been killed by their priests, and [they] baptize many times during the year. They do not join with the eastern Christians or with the Moors, whom they hate exceedingly, even though they live among them. When they marry, the couple is led to the river, nude from the waist up. Their priest or minister

3. That is, fled to Mughal India, a common place of refuge for highly placed Muslims.

4. Bembo's *Sabis* were probably the Gnostic sect of Mandeans.

5. That is, no mass.

unites them from the back part of the neck and, pronouncing some words, leads them out of the water and sends them separately to their homes, where they remain one month without uniting. When the time is up, he takes them to bathe in the river again, where he baptizes them, and the marriage is performed. Of this sort of Christian there are 30,000 families dispersed in the two kingdoms from which some passed to Muscat and to Ceylon at the time when the Count of Lignares was the viceroy of Goa.[6]

There are many bazaars, rich rather than beautiful, because of the quantity of merchandise from India that arrives there, carried not only by Gentile merchants but also by French, English, Portuguese, and Dutch, who every year dock there with their ships loaded with spices and jewels. These goods are sent throughout Turkey, and from there some go to Aleppo and then also to Venice. All the ships from India arrive in the month of July and leave at the latest in November so as to be in India before the winter, which begins there in May and ends in September.[7] The air is not good, and during the summer there is such a steady sandstorm that for many days the sun cannot be seen, and it penetrates so much that one must shut oneself in one's room because the storm weakens people very much. This storm is made by the wind from the sand of the desert. The city is rather well supplied with food, but sometimes fresh fish is scarce so they salt it, and it is taxed. The water is not healthy and almost salty. Little wine is to be found, and it doesn't last more than four months. It is made in the month of July so that the grapes will not rot because of the great heat. To celebrate mass the fathers have some sent from Shiraz.[8] They also make a raisin wine that is not bad, and they drink brandy made from dates and containing nutmeg, cloves, cinnamon, and other spices that is rather good. They also have good date vinegar. There are many date palms along the shores and in the countryside, and they send [the dates] throughout Turkey and India, and they keep them in baskets made from the leaves of the same tree, joined together, that they called *temera*.[9] They dry some, making them bake in a furnace, and they remain very hard. This fruit is gathered in November and December. The pasha earns considerably with them, because he gets a *saya*

6. Bembo's "Maschati" and "Ceilan."

7. Bembo seems to be referring to the major monsoon season.

8. The chief city of southern Iran, Bembo's "Xiras" has long been well known for its red wines.

9. *Tamr* is the Arabic word for dates.

per tree, that is, one twenty-fourth of a real. From some of the larger trees he gets up to one-half real.

Shortly after I had arrived at the house of those [Carmelite] fathers, a Frenchman came to visit me. He was dressed in the costume of his nationality. After lunch the Dutch agent came. He is like a consul who lives there for the interests of his country. I observed that they freely dress in every color, even green, which is something that the pasha permits for fear of the companies that arrive there every year. On the morning of the 7th I heard Mass in those fathers' church, which is not hidden, something that I saw in no other Turkish city. The clergy were only two: the superior, of Polish nationality [and] called Jerome, and a Frenchman named Toussaint who had been one of the four on our ship. In the same church the Christian Armenians also have their services. They are no more than fifty who live in that city, and some happen by in caravans. Those fathers have also a good, pleasant house. They are going to rebuild it since it was ruined in the last war of the Turks against the Arabs. The Father Superior [also] took care of the interests of the English and the French. On the 8th I went to see the bazaars, which are full of things from India. There are many Gentiles [10] who sell there. Some of them speak Portuguese. From this place to India there is always someone who speaks that language, as from Aleppo to here I found many who spoke Italian. On the 9th I made arrangements for a boat to take me to Kong [11] at the price of five *abbasi* per person; [12] three of these coins are a little less than a real.

On the 10th I was conducted to the house of a Turkish merchant who took me into a room that was full of strings of pearls. He showed me some very beautiful and large ones. They are brought there from [the places] where they fish them. Around the 21st hour I took leave of the fathers and

10. Bembo generally refers to non-Muslim and non-Christian Indians as "Gentiles" and seems to make no distinction between Jains and Hindus.

11. Kong is a small port, located on the Persian (Arabian) Gulf about 6 km to the northeast of Bandar-i Lengeh and about 140 km southwest of Bandar 'Abbas and Hormuz. It was the Portuguese commercial center in Iran from 1622 to 1711: according to the agreement established by Shah 'Abbas I of Iran (r. 1587–1629), the Portuguese were permitted to collect half of the customs receipts in Kong. The port was far less significant than Hormuz and Bandar 'Abbas, where English, French, and Dutch interests were paramount.

12. The Persian spelling for the coin would have been *abbasi,* derived from the name of Shah 'Abbas I.

recompensed them appropriately for their kindness to me. I embarked on a small boat in the lesser branch [of the river] by which I had entered. On going out I went into the large branch of the river, to the left of which are the three palaces in the shapes of fortresses built by a pasha of the royal house who had had three sons and gave each of them a palace. When I arrived at the boat that was to take me to Kong, the fathers said good-bye. They had insisted on accompanying me. We did not leave that night, nor on the morning of the 11th, because the ship's sail was still at the customs house, since those officials had not yet searched the boat to check its merchandise. They have the practice of keeping the sails of all ships as security. They return them when the chief customs officer permits it. After midday the agent of Holland came to see me in a rather clean little boat covered with a nice little cloth for protection from the sun. With his little boat he took me to a small stream that goes from the river on the right. It extends for two leagues inland, and on both sides are gardens of palms, oranges, and other fruit trees. In that plain are twelve water canals, close to one another and similar to one another. They are very pleasant because of the quantity of gardens that they irrigate. We debarked at one of those to eat. At the meal many toasts were proposed, as is the custom in that country. In the absence of wine we drank brandy. In another little boat we found the above-mentioned Frenchman with whom we wandered along those canals until evening. He returned to the city, and I to my boat.

On the morning of the 12th the search by the customs official had not yet been carried out, so I debarked with the Father Superior and went to the *sabandar*[13] to find out the reason for their delaying us. I found out that it was because of the insistence of the Dutchman, who had given him a present for that purpose, because he wanted to send another ship first with letters to his commander in Surat telling him of our trip. He had become suspicious that Father Giovanni was carrying letters to Goa with orders against his countrymen because of some comments made by the Frenchman. It was surprising that we did not run into some trouble because of this unexpected event; toward midday they brought the sail, and in spite of the fact that we gave them half a piaster, those officials searched our things and made confusion in our luggage with many discourtesies. We left only that night. The fathers and the Frenchman had come to see me after lunch, and I had gone with them through those canals for amusement. At sunset I returned to the

13. Previously defined by Bembo as the chief of the merchants.

ship, which had begun its journey with the current. But since there was no wind and since the tide grew again, they anchored in the middle of the river, which was about six miles wide. When the tide was going out to sea again, around midnight, we left in the company of three other boats.

At sunrise on the 13th we were in front of an island that divides the river into two branches, both of which flow into the Persian Gulf after a day's journey. One [branch] takes one to the coasts of Arabia and the other to [the coasts] of Persia where there are [only] a few small ports of little importance but many beaches, subject with all those ports to the king of Persia. The beaches and all the ports of the Arabian coast are under the Imam Arab Prince.[14] We entered the branch that leads to the Persian shores, and two hours after sunrise we were in sight of two castles called Afara, in front of which we anchored because of the contrary currents. I went ashore with the jolly boat[15] to see the castle nearest Basra. It is of earth with four bastions and is uninhabited inside. The other is larger and guarded by many soldiers and has its gate on the river that passes between the two castles and comes from Persia. [The river] is called *Qara Su,* that is, "Black Water."[16] I passed its source while in Persia. I went aboard again, and we resumed our journey with the current. When the current again became contrary, the jolly boat was put in tow behind the *terrada,* as they call these boats, which have some similarity with our *marciliane.*[17] I was stupefied to see that it had no nails or iron pieces, but that it was sewn together with mats and rope. It was not very big, but wide and short. In the prow it became narrow, almost like a *felucca,*[18] which cuts the waves. In the bow it also got narrow and somewhat higher, and there was a partition of palm wood that made a sort of room. They have no other covered place but are all full of merchandise on top of which the sailors and passengers accommodate themselves. The captain with some sailors sits on top of this room to hold the rudder so that it will not turn more than a foot from one side to the other. He pulls some ropes that are arranged on some boards. It is easily managed because the bow is so narrow. There is only one mast, closer to the bow, and near it they

14. The Ottomans had conquered the Arabian coast of the northwestern part of the Gulf in 1591 but lost it to local Arab rulers in 1669.

15. Bembo's word is *coppano.*

16. The Karun River originates in the Zagros Mountains of western Iran.

17. A seventeenth-century Italian sailing cargo ship.

18. A low, fast ship with two masts and a lateen sail.

make the fire for cooking. There is a lateen sail,[19] but they are so inept that when the wind changes, they remove the sail to attach it to the other side of the mast, since they do not know how to turn the sail. They have a small jolly boat that they pull behind. A sailor stays in it who makes sail so as not to slow down the terrada. They call such jolly boats *terranchini.* Our terrada had twenty-three Arab sailors; the captain was Persian, and there was a scribe. They do not use a map and infrequently [use] the compass, since they stay close to land and guide themselves through practice.[20] Sometimes they propel themselves by oars, turned backward, [and they sing] songs in their language in rather good style. However, they are lazy people and put up the sail at every breeze. They go nude, covering only their genitals. Their food is a stew that they eat with their hands and a paste of dates that they called *tamara,* eaten with little bread or biscuit. The weapons of our terrada were two cannons, six broken arquebusses, ten spears in bad condition, and several very old shields. Besides my group there were five Turks and five idolatrous Indians. Toward evening, when the contrary tide returned, we dropped anchor not far from shore. There we were bothered by quantities of flies attracted by the sugar of the dates.

Around midnight a north wind arose, and we set sail. At sunrise on the 14th we found ourselves at the mouth of the Persian Gulf. Due to the many sandbars there, we were obliged to use the sounding line constantly, since we were in only two arm's lengths of water. Those sandbars are made by the current of the river. When ships come from India, the captains are obliged to take aboard a pilot from a nearby island, called Kharg.[21] They go with him to Basra and out again with him to the Gulf. Around midday the wind calmed down, and we were twelve *terrade* waiting, but toward evening the north wind returned and continued all night.

On the morning of the 15th, with our prow to the southeast, we saw the island called Cari[22] by the Arabs and Larecca by the Europeans. It is governed by an Arab emir. Going by it on our right around midday, we passed close to it. We saw the city located at the foot of a mountain. With the wind continuing, we saw the shores of Persia at sunset, but from a distance, and the city of Balatfare, located on a plain. That night the wind shifted, and

19. Bembo writes *all Latina.*
20. That is, through familiarity with landmarks.
21. Bembo's word is "Carque."
22. Qarawah Island may be Bembo's *Cari.*

the sea came against our bow, which was a sign of an upcoming storm. We used the sounding line constantly to know how far we were from land.

But on the morning of the 16th, the wind having passed from the west to the northwest, we continued our voyage, always staying close to land, as is the custom of those ships, which do not go farther out than five or six miles.

On the morning of the 17th, however, the wind was very contrary and coming from the southwest, and we were prevented from traveling. We saw fourteen terrade going toward Basra, navigating without fear of Corsary pirates, who never penetrate that far. At the 22nd hour the west wind returned and lasted until the fifth hour of the night, and then came a north wind.

But on the morning of the 18th it left us becalmed until midday, when it arose entirely contrary from the southwest. Meanwhile, we amused ourselves fishing with hooks and lines for mackerel, of which there were many in that place. The wind having become cooler, we took cover by dropping anchor by some mountains, but about two miles from land in eight depths of water.

On the morning of the 19th a favorable north wind blew from those mountains that induced us to set sail, but when we had got farther from land the southwest wind started up again and obliged us to go back. We anchored about a mile from land not far from where we had been before, facing a town called Bander, which means "port of the large town."[23] It is situated on the shore and is under Persian jurisdiction. Upon anchoring we found only two terrade; the others had remained behind. Having gone ashore with the jolly boat to gather wood and water, we learned from [the people] of that town that there were twelve Portuguese vessels on the shores of Kong to gather the tribute that those lands pay to that country.

On the morning of the 20th we set sail with a slight north wind, but on changing course we again met the southwest wind; despite all our efforts, we were obliged to return to anchor where we had just been. Around the second hour of the night the sky became very dark and noisy with thunder and lightning, rain and angry wind, which had us tossing all night.

On the morning of the 21st we set sail with an east wind, but having

23. "Facing a town" presumably means that they are sailing along the Iranian side of the Gulf; there were and are a number of towns along the Iranian coast of the Gulf that bear the prefix *bander,* or "port."

again met the contrary wind, we anchored a mile farther ahead than before, facing another town of the same name of Bander, and that night we had a storm like the night before.

On the morning of the 22nd we set sail, and with great effort and the help of the east wind we got beyond the point. However, still finding the southwest wind, we took shelter in a small bay of that land. There was another storm that night, which lasted all the next day and night.

On the 24th after sunrise, when the wind had died down, we set sail. But as soon as we came out of the bay, we were pushed back in by that stubborn southwest wind and dropped anchor again. Thus I resolved to go to that town to look for horses to go to Kong by land, which is only five days' journey away. However, I did not find any. That town is on a plain, and it is made of [reed] mats. It is two miles distant from the city that is governed by the Persians. I observed that those women go covered with a long cloth that falls from the shoulder a distance of two or three arm's lengths.[24]

The Indians aboard the terrade went ashore to eat. They are all superstitious, as I will tell at the appropriate time. They made a circle in the earth around their fire, within which anyone who was not of their rite, who might have entered, would not be able to eat. Nor can they eat wearing the clothes of anyone who was not of their rite. I observed that they kill no animals, not even lice, which they throw onto other people.[25] They wear a little idol around their necks. But I will speak at length of these and other foolish customs of theirs at the proper time.

Once again the southwest wind stopped, and on the morning of the 25th we set sail with a northwest wind along with three other terrade. It got cooler toward midday, and at sunset we were in front of Shaykh Sho'eyb Island,[26] where the Portuguese usually get water. Since the wind kept getting stronger, and we were afraid of passing beyond Kong, we dropped anchor near the mountains. At around midnight we lifted it again when the wind was losing strength.

On the morning of the 26th we were between two small islands where vessels get water.[27] The wind became westward, and we continued our jour-

24. The *chador* is a single semicircular piece of cloth that covers the head and body.
25. These merchants were probably Jains.
26. Bembo's "Sexsieb."
27. Hendorabi and Qays Islands.

ney close to the land and enjoyed the view of beautiful plains with towns along the shore. Toward evening we saw the shores of Kong, near which we dropped anchor at the second hour of the night. Father Giovanni, without waiting any longer, immediately went to the Portuguese commander, who was there with troops, and remained there the night. [The Portuguese commander] sent four soldiers aboard the terrada so that those on land would not go aboard to search.

On the morning of the 27th I saw that the Portuguese armada consisted of six galleons not much bigger than are ours, called *navilii,* and of two small boats. Besides these, there were eleven boats of merchants of Surat[28] and the coasts of India, and many terrade. Kong is a port of the king of Persia, of good depth and not very open, and there is little good air there.[29] In ancient times it was a very poor town, located in a sterile countryside, a nest for poor Arab fishermen, as is that entire coast. They lived under tents until the time of the viceroy of Goa, the count of Vidigueira, when Rui Freire of Andrada was Captain Major of the Portuguese in the Persian Gulf and also General of Muscat.[30] He made rich merchants from India live

28. In southern Gujarat at the mouth of the Tapti River on the Gulf of Cambay, Surat was conquered by the Mughals in 1573. It became a major center for shipbuilding and for the export of textiles and gold from India to western Asia and Europe. The English established their first trading settlement in India there in 1612.

29. Since Bembo's contemporaries described Bandar 'Abbas and Hormuz at length, this detailed description of Kong is particularly useful. John Chardin left a valuable account of Hormuz from his visit a year later, in 1674, and his complaints about the bad climate and the brackish water are similar to Bembo's about Kong.

30. Portuguese Gombroon, a name derived from the older Portuguese *Gamru* (Persian *Jarun*), was the mainland transit point for goods that had been landed at the island of Hormuz and was the terminus for overland trade routes from the north and northwest. The Portuguese seized Gombroon in 1514, and it was a key element in their control of trade in the Gulf and the Arabian Sea. It was retaken by Safavi Iran in 1614. With British help the island of Hormuz was regained by the Iranians in 1622. The reference here is to Portuguese retaliation, conducted by Admiral Ruy Freyre, after the success of the British-Iranian alliance that drove them out of Hormuz and Qeshm: the British East India Company, the Dutch East India Company, and French merchants were given the valuable commercial privileges that the Portuguese had had; Gom-

there, while he was sacking the coasts of Arabia and Persia. To avoid this trouble, the Persian king established peace with the Portuguese and promised to pay them five horses yearly and agreed to divide equally with them the fees collected from a port set up for trade in that place. The Portuguese promised to [use] their armada to oblige merchant ships from India and Sind[31] to stop there instead of going to Basra. This was easy to do, since not only Persian and Arab ships but also a great many from India stop there. They have made it a considerable place, which can be called a city, since it has many good stone buildings, all of which have terraces for the heat. It is governed by a *devar aga.*[32] For the business of fees there is a sabandar and a superintendent for the Portuguese, called the *faccenda,* who is like a consul. On the roof of his house he flies the flag of his king. There is also an agent, some scribes, and several other Portuguese. For protection from Corsary pirates there is at the shore a fort, not a very large one, with four cannons. At the fourth hour of sunlight I debarked, and Father Giovanni took me to see the Superintendent, named Gaspar de Souza da Cerda, a noble and kind person. Since it brings many advantages and lasts three years, this post is given only to nobility who have served in wars or in the army. The said gentleman wanted me to stay in his house, but, since I wanted my liberty, I took [a house] near the marina not far from his. I could not, however, excuse myself from taking meals with him.

On the morning of the 28th I went to mass in the church of the Augustinian fathers, which is larger than that of Basra. They display a cross there. This was the first place where I saw that the infidels permitted public freedom to Christian churches. That Superior is the pastor of all the Christians there and is paid by the king of Portugal. At that time it was Father Francesco della Speranza who was there on a four-year term with the title of vicar. After the meal I went to see the cisterns behind the city where drinking water is kept. There is no other drinking water there, so they use salt water for washing and other household things. The cisterns are rather deep and have four doors that they keep closed when water is low, and they

---

broon was renamed Bandar 'Abbas, and it quickly became the most important Iranian port. Portuguese actions convinced Shah 'Abbas to grant them privileges in the smaller and more westerly port of Kong in 1622.

31. Controlling the vast delta of the Indus and an Islamic state since 711, Sind was part of the Mughal Empire of India from 1591 to 1700.

32. Official in charge of a village.

distribute the water to each family by measure. Although it tastes good, that water is harmful to one's health and causes dangerous quantities of dysentery and a certain worm that plagues the inhabitants of Bandar 'Abbas. This worm grows in the body and then comes out through the foot, arm, or other part of the body. When it begins to come out, they wrap it around a little piece of wood, little by little, so that it will not go back in, but without forcing it so as not to break it, which would leave an open sore and then it would try to get out somewhere else and perhaps die within the body. In this patient way, however, it comes out by itself in a few days, and they get well easily.[33] Not far from the cistern is the Temple of the Idols of the Gentiles,[34] in front of which is a court surrounded by a wall. In the middle of it is a very large tree from the top of which some branches grow out and down to the ground where they take root and thus make a new trunk. In this way many arches are formed, or, better said, many trees from one tree, which multiplies itself and yet remains one. This tree is one of their gods because they worship it. The temple is triangular. There are many idols there, among which I saw the effigy of the head and feet of a woman held by them to be a saint for having obliged everyone who desired her without asking for a fee or reward. Their worshippers guard her.

On the morning of the 29th all the Moorish vessels unloaded their weapons. On land there was gaiety, with dancing and music for one of their holidays. I observed that the natives of the country, as well as the Portuguese, have a straw umbrella carried by their servants behind them in the street to shield them from the sun.

On the morning of the 30th, being already the holy days, the chaplains of the armada and the other religious who found themselves there, united in the above-mentioned church where Mass was sung, and after the meal

33. Bembo's description fits the Medina worm *(Dracunculus medinensis),* also called the dragon worm or Guinea worm, a parasite known since ancient times in Africa, India, and the Middle East. Contaminated water is the source of the infection for both animals and human beings. The worm larvae mature in body cavities and visceral connective tissue and then break through the skin and infect the water that the carrier bathes in. Drawing water, washing clothes, and bathing can all lead to the dissemination of the worm. Its name, Medina worm, comes from the fact that its incubation period in human hosts corresponds to the annual Muslim pilgrimage, when pilgrims' ablutions infect others.

34. "Tempio degl'Idoli delli Gentili." Bembo refers to a Jain or Hindu temple.

there was the exposition of the blessed sacrament and divine office. In that gathering I noted a devotion or ceremony of the Portuguese that they make on that day, which was Holy Thursday. They stand all through the exposition that is the Mass of that day, and after the Friday Mass [they stand] dressed all in white with their heads covered and with two swords in their hands to lean on. It is in commemoration of the guard that was kept at the Holy Sepulchre.

On the morning of the 31st the Passion of St. John was sung solemnly, as is customary on Good Friday.

[APRIL 1673]

On the morning of the 1st of April, after the *Gloria in Excelsis*, the Superintendent and other Portuguese with the Persian commander went out several miles to meet the Prior of the Augustinians of Isfahan,[35] called Friar Emmanuel of Jesus Maria, who was coming from that court. He had been sent there by Antonio di Mello, General of the Portuguese in the Persian Gulf, to complain that he had not received the tribute of three years' portion of the merchandise fees from the officials of Kong that he expected to get, and that in the future the pacts should be kept, or else he would treat with hostility not only the port of Kong but all the Persian coast. On entering he passed by the shore and was saluted from the fort and from all the ships by cannon. Ahead of him went many people on foot, Persians and Gentiles, singing and dancing with drawn weapons in their hands, beating them together in the Moorish manner, a ceremony customary among those people in times of gaiety. Behind these went the envoy with the Persian commander and the superintendent, followed then by many Portuguese and Persians. He went to the house of the Superintendent, where the Persian [commander] also stopped for a time. When he had left, the other officials went to visit him there. When the visits were over, he took off the Persian robe with which he had come, all gold and given him by the court, and put on that of a missionary, in which he received the Portuguese and explained that he had obtained what he had asked for. He stayed to eat with that Superintendent and with many others of his countrymen. I was invited with them, and we drank much wine of Shiraz in small cups. We were not accustomed to drinking it, but [the

35. The capital of Safavi Iran.

weather] was very hot. [The wine] is very expensive, costing fifteen reales per case of ten ordinary flasks delivered to that shore. They also take some to Goa. One hundred loads that were brought for that occasion were all immediately sold in those taverns and on the armada as merchandise to be taken to Goa. While we were walking along the beach that evening, we felt an earthquake that did not last long and that did no damage. We passed some hours in the house in a game of dice called *Passadieci,* but different from ours.[36] It is the most popular game among people of that nationality.

After Mass on the morning of the 2nd, Easter day, the Superintendent took us to breakfast, since the Portuguese are accustomed to eat three times a day. That day the news came that a French ambassador had arrived on business of his company in Bandar 'Abbas, another Persian port, three-and-one-half-days' distance by land from Kong, traveling always along the shore inhabited by Arab fishermen who live in huts. During that trip one sees several mountains of white salt. The port is rather safe from winds, since it is defended by Qeshm Island and Hormuz, which are so famous.[37] The sea is so peaceful that it seems to be more of a pool than the sea. Due to the continuous calm, the sea water stagnates and produces a terrible air, particularly in the months of June, July, and August. At that time many people go to the mountains, since in that season many people die from the illness of that worm that I mentioned already. However, it is a port of much traffic for the Dutch and the English, who have half the rights over the merchandise that arrives there. This was permitted by the king of Persia as a reward for his having been helped by them with ships and soldiers to take Hormuz from the Portuguese. Caravans from Persia continually come there with much merchandise, particularly with silks, which are bought by the Dutch and English in exchange for their goods.

I was in the houses of many Gentile merchants who have business with pearls, an enterprise that is mostly in their hands. The islands where [pearls] are fished are nearby, are called al-Qatif and Bahrain,[38] and belong to the

36. Apparently a reference to the dice game pachisi.
37. "Queixome Islands" and "Ormùj" in Bembo's text.
38. Al-Qatif is a rich oasis on the Saudi Arabian mainland to the northwest of Bahrain: it stretches along Tarut Bay from Ras Tanura to al-Dammam. It was part of the Ottoman sultanate from 1534 to 1664. Though threatened by the Safavis in 1637, when it was defended by the Portuguese admiral Ruy Freyre,

Persian king, although they are inhabited by Arabs. Anyone who wants to can go fishing there, if he pays the fee to the king. There are officials there to exact it, and all pearls greater than a certain size belong to the king. Pearl fishing begins in June and ends in September. The fishermen anoint their entire bodies for many days before and stay exposed to the sun, so that the water won't harm them. The pearls of these islands are the best of all and better than those fished in Hainan in China, in Manor near Sri Lanka,[39] and in the Red Sea. This is how they fish them. Fishermen with ropes tied around their waists are let down into the sea with baskets. When they have filled the baskets with oysters and need to breathe, they signal with another thin rope that they have in their mouths. Those that are in the boat pull them up immediately and are very careful to do so. Those fishermen are so knowledgeable that, even at the bottom of the sea, they can tell which oysters have good pearls, and they hide them to steal them from their masters. Some boats go to fish on their own, some [go] for merchants, and sometimes they sell the catch as it comes, as is the custom with fishing catches. Those oysters are smoother than ours. When they have fished them, they leave them in the sun to rot, and then they wash them and gather the pearls, few or many, large or small. They give to the official those of the prescribed size that are the king's and, paying the fee for the others, they keep them. They say that pearls are formed by the morning dew of summer that falls on the oysters that come up to the surface at that hour and open themselves to receive it. And as many drops as fall on the meat of the oysters, so many pearls are formed, growing more or less in size. Those drops that do not touch the meat remain like small grains that are then the "ounce" pearls.[40]

Qatif was not part of the Safavi Empire. Many of the fishers working the pearl beds around Bahrain came from Qatif, and the oasis also exported large numbers of horses and quantities of dates. Portuguese merchants shipped both horses and pearls from Qatif to the Indian ports of Cambay and Surat, where they traded them for cloth. Al-Bahrayn (Bahrain), now a major petroleum producer and processor, depended on its famous pearling industry as the major source of export wealth until 1929. Bahrain was a powerful and rich state in the fifteenth century but was occupied by the Portuguese for eighty years in the sixteenth century. They were displaced by the Safavi Shah 'Abbas I in 1602, and Iran continued to rule Bahrain for the next century and a half.

39. The island of Heinan in China and the peninsula of Mannar in northern Sri Lanka.

40. Bembo refers to an early Italian measurement of thirty grams.

On the day of the 3rd many fishing boats came. Sometimes fish are scarce, but when the armada is there, there is plenty of food, since fishers come from nearby places to supply it. Even though the soil is arid, it does produce fruits and greens at certain times, and from Basra come many dates, which are like bread for the poor.[41]

On the morning of the 4th many terrade came with merchandise, since that shore is frequented by galliots[42] and ships from all the coasts of India.

On the day of the 5th I went to see the making of a rather large vessel that, as I said of the terrade, was without nails.

On the day of the 6th the commander of the armada and the Superintendent consulted and decided, although it was the end of the season, to give a galliot to Father Giovanni so that he could get quickly to Goa, since he had made them believe that he had important letters for the viceroy.

On the morning of the 7th we loaded our luggage on the destined galliot, and I saw some cats that were being sent as gifts to the viceroy. They were of a rare kind found only in the kingdom of Khorasan in Persia.[43] Their rarity consists of their having long, thin, shiny, and curly hair similar to that of poodles, and a long tail. After lunch, having first paid our compliments to the Superintendent, we [were taken] on the Persian commander's boat, which had a shelter at the bow, to board our own boat. When the commander of the armada left the ship, he was saluted by only one cannon, since there was only one on the galliot, at the prow. Around the 22nd hour the sail began to fill. With us came a warship with the Captain Emmanuel d'Andrada to accompany us to the mouth of the Gulf, as a precaution against not only the Arabs but also Dutch ships, because of the words of the father in Basra. Our ship was commanded by a captain called Antonio Suarez de Soza, a native of India who did not permit me to make any provisions for the trip and who took me at his [own] expense and even gave me his bed. We traveled all night with the square sail with a good wind. The ship has only one mast and usually goes by oars, which are twenty-five in all, and manned by Christians of India subject to [the Portuguese], forty in number. They are poor people, almost black in color. They get a set sum as pay for each trip. Their food is only rice cooked in water, and they are the servants of the Portuguese soldiers.

41. Fresh Basra dates are reputed to be better than those from Qatif, but the latter are superior in dried form.

42. *Galeatta.*

43. The province of Khorasan in northeastern Iran.

Two hours after sunrise on the morning of the 8th we remained becalmed, [and that] lasted almost all day. Around the 22nd hour we anchored between two little islands, [having been] carried there by a light wind.[44] In one of these we got water, which is preserved there for that purpose in some cisterns. On the walls of the cisterns I wrote my name, [for I could see that] at various times there had been many other passengers of various nationalities.

After the 20th hour on the 9th we set sail with a good wind that lasted all night.

We remained becalmed from the morning until the evening of the 10th, when a little wind arose that pushed us to the mouth of the Gulf, and the ship went backward. Around midnight we were in front of Cape Musandam,[45] where the kingdom of Hormuz begins: it ends at Ras al-Hadd.[46] That piece of land is 260 miles long and is called Hiaman by the Arabs and by us Arabia Felix.[47] Opposite Cape Musandum is the Cape of Jask, about thirty-six miles distant from the Indus River.[48] The two capes form the mouth of the Persian Sea. On the right one can see the Land of Arabia and on the left that of Persia.

The calm continuing, on the morning of the 11th we had not traveled far from the two capes, and around night a contrary wind blew that lasted a few hours and left us again in calm all the following day. At the second hour of the night a west wind rose that lasted all day the 13th, and by which we traveled much, but it became calm around midnight, and on the 14th we could not see any land. The calm continued until the 22nd hour of the 15th, when the southwest wind began, favoring us all night, but on the morning of the 16th it had nearly blown itself out. At sunrise the watch reported [ships] about eight miles to the north, which were immediately recognized as being Corsary pirates, who usually infest those waters. They are of three nationalities— Malavari, Sanganni,[49] and another cruel group that go armed with arque-

44. Probably the Bani Tunb islands.

45. The Musandam peninsula, projecting from the northern part of the Arabian Peninsula and separating the Persian/Arabian Gulf from the Gulf of Oman.

46. Bembo is referring to the province of Muscat in Oman; Ras al-Hadd, near the city of Sur, he identifies by the name Cape Roselgati.

47. Yemen is identified with Arabia Felix, not Muscat and Oman (Hiaman).

48. The Cape of Jask in Baluchistan in Iran. It is many hundreds of kilometers from the Indus.

49. The Sanganian or Beyt pirates came from Kutch, on the northwestern

busses and arrows and also throw balls of fine earth into the faces of their adversaries to blind them during the fighting. However, seeing that the sail was traveling toward land, they thought it might be a merchant ship of Sind or Arabia. They wanted to give chase, since the Portuguese are esteemed in these seas, and they oblige all the ships, boats, or terrades to get a license from the viceroy, general, or other Portuguese commander. Finding one without the *cartaz,* as they call the license or passport, they consider it a good prey.[50] But since the wind was starting up again, they judged it best to continue on our journey, since they would not be able to reach the ship before night.

The morning of the 17th we remained abandoned by the wind. I observed some flying fish of the size of mullets.[51] They do not fly more than two boat lengths, about an arm's length above the water. Once their wings are dry, they fall back into the water and then fly again. One sees schools of three to four hundred together. These poor little fish are chased in the water by large fish, and in the air by water birds that the Portuguese call *aleatras,* which stay at sea day and night and feed only on fish; they only go ashore to make their nests. Thus those poor fish that seem privileged by nature because they have wings to fly are exposed to more danger than other fish, since they are the prey of both fish and birds. Our sailors caught some good fish, until at the 22nd hour the wind came from Ostro Garbin,[52] which became a wind at the bow during the night and gave us a good voyage.

At midday of the 18th we took the height of the sun, and we found ourselves thirty Portuguese leagues above Ras al-Hadd. A Portuguese league is three-and-a-half [Italian leagues], and the Dutch is four Italian leagues.

The wind continued all night and became calm at the break of day of the 19th, but it came back after two hours and continued all day and night. On the morning of the 20th it became so much stronger that we were obliged

------

coast of India. In the seventeenth century they were active not only in the Gulf but also along the Malabar coast of India.

50. The Portuguese authorities in the western Indian fortified port of Diu sought to control maritime commerce in the Arabian Sea among Gujarat, Arabia, and Iran through issuing *cartazes,* or passes.

51. "Molli" in Bembo's text.

52. Bembo seems to have misunderstood as a place name an Arabic nautical term for a west wind. During the night the wind shifted to come from the northwest and move them well into the Gulf of Oman.

to close part of the sails, since it was pushing us a lot, although in a favorable direction. The worst was that everyone wanted to command, and they were such poor sailors that it took an hour to get them to pull a rope. The pilot was a Gentile, not very knowledgeable in his job, and the galliot was so old that it was to be feared, especially since we were close to the winter season.

[INDIA]

The wind continued, although more moderately, and at the second hour of day on the 21st, we saw that the waters were too calm. We saw various dolphins and many weeds in the water that look like snakes but are not animated, nor do they move except with the movement of the water, all indications of nearby land. Thus we took a sounding and found that we were in thirty depths of water. We resolved to get away and put the prow toward the south. At midday we took the height of the sun, and we were at twenty-two and a half degrees; thus we knew our position by latitude, but not by longitude. We headed east. At the 22nd hour we saw land to the left at a distance of seven miles, which was thought by some to be the pagodas of Kutch, one of the principal temples of that Gentile land.[53] Others thought it was Diu, the fortress of the Portuguese in the kingdom of Cambay, also called Gujarat, toward Goa, 150 miles beyond the said pagodas.[54] Others thought we were in a small gulf where the waters have an extraordinary current and where there are usually Corsary pirates, and around which are many sandbars. Having taken a sounding, we found

53. Bembo gives us the word "Giacheeti," perhaps his rendering of an Arab pronunciation of Kutch, north of Gujarat and in the seventeenth century still an island. His reference to temples *(pagodas)* would include the great temple site of Somnath.

54. Cambay and Gujarat. Cambay (Khambayat) was one of the most important Indian ports in the Middle Ages. It was absorbed into the Delhi Sultanate in 1298, and its Muslim merchants became famous for their wealth and patronage of architecture. Central authority from Delhi declined in the last decade of the fourteenth century, and in 1407 the first sultan of the Ahmad Shahi dynasty declared his state independent. Gujarat became part of the Mughal Empire in 1583. During the seventeenth century its importance as a port greatly diminished due to the silting up of the Gulf of Cambay and the resulting abrupt and dangerous high tides.

ourselves in twenty arm's lengths of water,[55] and since we didn't know the land, we turned out to sea with a wind from the west. All that night we kept watch for fear of pirates, and we kept taking soundings for fear of the land. In fact, on the morning of the 22nd we saw land, and we were in only sixteen arm's lengths of water. But since we did not know the land, we went toward the southwest, and after two hours of sunlight we saw two sails coming toward us about a mile distant from one another. Immediately they were thought to be ships of *Sanganni* pirates, or *Sangari,* or *Sangalli,* as they call them. There was a light wind from the west, and we made every attempt to use the wind's advantage over them. We prepared all the arms, and I noticed that those few Portuguese put themselves with much courage in the places assigned to them by the captain. On the contrary, the black sailors showed laziness and cowardice! Like animals destined for slaughter, they watched all the preparations without studying how to defend themselves. From the resolute manner in which the ships approached us, we thought that a fight was certain. But when they were within a mile, the one, having recognized our Portuguese ship, turned her prow and fled with the wind at her bow and also using her oars in desperation. When our men saw that, they followed them, but all the effort was in vain, since our galleon could not make it with only the oars. Having lost hope of catching up with one or the other boat, we returned to our voyage. Those soldiers wanted to pursue them to take booty, since they get from the king as pay only twenty *pardaos,*[56] six of which are an ongaro. They get them when they leave Goa, and then another ten after six months. They get three additional pardaos a month for food, which the captain takes, since he does the shopping for everybody. Provisions are more or less abundant, according to the generosity of the captain. That day and night we had a rather good trip with a favorable wind.

On the morning of the 23rd the wind became a north wind. We were about four miles from shore. Around midday the wind changed to the south, and the captain resolved to go toward land and go into port by the fortress of Diu. It was near the full moon of April, three days before which there is usually a terrible storm in those seas. Thus the king commands that all his ships and vessels be secure in time, under punishment of the captain's having to pay for damages. Around an hour after nightfall we dropped

55. An arm's length was 65–70 cm.
56. A coin in use in Hormuz.

anchor in sight of the said fortress of Diu, [which is] in a strong natural position, since it is at the water's edge. It is called Diu by the Arabs and Persians, and Debissa by the Indians. It was built, according to the Chronicles of Gujarat (Thus is called the kingdom of Cambay.), by Darya Khan, king of Cambay, and then was made famous by Malik Ayaz, of heretical Russian nationality, made a slave by the Turks when he was young and bought by a merchant who did business in the kingdom of Cambay.[57] This man gave him to the king of that time as a rare man because he was practiced in arms and was an especially excellent archer. This was the beginning of his fortune, because it was then the custom of that kingdom that valor in arms exalted people so much that from being slaves it made them free men and great lords.[58] He acquired with the nobility of his talent a rather glorious name in the wars of Cambay in the service of his king. But he was also favored with distinction by fortune, which gave him a most happy opportunity to earn for himself the full gratitude of the king, his lord. The king being on a campaign with his soldiers, a kite flew over him and dropped excrement on his head. He was so displeased by the incident that he thought it was a bad omen for the war. The Gentiles are extremely superstitious about conjectures [having to do with] things of the air. The king said that he knew of nothing he would not give to anyone who would kill the bird. Ayaz was present, and he immediately prepared his arrow and pointed it so well against the kite, profaner of the royal head, that the bird fell with an arrow through it. In a spirited fashion he presented it to his lord, who with magnanimous gratitude gave him his freedom. He [also] made him one of the principal captains of his army and honored him with the title of Malik, which among those people is a sign of highest esteem. He

57. In his citation of the *Chronicles of Gujarat* Bembo is apparently referring to a book, not an oral account: it is possible that his informant was relying on the A.D. 1611–1612 *Mir'at-i Sikandri* of Sikandar ibn Muhammad, which makes use of several earlier chronicles. Bembo renders Darya Khan as "Dariar Ham," and Malik Ayaz as "Melique Az." The first sultan of Gujarat was Muzaffar Shah, who expanded the fortified city and made it a prosperous port after 1407. It became the capital of the district in 1510 under Malik Ayaz, who governed until 1522: he developed it into a commercial center and improved its defenses in order to resist Portuguese military expansion.

58. Social mobility was the norm in Islamic societies. The first rulers of the Delhi Sultanate (1192–1526) were manumitted warrior-slaves.

then gave him, as recompense for services rendered in that war, the command of Diu.

This fortress is on a point of land separated from the mainland by the sea. Yet the sea there is more like a shallow pool, and thus it is called an island. It was built, as has been said, by Darya Khan for a famous victory that he had against the Chinese.[59] Before then it had been a small fishing spot. Although even when it was given to Malik Ayaz it was not a very important place, he managed to bring a great deal of commerce there, so that besides the tribute that they paid to the king, he was able to accumulate great treasures. He surrounded the city by walls and made it very strong. Since the port is perfect, ships from everywhere go with merchandise there, taking all the commerce of the other cities of Cambay. When this Malik Ayaz was in command of that port, the first viceroy of India, Don Francisco d'Almeida, won a bloody battle against Mir Hashim,[60] General Captain of the Sultan of Cairo, who was allied with the king of Cambay against the Portuguese. After that, Almeida took possession by force of this fortress of Diu. Now it is governed by a captain by the grace of the king, as are the other offices. In good times it produces [revenue of] about sixteen to eighteen thousand reales. As soon as we had dropped anchor, a new

59. Presumably the Mongols or Chaghatai Turks, who frequently raided northern India.

60. Francisco de Almeida (c. 1450–1510) was appointed viceroy of India by the Portuguese king in 1505, as part of that country's aggressive policy following Vasco da Gama's successful voyage around the Cape of Good Hope to Calicut in 1498. With a fleet of twenty-one ships Almeida rounded the Cape, seized the major Arab trading town of Kilwa in East Africa, and then set up his official residence in southwestern India at Cochin, where Alfonso de Albuquerque had built the first Portuguese fort in India in 1503. Almeida constructed a series of forts along the west coast of India and effectively broke Egyptian and Arab control over trade with India and Southeast Asia. An Egyptian fleet sent by the Mamluk sultan in Cairo defeated a Portuguese fleet at the battle of Chaul in 1508; the Portuguese commander, Almeida's son Lourenço, was killed in the action. In February 1509, Francisco de Almeida commanded a second fleet that avenged his death, defeated the Egyptians under Admiral Mir Hashim at Diu, and effectively ended Mamluk power in the Arabian Sea. Albuquerque succeeded Almeida as viceroy of the Portuguese territories in India in 1509 and conquered Goa from its Muslim ruler in 1510. The struggle between Portugal and Muslim states for control of the western

northwest wind arose that pushed toward Goa. Thus the captain, without saying anything, nor advising those on land, lifted anchor and opened the sail, in spite of the fact that many thought it best to await the morning and continue the trip then, if the wind was still strong, because, if it calmed during the night, we would be in great danger due to the nearness of the time of the full moon. But the captain, without paying attention to those reflections, wanted to leave. We traveled with a good wind until the seventh hour of the night, when the moon went down and left us becalmed. Since the current was taking us toward land and was at times so swift that the ship was not secure, we anchored in twenty-five arm's lengths of water.

The calm lasted through the morning of the 24th, and the captain repented of his decision. Then they had recourse to vows, promising to have two masses celebrated to St. Anthony of Padua, if he would send wind so that we might enter a port somewhere, that is, in the land of Cambay or returning to Diu, until the bad days had passed. I saw on that occasion a very bizarre and curious thing. After the prayers and the vows made to the saint, for whom they have great devotion since he was a native of Lisbon, they tied an image of him as if to lower it into the sea. It is their custom to do this when they ask for favors, threatening not to untie it until he has sent the wind. But they untied it almost immediately because a soldier said that that saint was so honorable that he would have listened to them even untied. I can't think of any simplemindedness or stupidity to equal this. Then they asked everyone for alms in order to have the masses celebrated at our arrival on land. Around midday a west wind rose that lasted until the eighth hour of the night. At that point the moon went down and left us becalmed in sixteen arm's lengths of water forty miles from land.

On the morning of the 25th a north wind rose, and we saw land around midday. The wind turned and came from the west, and they handled the sails so as to be able to reach land that night. Some said the land was

---

Indian coast continued for decades. In 1528 the Portuguese inflicted a major naval defeat on the Ahmad Shahi dynasty, which at its height between 1526 and 1555 controlled a large kingdom stretching from the Indus delta to just north of Mumbai. Under pressure from the expanding Mughal state the Ahmad Shahis in 1535 signed a treaty with the Portugese, who then built their fort at Diu. Three years later an Ottoman fleet bombarded Diu but was unable to take the city, which subsequently became the center of Portuguese control over shipping in the Arabian Sea.

Chaul, others Mumbai, and others Daman, and others [said] other forts of those coasts.[61] Since everyone was firm in his own opinion and no one agreed, the captain turned the prow toward the sea, because no one really knew what land it was. We continued then to travel with the same wind, not separating ourselves from the land. Around the third hour of the night we saw a ship at our bow that was coming toward us full sail. When we saw it, we continued the trip and prepared our arms, even though we thought it was a friendly ship going to one of the above-mentioned fortresses. When it arrived close to us, it continued on its way without giving any greeting, and thus our ship behaved the same way. When the moon went down, the wind changed to southwest, the opposite direction, which obliged us to drop anchor in little more than eight arm's lengths of water.

The morning of the 26th, having ascertained that that was the land of Daman and that we had gone about six miles beyond the fortress, we set sail and tried to navigate past a point. But since we had got rather far from land, we began to fear the upcoming full moon and lost hope of getting into port with that wind. We decided to try to take shelter at Daman, since the night before we ran the danger of getting stuck in a sandbar. Then the wind calmed, and that put everyone in a state of great apprehension. But it started up again, and we went toward Daman, but in great confusion, since everyone wanted to be the pilot and say where the port was. Some said they saw it, others disagreed and said it was somewhere else. The reason for the various opinions is that along that shore there are many canals that resemble the port, but which are dangerous due to the many sandbars. With such a variety of opinions we made a mistake in entering the port, and around the 22nd hour we found ourselves above a sandbar in two arm's lengths of water, and then in only one! We thought we were really lost, but turning the prow we found, with God's help, four arm's lengths of water. The sandbar extended for six miles and was well known and marked on the map, but the error had been in thinking that that was the port. At sunset we recognized the real port and the fortress, and at the second hour of the night we dropped anchor in four arm's lengths of water. As is the custom, we signaled to the fort so that they would send us a pilot to conduct the ship securely, since there were many sandbars at the entrance of the port. When they did not respond, we lit the ship's lantern, but there was no sign from the fort, which made us fear that we had made a mistake in thinking that

61. Chaul and Daman were Portuguese settlements.

that place was Daman, and we were very apprehensive. Our fear grew when around midnight a southeast wind rose, and we began to worry that it might be the beginning of the storm and that that fortress was not Daman and that we would not be able to make a safe harbor elsewhere. That night we signaled many times, and the fortress answered none.

On the morning of the 27th we saw that it was Daman, and the wind calmed. We put the *almadia*, which is a long and narrow little boat made from a single tree trunk, into the water and sent a man to get the pilot. We meanwhile moved toward the port. When the pilot came, however, he made us go back because there was not enough water, which was why he had not come the night before. At the second hour of the day he took us into port. This is a river that comes down from the land of the Moors and enters the sea, forming this port.[62] There they build galliots and small merchant vessels. It is deep enough for large ships, but they cannot enter if they are not empty and almost out of the water, because there is a sandbar at its entrance. It is called Banco d'Area. Out to sea it is again deep but exposed to all the winds. To the right is the fortress, or the city, and on the left is a fort called St. Jerome's, made by the viceroy Don Girolamo d'Assavedo. The fortress was the next after Diu to come into Portuguese possession, and it is set in the land of the kingdom of Cambay, which begins with a city of the same name and ends at Chaul, a Portuguese fortress where the kingdom of the Deccan begins. That stretch of coast measures 210 miles. Along the coast is principally the said city of Cambay, then Machigam, Ghandhar, and the city of Baroch, where an important river called Narmada enters the sea.[63] Twenty-four miles farther, another river, called the Tapti, comes out, on which is the famous city of Surat. South of it are Navsari and Ganevi, which belong to the Great Mughal,[64] then Daman and the settlements of Dahanu, Tarapur, Mahim, and the city of Bassein, Tana, the fortress of Mumbai, and finally Chaul, which are all Portuguese. The fortress of Daman is one of the

62. Here Bembo may be using the term *Moors* to designate any and all dark-skinned non-Europeans, or he may more specifically be referring to the Mughals. In either case he is saying that the Damanganga River emptying into the sea at Daman does not lie wholly within Portuguese territory, a correct statement, since the river's source is in the mountains known as the Western Ghats.

63. These ports are on the northern and eastern shore of the Gulf of Cambay.

64. At this time the Mughal emperor was Awrangzeb (1658–1707).

principal ones that Sultan Bahadur, King of Cambay, had.[65] First it was burned by Antonio di Silviera, then destroyed by Alfonso Martin di Soza, and then acquired by Don Constantin di Braganza, viceroy of India, who occupied it with a sufficient number of soldiers. From that time until now, as I saw, they have been working on the fortifications to make the city more secure. After it was taken, it was besieged by the Great Mughal two times. Each of the attempts was in vain because of the good defense of the Portuguese, in whose power it now is. It is governed by a governor or captain; and in spiritual matters by a vicar called *Dalla Varra,* that is, *Verga,* that is, the symbol of authority,[66] granted by the archbishop of Goa. Justice is done by an Auditor. Taxes and fees are collected by an agent whose position lasts three years.

As soon as we had anchored, Father Giovanni went to visit that Captain, who immediately sent to invite me. I got out of it for that morning, but after lunch I went ashore with those knights who were aboard.[67] Not far from the gate of the fortress I saw a loggia covered with wood where the Captain received goods and news from the ships that arrive there. I entered the fortress and saw a long street, at the end of which one sees the other gate. At the left are a convent and the church of the Reformed Fathers, where ten priests live. At the midway point of that street, on the right, is the castle, which is nothing more than a closed plaza, where the house of the Captain is, as well as the munitions' storage and a few other houses, and on one side there is also the church of the Jesuit fathers. With the said knights I went to visit the Captain, who sent his son, named Enrico, a rather self-possessed youth, to meet me at the stairs. I was then received by the Captain himself, who after many courtesies obliged me to remain with him until the departure of the ship.

65. The Ahmad Shahi dynasty controlled a western Indian sultanate centered on Gujarat from 1391 to 1583, when Gujarat was absorbed into the Akbar's Mughal Empire. Sultan Bahadur Shah (1526–1537) was one of its most energetic rulers, on the offensive both against neighboring Hindu states and against the Portuguese, who sought to break the commercial alliance of Gujarati Muslim merchants and the Karimi merchants of Mamluk Egypt. Though Bahadur Shah subsequently entered into a military alliance with Portugal and granted them the fortress of Diu in 1535, the Portuguese treacherously arranged his murder in 1537.

66. *Verga* means "rod" in Italian.

67. "Fidalghi" is Bembo's rendering of the Portuguese word for knights.

I was led by those gentlemen through the city, which is not very large. It is surrounded by walls thirty feet high and twenty feet wide with ten bastions. One part of the walls is by the sea, and another part on the river, and on the land side it is surrounded by a deep ditch through which flows water from the river, and the entire city is protected.[68] All the streets are straight from one side to the other of the city, which has three gates, but one is always closed. I went out by the land gate, opposite the one through which I had entered, over a drawbridge. The moat is all of stone and [is] one and a half spear lengths deep.[69] The houses of the city are all of the same height, but by order of the viceroy lower than the walls so that they will be less exposed in case of assault. In the city are four religious orders—Dominicans, Reformed, Augustinians, and Jesuits, who, instead of a hat, wear a cloth beret, not very different from ours [worn by] Venetian gentlemen. Throughout all the Indies they are called Paulists. In addition to these [individuals] there is the cathedral and another priests' church, where there are twelve priests.

That evening I stayed in the house of the Captain, where most of the knights of the ships also were entertained. We were treated with great luxury, since that Captain had an honorable office. Besides the fact that all the utensils were of silver, we ate off dishes of fine Chinese porcelain, much esteemed in those places also.

On the 28th there was a feast of the Madonna. In the procession the horses of the principal knights went first, and the number of Portuguese in the city is not greater than one hundred families. In the entire jurisdiction of Daman there are not more than 6,000 armed men, from foot soldiers to cavalry. Most of them come from the towns, called *aldee* by them, which are subject to the city and which belong to various knights of the country to whom the king has given them since the time of the conquest. The lands pass to their descendants, each of whom has the obligation to keep a precise number of squires and horses ready to go to the fortress at the captain's request. In addition, they pay to the king the quarter part of the earnings of each township: these townships number three hundred under Daman's jurisdiction, which extends twenty Portuguese leagues in length. It begins on the Surat side at the river called Pandel that divides [the Mughal Empire]

68. The Damanganga River divides contemporary Daman into Moti Daman and Nani Daman.
69. Bembo uses the term *pica*, "a pike or spear."

five leagues distant from the city, and it ends at the Antora River.[70] In that space are four captainships[71]—Sanjan, Dahanu, Tarrapur, and Mahim—and four fortified places. Inland it extends two and a half leagues and borders with the feudal lands of the Great Mughal: Vergi, Colle, and Chota, [whose ruler] has the right to a certain fee [from Daman] called a *chouto,* which was paid to it before the city belonged to the Portuguese, as a result of which there are often confusions.

Each day that Captain gave us different food, since the food was not expensive; only sometimes there was a scarcity of fish. Because of that and because of the lack of olive oil, they are permitted to eat dairy products during Lent and on days of abstinence. He had me taste some choice fruits of the country—all different from ours, but of a flavor so sweet that I did not like them. However, the Portuguese love sweet things, and as the last course they bring in sweet things, hot or even cold and seasoned, like fruits or other things. They have the custom of putting sugar even in soup, and they eat it before drinking water, which everyone drinks in the absence of wine, since vines do not grow in those parts, and the wine brought from Persia or Portugal is very expensive. They use it only at banquets or in the most important conversations, and they drink it in very small glasses; [they do this] also due to the climate, which is rather hot and doesn't allow for much drinking without danger of enflaming the blood. Before going to the table, everyone washes his hands. The nobles wash several times during the meal, because they eat everything with their hands, placing in the center of the table only two or three spoons, as many skewers, and several more knives. Thus most of the food is brought in for each person in separate plates, as is done for the clergy, so that no one individual will be nauseated by another. Each evening they wash their feet and bodies, not only to clean away the perspiration, but also for health and pleasure.

After lunch on the 30th I went out of the city with the Captain and his son and many other knights, some in carts and some on horses whose equipment was of silver and who had silver rings at their feet as well as many little bells of the same metal that hung from their bridles. Similar silver rings are worn by noble ladies on their arms and feet in that country. The Captain usually has ten horses in his stables, most of which belong to the knights, who have the duty to keep them in their villas and to leave them in the cap-

70. His term for the Mughal state is "Mogor."
71. *Capitanati.*

tain's stables as a courtesy. We went about two miles out of the city along the seashore, where those few knights who were with us took part in a race. At that time most of the nobility were hunting or at their villas collecting their tribute. When they are in the city, they pay court always to the Captain, who signals with a bell before going out, and all go to serve him. These knights are the best in all of India for managing horses, which are mostly of Arabian stock; there are few such horses in the country. The Captain himself, though of advanced age, rode rather well. His name was Emmanuel Fortado di Mendoza, a knight of Lisbon married in Goa. He had many captainships, some [that were] his son's, and some [that he had] received as the dowry of his wife. Before leaving that beach, a knight named Emmanuel de Soza, possessor of a town called Upper Daman, one mile distant from the city, sent to invite the Captain to refresh himself at his house. The Captain accepted the invitation, and we all went with him while the sun was setting. At first we were given melon, which is in season all year, and then was set out a worthy supper. Among other things there was a dish of marzipan cakes, some filled with salt and some with cotton, which amused everyone since almost everybody was fooled by them! After supper an Indian lady appeared who performed some dances accompanied by instruments and sang rather strange songs in their language. We finally left at the fourth hour of the night. Before entering the city, we stopped for devotions in a small church, called the Madonna of the Assumption, where a hermit lives. There was a religious celebration of many days' duration, which is why it was open both day and night.

[MAY 1673]

The 1st of May I went to see the Dominican convent, where there were only four priests and two laymen, although there is room for many others. Among the first I met was a certain Father Antonio Vellose, one of the most important of that province and a noble native of India, who gave me many stones and medicinal herbs and even offered me some money. Each day several nobles appear at the house of the Captain, some of whom are dressed in French style, though the older ones keep to the older style of dress. Instead of carriages or seats, all use a *palanquin*, as they call it. It is like a bier or litter in which a man lying on a rug and pillows is comfortably carried supported by a thick and long rod carried by four men, two in front and two behind, as is seen in the drawing. So that the rod will not bother the person in the palanquin, if he should want to sit up, it is

FIGURE 16. Bembo riding in a palanquin.

curved in an arch in the middle. Since not all rods are appropriate for this use, they are sold for up to seventy escudos apiece. These palanquins are very comfortable and dignified. For rain and for the sun they have a covering of palm leaves thrown over the rod that covers everything. A little window on each side remains, which is lifted or lowered with a stick. Women usually travel that way. The men usually travel uncovered and have themselves protected from the sun with umbrellas carried by servants walking alongside the palanquin. These [umbrellas] also are usually palm leaves, but there are some of silk and gold for ceremonies. The men who carry the palanquin are called *boi,* very humble people who go naked and serve for a very low price, not earning more among all four of them than seventeen pardaos a month, that is, three ongari less a pardaos.[72] Nor is there any obligation to feed them or dress them. Nevertheless, many nobles, and especially on the occasion of weddings, dress them in livery

72. According to Florio's 1611 Italian-English dictionary, an *ongaro* was a Hungarian ducat, and a *pardaos* was "a certaine coin in Ormuz."

for decorum and kindness. They do the same for the ones who carry the umbrellas. There are other instruments for having one carried, called *reti*, being, in effect, a net of rope the length of a man, hung by both ends on a straight rod. Inside them the person stays comfortably but curved, with a pillow under the head. These are always covered. Since they are lighter, they are carried by only two men. A third kind of carrier is the *andor*, a carrier similar to the palanquin, but rougher and more ordinary, with a straight rod. They are lighter and serve for travel. The andor as well as the palanquin are woven like a net, with canes divided lengthwise into thin pieces. In the evening I was unable to excuse myself from washing my whole body outdoors with warm water in the company of those knights who have themselves washed by *kafri*, who are African Moors and their slaves.[73]

On the day of the 3rd, since the weather was better, we decided to leave, although those gentlemen wanted me to remain there that winter. After many compliments that Captain gave me a rod with a massive gold handle with his coat of arms on it. It was all covered with a woven covering of elephant hairs, a thing esteemed for its rarity, since those animals have only a few hairs in their tails. It is also believed that [these rods] preserve unharmed the person who carries them. I have kept this object always and took it with me to Venice. Not having anything to repay such generosity, I gave him in gratitude some glass tobacco cases and a piece of silverware for the table that I had with me by chance. It is unbelievable how much those trifles were appreciated by the son of the Captain. Only coarse glass made from rice is worked in those parts.[74] It breaks easily, and they use it in Cambay and in Bengal. After supper we took leave of the Captain, and after I had left tips for the servants, we went aboard ship and waited for the current to go out of the port. But a wind rose from the west and lasted all night so that we were not able to leave.

On the morning of the 4th, since the wind did not let up, Father Giovanni went to the city to find out about going to Goa by land, should

73. Bembo's term *kafri* is derived from the Arabic *kafir*, an unbeliever. Bembo refers to them with his generic label "Moors," though they are non-Muslims. They may have come from the Portuguese colony of Mozambique.

74. Daman is known for the production of *ghol*, a fish powder used in making isinglass. This seems to be the likeliest explanation for Bembo's reference to glass made from rice.

the wind keep up. Meanwhile, I went to see the fortress of St. Jerome, mentioned above. It is triangular in form and on the highest part of the fortress. It is surrounded by a moat. On the walls it had eleven iron cannons and four bronze ones, with sixty soldiers and a captain appointed by the viceroy but subordinate to [the captain] of Daman. Since the contrary wind continued, the Captain again obliged me to dine with him and gave me quantities of oysters in vinegar. Since the wind had died down toward evening, I embarked again after supper. Guided by a pilot, we got out of port with the current after midnight. But we traveled little, so that in the morning of the 5th we were not farther than two leagues from Daman. Since we met with the contrary current, we dropped anchor in only twelve lengths of water so as not to make leeway. At the 23rd hour we set sail again to move with the current, but because of a west wind, we did not go far. Again we dropped anchor so as not to drift with the current.

On the morning of the 6th we tried to move again with the current, but the contrary wind made us begin to think of going back to Daman. The Captain was not of this opinion, but Father Giovanni opposed him vigorously and used as an argument the need to keep secure the letters for the viceroy. After much discussion and difference of opinion we went toward the city, and before midday we anchored in front of the port. We signaled for a pilot, and without one we entered at the 23rd hour with the current. I found the gentleman Enrico at the marina, who under orders of his father took me to his house so that I would stay there until a new occasion to go to Goa should arise. But Father Giovanni on the morning of the 7th went with an andor[75] toward Bassein,[76] expecting to arrive there in time to be able to go with a small boat to Goa. I gave him some letters for the Carmelite fathers, since I was not able to go with him because we were unable to find enough andors for me and my party. Father Giovanni told me that the Captain would tend to my needs and could be repaid on my arrival in Goa.

After Father Giovanni left, there was nothing more than could have been desired in the courtesy and kindness of all those gentlemen. They provided me with constant entertainment, as if I were one of their dearest relatives.

The day of the 8th there was a joust at the marina. That evening many ladies came to the house of the Captain, and they were entertained by

75. A carrier similar to but simpler than a palanquin.
76. Bassein is 35 km north of Mumbai.

some very funny buffoons, especially funny in their gestures. Then there was a magician who made many dolls dance without speaking and who performed various other hand tricks. But I thought that it was not convenient that I should stay so long in the house of the Captain. Thinking how to excuse myself, I thought of going to visit the city of Surat. I ordered that some carts be found for the trip, but he would not permit my going for several days.

On the 11th there came an ambassador from the Great Mughal who was going to Goa on business of his king.[77] The Captain sent his guard to meet him. The guard is consisted of ten musketeers and one drummer, who ordinarily walk in front of him when he leaves the house, as well as many knights who pay court to him. He also sent his own palanquin for the gentleman. That man came to present himself with a dragoman and two other people and asked for carts, or andors, to take him quickly to Goa, without saying what his mission was about. On leaving he put his hand on his breast and bowed his head, as is the custom of the Turks, and took leave. This ambassador was a pious man, a rather polite person, self-possessed and nobly dressed.

The next day, the 12th, came another ambassador, from Shivaji, the king of the neighboring kingdom, who had been subject to Afdal Khan, against whom he had rebelled seventeen years before.[78] Then he had made himself

77. The Great Mughal was the emperor Awrangzeb.

78. Shivaji (Bembo's "Survagi") was the brilliant Hindu Maratha leader whose resistance to Mughal authority was at its height during Bembo's sojourn in India. Shivaji's father, Shahji, had been a powerful Maratha chief and an officer at the court of the Muslim 'Adil-Shahi dynasty in Bijapur in India's Deccan. First resisting Bijapur, Shivaji in 1659 destroyed a hostile army and its commander, Afdal Khan (Bembo refers to him as "Hidalchan"). Four years later he humiliated the Mughal emperor Awrangzeb's uncle, Shaista Khan, the viceroy of the Deccan. In January 1664, he took and sacked the great port city of Surat, one of the centers for European commerce with India. Briefly brought back into the Mughal fold by the military success of the Mughal general Jai Singh in 1664–1666, Shivaji again rebelled. Using brilliant guerrilla tactics he built up a sizable Hindu kingdom in the area around Mumbai and through a combination of military daring, diplomacy, and political maneuvering was a major power in western India until his death in 1680. Due to the successful assault on Surat, any Portuguese commander would accord careful respect to an emissary from Shivaji.

chief of one hundred people and had become a robber. He was so successful that he took possession of several cities and riches so great that he was
feared by the neighboring rulers and even by the Great Mughal. He attacked
and sacked many cities, and three times even Surat; and he threatened to
do the same with the fortresses of the Portuguese. Thus he has become very
powerful and formidable and finally usurped the title of king, although he
was born of a very lowly family. He is idolatrous in religion and among the
most superstitious; he cooks his food with his own hands. This ambassador
was received with more decorum than the previous one, because the delegation was directed to the Captain himself. He sent many other people to
receive the ambassador, besides the palanquin and the guard. He received
him in the hall, which was all decorated with rugs, and met him at the stairway with his sword in his belt and attended by most of the knights. The
ambassador had with him more than twenty armed people. The Captain
seated himself on a velvet chair and had in front of him a stool with cushions on it. On his left he accommodated the ambassador on an ordinary
chair. After some general speeches the ambassador requested a private audience with the Captain. Then everyone went out, the two remained alone,
and the ambassador presented his message, after which he was again accompanied to the stair with great dignity by the Captain. The ambassador was
young, handsomely tall, and almost black in color, lively and ready with
words, richly dressed in clothing of silk and gold in the manner of his
country.

The morning of the 13th, since the carts had been found, I left for Surat,
leaving my luggage in the custody of the Dominican Fathers, the Superior
of whom, named Francesco Salema, was a close relative of the Captain.
Before leaving, I took my leave of the Captain and of those knights and of
the captain of the ships with whom I exchanged only compliments. I did
not know how I should comport myself in giving him gifts. The Portuguese
are of high tastes, and my means at that moment were few and not adequate
for my intentions. On reflection I decided to use all the civility possible in
my expressions and to take other measures once in Goa.

Having heard Mass, I crossed the river on the side of the fort of St.
Jerome and went to the carts. Since they were returning, I was able to rent
them at a good price, giving four rupees for each one; another half-rupee
would make an ongaro. These carts are pulled by oxen, so agile that they
travel like horses. [The carts] are, however, rather uncomfortable, because
they have only two wheels, and the body of the cart is nailed to an axle, so
that at every bump or obstacle that the wheels find, the cart shakes and with

it the person inside, who suffers bother and annoyance considerably. They are covered like our carriages, but the covering is so low that one can only stay under it seated with legs crossed in the Turkish manner, and they hold only two persons. The cart guides are idolators of Surat.

I left at the second hour of daylight with Giuliano and two servants, having left Padre Giacomo in Daman, and we divided up into three carts. The roads were dusty, and the country was cultivated on all sides. It was green, and thus it stayed all year, because in India the leaves do not fall all at once, but a few at a time, and new ones always grow. The reason is that there is no snow nor frost nor cold, only a hot fog sometimes that dries the fruit before it can ripen. We passed through two streams of water, and after four hours we stopped the carts in the shade of a mango tree,[79] which protected us from the sun with its vast branches. We stayed there until the 21st hour, eating a little snack, since along the road one finds food in many straw houses that are the dwellings of the poor Gentile peasants. All of them, men and women, go naked and only cover their private parts with a cloth held and tied by a cord. They anoint their skins with various oils to protect themselves from the burning of the sun. Having left there, I saw during the journey several tombs of Mohammedan Indians, similar to those of the Turks.[80] Half an hour after nightfall, we arrived at a large and populous town, which perhaps cannot be called a city since it is not surrounded by walls. It is under the jurisdiction of the Great Mughal. Sleeping in the carts, we passed the night under some palm trees, which are very common in the Indies.

At daybreak on the 14th we continued our journey, and we found seven carts going to Surat, and many others that would go from there to other places. Along the way there were many streams, and at the hottest hours the carts stopped in the shade of a great tree, since the sun was very hot. We left at the 21st hour, and after an hour we reached a large town where the cart guides insisted on remaining until the second hour of the night, when we continued the trip, stopping only a little to refresh the animals. We traveled that night going along a narrow, but rather long road through a very dense wood.

On the morning of the 15th we made a short stop in a town after two

79. The mango tree can grow to immense size. Bembo's "manghe" is a rendering of the Portuguese *manga* derived from the Tamil word *man-gay.*

80. It is unclear whether he is referring to tomb buildings or to grave markers; in any case, there were some architectural and artistic traditions shared by the Turks of the Ottoman Empire and the Turks of India.

hours of sunlight. At midday we made another so that the oxen could drink at a fountain. When the heat, which was insufferable, had let up a bit, we continued the trip. During the whole three days I ate only bread, perhaps because of the heat and discomfort of the cart that took away my appetite, or perhaps because the food made by those filthy people gave me nausea. But what bothered me most was the water, which was not very good to drink, and the most insolent behavior of my cart man. In addition to having stolen a fur and other things from me during the trip, he slept in the cart with me during the night, even though I told him not to. He did not understand much, or did not want to understand in Portuguese, so I was unable to make him get out. He was so smelly that I couldn't put up with it, and since he did not want to get out, I had to, and I went on another cart and sent the servants to keep that beast company.

At the 22nd hour we entered a plain and on the 24th crossed through a town and then shortly afterward reached Surat. We were immediately taken to the Customs, which is the strictest of any I saw. Since it was late, they wanted to keep the carts until the next day and did not permit me to take my own coat, so that I decided to leave the servants to guard the things as well. Surat, which in ancient times was an unknown port, used to be a poor city. Today, due to the Portuguese, Dutch, English, and French, it is the richest city and the most famous port of the whole dominion of the Great Mughal, who can be called without difficulty the emperor of India, since most of it is under his direct rule, and part of it pays tribute to him through rulers dependent upon him. According to Persian histories, this Mughal is descended from the family of Magog, nephew of the Patriarch Noah and son of Jiafet, who was the powerful king in the parts of Tartaria. As long as Magog and his son Tarazan lived, his subjects adored one true God, observing the religion left them by their progenitor Noah. But zeal grew cold in their descendants, and it became permissible for the subjects to join various sects. They went to inhabit new provinces like vagabonds and became dispersed. However, the descendants of Mughals remained in the province they call Mogolia, or Mogostan. The Tartar histories say that the Mughals derive from Ture, nephew of Noah and also son of Jiafet. They tell that in the hundredth year of our salvation, the Mughals passed to India and took possession of most of it and have kept it until now.[81]

81. The acquisition of an impressive and ancient genealogy was an important part of political legitimacy, though it is as spurious here as is the claim that

They have in their power what is most rich and precious in jewels and spices. The king, or emperor, at present descends directly from the Great Tamerlane, so famous, who made prisoner the Ottoman emperor Bayazid. He left four sons at his death: Jahangir, 'Umar Shaykh, Miranshah, and Shahrukh. He left the empire to this last, Persia to Miranshah, and the Indies to the son of Jahangir, who had died before his father. From this one, who was called Pir Muhammad, the living Great Mughal descends.[82] He has his residence in Agra, a great city, twenty days' distance from Surat. The present Mughal, although his ancestors were idolators, is of the Muslim religion and conforms more with the Arabs and Turks than with the Persians,[83] although Persian is spoken in the court and also Hindustani, the native tongue. The subjects are in part Muslims and in part idolators or Gentiles, which is the same thing.[84] These [latter] are more numerous than the first, but [are] people of little spirit, weak and not lovers of fighting.

Surat is a very famous city, situated on a river called Tapti, which cannot be traveled by ships unless they are empty. They drop anchor in Soali,

---

the Mongols entered India around A.D. 100. The Mongol invasions of the thirteenth century ravaged Iran but spared most of India, although there were periodic incursions by Mongol and Chaghatai Turkish forces in the thirteenth and fourteenth centuries, culminating in Timur's 1398 invasion of northern India. Babur, the first Mughal emperor (1526–1530), was of Mongol and Turkish descent and was proud to identify himself as a direct descendant of Timur, who had defeated the Ottoman sultan Bayazid in 1402 at the battle of Ankara.

82. Timur's 1398 invasion of northern India and sack of Delhi laid the basis for the Mughal claim to India. Bembo's account of the origins of the Mughals is inaccurate. The first of the Mughal emperors, Babur, was descended on his father's side from Timur through Miranshah and on his mother's side from Chengiz Khan.

83. A reference to the fact that Iran under the Safavis (1501–1722) was a Shi'i state, whereas the Ottoman Empire, like the Mughal, was Sunni.

84. Mughal India was the most religiously diverse Islamic state of its day. The ruling elite was largely Muslim, though Hindu Rajputs were prominent in the military, and other Hindus, Jains, and Parsees occupied positions of power and responsibility in the bureaucracy, particularly during the reigns of Akbar (1556–1605) and Jahangir (1605–1627). The vast majority of the population was Hindu, and the empire's health depended upon good relations among its different religious and ethnic communities. During the second half

a town seven *cos* distant from Surat. A *cos,* or *corù,* is half a Persian *fersegna,* and a little less than two Italian miles.[85] There the Dutch and the English have a special customs house for their goods when they unload ships. The water of that river, or canal, is not salty when the tide is out, but salty when it comes in. The city is longer than [it is] wide and surrounded by walls of bricks on which are several cannon. It has only four gates, at which there are always guards to take everything that enters to the customs house. Likewise, they do not allow anything out, not even anything used, unless it has been sent out through the customs house. There are two customs houses, one across from the other. One is for things arriving by land, and the other for things arriving by sea. They are both well constructed. There is then another one for things going out. The houses are mostly low, with palm-thatched roofs with tiles over them. The doors of the houses are, in proportion, very tall, because in ancient times the water ran through the streets during the winter. The streets are neither long nor wide, and little boats went from one house to another. There are good buildings for the lodgings of foreigners and for the deposit of merchandise, called caravanserais by the Persians.[86]

There are many baths and many mosques, not only for the Moslems of the country, but also for foreigners, and every nationality has its own particular mosque, as the Jews in Venice have synagogues for the various nationalities in their ghetto. The most beautiful [mosque] is near the gate toward the east, which is guarded by a *sherif.* Almost in the middle of the city on a canal is the castle or fortress. It is not very big and has three bastions and an elevated place with twenty cannons on it, many of which [are] of bronze. The cannoneers are Europeans who go there for the good pay. Most of them are exiles or fugitives from their countries. There are some French, Flemish, Portuguese, and a Roman. The head of them all is a

---

of his reign Awrangzeb did much to undermine the political tolerance that had been the cornerstone of the internal policies of his predecessors, particularly when he instituted the *jizya,* the head tax on non-Muslims.

85. A *kos* was the common measure of distance in Mughal India and amounted to about 3.2 km. A *farsakh,* or *parasang,* was the distance that could be comfortably walked in an hour, i.e., about 5.5 km.

86. *Caravanserai* was the Persian equivalent of the Turkish *han,* a fortified structure that could house and protect whole caravans during the night and serve as an emporium for their sales during the day. They were an essential link in overland trade, and their maintenance and support was a vital element in commercial prosperity.

Portuguese who gets thirty rupees a month as pay. The castle is surrounded by a narrow and deep moat through which passes water from the river. It is guarded by two hundred native soldiers directed by a captain who is independent of the governor of the city and who is sent by the king and is called *nabob*.[87] This nabob is treasurer for the king and guards in the fortress money gathered from taxes there. He cannot go out of the fortress without permission of the king, nor does he let any foreigners in. The same defenders do not enter there except in times of emergency, which happens only a few times, as in the time of King Shivaji, who sacked the city three times and took away the treasure. On the land side there is a drawbridge that goes to a great plaza without houses, where the fair is held. The city is very rich and abounds in inhabitants, not only in native Mughals, Moors, and Gentiles, but in very many foreigners, who are French, English, Portuguese, Dutch, Flemish, Italians, Poles, Swedes, and other Europeans. In addition, there are Turks, Arabs, Persians, Tartars, Georgians, Scythians,[88] people from Malabar, Bengalese, Singalese, Armenians, and other Asian and African nationalities that are not well known. They are attracted by the great traffic by land and sea from all of Europe, from Africa through the Red Sea, and from Asia overland by caravans. From that port, then, ships go to Europe, China, Malacca, Ache, the Molucca Islands, Jakarta, the Maldive Islands, Bengal, Sri Lanka, Cochin, Cananor, Calicut, Mecca, Aden, Suez, Mogadishu, Qishn, Muscat, Madagascar, where the French have a fortress, Hormuz, Basra, Sind, and other places.[89] The city is governed by a pasha who is subject to the principal rulers of the empire and who is regarded with respect. There are other minor ministers; in addition, the king has a Moor whose office it is to spy and to report all the goings-on of the nabob and other ministers once a week.

The dress of both the Moslems and the Gentiles is usually of white cotton, since there is no linen in those parts. Some wear it in various colors, and others use silk with silver and gold, according to their wealth. They wear one piece of clothing over their skin, tailored and tight at the waist to

87. A *nabob* was a high-ranking military officer.

88. That is, Crimeans.

89. Malacca on the southwest coast of the Malayan peninsula; Aceh, the great Muslim trading center in western Sumatra; Calicut in southern India; Mecca (through the port city of Jiddah); Mogadishu in Somalia; Qishn on the southeastern coast of the Arabian Peninsula.

FIGURE 17. Indian men.

the hips, where they tie themselves with bands of silk of various colors and gold. Below that, the dress is calf-length and rather wide, forming pleats. The pants are of the same material as the robe. They are tight around the leg and very long, since they remain bunched at the top of the foot. The sleeves of the robe are also long and bunched the entire length of the arm. The feet remain bare, but they wear rather beautiful and light shoes, of which I wanted to have a pair to show. They keep them on without tying them, so as to be able to take them off easily each time they go on rugs in private houses. They have many arm's lengths of fine silk, of various colors or with gold, wrapped around their heads. The binding in many turns makes a flat shape around and over the head. Most of the people wear earrings as ornament. The Gentiles have their hair under their turbans, as distinct from the Moslems who are shaved, as one knows. They also wear at their belts a very strange weapon, called a *khanjar*.[90] In the blade it is rather

90. What follows is an excellent description of the Indian *katar*, though Bembo calls it a "gangiar."

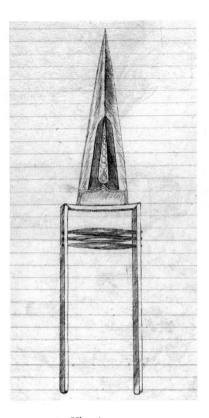

FIGURE 18. Khanjar.

similar to the Turkish dagger, but it is about an inch broad in the center and very sharp at the point, and it cuts on all sides and is a little more than a palm long. The handle is all of one piece with the blade and is divided into two parts that reach almost up to the elbow to protect it from a sword blow or any similar attack. These two parts are crossed by three pieces of iron at the point near the blade. These serve as handles, since one puts the four fingers between these pieces of iron and the blade. The blow of the point of the weapon comes from the entire arm and gives it an incredible strength, so that in the hands of a strong man, I think it would be sufficient to break a block of ice. One can see its shape in the drawing, but I wanted to take one with me as a very rare curiosity. Some have them gilt or with silver, but most are bronze, as is mine.

The Moslem women do not dress very differently from the men, and some wear the same binding around the head, but with brighter colors.

When they go through the city, they wrap themselves in white mantles and cover their faces. Some women of the Gentiles dress in the same way, but most of them wear a white shirt or a shirt of various colors. It extends to the waist, and the sleeves [extend] to the elbows. They cover the rest of the arm with many gold, silver, glass, and ivory bracelets according to their wealth, and wear similar jewelry on their ankles. From the waist to the ground they cover themselves with a skirt of many folds and many colors. When they go out of their houses, they, too, cover themselves with a white mantle, but not their faces, which they allow one to see with freedom. They adorn themselves completely with jewelry and wear large circular earrings. All the men and women wear a white cloth under their clothing and over their private parts, which, as we have said, is the only clothing of the poor people. In many parts even civilized persons do not wear any other clothing, and they anoint their skin with oil to make themselves shine and also to protect themselves from the sun.

In the city there are French, English, and Dutch companies. These merchants live in large palaces, built according to their own customs and with the flags of their kings flying over them. They live with much freedom and are esteemed and honored by the natives. They pay 5% on their merchandise, except the Dutch, who were exempted from 1% in gratitude for a sumptuous gift that they made to the king in 1661, as Padre Godigno, S.J., relates.[91] All the Dutchmen who are in Surat live together in a house with great respect and obedience to their chief, who has the title of Commander.[92] But the principal director of the company is in the city of Batavia from whence they receive all the orders. It is a rich and powerful company because they own many sources of the most esteemed spices. The English are all united and are also obedient to one chief, called a president, who has the supreme direction of the company with two others. From him go all the orders to the fortress of Madras in the Gulf of Bengal and to the island of Mumbai, which is what the English own in India.[93] When they return to

91. It seems that Bembo is referring to *De Abassinorum Rebus* by the Portuguese Jesuit Father Nicolao Godigno; but this is a confusing reference, since Godigno's book was published in 1615, and the author died in 1616.

92. *Comendatore.*

93. By 1652 the English fort in Madras had become a major commercial center on the east coast of India; the English began to exercise effective control of Mumbai in 1672.

Europe, all their ships receive their last orders in Surat. The French also keep order. They are governed by five directors who manage the whole company, which was the last to be introduced there through a Capuchin father named Ambrose, who enters into all the deliberations of the company, and it is practically governed according to his opinion. He has been in that mission for thirty years. There are no other clergy in that city, other than the Capuchins sent by the Sacred Congregation of Propaganda Fide. I went immediately there on my arrival and left the servants at the customs house with my things, as I have said. Before arriving, I met the pasha along the road, who had many people on foot and on horseback marching in front of him and also had many lanterns. He was in a very beautiful palanquin covered with velvet, and there was a silk ribbon with a silver ornament in the center. He was dressed all in white brocade. When I arrived at the Fathers' house (there were three of them as well as a rather active layman who was better than the others), they immediately recognized me and showed me much courtesy, but since it was a Fast Day, I did not ask for anything but some wine, which was quickly brought, and they gave me a room.

Since I learned that Father Ambrose did not like strangers and that he was rather avaricious, on the morning of the 16th I sent for the banian Oudodaj or Gogiudaj Sougy,[94] and gave him letters that the Captain of Daman had given me for him. When he offered to help me in whatever I needed, I asked him to find me a house and to rescue my things at the customs house, which is very strict.

When the house was found, I wanted to go there immediately, but Father Ambrose obliged me to stay with him to lunch. He told me that the head of the French company wanted to visit me. I asked him to excuse me since I was without appropriate clothing and I would not be able to receive him personally, as I would do as soon as I got my clothes. The Father answered that it would do no good [for me] to excuse myself because that gentleman absolutely wanted to be the first one to visit me. That evening they also asked me to stay to supper with them, after which I went to my house [which was] not far away. The Fathers lent me beds, chairs, and tables. While those things were being carried, I saw that the women were luggage carriers, bearing wood, water, and everything else.

The morning of the 17th I bought clothes from the banians, who are

94. *Banian* is a term for "merchant."

merchants and more thieving than Jews. In truth, there are no Jews in India, except for some peddlers.[95] Since there are many idolaters in this city and in the kingdom of Cambay or Gujarat, it seems to me appropriate to tell here with some clarity what I can about the various rites and superstitions that they have, without obliging myself to put them in order, however, but only putting down what I remember of what I saw or of what I was told by those who stayed a long time in those parts and who observed more carefully. It is true that under the Great Mughal they are persecuted, since he is a great enemy of idolatry and has had many of their temples destroyed.[96] If it were not for his nearby vassal kings who support them, he would have forbidden idolatry in all his states. In this he does not imitate his ancestors, who accepted equally Moslems and idolaters. These are divided into various and different rites, all agreeing, however, with the opinion of Pythagoras about the transmigration of souls, not only from man to man but to every kind of animal. All have great veneration for and adore bovine animals, although they respect other animals more or less. Doing good to animals therefore, they esteem a work of charity of no less worth than doing good to human beings. They say that all the Gentile people of India were divided into different groups. Although they lived together in the cities, they could distinguish one another, like the Jews of the tribes. There were as many as eighty-four, each with a particular name and work. They did not marry outside their group, nor did they rise to a condition higher than the one in which they were born, nor change their work, be they farmers, soldiers, merchants. They make fun of our ceremonies as much as we do of theirs. Others say that India was divided into seven parts. The first and most honored by the kings were the Brahmins, or philosophers, who at the beginning of the year predict rains and droughts, winds and sicknesses, and who are therefore esteemed by everyone. The one who made a false prediction had to be silent for the rest of his life in punishment. The second place was held by the workers of the earth, who were very many. They lived in the coun-

95. By the seventeenth century there were important Jewish communities in Mumbai and other Indian cities.

96. The emperor Awrangzeb departed from the politics of tolerance that had characterized his Mughal predecessors and sought to make India a thoroughly Islamic state. His strident anti-Hindu policies were more characteristic of the second half of his reign than of the first, and Bembo's account here may reflect knowledge gained after his return to Venice.

try with their wives and families and had no other work than to gather great harvests of grains. The third was of the hunters and shepherds who never stayed in the cities. They went with their tents, now in one place and now in another, keeping the country free of wild beasts and animals harmful to men and to farms. The fourth place was held by the artisans who made arms and farm instruments and other necessary things. The fifth was of the soldiers, who, after the farmers, were the largest group. The king gave them [money] to live on and for the horses and elephants that they needed for war. The sixth place was of the governors of the provinces and of the cities, who had the office of letting the king know of everything that happened in all of India. The seventh and last place was that of the public counselors and officials in the cities. As I said, it was unlawful for anyone to take a wife from a group other than his own, [a rule] which is still observed in some places.

The rites are various, as various as are the parts of the country. Rather, they are many and very different even in the same place. However, in the principal things they are alike, as in the belief in the transmigration of souls, which upon death they think are sent by God into other bodies according to the merits or transgressions. From a life more or less difficult, or from rich, poor, noble, and common men, [the soul] can be sent into other men or into animals, all according to the life just passed. Some Gentiles told me that ordinarily the souls of kings pass into the bodies of lions, those of talkers into dogs, those of high livers into pigs, those of thieves into cats or tigers, those of avaricious men into ants, those of cruel men into wolves, liars into foxes, weak and frightened men into chickens, prudent men into elephants, generous men into horses, those who give alms into the animals they most like, women into vipers and serpents, their Brahmins into cows, which is the best fate of all, since it is the animal most respected by them. Each one of them on his deathbed tries to give up his spirit with the tail of a bovine animal in his mouth or in his hand. They anoint themselves with cow dung, and they wash their faces with cow urine as devotion. Some, when they have sinned with women, cover their member with dung as if to cleanse themselves of the committed sin. No bovine animal is ever killed by any Gentile but rather is held in veneration, since they believe that in those animals are the souls of their best ancestors. In the whole kingdom of Cambay anyone who killed a cow, even if he were Moslem or of another religion, would be punished severely, even by death. The Gentiles pay a great sum to the rulers of the cities to keep this rule. They also all believe that there is a Paradise, but only souls of their nationality go there that are without sin after many transmigrations. They say that the souls of other religions pass finally into the bodies of Gentiles and then they are saved. The most observant and superstitious do not kill nor do they eat any kind of animal, whether meat or fish. They eat only fruits of the earth. Others eat fish and not meat. Others eat meat of one kind, others of another, but none eat beef. They are so averse to killing animals of any kind that they don't keep cats in their houses so that they won't kill mice.

They consider themselves obliged to spend their money to save animals from death, otherwise their blood will be on their heads. Thus there are public hospitals for taking care of animals. In Cambay there are hospitals for every sort of animal, whether flying or land animals, where crippled or sick animals that cannot take care of themselves are cared for. When they are well, they are set at liberty, if they are wild. If they are domestic, they are put into the custody of a good person who will take care of them. These hospitals are kept by public alms. When he was in Cambay, Pietro della Valle went to see those hospitals where among the many animals kept there he saw some small mice. They had been found orphans and were being taken care of by an old man who kept them in a box wrapped in cotton. He handled them carefully with his glasses on his nose and gave them milk through a goose quill, since they could not yet eat by themselves. They said that that good man had the intention to set them free when they were grown. In another hospital a clever Moslem got his living. He had been caught stealing and had had both hands cut off. But the Gentiles felt pity for him at seeing him incapable of earning his living, and they kept him among those animals and did not allow that he should lack anything. Even fleas and lice are secure in their hands. They remove them from themselves, but they throw them on a companion; they do not kill them.

In the kingdom of Cambay there is the custom of giving alms to flies. They throw rice, milk, and sugar mixed together, and clouds of flies gather there to banquet. In Hormuz a Christian dressed like an Indian met a hunter and bought from him some birds that he had in a cage in order to eat them. He gave the hunter the money; and the hunter, thinking that as a Gentile (for as such he had judged him from his clothes) he had bought the birds to give them their liberty, opened the cage as soon as he received the money and let them fly away. The Christian shouted and protested that he had had no intention of performing such a charity toward those animals, and the hunter was obliged to return his money.

They say that the souls, before entering another body, pass through a branch of the Ganges River whose water, as the poets pretended of the river

Lethe, has the faculty of erasing the memory of all past things. But they say that God does not grant his grace to bad souls, but rather makes them pass the river dry and thus have the trouble of remembering what they had been before. On this matter a Gentile told me of this strange case: a rather old ox, although he was very well cared for and lacked for nothing, continually bellowed. It was said that he was the soul of a tyrannous king who by God's punishment had passed into that animal without having touched the waters of forgetfulness. Thus he bellowed, remembering what [had occurred] before he became an animal.

They are so foolishly scrupulous that they cannot eat food that was for others [who are] not Gentile and [are not] of their same rite. When they cook their food, a thing that I have mentioned elsewhere, each one does for himself, they make a circle around the fire. If anyone of another religion should put his foot inside the circle, they can no longer eat but throw everything away. Their holy men not only do not eat of any meat but also abstain from fruits and vegetables whose color is like blood. Others of more broad conscience eat fish, as I have said. Others, although they do not slaughter any animals, eat meat, except beef, because they say that the cow is their mother for her milk and for the dung with which [cows] fertilize the earth.

They all carry their idol on a string around their neck. The idols are various, as they were for the Romans. They also believe a lot in witchcraft. Principally, however, they believe that there is a God, Lord of all things, from whom all good comes. They also believe in devils that can do evil, so they try to be on good terms with them, paying them honor and making them houses and temples called pagodas, of which there are many throughout India, very splendid and wealthy. Religious men usually look after these. They are held to be saints. They make vows and live very strangely; some live eight to ten years or, even, their whole lives with their hands behind their necks without moving them. Others remain seated; others standing in the cavity of a tree; others put an iron ring through their phallus; others never cut their nails nor their hair and never clean it; others observe other crazy and dirty practices.[97] These are kept and fed by the women, who let themselves be impregnated by them for devotion. A husband is considered fortunate if his wife has been enjoyed by one of these holy men. They usually go completely naked, and the women go to get

97. Bembo is here describing mendicant *sadhus*, not Brahmin priests.

blessings from them, touching their member and then kissing their hands. All of them are sad, clever, and malicious people.

Many pagodas are kept by prostitutes who earn with their bodies and raise beautiful daughters to keep the pagodas in their absence and old age. The people of the kingdom of the Deccan abstain entirely from animals.[98] They believe there is only one God, but they nevertheless also adore the devil so that he will do them no harm. They believe that there is a paradise that has a sensual beatitude of eating, drinking, and other things. They also believe that there is a hell under the earth, where the souls are purged of their sins for a certain time, after which they pass to other bodies.

They have some notion of the birth of Christ our Lord, of his passion and ascension. They say that he was born of a holy woman and that it was never known who was his father. He grew in age and goodness. When he was grown, very wicked and ungrateful people tried to kill him because he was too good. He hid himself and has never been seen again. The mother cried so much that she died of sorrow, and thus they hold images of the Madonna in great veneration.[99]

Some have a fast, like Lent, during which they only eat in the evenings, in imitation of the Turks.[100] They respect Fridays as we respect Sundays.[101] They also celebrate feasts, among which a solemn one called "of the line" when they receive the sign of their religion, as is Baptism the sign of ours. This rite was anciently celebrated with much pomp in Goa in a pagoda called Zapatu, situated on the Island of Var. Many people from various countries went there. They washed themselves in an arm's length of sea that is between the two islands and held that water to be holy; and they said that on that day they saw the pagoda walking on it. Thus they threw betel, areca, figs, and sugar cane into the water, since they thought that the pagoda ate those things.[102] This ceremony was called "of the line," because when their

98. Bembo renders the Deccan (Dekkan) of central India as "Daquen" or "Dachen."

99. Jesus is revered in Islam as a prophet, and Bembo's account in general tallies with Muslim views of Christ and Mary.

100. Under normal circumstances all adult Muslims in good health are required to keep the month-long Fast of Ramadan during which they are not supposed to eat or drink from sunrise to sunset.

101. Friday is the Muslim holy day.

102. Goa is referred to in the *Puranas* as Govapuri or Gove and is considered the site of Paradise.

children are eight years old, they put some strings around their necks, which they keep their entire lives, and these serve as the visible sign of their religion, as with us Baptism leaves an invisible character on the soul.[103] Some of their holy men wear a stone around their necks the size of an egg with some lines on it, and they regard it as their idol. But there are few of these now, and perhaps none. Because of that stone, called *tambarane,* they were venerated by everyone, and they carried much merchandise from ships from one country to another without paying fees, since they were not inspected by the customs men nor by other officials. But when the fraud was discovered, they tried to correct things. These men did not eat fish or meat. They took only one wife for their whole lives. At the time of the wedding the relatives of the couple dye their clothes yellow and put a sign on their foreheads and faces with various colors, which is the symbol of their idols.

Most of the princes do not have wives but instead an infinite number of concubines who are the daughters of the principal barons and lords of the kingdom. These women live in the palace only a few months of the year, and for the rest of the time they stay in the houses of their own fathers. When they are in the king's [house], they all go every day to bathe in a pool, where the king watches them and throws a jewel to the one he likes best, which is a signal to her that he wants her to sleep with him that night, as is the custom among the Persians and Egyptians.

When they die, their bodies are burned. Those of the kings and nobles are burned in fires of sweet-smelling and very expensive wood, such as sandalwood and others. It was still the custom that most of the concubines, favorite friends, and court officials should be burned with the king. At the same time silver and gold coins were thrown on the fire, which were to keep them company and to serve for provisions in the other world, since they believed that everything thrown into the flames with the body went to the other world. The women of a certain rite are not thought to be honorable if, within some days after the death of their husbands, they do not burn themselves on his ashes. They do it with much solemnity, accompanied by friends and relatives. The widow gives all her rights to the heirs or to whomever she wishes if she has no heirs. Then she mounts a white horse and goes around the city or country for three days, preceded by trumpets,

103. Distinctive of the Brahmin caste, the *jagopavit* is a thin cord worn around the neck.

tympana, and various instruments, and many people and buffoons go along jumping and performing tricks, with songs of praise for that woman for the honor that she is doing her dead husband. On the third day she dresses in her most sumptuous gown and adorns herself with her most precious jewels, and after having gone around the city, she goes to the place where her husband was burned and where a great pile of wood, pitch, and oil is prepared, surrounded by a great platform with many steps on which the relatives and people stand. Here the most important [person] tells her how much she owes to her husband and how by means of a pain that is over in moments she can acquire an honor and fame that is immortal. Then she takes leave of everyone and throws off the ornaments, jewels, and clothing and remains naked. Weeping and with her arms upraised, she walks three times around the platform, and the last time she picks up a jar full of butter and places it on her head and faces the sun, recommending herself to her idols. Finally, she goes toward the fire and throws in first the vase and then herself, while over her all the relatives throw butter, oil, and pitch so that the flame will burn better, making at the same time loud noises with songs and sounds until she is turned to ashes, and so as not to hear the screams of the miserable woman.

Those who cannot afford this ceremony burn themselves with their husbands, although there is no law that obliges them, only the zeal for self-respect, since they are remembered as infamous if they do not do it, as if they had been caught in adultery. Such folly, however, is almost gone today after the contact with other nations. It was brought to India in ancient times by the Aryans,[104] barbarous people who believed in many gods, and therefore they had many priests and many ceremonies. Among their most famous customs that they considered very pious [was this one]: when someone became old and was so decrepit that he was no longer able to take care of himself or so sick that the doctors judged him incurable, they immediately put him on a great pile of wood and killed him. His relatives set fire to the pile, and his wife threw herself on the flames to honor the ashes of her husband. There are some women who offer the virginity of their daughters to an appointed pagoda. When the girls reach the age of ten years, they are given solemnly to the pagoda as if they were getting married. Inside the door of the temple there is a square column two arms high surrounded by steps and candle-holders. On top of the column there is a sharp pole where those girls leave

104. Bembo uses the word "Eruli."

their virginity after various ceremonies made by the mothers and other women. At that time the column and the steps are covered by a cloth so that the girls will not be seen by anyone while performing that act. Likewise in Cyprus, they had the custom of exposing their daughters on the shore of the sea to earn their dowry before they got married. With the pretext of paying to Venus the first fruit of their chastity, or rather dishonesty, they submitted to foreigners who sailed by there. According to Herodotus, the Babylonians used to send their daughters to earn money with their bodies when they had run out of funds. Some Gentile kings bring four thousand or more women with them to war as prostitutes, but [the kings] pay the soldiers first. And they say that with those [soldiers] they are able to wage more war than if the army were six times its size, because the men fight with more courage in order to have the women, and the young go willingly to war. Among those women there are some wealthy ones, because they take beautiful girls with them, and these [wealthy women] go with them in the evenings to the soldiers' quarters with songs, music, and dancing. They leave there those girls the soldiers like best, and they make a lot of money from them. The kings have many foreign soldiers attracted by this sort of loose living.

In the famous city of Cochin, which first belonged to the Portuguese and now belongs to the Dutch,[105] the natives are people of arms, but otherwise very lazy and enemies of effort. They leave to the women the exercise of work. These women are so used to it that they willingly do the work of men. These [men] are so poor that they do not have enough to support a wife, and so five or six join together to maintain one wife. She stays very faithful to them. So as not to meet one another, they hang their shields on the door of the house when they go to sleep with her. When the others see it, they wait until the first has come out, and thus they enjoy her one after another peacefully. Since they have a wife together, their sons are not heirs to their goods, as they cannot be certain who is the father of a child born to the woman. But the sons of their sisters are their heirs, since they can be sure that they are of the same blood. It is the same way with the succession of kings. Thus among them it is important to be a nephew [who is] the son of a sister rather than the son of a brother.

105. Vasco da Gama established the first Portuguese factory in 1502 in Cochin, the principal city of Kerala in south India and one of the finest harbors on India's west coast. Albuquerque built the first Portuguese fort there in the following year. The city was seized by the Dutch in 1663.

Among the most superstitious idolators are those from a city on the coast of Malabar[106] who, if they meet a Christian along the road, shout for him to stop and go by another way, since they cannot even pass close to anyone not of their rite. In another city the women go nude, covering only their private parts with leaves of trees. In the event that one of those leaves falls on the road, they have to remain there until the husband comes to put back the leaf where it belongs. They pay a great deal of attention to augury, especially of the air, as in the flight of birds and other things. When kings have ordered their armies, and they see in that instant some bad omen, they change all their plans until there is a new deliberation of their sorcerers and wizards to whom they, full of faith, pay heed. They say that there was a king 'Adil Khan[107] who during a dangerous illness made a vow to weigh himself and to give his weight in gold to a pagoda, which he did and was immediately healed. As he went out of the temple, he took off his rich robes and gave them to a Brahmin to put on, who died as soon as he had put on the clothes. The wizards made the king believe that he would have died of that illness but that he was freed because of his alms, and the pagoda made the Brahmin die in his stead. Many alms are given by the kings, especially to the temples and to the priests. Among these the most esteemed religious are the yogis, little different from the dervishes of the Turks.[108] Mostly they are on continuous pilgrimage, but usually they do not go beyond Persia and rarely arrive in Aleppo. The second sons of kings usually take up this religion to keep themselves secure from death, with which they are usually threatened by their older brothers upon their succession to the throne. But often it happens that the yogis rise up and remove the firstborn from the throne and take his life. Many of these yogis are people who know herbs well and know how to use them for medicine, and by them is made the snake stone called *Cobra di Die,* which serves against the very poisonous bites of some snakes.[109] They put it on top of the wound, and if there is no

106. The Malabar coast extends along the west coast of India south from India and includes the coastline of the modern states of Mysore and Kerala.

107. Bembo renders his name as "Hidalchan," a common name among Muslim Indians and not necessarily to be identified with the ruler named Afdal Khan mentioned in footnote 78. There are frequent Hindu stories of Brahmins providing life-saving advice and beneficial counsel to Muslim sultans, and the sultans of India sometimes figured as patrons of Hindu architecture.

108. Bembo's transcription is "Joques."

109. He seems to be describing the bezoar.

blood, they make some come out and put the stone on it, which attracts to itself the poison and cannot be removed until all the poison has been absorbed; and then it falls off. It is then placed in milk where it is cleansed of the poison, which it completely releases. Thus it is a perpetual cure. If it were not placed in milk, it would no longer be any good.

On the morning of the 18th I went to some Armenians to try to change some money. I was unable to [do so], because Father Ambrose had not wanted even to give them assurances about my social position. Some would have given me the money to invest in merchandise. I would have had to pay a large interest—50% from Surat to Aleppo—and mine would have been the risk of the merchandise. That day I experienced the most [intense] heat that I did in any place. I had to change my shirt three or four times, and each time it was as wet as if it had been in water. Without any exercise I was sweating like a fountain, something that leaves a person very tired.

On the 19th I bought myself a French-style suit of clothes, which gets one more respect from the natives. European things cost me very dearly, since it was not the time of year when the ships arrive, and the merchants want to earn at least twice what things are worth. The worst thing is that if one needs an arm's length of cord or material, one must buy an entire piece; and if one wants a pair of European stockings, one must pay for them before trying them on. Once they are tried, the merchants don't want them back, even if they didn't fit; in other words, one must pay to try them on. The same was true for the rent of the house. If one wanted it for ten days, they asked for the rent of several months. Nor can one deal with anyone other than these banian. One day I asked them how they expected to be saved, if they stole from people. They answered me that they had been born naked, and that naked they would die, and thus they would give back to the world what they had taken from it. They said that all that was in the world had been put there by God for the service of man, to whom he had given the brains to know how to take advantage of it for himself and for his ease, and that everything they had would have to be left behind at death. The profit on things from Europe is high, but there is not much business. A pair of English stockings costs four zecchini; a ream of paper, fifty lire; a cup, five lire; a tobacco pouch of a soldo, four lire; and thus proportionally everything else.

On the 20th many Gentile merchants came to visit me. One of them brought a forty-five-carat diamond to show me, which a servant of his held in his hand. It was a rough octagon that seemed like a piece of crystal. He was asking 25,000 rupees for it, but he would have given it to me for 18,000, which equal 4,000 ongari. They said that once worked, it would be thirty-five carats. They told me that the little success of our goods was due to a rule of the Great Mughal that provided grave penalties for those who transported them, saying that through them much money went out of the kingdom and things of little value remained there.

That evening I went to visit the Capuchin fathers in whose house I found the captain of the French company. He was a young man who directed the company with Father Ambrose until the return of some of the directors, two of whom had recently died: Monsieur Caron, who had been called to France by the king to give an account of that company, went down with the ship in sight of the port of Lisbon, and thus rendered his accounts, although he was the best director of them; but he did not get along well with Father Ambrose, who was much esteemed by the king. Monsieur Baron, another director, who had been consul in Aleppo, had left for San Thomé, a fortress that had recently been taken from the Moors in the Gulf of Bengal.[110] It was by them once again besieged with the help of the Dutch, who were then enemies of France, from whom they had taken a place called Trincomalee, which was immediately taken back, however.[111] The other of the five directors had gone to Persia to treat of some matters with the king, but he died before being able to accomplish this task, in which he was replaced by his secretary.

On the 21st day, the day of Pentecost, I went to Mass in the church of the Capuchins. It is in the house, not very large, but well kept with only one altar and a hidden place where the directors stay to hear Mass. After lunch I waited for Father Ambrose, who was going to take me with him to see the city. When he came, he brought with him the French captain without having warned me first, for which I was sorry, not so much because I was in a house without furniture or things, since as a traveler I was not held to anything much better, but more because I thought that he might think that I wanted to be visited first by him rather than vice versa. After some compliments we went out together. When we arrived at the French house, two carriages of the French type were ready. They had four wheels; one [carriage] was upholstered in velvet, and the other in cloth, and they belonged to the company. The English and the Dutch had some of the same kind. The natives used carriages with two wheels, as I have already said, decorated with

110. San Thomé, just south of Madras on the Coromandel coast.
111. The great natural harbor of Trincomalee in northeastern Sri Lanka.

rugs and silk and gold cushions. Some rode Arab horses, and some have the palanquin. The Gentiles maintain decorum and luxury for themselves and have many servants. We entered in the carriages which, like most of the carts of the country, are pulled by oxen of a kind found only on the coasts of Bengal. They are more than ten hands tall,[112] white with a hump on their necks which is funny to see. They run and gallop like horses and are greatly esteemed, since they are scarce. They are taken care of daily with solicitude. Their food is a mixture of flour and sugar and sometimes vegetables like chickpeas or some similar thing.

We went out of the city by the same gate by which I had entered. Going to the left, I saw a very large pool or uncovered cistern made of marble carried from Diu. Its form was polygonal with many faces and angles, but with steps that go down and around to the level of the water from the field where it is [situated].[113] In the middle of it is a little island to which one can only go by swimming or by boat. The diameter of the whole thing must be two ample horse race lengths. They say that it is the largest pool in India and among the oldest. It is called Cisterns of Goppi,[114] which was the name of the man who had it made at his own expense, as many rich people do in various places for the public good and as a work of charity, since there are few rivers in the country, few fountains, and scarce rains, except in the season they call *Pausecal* or *Pauecal,* which means "time of rains."[115] It is of three months and begins in June, during which time the rains are abundant and continuous. Nevertheless, in India and farther north these are the hottest months of the year, but because of the rains they are called winter months. If the providence of nature and of God did not send that great abundance of water in that hot season to extinguish the excessive heat, that large part of the world would be uninhabitable for the drought, as many of the ancients believed it was. They argued thus because of its closeness to the sun. But the conclusions reached through theories by those seated at

112. Bembo uses the term *quarte;* ten hands would be about 100 cm.

113. Large stepped cisterns *(baolis)* were a major element in India's complex traditions of hydraulic architecture. Without them communities might not survive the postmonsoon periods of heat and drought. Like *sabils* (fountains) in the Islamic world to the west, these cisterns were often built as acts of public piety and service by rulers, officials, and wealthy merchants.

114. Bembo writes "Goppi Tellau."

115. Bembo is describing the South Asian monsoon.

their desks who travel only in their thoughts, which seem at first sight self-evident and necessary, are discovered false in practice. Those who personally travel to those countries discover the opposite to be true. Particularly in Goa, over which the sun is in its highest zenith at this time and sends on that city and kingdom perpendicularly all the burning of its rays, not only is it inhabited but there is everything necessary in abundance and much fertility and growth from the land, thanks to the many rains, whose waters, conserved in only one pool, are sufficient for the needs of a whole year of an entire populous city, not only for the thirst of the men and the animals, but also for cleaning. This latter is, in fact, the use for this water, because in many places it is dirty, since the Indians care little for hygiene. In Surat, however, the Gentiles do not use the water of the pool but rather that of the river. Once they found a cow drowned in the cistern, and thus they vowed solemnly to drink no more of that water, an oath that they still observe.

We went to see the garden that they call "the Queen's." It is greater in perimeter than the fortress of Daman. One enters the garden through a majestic portal of stone. At the end of a very long road, proportionately wide, there is a house with four façades and a hall in the center. There is a room on each of the four sides. At each façade there are delightful fountains that serve to tempt the heat of the air that comes in on summer days. The garden is full of flowers and fruits. Many peacocks and other birds fly about. They took me then to see the tombs of the Europeans. These are in the country and are very beautiful and rich, especially that of two English brothers made in the shape of a tall square tower in the middle of which are the two tombs. It has stairs to climb to the top of the tower from where one can see the city, the country, and the river as far as where the ships anchor. There are other tombs of Dutch and English men in stone with statues and inscriptions that tell the rank and office of the deceased. The tombs of the natives are like those of the Turks: a stone at the head and one at the feet.[116]

On the morning of the 22nd I went to mass and saw the wedding of a *cafro*, that is, a Moor of Africa, but a Christian and the slave of some Portuguese who do not give them their freedom, even if they accept the faith. The bride was a half-breed Christian, that is, born of a European and of a native woman. After lunch I went with Father Ambrose to visit the French captain whose house is not far from that of the Fathers. (That of the

116. The "natives" he speaks of are Muslims.

English is also nearby, but that of the Dutch is near the gate of the city that I have already mentioned.) On entering I saw two palanquins, one upholstered in velvet and the other in cloth with the ends of the rods covered with silver and with a ribbon where the rod curves. The captain himself came to meet me almost at the door, treating me with every courtesy and having me walk at his right. He led me into a great open hall with a fountain in the center filled with every kind of fish. The palace is quite large, with many apartments, since almost everybody of that nationality lives there. They eat together like clergy, nor can they go out of the house without the permission of the captain. They told me that all the directors together with some counselors have authority to judge even on the life of the French. Throughout the palace they have some pieces of artillery for protection in case of an invasion by Shivaji. The cannons were narrow at the mouth but broad in the body, and they shoot farther and with more strength. Some of these cannons with a beautiful carriage and with many other rich curiosities had been given to them as presents for the [Mughal] king. They were to be presented to him when the Company first came, but at that time the Great Mughal changed his mind and did not show up.[117] Since the person who was to present them had died, the directors had sent to France to ask for new instructions from their king. When I had toured and seen carefully the entire palace, I found in the first hall a table set with very fine silverware and tablecloth. Various candied fruits were brought in and cheese from Piacenza, which is a very rare thing in those parts. Then we drank wine, which costs an ongaro the flask and is Portuguese and Persian. We drank to the health of the rulers and of friends, even though in that hot climate it is not very healthy.

When we had finished the refreshment, we went out of the city toward the river, and, walking by the marina, I saw several shipyards, but [they showed] little skill in either the design or strength of the boats. Returning to the city and coming to the French house, I insisted that the captain remain, though he made every effort to accompany me back to my house. He sent some servants with me, however. They have many who always walk ahead of them on foot. I gave them tips as is the custom.

117. The French securely established their company in Surat in 1663–1664 during the reign of Awrangzeb. Their competitors—the Dutch, Portuguese, and British—had already had commercial establishments there for some six decades.

Talking with Father Ambrose about the business of that company, he told me that they were in a very bad state. With much merchandise and many ships in the balance, they had only ten reales as earnings the first year, after deducting their expenses. The reason was that the Dutch competed with them by paying highly for native goods and giving European goods cheaply, since they had much money. This obliged the French to lose in both buying and selling, and they had contracted many debts and had even sold some ships to make them up.

On the morning of the 23rd I saw many elephants in the city. They use them for various things. Kings have many of them for grandiosity in public events and for trips; they decorate them richly with many jewels, thus exhibiting their wealth and power. They also use them in war. To their two tusks, from which ivory is made, they bind two large cutting swords, one on each side, and they send them among the enemy, where they reap death and confusion. If they return, however, they do the same to the king's own troops. Also in war they sometimes put on their backs certain wooden castles that hold eight or more people and that are well bound, so that, even if the elephant should walk or run, they will not fall. To take the wild elephants and domesticate them, particularly in Sri Lanka, where there are many of them, they use this artifice. They tie some domesticated ones by the feet to some trees. Nearby they make a huge pit and cover it with branches and grasses. Inside these pits the wild elephants fall as they try to approach the domestic ones that they see tied. Once they have fallen, they cannot get out, and they leave them there for seven to eight days, always watching them and giving them leaves to eat. Every day they throw some earth into the pit, on top of which the elephant begins to rise. When they are about to get out altogether, they put some chains on their feet. They leave them without food for two days and beat them so that they will stay calm, until they understand the language of those who command. They are very docile animals and very attached to their custodian, who gives them food and tames them. Their food is rice and cooked vegetables. When these animals are sold, they are paid by the cubit. They are measured from the feet to the height of the back, and they are worth large sums. One can cost up to 1,000 pardaos the cubit. As I said elsewhere, six pardaos make an ongaro.

I found in the city the son of the pasha with many people on foot with unfurled flags. He himself was in a palanquin with a silk umbrella attached to the center of the rod, which turned easily to every side so that he could protect himself from the sun. They say that the custom of having oneself carried on the shoulders of men in palanquins was introduced by the ancient Gentile kings to distinguish themselves from other people, since they thought of themselves as almost divine and boasted that they were descended from the sun. They tell the following fable, which those ignorant people consider to be true. They say that in those parts people used to wake up early in ancient times to adore the rising sun. One morning they were all together in the country awaiting the birth of the sun. When the sun came up, the ground opened, and they saw a man of perfect age arise from it. He was taller, stronger, and more beautiful than all others and was accompanied by such majesty, grace, and pleasing looks that one felt obliged to love and adore him. They tried to recognize him and asked him who he was and what he wanted. They say that he answered that he was the son of the sun and of the earth; he had been sent by God to rule and govern them. They prostrated themselves then and adored him and received the laws from him. He built the cities and introduced commerce. Through this means and through arms he enlarged the empire and took possession of all the eastern provinces. They think and blindly believe that all the kings of India are descendants of this man.[118] I also saw throughout the city some persons called Parsis, who are Gentiles in the ancient manner, most of whom fled from Persia at the time when that kingdom became Moslem.[119] They adore fire, the sun, and the moon. They keep a fire lit all the time, as the Vestals did in Rome. If their houses catch fire, they let them burn, since they believe that they offend the god they adore if they put out the fire. In those days the news reached us that the king of Japan had expelled the Dutch from his state and had forbidden them to do commerce there. But the news was not verified immediately.[120]

118. The reference may be to Vishnu.

119. The Parsis (Bembo's "perseos") are Zoroastrians who fled from Iran to western India after the seventh-century Muslim conquest of Iran. They have remained a powerful community, particularly in commerce, to the present day.

120. The report was inaccurate and may have been based upon the Tokugawa shogunate's restrictions on European learning. But it is not difficult to see why Bembo and his friends would have believed what they heard: Christianity had been prohibited in Japan after 1612; in 1635 the Japanese were forbidden to travel abroad, thus making it impossible for Japanese merchants to engage in international trade; and in 1639 Portuguese merchant ships were forbidden to land anywhere in Japan. Only the Dutch and Chinese retained trading privileges, limited, however, to the city of Nagasaki.

On the day of the 24th I went to see the mint. There anyone can have coins made who pays a tax to the king. All coins, both gold and silver, are of good quality. Around midnight a southeast wind arose and brought such a heavy rainfall that I doubted I would be able to return to Daman that winter due to the mud and water that disrupt the roads.

Thus on the morning of the 25th I decided to try to get carts for my return without attempting to go visit the city of Cambay, which is four days' journey from Surat. I thought that more delay would make my trip very difficult. It was hard to find carts because the commander had conscripted them all into public service for an expedition to a nearby city to get lead. They buy [lead] from the Dutch and the English, from whom they also get cannons that show the latter's arms on the walls of the castle. Yogidas, the banian who always assisted me, went on my behalf to the commander to get a license for only two carts. The permit was not given for rented carts, but it was given for private carts of merchants. Nevertheless, when the license was signed, I secretly made arrangements for two for rent. They went to wait for me two kos distant from the city where I went with the French carriages. I went out of the city at the 22nd hour, accompanied by the Capuchin fathers and by the banian. As I was going out the gate, I met with a feast they make when they marry. Many men went on foot playing fifes and drums. Behind them came many others on horseback, and then many carts and some Dutch carriages. There were many unfurled flags. Finally there were some palanquins with many children, boys and girls, who were younger than five years old. Around them went many people dancing and celebrating that marriage. I was told on that occasion that, although women whose husbands have died cannot marry a second time, the contrary is not true. The man is not bound by the same law and can marry again. When we had arrived at the carts, I took leave of the fathers in the proper form, and I thanked them for the many courtesies and honors that they had paid me. The banian would not go until I had left him a letter signed with my seal attesting to the good services that he had given me and to the goodwill that he had toward Venetians, so as to acquire credit among European for-eigners who would come to those parts. After an hour's travel we stopped to sleep in a town not far from a running stream that we had crossed by means of a stone bridge.

One and a half hours before daylight on the 26th we began to travel. We had difficulty passing a stream because of the mud caused by the previous rain. We did not stop until the 19th hour, resting briefly. I observed then, as I already had in Surat, that those filthy Gentiles are not ashamed to take care of their necessities in the public street. They use the reasoning of the cynic philosophers that nature has not made anything dirty and that therefore it is not shameful to show any part of the body. At the 21st hour we picked up our journey again, and after sunset we spent the night near a small river.

On the 27th we continued the trip until the 22nd hour and then stayed at the town of Bulsar,[121] where I had slept the first night after I left Daman. As soon as we arrived, a servant of that aga came and ordered that we should present ourselves to him, all the people and all the baggage. When he was asked about the reason, the man answered that the captain of Daman had taken as prisoners a few days ago some men of that town and that thus the aga wanted to stop all the Portuguese who passed through there. Thus I alone went with the dragoman to the aga, leaving the servants and the things. We had great difficulty in making ourselves understood because there was no one there who understood Portuguese, and the dragoman did not understand their tongue. However, when we asked some things in Arabic, we were understood by one of those ministers, who asked us who we were and where we were going. When he understood that we were Venetians, he let us go immediately with great courtesy and even let go a poor Portuguese soldier whom I had taken with me after having met him along the road. We then stopped with the carts near the cistern of the town. It is so large that it serves the needs for the entire year.

At midday of the 28th we arrived at the river of Daman; precisely as midday was sounding we crossed it with the boat of the king, which does not charge for white men, as Europeans are called. Moors and Gentiles pay something each. The boatmen are obliged to take people only until midday, and after that they are off until another determined hour. Once passed over, I went to see the Dominican fathers. I thought that they would have found me a house, as I had asked them to do before leaving for Surat. Since they had not been able to, however, I stayed in the convent. I went immediately to the fortress to pay my respects to the Captain. From him I learned that a boat had left for Chaul, which was a trip about which they had known nothing beforehand. With much courtesy he offered me his house until I should have got one. However, since I was already being put up by the fathers, I thanked him and declined.

On the 29th I went to see a house. Although it was small and not com-

121. About 20 km north of Daman.

fortable, I took it, since there were no others to be found. The only good thing about it was that it was near the walls of the fortress. Before taking it, I asked if the prior of the Dominicans would let me stay in the convent if I gave him something every month. He would take no money and offered me every hospitality free, but I did not want to be obligated by such a gift, and so I moved into that house. I had to have it fixed, because it had not been inhabited for a long time. Father Francesco Salema, the superior, and all the others provided me with beds, tables, chairs, and every other necessity.

On the 30th I was invited by the Captain [Emmanuel Fortado di Mendoza] to go to his house the next day for the yearly visit made in the towns subject to the king. He goes with many foot soldiers and others on horseback. The king provides him with one hundred reales for the occasion, since the captain has to cover the expenses of everyone. On the morning of the 31st at the second hour of sunlight I went with a small cart sent by the Captain to the house of that gentleman, Emmanuel di Soza [who held the nearby fief of Daman di Cima (of the Heights)]. The captain had arrived shortly before, accompanied by thirty knights, some on horseback and some on palanquins, all going with unfurled flags. We passed the time in talking, dice games, and rested in the shadows. The meal was rather splendid, with much food and sweet things, which is the greatest expense. At the first table we were thirty-three. After lunch we all went to the marina, where they raced for the ring with good horses and rich trappings. After the entertainment we all returned to the house for more games. After a good supper we went to rest. The meeting was bothered by a rain that continued all night and that obliged many of those gentlemen who were sleeping in the open to take cover.

[JUNE 1673]

On the morning of the first of June, a solemn day because it was the feast of Corpus Christi, we heard mass and then passed the whole day in games and a lunch not less good than the first. Because of the rain, we were unable to ride horses or to go out. In the evening two Englishmen from Surat on their way to Mumbai came and were kept to a sumptuous supper by the captain.

On the morning of the 2nd, since the rain continued, the Captain decided it was impossible to continue the visit and thus decided to return to the city. This was done at the second hour of the day, while it was still raining. When I arrived at the convent, I found letters from Father

Giacomo and from the captain of the ship, which advised me that they had arrived within sight of Goa but that they had been pushed back by the wind and only, almost miraculously, were they able to reach the port of Chaul, where they would pass the winter. They asked me to join them by land, so as to be able to go to Goa together the first days of September. Since I was not comfortable in my house, I answered that I would go there before the winter was finished and that I would gladly continue the trip with them. As much as I was deceived by Padre Giovanni, I was indebted to Padre Antonio Velloso, a Dominican, who with great generosity gave me money that I was to pay back in Goa. He did not ask for, nor want, anything in writing. I took the money because I had great need of it. The Captain, who, according to Padre Giovanni, was going to provide me with money, told me that he could not give me any, because money was scarce even for him. Whether that was true or whether he was worried that he would not be paid back, I could not get money.

That Father [Antonio Velloso] was a noble native of India, of a city in the kingdom of Sri Lanka, which, like all the others of that kingdom, first belonged to the Portuguese and now to the Dutch. Sri Lanka is one of the most fertile and rich islands of the world. It is seventy-eight leagues long and forty-four leagues wide, and three hundred miles in perimeter. It is called Ceylon by the Arabs and Persians, and by the Indians it is called "*Hibenaro*," which means "fat earth," which it truly is. On it are found the most precious forests of cinnamon, pepper, cardamom, and other fruit trees. Rice is harvested three times a year. There are fruits of every kind in abundance. The waters of its rivers are sweet and healthy. In the mountains there are precious stones. In the sea are pearls, although, through the fault of the inhabitants who did not take sufficient care of them, the beds of oysters are depleted. The air is very good, and there are rains in every season. It is subject to various kings. The people are tall, cruel, friends of novelty, sensual, and dishonest. They have their wives in common and are permitted to marry their own sisters; also marriages are easily dissolved. Four or five brothers take only one wife. At the time of the Portuguese it happened that a woman asked the Portuguese judge to exempt her from serving seven brothers who were her husbands. She said that she did not have enough strength to satisfy them all. The judge asked her if two were enough, and she answered that she thought she could manage with as many as four.

From some buildings that are on the island, the conjecture is made that the Romans had something to do with the place. At the foot of a very high mountain that the natives call the Mountain of Adam, there is a large stone on which is seen the imprint of a human foot. They say that Adam left this when he ascended to heaven. Nearby there is a river that divides into four branches, and its waters are said to be medicinal. Likewise, there is a hermitage with two tombs where they say that Adam and Eve are buried.

That evening I retired to my house. It consisted of four rooms, three on the ground floor and one above, in which I slept. There was a garden that did not merit such a nice name, since it was more of a dump than anything else. The first night I had a rather numerous company of mosquitoes, spiders, lice, fleas, and ants that did their best to keep me awake. During the day they also kept me busy. Then, too, there was a crow so domestic and impertinent that he would even steal food from the fire. Despite everything, the liberty one has in one's own house was worth more than all the inconveniences. It also had a reasonable price, because, as I have said, food is inexpensive, except for wine and sweet things. There are many hens, but not much beef, because of the Gentiles. Instead of that, one eats pork meat. Salted hams and salami and other things come from Portugal. [The local people] do not know how to make them, or perhaps they cannot because of the heat. Fish is sometimes abundant. There are many fruits, all different from ours and too sweet. Among them I liked pineapple, which I considered the best of them. They use yellow wax with pitch and other ingredients to make candles that give a very bad light. There are no stores in the city. All is bought in private houses. The reason is that the Gentiles, who cannot pass the night in the city, have their stores in the [smaller] towns. There one finds everything, and especially they make cotton cloth that is very fine and cheap. The water one drinks is rainwater, which is conserved in a great ditch outside the city. They first filter it through cloth and then let it sit and drink it after a few days, when it is good and fresh. The best is that of the Reformed Fathers, from whom I got my water.

On the 7th the Captain honored me with a visit, accompanied by a gentleman whose name was Bento, that is, Benedetto Tesseira, who seemed very partial to me. He told me that he had a great desire to see Italy, but that he was prevented by his wife. He gave me several things, particularly some Italian books about which he was very curious. I judged him to be a man of great goodness.

The next day I went to return the visit to these and to other gentlemen who had been to see me. I saw that their houses were well furnished but small and limited in comforts. In the windows, instead of glass, they have pieces of oyster and clams that are very thin and polished, but they let in little light. The women mostly remain behind screens and let themselves be seen rarely, since the Portuguese are very careful with them. They always go in covered palanquins. When they go out to go to mass, they are accompanied by their relatives and servants, and they always go before daylight. They are almost all dark in coloring, and they wear the same clothes as the Gentiles. Their children, both boys and girls, even if noble, or older, go naked in the house, as I saw in the Captain's house and elsewhere.

The day of the 10th, since I had had a headache for many days, I had my beard cut. I let it grow again at my departure. My headache was attributed to the bad air of the place.

On the 13th was solemnized the feast of St. Anthony of Padua at the Reformed Fathers' house. On that occasion it was the custom to invite some laypeople. I was honored to be among them. The meal was generous and proper. In the evening I went, as I did almost every day, to greet the Captain. There I found the gentleman Bento Tesseira, who invited me for the next day to one of his houses in company with other gentlemen and the Captain to amuse ourselves. So that I would be ready to leave early in the morning, he invited me that night to stay in his house. Meanwhile, as we were dining, we heard a serenade by musicians and players who were celebrating the birth of a son to a servant of the Captain's. This is a custom practiced in all India for eight evenings by everyone. The ceremony is more or less rich according to the class of the parent. Even the Portuguese are taking up some of these customs. On that occasion it was said that Indian women give milk to their children to the age of three years and more. It was also said that in Goa a woman had had a child in her womb for twenty-two months. When she delivered it, it already had long nails, teeth, and hair. I laughed about that and would not believe it.

The morning of the 14th, at an early hour, we boarded a ship with eight oars and covered at one end. After an hour's trip against the river's current we arrived at a town of the gentleman Tesseira. It was called Verecundia and was located on the side toward Surat. The house is in a delightful and cool place. It is not very big, but it is divided into two parts, one of which is for the women. We heard mass in a nicely kept chapel. After lunch, which was worthy and abundant in everything, we went walking through the town and stopped in various gardens and orchards. Around the 23rd hour we returned to the fortress with the same boat. Because of the small size of the place and because there is not much to say, I will not continue to note all the days, most of which I passed in the house or in excursions outside the city or in the gardens of the Dominicans or Reformed Fathers.

On the 15th I met the minor king Chotia, whose state had been sacked by Shivaji. He was living under the protection of that captain who was trying through ambassadors to get his lands returned and to ensure him the dominion of them. At that time they were being ruled by no one, since for Shivaji it had been sufficient to ravage them, and Chotia would not return for fear of other attacks.

On the evening of the 23rd, the vigil of St. John the Baptist, which is a very solemn feast for the Portuguese, there were fireworks in all the streets and in front of the houses of the nobility. The fanciest were those of the religious in front of their convents. Among these the best were those of the Jesuits, who, after [a display of] a very beautiful ship all in fireworks, staged a fight among many people with rays and trumpets of fire. They are wealthy and receive much rent and have villas in that jurisdiction. Besides, they take care of the public money of the city, and the ministers must go to them in case of need. They are five priests, and their superior is the head of the Inquisition, in which the Portuguese are quite rigorous.

On the morning of the 24th I went out of the city early with the captain and all the knights in a solemn cavalcade to hear mass in a church dedicated to the saint; [it was] a mile's distance away. On our return, after races, they went throughout the whole city displaying rich clothing and fancy trappings. They even had silver on their lances. After having gone through all the streets, they divided into two groups, pretending to fight. The war consisted of throwing fruits at one another! When that was finished, they did more tricks with their horses, and all of it lasted until midday.

[JULY 1673]

On the 2nd of July I received by foot courier[122] letters from Goa from Father Valerio, a Carmelite, with the news that Father Seabra had arrived in that city, and more news from Europe that had come in a caravel used by the king [of Portugal] to send messages to India, since they are rather fast and arrive a month earlier than the regular ships. I also had news about my particular interests, which made me resolve to begin my journey before winter should begin and to go to Mumbai or Chaul, so as to go from there to Goa on the first occasion, since the rains had let up some. The wind, on the contrary, got always worse and made navigation usually impossible during May, June, July, August, and part of September, which

122. *Patamar.*

is winter in India. On the other side of the Ghats, however, in the Gulf of Bengal the winter is at the same time as in Europe. This winter, however, is not cold. It is only somewhat bothersome because of the humidity. That year winter began earlier than usual, and thus many ships of Gentile merchants and of Moors of Surat were lost. They ended up on Portuguese shores, and the captain had the right to the wrecks, as the Great Mughal had the rights to Portuguese wrecks that came to his shore.

On the day of the 26th I began to take leave of those knights who were my friends, from the clergy, and from the Captain. On the 27th Father Velloso provided me with two palanquins without any obligations besides that of providing for the poor people that bear them. I had letters for some gentlemen who were owners of towns we would pass, and others for the superiors of some convents. At the 24th hour I took final leave of all the Dominicans and left the city with Father Velloso, who wanted to accompany me to the town of Upper Daman,[123] because Emmanuel di Sozo, whom I have mentioned other times, had promised him that he would give me lodging. But perhaps the message had arrived late, or he had repented of his promise. Nothing was ready when we arrived, and the Father was very disgusted and told me at that time of the aversion that he had for those gentlemen, because of the facility with which they told lies and behaved in ways that were not worthy of their station. With the provisions that I had with me and with some others that we bought there we passed the night as best we could. On the morning of the 28th, four hours before day, after having thanked the good Father for all his favors, I got into the palanquin, and the servants [got] into two carts, and we began the journey. We went along the beach and enjoyed the view of the sea, as we did most of those days. We arrived at Nargol, a villa of the Jesuits of Daman, around midday.[124] When the bearers of the palanquin had eaten, I passed the river, called the Nargoli, in a boat, and the carts passed through the water, as do the palanquins when the waters are low. Those bearers are like beasts and can travel all day in the rain and wind without stopping and actually make a lot of headway. At the 23rd hour we arrived at the Villa Devier, which belonged to a widowed lady of Daman, from whom I had a letter for her overseer, named Giovanni d'Almoida, who received me with courtesy. The villa is poor, and the house itself is rather small and covered with palm leaves. Since it was Friday, and

123. Daman of the Heights.
124. Nargol is about 20 km south of Daman.

no bread was to be found, because it is not made in the town, our supper was of rice and water and salt fish. The beds were as poor as the supper. I found in the people there the crazy idea that all Italians are doctors. As soon as I arrived, I was assaulted in the house by all the sick people of the town. Since I could not get rid of them, I gave most of them some medicine[125] that I had with me and told them that it was the cure for whatever malady they had.

On the morning of the 29th I left under a bit of rain. Around noon I arrived at Dahanu, a big town, which is on a high hill. The place is governed by a captain subject to the [captain] of Daman, with an artillery officer, four Portuguese soldiers, and some natives. There are a little over fifty native houses in the town and ten of the Portuguese. I stayed only enough time to let the bearers eat an abundant meal that consisted only of rice, which cost ten *bazarcuchi*—small coins, four of which equal a *paisà*, and forty-five paisà a pardaos. Then I crossed the river, the entrance to which is guarded by a round fortress with some artillery. I left the carts because they could not pass the water, which was too high. I gave them their leave after paying them the right amount and carried the things to the other bank with boats that are there for that purpose. They charge a reasonable price. I left the servants to watch them. I went with haste to Villa Barapocrana with the palanquins and arrived around the 22nd hour to the house of the nobleman Valentin Falcon, who was the master there, and the owner of the palanquins that I was using. He had lent them to me at the request of Father Velloso. He received me with much courtesy and immediately sent carts to pick up my servants and things that I had left. The town is big and provides much revenue from palm trees of the same kind as those of Persia. Instead of dates, they give nuts, called "nuts of India." The most impressive thing is that one of these trees taken to Persia will give dates, while in India it makes nuts that are very big and of two kinds.[126] Some of them are good for eating, and others are good to make oil. Before being fully ripe, they have a green skin, somewhat like ours, and inside they have a sweet water similar in taste to milk and refreshing. As they mature, this water hardens to a substance

125. Bembo's term is "theriac."
126. There are many different types of palm, and Bembo is mistakenly identifying the coconut palm with the date palm, which, though similar in height and general appearance, is not the same. The palm wine that he describes is made, not from the trunk of the tree, but from the flower buds, as is arrack.

about two fingers thick. It remains attached to the inside of the skin. This can be eaten or oil can be made from it, depending on what kind it is. From the tree itself, when it is pierced, comes out a water called *sura,* which serves as wine for the natives. It has a sweet taste, but it is very strong, and one can easily get drunk from it. I do not think there is any tree in the world so useful as the palm, which gives to men what many other trees together do not. From the trunk boats can be made that are bound, instead of with nails, with strings that the tree produces among its leaves. From [the leaves] bags and rugs and other things are made. The skin of the fruit when it is dried and beaten is like linen that can be spun, and ropes and sails can be made from it. The fruits and the juice are the cargo of the boats, as well as the provisions of food and drink for the sailors. That gentleman received me with good manners and gave me without ceremony a good supper that lacked for nothing except bread, which is not made even there. If it hadn't been late, he would have sent for some in the land of Tarapur, but we made do with flat cakes, cooked on copper sheets, which are good if they are eaten warm. He gave us good beds to sleep on.

On the morning of the 30th, as is the custom of that nationality, he gave us an abundant breakfast. He changed my bearers and gave me some who were not so tired out, as well as two carts. I was infinitely sorry not to have been able to give him my weapons, since I had noticed that he liked them very much, but I could not do without them for the journey. Thus I took leave with many thanks and expressions of gratitude, and a little before noon I was on my way under such heavy rain that I had to stop for the carts and stay in a town on the river of Tarapur until the 24th hour. At that time the rain stopped, and I passed the river with the palanquins and arrived in the same land of Tarapur, where I did not know anyone; nor did I have recommendations for [that place], since I had not thought that I would have to stay there. I did have a letter for a Portuguese Dominican Father, a native of Portugal, and so I went to the convent. He was the only one there, and I took the liberty of asking him for a night's lodging and had no difficulty in persuading him. In fact, he himself offered it with courtesy and then treated me regally.

Tarapur is a big place with two bastions, governed by a captain, appointed by the king, with six soldiers and one artillery officer. It has the obligation to assist the fortress of Daman in time of need and to go there with four hundred armed persons who are taken from the subject towns. It is situated on the river, the mouth of which is protected by the two bastions mentioned. It has about two hundred native houses and fifty of the Portuguese. There are two other convents, one of the Franciscans and another of the Paulists, that is, the Jesuits.

On the morning of the 31st I waited for the carts to arrive that had remained behind. Meanwhile, that good friar kept me courteous company and demonstrated the liking that he had for Venetians. When the servants arrived with my things, I took leave and continued the journey, even though the rains did not let up. We forded a few rivers. The bearers would put the rods of the palanquin on top of their heads, and I did not have to be incommoded. These rivers can be passed only when the tide is out. Thus several times we had to wait to cross until the water was low. At the 21st hour we passed over another rather wide river, called Cerigon, with some large boats.[127] At sunset I arrived with only the palanquins—since the carts were not able to cross the river because of the high water—at Mahim Quelme,[128] so called to distinguish it from the other Mahim, which is on the island of Mumbai. This place is located on a river that is navigable for galliots. It is governed by a captain, appointed by the king, and six soldiers. It has the obligation to help Daman and to depend on the orders of the Captain of Daman. It has one hundred Portuguese houses and many other native ones. There is a Franciscan convent, and also a Dominican convent, to which I went immediately upon my arrival. I presented to the superior there the letter of Father Velloso. He did not pay much account to it and put us up without much courtesy. He gave us some rooms, hardly presented himself, and showed in his manners and in his face a low birth. At the proper time he took us to the refectory for a poor meal, excusing himself that the country did not give [enough donations] for more. The tablecloth was so old and ragged that it corresponded well with the meal. It was more of a net than a covering for the table. He insisted on being seated with us, although I could not understand why.

[AUGUST 1673]

On the morning of August 1st the carts arrived. Due to the rain, they had passed the night in another town. The lunch of that day was fairly good, though that friar showed in his face his real feelings that he found little satisfaction in our presence. He did not want to eat in our company and

127. Probably the Sarya River.
128. Mahim.

pretended that he had a pain in his stomach, which I think was in his purse instead. I could not leave as soon as the carts arrived, as I would have wished, because the men of the carts, who had been paid ahead of time, went back with their animals. I think they did it because they were worried about all the mud that there was. I sent around the town to look for palanquins for the servants and things. Since I was not able to get them for that evening, I resolved to go from there with only a servant so as not to see any longer the unpleasant face of that friar, who with great impoliteness had gone to visit a gentleman and had left me alone in the convent. About two hours after midday I took up my journey with the usual accompaniment of the rain. I crossed two rivers by boat, and after sunset I arrived in a large town called Dadra,[129] where that night, since I did not have lodging, I slept in the palanquin under the shelter of a shop roof and did not eat anything.

On the morning of the 2nd, after daylight, I crossed a river of the same name, which is where the jurisdiction of Daman ends. This Dadra River is the largest and most dangerous of all that I had passed. At its mouth there is a fortress that keeps the Corsary pirates from entering. They infest those shores and plunder goods and people. When I had passed it with boats at midday, I found myself two miles distant from Bassein in a town famous for its temple to the Madonna of Remedy. She is very miraculous and is very venerated. The church is in the custody of the Dominican fathers, for one of whom I had a letter. His name was Father Giovanni of S. Michele, but he had left a few days previously with the superior of the place. Nevertheless another missionary who had remained (They were only three there.) readily showed me every favor. He showed sorrow that the cells of the fathers who were gone were closed and that he could offer me only his own, which I did not want to accept. It was, besides, small, and we would not all have been able to fit. Thus I took lodging near the convent in one of the places where people stay who come to make a novena to that miraculous Madonna. I took several rooms, which, although they were the best, were dark and humid like a cellar. That father immediately sent me chairs, beds, and tables and also some food that he insisted I accept. He sent me some food again in the evening.

On the morning of the 3rd the servants and things arrived. I found a woman who would bring me food at the appropriate hours of the day, if I

129. Bembo calls it "Dantora." It is 16 km southeast of Daman.

gave her something daily. On the 4th I went to hear mass and to the adoration of that image to which not only Christians go but also Moors and Gentiles.[130] Although infidels, they receive many graces and in return make many alms of money, grains, eggs, hens, and oil. On the day of the 6th, since the weather had got better, I looked for a boat to go to Thana,[131] where one arrives after four hours' journey. One awaits the correct tide, as also for returning. When I had found the boat, I had the things loaded and took leave of that courteous father. I walked to the city, since there was no other way to get to the river, where the boat was.

This city called Bassein, or Bazain, is situated on the Indian coast on the land of the kingdom of Deccan on the north side.[132] It is surrounded by thick, high walls with eleven bastions and about 1,000 steps in perimeter. On one side the river serves as its moat; on the west the sea [does]. The sea also bathes its other sides but only at high tide. When the water comes in, it covers the plain and leaves it as an island. Before belonging to the Portuguese, it was destroyed by them two times: the first time by Ettore de Silviera and the second time by Nuno da Cugna. Finally it was given to them as the price of peace by the Sultan Bahadur, king of Cambay.[133] Its jurisdiction begins at the River Antora, eight Portuguese leagues' distance from the city, and goes to Caranga, where it ends. There are another eight leagues where it borders with the minor kings—Melique on one side and those of Colle and Chota on the other.[134] At the frontiers the Portuguese have several fortresses for the security of their towns. These are inhabited by 2,000 Christians and some Moors and Gentiles subject to them. The towns belong to the nobles of Bassein [and were] given to them by the king for their services in war. The knights of this city are the richest and most famous of all India. They are related to all the best families of Lisbon. The

130. The Virgin Mary is venerated in Islam, and one *surah* (chapter) of the Qur'an bears her name.

131. Modern Thana is located on the Kalu River about 25 km to the northeast of Mumbai.

132. Bassein is on the Kalu River delta (apparently Bembo's Antora River) about 40 km north of Mumbai. It is now known as Vasai. Colle is probably to be identified with present-day Kalyan. I have not been able to identify Bembo's "Melique."

133. See footnote 65.

134. I have been unable to identify the present-day names of Caranga and Chota.

younger sons go to India to better their fortunes and take as wives the daughters of half-breeds with rich dowries, since they have the ambition of becoming related to them. With this and with the service they give in the army they ascend to the first places in honor and wealth.

Bassein is governed by a captain appointed by the king, as are the others. He commands twelve captains subject to him who are in the forts and islands of the jurisdiction. In the spiritual realm there is a vicar placed by the archbishop of Goa, and the present one is named de la Vara. Justice is administered by an auditor; money and tithes by an administrator placed by the king. All the positions last three years. There are various palaces and good houses. However, the streets are narrow and short. There are also four convents of religious, that is, Franciscans, Dominicans, Augustinians, and Jesuits, and two churches of parish priests. The Jesuits have, in addition, a seminary for catechumens erected at the time of St. Francis Xavier, where are raised the Gentiles that receive baptism, who are many, since that jurisdiction is very populated. Fifteen thousand armed men come from there. There are besides in the city four hundred houses of native Christians, many of Moors and Gentiles, and three hundred of the Portuguese. The water, which is good in the entire city, comes from a fountain on the Island of Salsette, called Salsette of the North, to distinguish it from a similar one in Goa. The water is carried by boats, but ordinary people use some wells that are not good. Outside the city there are some fruit orchards and particularly sugarcane fields. They sell the cane to the English and the Gentiles of Surat. They also have much rice, but not much wheat, which comes to them from elsewhere. After I stopped for a while in the city, I went to the marina where I observed many pieces of wood to make galliots and boats for the armed forces. They make them of a very strong wood called teak.[135] I boarded the galliot, and, since there was a little wind, we set sail. We were traveling with the current of that river, which has several islands. After half an hour I saw on the right on top of a hill a delightful place called Cormandel, in the jurisdiction of a nobleman of Bassein. Farther ahead I saw a mountain that seemed cut. They say that in ancient times it united that island to the mainland; it is two hundred miles in circumference, and Alexander the Great had it cut when he went to India.[136] Thus the river was

135. Bembo renders the Malayalam *tekka* as "techa."

136. Alexander halted at the Indus River, but legends about him and his deeds abounded in Iran and India.

made to pass into the sea through that cut. At its beginning the river is a mile wide, but at this point it narrows to only about six meters. After another three hours we anchored at the island of Thane on the right of the river. I went immediately to the Dominican convent. I had a letter for the Superior that turned out to be superfluous, since he was a gentleman of good breeding. His name was Father Emmanuel of Santa Caterina, a native of Portugal. I was welcomed and treated with sincere cordiality by him. I also found there the vicar of the convent of the Madonna of Remedy and Father Giovanni of S. Michele. I passed some days happily with them, since it was necessary to wait for the moon to grow full so that the water level in the smaller branch of the river would rise. In bad weather it was not possible to travel in the larger branch.

Thane is a large place but without walls. It is governed by a captain appointed by the king and by the usual ministers I have mentioned elsewhere. Many knights live there and get rich produce from the island. There are five churches: the cathedral and churches of the Franciscans, the Dominicans, the Augustinians, and the Jesuits, who are very rich throughout India and not much loved by the others. On the 9th I stopped a galliot so as to be able to go in it to Mumbai immediately while the water permitted. On the 10th an astute man came to visit the Father Vicar. He pretended he was the Portuguese Count of Sargedas and that he had arrived in India with an English ship. It had first anchored in Madras in the Gulf of Bengal, where the English have a fortress. Then he had passed near Goa without entering the island, and now he was going to Bassein with the intention of then going to Goa, where the father of the real Count of Sargedas had been viceroy. He was courted by all those gentlemen who held counts and marquises of Portugal in high esteem, since these rarely go to India except by order or for grave crimes. When he arrived at the convent, I had occasion to speak with him. He told me that he had visited Italy and that he had stopped in Venice, where he had the friendship of a nobleman of the Cornaro family who had been ambassador in Rome, and that he had stayed as a guest at his house. Besides the fact that I cannot find any account of any Cornaro having been ambassador to Rome at that time, the rest of his conversation also did not have much solidity.[137] This was thought to be

137. The Bembos were closely related to the Cornaro family, so Ambrosio's doubts are well founded. He is too polite simply to say that the man is a liar and a fraud.

because of his age, since he was not older than twenty-six or twenty-seven, but that was the age of the real count as well. Then, too, I observed that his clothing with some gold ornaments seemed more that of a charlatan than of a gentleman. Around the third hour of the night I boarded the galliot, since the water was favorable. I was accompanied by four Englishmen of ordinary class, who were also going to Mumbai. We traveled in the small river for greater safety.

We did not have enough water at some point, and we remained on a sandbar until the third hour of sunlight of the 11th. With the new tide we resumed our journey, partly with oars and partly with sails. Around the 21st hour we arrived at the *Bara* of Mumbai, which is what they call the port of that island.[138] It is very beautiful, safe, and large enough for an immense number of ships—more than any other [harbor] in India. In addition to the English, who own it, it is frequented by Portuguese who pass to the city of Chaul, situated farther downstream on the mainland.

The Portuguese took possession of this city (Mumbai) or fortress of Chaul[139] by arms. They took it from the Great Mughal. It is located at the mouth of a river that forms that famous port when it enters the sea. It is the last that the Portuguese have in the north, but the first in the kingdom of the Deccan, coming out of the kingdom of Cambay. In ancient times it was very populous and did much commerce. But now it is almost uninhabited due to the bad air and because the Dutch have taken their traffic to their own ports. Not far from the city there is a rather strong castle that defends it. It is located on top of a mount called the Moor of Chaul. The [territory of] Shivaji also borders on this port, but although there is no armada of his there, he has some jurisdiction over it, even though the English have called themselves the absolute owners of the place. The strength of an opposing wind kept us from dropping anchor until the 23rd hour. As soon as I debarked, I went to the Franciscan convent. Only one priest lives there, with the title of Rector. His name is Father Giovanni di S. Michele. He took

138. *Bara* means "mouth of the river."

139. The Portuguese settlement of Chaul was 30 km to the south of Mumbai. Despite this confusing introduction, Bembo is clearly describing the city of Mumbai. The Portuguese had first attempted to seize the area of Mumbai in 1507 and were eventually ceded the harbor in 1534 by Sultan Bahadur of Gujarat. They divided the territory into various fiefs, with which they rewarded both military followers and religious orders.

me in affectionately. My things were kept at the customs house by the ministers of the place. They are Christian natives and look at everything carefully and rigorously and want to take everyone's name and keep in custody any firearms.

On the 12th a certain Enrico Gary, who had been informed by a letter from Padre Velloso, came to visit me. He said he was Venetian, born in the S. Giovanni quarter in Bragora of an English father and a Venetian mother. A sister of his father, who had been abandoned by an Englishman, then became wife of the gentleman Lorenzo Contarini, who lived in Santa Ternita, and he had been Chief Magistrate[140] in Capo d'Istria. He told me that he had left Venice at the age of twelve years. He walked through part of Europe and stayed some time in England. From there he had passed to India with merchandise, and there he had [held] worthy offices among the English. He had been the first captain of this fortress for his king, and the island had been made English through his negotiations. He was the man who negotiated with the Portuguese viceroy Antonio di Mello di Castro when it was given as dowry by King Alfonso of Portugal to his sister Catherine, married to King Charles II of England.[141] It was then sold by him to his merchant company in India who now own it. At present Gary is without office and attends to his own business interests that he has in all those places. He traffics in much merchandise and has several merchant ships, as big as marciliane.[142] He also has property on the island and is not an insignificant figure among the English. He knows many languages: Arabic, Hindi, English, German, Portuguese, French, and his native Italian, and [he] writes in all of them. He has a very beautiful library and delights in study. He was at that time about fifty-eight years old and had had an English wife. After her death he married again in Surat, since he had fallen in love with a Christian woman of that country. From her he had one son who was born before the ceremony, and he was a Roman Catholic even though he lived in the English manner. He said that he was Anglican only

140. *Podestà.*

141. The British and Dutch had attacked and burned parts of Mumbai in 1616. In 1661 the city was ceded to Britain when Charles II married Catherine of Braganza, the king of Portugal's sister. In 1668 the port was granted to the English East India Company, which established its headquarters there in 1672, shortly before Bembo's visit.

142. A type of Venetian cargo ship.

externally, being really a Catholic. He called upon the Blessed Virgin to witness it. He said it was necessary for him to live the way he did so as not to be bothered by the English. He showed much consolation at my arrival. He talked of Venice and called it his homeland with such tenderness and affection that tears often came to his eyes. He expressed the strong desire to end his days there, where he first had breathed. He was very courteous and would have offered me his house except that it was very small and occupied by women.

Another Venetian also came to visit me as soon as he learned of my arrival. His name was Francesco da Venezia. He was born in Castello and baptized in St. Peter's.[143] He had been away from his country already for twenty-four years. He had left as a sailor on the Republic's armed ships in the War of Candia expeditions. He had deserted and gone to England, leaving behind in Venice a brother named Andrea Brisiola with many sons. From England he went to Portugal, and with the ships of that king he had often gone to America in the office of pilot. In the expedition of some ships from Lisbon to the Indies at the time of the war with the Dutch he found himself in various encounters and battles with the enemy. He acted as a courageous and good soldier, as many Portuguese assured me. He received many wounds, however, particularly during an encounter with two Dutch ships. He defended himself from them for two entire days and finally saved himself with the special help of God. During that fight the Portuguese recognized that their vessel had been saved by heaven and by twelve Italian soldiers who defended it. They were of four nationalities: Florentine, Genoese, Livornese, and Venetian. During that encounter Francesco received many wounds in the head. From these they removed thirty small pieces of bone when he was taken care of in the royal hospital of Goa, where he was attended with every care. When he got out of the hospital, however, he was obliged to go begging, leaning on his crutches, since he had not even got his salary as reward for his courage and fidelity. The viceroy excused himself, saying that he had no money. Thus the poor man was reduced to sleeping in churches, since he also lacked clothing. After a few years of such an unhappy life, Divine Mercy took pity on him, in the absence of Human Justice, and his health got so much better that he threw away his crutches and left Goa without even taking leave. He went to the country of the

143. Located behind the Basilica of San Marco, St. Peter's is one of the oldest districts of Venice.

Moors and from there to Surat, where he served as pilot in several business voyages on the ships of those Moors. He even substituted for captain sometimes and was recognized with a large salary, since the Europeans are much esteemed in that work. He gathered thus a small sum of money, which grew until he had 8,000 ducats. He began to traffic in merchandise, and his ventures always went well. Encouraged by this good fortune, he left the profession of navigation and stayed in Surat. There he took a Christian woman of that place as wife and with her retired to Mumbai five years ago. There he built a house proper to his position. Every summer, however, he returns to Surat with some merchandise. In the winter he retires to his house with his wife and there lives civilly, wearing silk and having Moorish slaves in his service. He speaks Portuguese well, but he has almost forgotten his native language for not having exercised it in those parts. What matters most, however, is that he has remained a good Christian, and thus one sees clearly that Our Lord God has always assisted him and blesses his business and his honest efforts.

Enrico Gary suggested to me that I go visit the English President,[144] since this was the custom of persons of quality who arrived in that place. Since the next day was Sunday, a day when they do their praying, I decided to make the visit on Monday.

Meanwhile, Gary invited me on the morning of the 13th to his house to eat with the Father Rector. He sent for me a beautiful horse. He has not a very big house, which he built, but it is quite clean and well furnished with some fine things, among which I observed some door screens of very thin Indian cane bound together with silk threads of many colors. Small openings are left between the canes so that one can see through them. The meal was very worthy, partly Italian and partly English, but all on very fine Chinese porcelain, which is esteemed more than silver dishes are. He also had much silver and was served by Kafri slaves, that is, black Moors of Africa. At the same meal there was a certain German colonel named Bach. He has the direction of the artillery and also serves as engineer. He had been in that office for three years. He showed that he was a man of spirit and said that he had been in Milan at the time that that state was at war with France. He had seen Venice twice and had also spent time in Turkey. That day my firearms were brought to the house by the servants of the President. Gary offered me one of his boats to go to Goa as soon as the weather would permit.

144. The head of the East India Company in Mumbai.

On the 14th, with Gary and with the Father Rector, I went to visit the President. When we arrived at the gate of the fortress, we waited until the President had received news of our arrival, since no one can enter without his express permission. Since he was in council, which often gathered due to the troubles with the wars with the Dutch, and since the guard who had gone to advise him was not able to see him immediately, a Portuguese confidant of his came out to entertain us. He told me that he had orders from the President to ascertain when I would come so as to bring me to the fortress and send me a carriage with horses, since the streets were full of mud because of the rains of the winter. Shortly thereafter, he took us into the fortress and then into the palace, which had belonged to a Portuguese nobleman before the English had become owners of the island, although the [Portuguese] king had already confiscated it from him because of various crimes. Now the English have left a small courtyard around it and have enclosed it in the fortress, which is not yet finished, and made it the residence of the President. The fortress is set on a point of land toward Goa and is called by the name of the whole island, Mumbai. The island is not very large and is divided from the island of Salsette where Thane is by a small river. The entire island has nothing but three settlements—Mumbai, Mazagaon, and Mahim—of which Mumbai is the most important, since the fortress is there.[145] Having climbed the stairs of the palace, I entered on the right into a very long hall divided in the center by two curtains. The first space served as an antechamber, and there were various English gentlemen. When the curtains were parted, I saw at the end of the hall a majestic chair from which rose the President. He came toward me and greeted me with kindness. He had me sit at his right on a chair different from all the others with a green velvet cushion, like the one that he had on his own chair. With his good manners he kept me in conversation about my trip as well as about several things to do with Venice. He then passed to talk of India and told me that his company was no longer finding the earnings there that it had at first, when they were earning fifteen and twenty for one. Now the Dutch had taken some of the profit. His name was Gerard Aungier, a rather civil man of good height. He wore a wig and black clothing and had velvet slippers embroidered in gold on his feet and a sword at his belt. He had the title of Governor of the Island and Port of Mumbai, President of the English in

145. Modern Mazagaon is 3 km to the north of the fort; "Main" is Bembo's rendering of the district of Mahim in the city of Mumbai.

the East Indies, and head of the whole company in the north, who with the two presidents of the south together govern the whole company. He spoke good Italian and had learned it while traveling in many places in Italy. He had gone, however, neither to Rome nor to Venice, since during his travels he had received orders to embark immediately for the Indies, where he had arrived seven years ago. He had, though, seen the islands of the Republic [of Venice] at the time when Girolamo Grimani was Captain of the Ships and had received many honors from him. When the talk settled on the War of Candia, he exalted with high praise the constancy and valor of the Republic in defending it for so many years from the exterminating power of the Turk. He said that our homeland received real and well-merited praise for everything [it had done]. He added that if it had not been for the pullout of the French [troops], Candia would not have fallen. On this point he related the fable of the giants. When Jupiter saw their pride and their attempt to make war on heaven, he resolved to call the Council of the Gods, during which was declared the first war of Athens, in which many of them died as a punishment for their audacity. Then when their insolence was renewed in their descendants, the gods were again called to council, and the war of Troy was set upon during which an infinite number of heroes and soldiers fell. With good reason, then, he applied the fable to our case and said that it could be said that Jupiter had for the third time called a council to punish the Ottomans and had decided on the assault of Candia, during which the boldest and most experienced of the Turks died. However, the same could be said of almost all of Europe, since every Christian nation had lost in that war its best subjects in the profession of arms. He accompanied this discourse with many felicitous phrases. When he saw that I wanted to take leave, he asked me to stay with him to lunch. When the Father Rector observed that it was the Eve of the Assumption of the Blessed Virgin, [Aungier] ordered some fish to be found. It was in vain, however, since the hour was too late. He excused himself that he did not know that it was a day of abstinence, since the English have more sinners than Roman Catholics do. Nevertheless, he wanted us to drink something before we left. He had some wine from the Canary Islands brought and then some *Poli Pong,* which is a mixture of white wine, water, lemon, toasted bread, and nutmeg. With that we made many toasts, and he invited us to eat another day. I finally took leave, and he accompanied me to the stairway.

The governor, who has care of the fortress and the island in the absence of the President, went with me to the carriage that the President had ordered readied to take me home. It was constructed in the French manner and pulled by two oxen of the Bengal type. The soldiers of the fortress accompanied me. Since I needed some money, I resolved to accept the good will of Gary. I offered him some jewels for security, but he did not want to receive them and was content with a written account of the debt, which I gave him; I would pay him back in Goa. Nevertheless, it seemed to me that he did the favor coldly. In the meantime it had been discovered that the above-mentioned Count of Sargedas had been an impostor. Under that name he had received some money from the English in Madraspatan who owned that fortress in the Gulf of Bengal. When he had arrived in Bombain, he had pretended to be French, and when he went to Tanà, he had again taken that name. I thought that this example might have prejudiced my case, since I was going as a traveler in the same condition.

On the 15th the Father Rector did me the honor of inviting Gary to lunch. On the morning of the 17th in the church of that Father, and by order of the President, and with Gary assisting, all the Christians subject to that church were made to swear loyalty, swearing over the Gospels that in case of war they would take up arms in defense of the Company and of the King of England against any prince, without exception, and that they would fight to the death and be obliged to obey his officers, and [they] promised not to flee or show any kind of treason. Thus they all swore one by one. The Moors made the same oath on the Qur'an, and the Gentiles on the heads of their sons. In all, there were a great many people, since the island is very populous, not so much because of the freedom of worship that allows all rites the peaceful use of churches, mosques, and temples, as much as because they give shelter to all the criminals and deserters of nearby princes for all grave deeds that might have been committed. Among these [persons] are many Portuguese. When the ceremony was over, a high-ranking Englishman came with the President's carriage so that I would go to his house to eat. The day before, the invitation had been repeated. The Father Rector also came with me, as well as another religious. On entering the fortress I found that the troops presented arms in my presence. This is a distinguished honor and a sign of much esteem. On the stairway I was received by the President himself, who led me to a large room behind the hall. The windows had a beautiful view toward the sea. He told me that it was the intention of the Company to set up a city in that place, which would be bathed by the sea on three sides. In the same room a long table was set. Before we sat, several toasts were proposed, a custom of that nationality. The dinnerware was all of silver. There was a great abundance of meat and fish, mostly roasted. It would have been enough for a much greater number of people, since they brought in whole quarters of veal and beef. When the dinner was finished, we passed some hours in pleasant conversation, and I was sent home with the same carriage.

On the 18th Enrico Gary wanted to take me to Bandra, a town of the Jesuits, to whom he had promised that he would take me one day, since they had come to visit him.[146] We left in two palanquins, and in two and a half hours we arrived at the river that divides the island. When we had crossed the river in a boat, we were in Bandra, on the island of Salsette, where the Jesuit fathers command in the spiritual and in the temporal, except for death sentences. Around the walls of the church and convent, which is situated next to the sea, there are several bastions armed with many cannons to defend the entrance of the river against the Corsary pirates and others. When we had arrived at the gate of the convent, we had the Father Superior called for. He had us wait for quite a while, and [he] finally appeared with a sad and mortified face. His habit was so torn and worn, and his beret was so dirty, that he seemed to have come from the kitchen to frighten us, rather than from his cell to welcome us. He kept us at the door for a good while with a thousand affected ceremonies. Then he took us into the convent, which is handsome and big enough for twenty-six religious, even though usually there are only two there. One has the title of Vicar and keeps the church and the spiritual side, and the other is called Rector and is the Superior and has charge of the town and the production that is carried out by many subjects subordinated to him. He let us see the church, which has three altars. Meanwhile, a table for two was prepared in a corridor. He excused himself that they had already dined. The meal consisted of eggs and a few other trifles, which greatly surprised Gary, who had imagined a meal equal to their power, as he told me on our return. Those good fathers excused themselves, however, because of our unexpected arrival and [because it was] a day of abstinence. Thus after many and varied conversations we took leave. We crossed the river again and on our way back to the fortress went through the town of Mazagaon, not far from the sea, where Francesco da Venezia has his house.[147]

On the 19th Father Giacomo, whom I had sent for, arrived from Chaul, since the galliot of Antonio Suares di Soza, with which I had left Bandar-i

146. Bembo's "Bandorà" is on Salsette Island north across the Mahim River from Mumbai.

147. The district of Mazagaon is on the east side of Mumbai.

Kong, had not departed yet. On the 20th the weather began to improve and gave me hope that I would be able to leave soon for Goa. After lunch I went to see a very large avenue of palms, some of which are males and others females. So that they will be fertile, salt fish and other foodstuffs are buried in a ditch at their roots.

On the 21st a man from Candia who had been taken as a slave to Constantinople during the War of Candia came to visit me. He had been in the service of the Republic on a Paduan ship. Having fled from Constantinople, he had passed to these parts, where he had established himself in a sailing office and had done well. It is easier for such people than for people of higher position to better their fate.

On the 22nd Francesco da Venezia wanted to invite me. I did not know how to deny him this satisfaction, especially since every day he came to Mumbai and insisted. I went that very day to Mazagan to his house and heard Mass in a Catholic church, which is permitted by the English through the [treaty's] requirement set out in the transfer of the island.[148] In that town lives an English captain with some soldiers, which form a whole company. On a little hill not far from the town there is a half-destroyed palace similar to the one that is in the fortress of Mumbai. It belonged to a Portuguese gentleman and is going into ruin because of his negligence. The English, who have made Mumbai into a city, want to make this [place] into a fortress because the location is very apt. The said Francesco gave me a good and well-prepared meal. Since it was like our meals, I enjoyed it more than any other. All the servings were on fine porcelain, of which he has an entire set. The house itself is well kept and provided with all it needs. He keeps his wife dressed decently with gold and jewels, as is the custom of the country.[149] He is served by his slaves and governs himself in everything with prudence and is a good Christian. Since he is happy with his lot, he has abandoned entirely all desire of going back to his homeland. After dinner I went to walk along the marina, where I saw that several ships and boats

148. The Portuguese had seized the Mumbai islands from Bahadur Shah of Gujarat in 1534. In 1661 they were ceded to Charles II of England as part of the dowry of Catherine de Braganza. Seven years later he leased it to the English East India Company. Under company control the city grew rapidly from about 10,000 in 1661 to about 60,000 when Bembo visited. Among the city's rights granted by the British Crown were the following: to expand its territories, mint money, conduct military affairs, and exercise criminal and civil authority.

149. This reference indicates that she was probably Indian.

were being constructed so as to be ready to leave as soon as the weather permitted.

On the 23rd Enrico Gary had one of his *cibars* (as they call some small boats) put into the water. This cibar was to serve for my passage to Goa. Thus I lost no time in making the necessary preparations. On the 24th the President commanded drills involving all the persons capable of bearing arms who had sworn the oath of loyalty on the 17th. The muster field was under the windows of the convent where I was lodged. First, they ordered all the troops in the fortress that morning to pass by in general review. At that time they had taken weapons away from thirty Portuguese because they had asked to make an exception in their oath so as not to be forced to fight against the Portuguese. They had to leave the island immediately and returned to the mainland to the service of those petty kings. After lunch an official of the fortress put in order all those people, who were 1,500 persons, including about three hundred English. The rest were Portuguese, Moors, and Gentiles of every station; most were farmers and fishermen who were so poor that they could not even provide themselves with arms. The drill continued for some time, and when it was over, the President arrived on horseback, preceded by one hundred Moorish foot soldiers, paid by the Company as his particular guard, and accompanied by twenty of the principal Englishmen of the island on horseback. When he had arrived at the field, he looked it all over and went all around it with attention. Meanwhile, he was saluted by all the muskets and by the cheers of all the soldiers, who applauded his name, that of the King, and that of the Company. At the same time I was treated very politely by some English ladies who had come to that convent to see the ceremony. They had come from England with their husbands, who dealt in commerce. I conversed with them gladly, since they were very free and at their ease.

On the morning of the 25th I went to the fortress with Gary to take leave of that President. Although he had taken some medicine for a certain indisposition of his, he insisted on receiving me in his private quarters. He met me in a gold robe with a matching cap. When he heard of my resolution, he offered me for the passage to Goa a frigate of his that was already destined to go there. This was, however, only a compliment, because, besides knowing very well that I had the cibar of Gary, he had already offered the frigate to the Jesuits who were gathering in Goa to elect a Procurator for a chapter meeting in Rome. Nevertheless, I thanked him, as was appropriate because of his courtesy. Before letting me leave, he obliged me to join him in some toasts that he proposed to my good voyage. I do not know how good that was for him, since he had been taking medicine. When I had left the President, I went to take leave of Colonel Bach, who was sick. I thus went through the ceremony of leave-taking with his wife, a rather spirited English lady, from whom he had in dowry 20,000 pardaos, which was one of the most considerable sums on that island.

On the 28th, the weather being normal, I embarked around the 22nd hour, after having taken my leave of Gary and of the Father Rector, to whom I left a small token of gratitude for all the courtesy shown toward me all those days that I had stayed with him. Having left the shore, we went with the ship near the gate of the fortress where at that moment eight Jesuits were boarding the frigate of the President. All were from the north. I observed that the fortress was not yet finished on that side, although the President was using great diligence to continue the work with many workers.[150] I also saw that behind the fortress on the sea side there was the cemetery of the English. We were already away from land when we met the contrary current of the water, so we were obliged to drop anchor and wait for the current to shift [which occurred] about four hours before daylight on the 29th. Then we set sail with a good wind. At sunrise we saw the city and fortress of Chaul at a distance, which is 180 miles from Goa. Favored the whole day by the west wind, we went quite far in our voyage, also because that kind of boat is rather fast. Furthermore, to favor me even more, Gary had not only given me the boat but had not even loaded it with any merchandise, except for some melons of that island that he was sending as gifts to the viceroy of Goa and other friends. They are highly appreciated there, even though the flavor of even the best does not compare with that of ours. These cibar are not very different from the terrade of Persia mentioned above, except that in the prow and the bow they become quite narrow, like our felucca. In the middle, however, they are very wide and capacious. They have only one sail and ordinarily serve as transport for merchandise. If one wants cover, they join together several mats. The captain of the boat told me that the frigate could not leave port with that wind, and that traveling by cibar through these waters was more sure than with ships, because in a contrary wind one could take shelter in all the rivers, of which there are many along that coast. Large ships, however, had to go out to sea and lengthen their voyage and increase the danger. Around evening we found

150. The British had only recently gained control of Mumbai, and the paucity of Bembo's description is due to the fact that there was little to describe.

ourselves in front of Dabhol, which is twenty leagues distant from Chaul. Since the wind continued to be good all night, we found ourselves in sight of Rajapur on the morning of the 30th. This is the city of Shivaji, which is another twenty leagues distant from Dabhol. The wind from the west took up again, and around the 23rd hour, half the sail was furled for fear that we would pass beyond the port of Goa during the night. Although around the third hour the wind became somewhat contrary, bringing with it some rain, it ceased after a short while.

At midnight we happily entered the port, having recognized it through the call we were given from the fortress that is at its mouth. Guards are on duty there continually. Although all night there burns a great light on the tower as a signal to ships that are looking for the port, we were not able to tell the difference between it and many fires and lights that we saw along the entire shore. As soon as we entered the port, the guard who had called to us obliged us to stop. At daybreak on the 31st officials came to search the merchandise. Since there wasn't any, we were immediately dismissed. Since the cibar had to load some wine for its return, it entered a river on the left that does not lead to the city. Therefore, I took an *almaida,* which is a small boat made out of a single trunk. With it I went toward Goa, which is situated on an island divided from land by a very narrow river or canal of salt water. At its mouth, which the Portuguese call the port of Goa, there are two forts, one in front of the other, one on the island and the other on the mainland. The port, however, or river mouth, remains closed at the beginning of winter due to the quantity of sand that the wind carries there. It only opens at the end of winter with the north wind that disperses the sand. A little vessel can navigate the river up to the city then. Along that section [of the river] there are on both banks many palaces and gardens in good order. Once in a while there is a fort on the island and on the mainland that defends the entrance of the river, which is six miles long from the port to the city. The city is built on the most internal part of the island toward the mainland. In the outskirts it extends on the plain along the river, then it rises on various hills where there are mostly the convents of the missionaries, from which one enjoys a view of the island and part of the mainland.

When I arrived at the city, I went straight to the monastery of the Carmelites on one of those hills, where the air is better than in any other place. When I arrived there, I was welcomed with all affection by Fathers Valerio, Celso, and Giovanni Maria, who had come from Venice to Iskenderun on our ship and from there to Aleppo in our company. While they demonstrated every kindness because of our past friendship and because of the letters that I had from their superiors in Aleppo, the other clergy were no less kind, even though they had not seen me before. They immediately prepared for me the best rooms and were sorry about the bad manners that Padre Giovanni Seabra, mentioned above, had shown toward me. Because I wanted to disturb them as little as possible, I encouraged Father Giacomo to go to his own monastery.

[SEPTEMBER–OCTOBER 1673]

On the morning of the 1st of September the said Father Giovanni came to visit me. He was not living in his own monastery but in that of the Dominicans. Meanwhile, he had been appointed Inquisitor by the Viceroy with whose assistance he had excommunicated the Commissary General of the Dominicans with much scandal in that city. The Viceroy, who was not fond of that father, sent him after that in chains with another priest to Lisbon to render accounts for various acts. Father Giovanni paid me compliments and went through ceremonies as if it were the first time he had seen me. He told me that soon he would have to return to Europe and that he would go through Cairo and not through Aleppo or Jerusalem. After a few days I tried to take leave of the Carmelites and retire to a private house, but it was not possible, since they would not permit it and assigned me ample quarters in the convent for my greater comfort. Since their rule obliges them to eat Lenten foods all year and does not even allow meat to be brought into the refectory for guests, they would send me a generous provision of meat in the morning to my cell, and in the evening I would go with them to the refectory to eat fish, which all the Portuguese eat because it is a light food. They also immediately found me some money so that I could take care of some debts I had contracted in Daman and Mumbai. During the first days after my arrival most of the clergy came to visit me, and all the Italians. I then returned the honor they had done me.

The day of the 5th I went to the Theatine Fathers, who were only two Italians. The Superior is called Padre Carlo da Modena and is a very old man; the other was from Piacenza and had arrived there a short time before. They have a rather beautiful church, built with alms by the same Father Carlo. He is also beginning to build the monastery with the intention of establishing there a notiviate when it is finished. Meanwhile, they only have a hospice for their missionaries who pass by those parts. They are the best for religious ceremonies, since they do them in Italian fashion, with much admiration from the Portuguese. I also went to visit the Commissary General of the Franciscans and recommended Father Giacomo to him for the duration of my stay there. He seemed to be a very civil person. Also the Provincial of the Augustinians seemed very affable and talkative, unlike the Portuguese, who are by nature grave and serious. He has had dealings with many nationalities in the missions of those parts. Their monastery, which is ample, is a magnificent structure. It ordinarily holds forty clergy and is situated on a hill and enjoys the best air after that of the Carmelites.

The city of Goa is the metropolis of the King of Portugal's conquests in India. There the viceroy lives, and it is an archepiscopal seat, although it has been twenty years now that the church has been without a pastor, since the Pope had suspended the election of [a new] one due to the war with Spain. Afterward, an Augustinian was elected who died two years ago on board ship not far from port, while he was going to his residence. They were waiting for a new appointment. The city is situated in a land called Kanara by the natives [and is] on an island named Tizzuarin, which means thirty towns, because there were that many when the Moors went to live there.[151] The island is located in a small gulf formed by the mainland. It is surrounded by two pools of salt water that enter through two entrances made by the sea, one on the north side where the city is and one on the other side where it was in ancient times, which the Portuguese call the Port of Old Goa. These two meet and form the island of Tizzuarin. Then they enter the land and spread out in many canals that receive many small rivers, coming from those great mountains called the Ghats, and form various little islands. The island of Tizzuarin, or Goa, beginning on the point toward the sea [and extending] to its opposite side, is nine miles long and three miles wide at its greatest width. In all it has a perimeter of twenty-three miles. The entrance of the port is very famous, because it is capable of holding many

151. Kanara extended south and east of Goa. When the great Arab traveler Ibn Battuta visited the western coast of India in 1343–1344 on his way to China, he stopped in Sandabur, modern Goa. He describes it as an island bounded by a gulf and containing thirty-six villages and two cities, one being the older pre-Muslim Hindu city, the other being the Muslim city constructed after 1472, which contained a large jami' mosque that resembled the mosques of Baghdad. (*Voyages d'ibn Battuta,* Arabic text with French translation by C. Defremery and B. R. Sanguinetti [Paris, 1854], vol. 4, pp. 61–62.) Bembo's definition of *Tizzuarin* seems to be an error. The Arabic "thirty" is *thalathun.* *Tizzuarin* would mean "ninety."

sailing ships. It is formed, as can be understood by what has been said, by two points of the mainland that extend out in the form of a half-moon. At the innermost part is the point of the island that divides in half that ample gulf into two ports that are very large and very safe. On the western point of the mainland, called Salsetti, or coast of Calicut, the Portuguese have a considerable fortress called Marmagao.[152] Under it the place is very safe for any ship. On the other point, called Bardese, there is another fortress that they call of the Aguada.[153] In fact, there the ships get provisions of water before going out of the port. On this fortress is the light mentioned above. Another fortress is on the point of the island, and on a hill there is a church called the Madonna of the Point, from which one sees the sea on all sides. On the side of Bardese, the river gets narrow and forms the *bara,* or mouth of the river, which must be a pistol shot long. There are two more fortresses, one in front of the other. That on the island is called Gaspar Dias, and the one on the mainland is called "the Wise Men's,"[154] which was built by the viceroy Don Alfonso of Norogna, nephew of Don Alfonso of Albuquerque. Besides these, there were all around the island several other forts to prevent passage from the mainland. The principal ones were five, called Panjin (or Panjì), Agacaim, Banestarim, Goltim, and Domgrim (or Daugì),[155] which now have become seven with different names, that is, Panji, Ribandar, Domgrim, St. Blase, St. James, St. John Evangelist, and St. Lawrence. Some say that when the island was taken by the Portuguese those pools were full of *ramari,* animals similar to crocodiles, which in an instant devour a large calf or other animal that they might find in that water.[156] They had been placed there to protect the island so that people could not get there by swimming. Sabaggio, the lord of Goa, condemned those to be executed to be thrown into that water while trumpets were sounded as a signal to those

152. Marmagao protected the southern shore of the port.
153. Aguada guarded the northern shore of the port.
154. That is, the Three Magi.
155. *Panjì* is the Persian word for "five." On the northern shore of the island of Goa, Panji protected the mouth of the Goa River. Agacaim guarded the southern shore and a narrow passage of the Mar de Marmagao separating Goa from Salsette. Located near Ponda, Banestarim watched over the eastern land approach to the island. Goltim was in the island's northeast on the Goa River, and Domgrim protected the island's center.
156. *Gavials.*

beasts to come for their prey. Although they had multiplied considerably, these [reptiles] are now completely destroyed.

The island is very ancient in the histories of the Gentiles and the Moors, although when the Portuguese came to the Indies it had been but forty years since a Muslim Moor by the name of Malik Hasan had built there. From some signs and memorials that were found there after the conquest, however, it is believed that in ancient times it was inhabited by Christians. Among other things a bronze crucifix was found in the foundations of a house. It was sent by the viceroy Don Alfonso of Albuquerque to Portugal to King Emmanuel. They had a stone with a cross put up in that place with an inscription telling about this event. I saw that stone, which is in a street near the church called the Church of Mercy. At the same time there was also found a copy of a donation or gift of tribute made by a king called Mandtrasar to the priests of a temple. It began with the words: "In the name of God, creator of all the worlds, sky, earth, moon, and stars who adore Him, and in His name make their good shade, and His name is what sustains them. I render Him thanks and believe in Him who for love of his people desired to take flesh in this world." It follows then with the donation and admits in other words of the Incarnation of the Son of God and the mystery of the Trinity. From it one judges that they were Christian descendants of those converted by St. Thomas the Apostle, who brought the Gospel to India.[157]

When the Portuguese won the island with arms, it was ruled by King 'Adil Khan, son of Sabaggio (Çabaio), who had taken it by force from the Muslim Moors. Their entrance in the Indies is described differently by the Moors and by the Gentiles, but the Persians say that they entered there by force of arms in the year 707 of the Mohammedan empire, which is 1300 in our reckoning. They came under the command of a prince of the kingdom of Delhi, called Shah Nasr al-Din.[158] This man, as they say, passed to

157. The Syrian Malabar Christians (or Christians of St. Thomas) in southern India cite the apostle Thomas as their founder. The crucifix could also have belonged to a Christian—either Arab, European, or Indian—in Goa before Albuquerque's conquest. It was obviously important for the new rulers of Goa to establish their claim to legitimate rule through as ancient a Christian heritage as possible.

158. *Shah Nasr al-Din* refers to the Delhi (Bembo's "Delin") sultan 'Ala al-Din Khalji (A.D. 1296–1316), who used the traditional regnal title of *Nasir Amir al-*

the conquest of India with a powerful army from the north. Conquering the neighboring countries, he then entered victoriously into the kingdom of Kanara, which begins at the River Bat, not far from Chaul, and ends 270 miles farther down the coast at Cape Camorin, which is also called the Coast of Malabar. Engaging then in wars throughout all India, he introduced the impious sect in various kingdoms. Since it was all very odious to the Gentiles, they rebelled in 1479 and made a great massacre of Mohammedans, part of whom fled to take refuge on this island. Here, due to the convenience of the port, merchants from everywhere came with rich commerce, taking it away from other ports. Thus this city grew in fame and strength. When the above-mentioned Sabaggio took possession of it, it was dominated by Malik Hasan, the same who had built the ancient city of Goa, in defense of which he had 12,000 men. This Sabaggio was of low birth, and it is commonly thought that he was a native of Persia, from a city called Sabzavar, where his father made a living selling fruit. There he put himself at the service of a rich merchant, who, when he saw that the youth had spirit and diligence, sent him to India with twenty horses to sell. Since he had good fortune, he returned to his master with earning of 500%. The latter was so satisfied that he sent him the next year with another fifty horses. Since more than two-thirds of them died during the trip and he was ashamed to return with a loss to his master, he stopped in the kingdom of the Deccan. Through his brightness he introduced himself in the court of that king, called Mand, and fortune opened to him the road to extravagant prosperity. Others say that the master himself, very pleased at his good will, presented him to that king because of his talent. However it may be, it is certain that, taking up arms in the service of that king, he comported himself with such valor and fidelity that he received as prize the city of Gulbarga, of which he became absolute lord. There he governed with complete prudence and saved his revenues until he had gathered a good number of people. Then he began to take possession of many lands of the king of Vijayanagar that adjoined his. Afterward he enlarged the army and besieged

---

Mu'minin (Helper of the Commander of the Faithful) to indicate his nominal obeisance to the 'Abbasid caliph in Cairo: this designation may be the source of Bembo's name of "Nosaradin" (a combination of *Nasr* and *'Ala al-Din*) for the sultan. He initiated his invasion of the Hindu states of southern India with the conquest of Devagiri (Deogir) in A.H. 695 (A.D. 1296). The Muslim date A.H. 707 corresponds to A.D. 1307–1308, not 1300.

Goa. On the death of the above-mentioned Malik Hasan he took it and also the places adjacent to it. Thus he had established quite a vast and considerable state.

From the single district of Goa he gathered every year 500,000 pardaos of tribute, that is, 100,000 from the city, including the tax on horses, which amounts to forty pardaos each; 6,000 from the thirty towns of the island; and 3,900 from the nearby islands. From the passageways from the island to the mainland he collected 2,300; from the sale of spices in the city, 3,000. He got a large sum from a gambling house outside of which it was severely forbidden to gamble. The rest he got from many other taxes. The Sabaggio was one of the eighteen captains among whom the king of the Deccan had divided his kingdom. At his death he had him made tutor and governor of the kingdom and of the child who was to succeed him to the crown, who was at the time twelve years old. He then gave him one of his daughters as wife, with considerable riches.

When finally the Sabaggio died, full of glory, 'Adil Khan succeeded him in the kingdom.[159] He was peacefully enjoying his rule, until the viceroy Don Alfonso of Albuquerque arrived in those seas and deprived him of it

159. Bembo's account of Malik Hasan, 'Adil Khan, and Sabaggio is engaging but presents a confusion of names and histories, presumably derived from his unidentified source, reporting events of two centuries before. I have attempted to set out the principal historical facts and characters on which it seems to be based.

Malik Hasan is probably a reference to Hasan Nizam al-Mulk Bahri Malik Na'ib, a powerful official and vizier at the Muslim Bahmani court in the Deccan in the late fifteenth century. The Bahmanis controlled the dominant Muslim Decanni state, and Gulberga was one of its principal cities. Its chief Hindu rival was the powerful state of Vijayanagar. After the execution of the great Bahmani vizier Mahmud Gawan in 1481, the Bahmani kingdom entered a period of turmoil and disintegration, during which various local dynasties became autonomous. Sultan Muhammad Shah III died in 1482, the year after the execution of Mahmud Gawan. (Originally from Iran, Mahmud Gawan had been honored by the king with the title of *Malik al-Tujjar;* among his other accomplishments was the seizure of Goa from Virupaksha II, the Hindu king of Vijayanagar in 1471–1472.) Muhammad Shah III was succeeded by his son Shihab al-Din Mahmud (1482–1518), who was placed under the tutelage of Hasan Nizam al-Mulk Malik Na'ib, who was murdered soon afterward.

Goa was a flourishing city at the time and served as the principal western

by force of arms. When he arrived with his armada in sight of the island and wondered whether he could enter that port with his ships, he sent his nephew Don Antonio di Noregna with some troops. They met some enemy ships and fought so well that he put them to flight. He followed them inside a fortress where they had taken shelter and made himself master of it. All the Moors who had been in it brought such an account of the valor of the Portuguese to the city that they frightened the citizens, who immediately surrendered, so as to be able to plead for their lives with the victors. A principal instrument in the surrender was a certain Gentile of Bengal dressed as a yogi who had predicted some time before that that city would fall to a foreign people against the will of the inhabitants. Due to the respect for this prophet and because of their fear of the Portuguese, they sent to the viceroy an esteemed man named Mir 'Ali to ask for peace and offered themselves as good subjects of the king of Portugal. They begged the viceroy not to allow the sacking of the city. He gladly accepted the surrender, and on the 17th of February 1520, the principal citizens went to the shore to give him the keys of the city and the rule over their lives and goods, and [they] swore perpetual fealty to King Emmanuel, who was then reigning. After this ceremony the viceroy entered victoriously into the city and went to live in the

---

Indian port, a center of trade with western Asia and Africa. The dynasty's purported place of origin, discussed below, is the likeliest source of *Sabaggio*; the name of his famous vizier, Mahmud Gawan, is just as likely a source for Bembo's report of a "king, called Mand." The Bahmanis lost Goa to the breakaway and rival dynasty of the 'Adil-Shahs, based in Bijapur. As the Bahmani sultan, Shihab al-Din Mahmud *(Sabaggio)* had controlled Goa, and the purported death of the city's ruler in 1510 in Bembo's account may be a reference to the disintegration of Bahmani power and the assumption of power in the west by the new 'Adil-Shahi dynasty. This dynasty's founder, Yusuf 'Adil Khan, initially a slave in the service of the Bahmani vizier Mahmud Gawan, had risen to positions of great power in the Bahmani state before declaring himself an independent ruler in 1489. Subsequent 'Adil-Shahi dynastic histories claim that Yusuf 'Adil Khan was a son of the Ottoman sultan Murad II and was condemned to death when his brother Muhammad II became sultan, but through his mother's efforts he was smuggled to safety and subsequently educated by a merchant from the city of Sawa *(shahr-i sawa = sabbagio)*, a center for fruit-growing in northern Iran. Bembo's source attributes this history to *Sabaggio*.

palace of the Sabaggio, or of the defeated 'Adil Khan, which is now the house of the Inquisition.[160]

The first sign of peace and justice that the viceroy gave to those new subjects was an edict that he had published in Portuguese and Hindi[161] with which he assured all the inhabitants the rights to their property and permitted them to make commerce in whatever kind of merchandise and threatened grave punishment to those Portuguese who might dare to take anything from their rightful owners or otherwise molest them, be they Moors or Gentiles. With that edict he consoled the inhabitants and won himself their affection. After he had reflected upon the position and size of the city, he designated it as the metropolis of all the territory gained in India. Thus he decided immediately to fortify it, not so much because the dignity of a city that was to be the viceroy's residence demanded it, but rather because he feared that King 'Adil Khan, who had retired to the mainland and who had not given it up willingly, would soon make every effort to regain it.

This is what happened, because in a few months the subject cities began to deny tribute. They had heard that 'Adil Khan was coming with a powerful army to recover his states. In the city they had secret intelligence, so as to be able to betray the Portuguese. When they realized what was happening, [the Portuguese] began to prepare themselves with fortifications and to jail traitors so that they would betray their accomplices. Meanwhile, a captain of 'Adil Khan's tried to cross over to the island during the night with many troops on some barges and in some large baskets covered with

160. Bembo's summary of the capture of Goa exaggerates the lack of resistance. The unnamed Brahmin's prediction of foreign conquest is in line with other after-the-fact accounts of Brahminical predictions. Bembo's Mir 'Ali may have been the city's governor in the absence of Yusuf 'Adil Khan, but the city surrendered on March 4, 1510. Yusuf 'Adil Khan recovered it in May of the same year and held it until November, when Albuquerque seized it again with great cruelty to its inhabitants. Albuquerque was impressed with the beauty of the palace built by Shihab al-Din Mahmud and Yusuf 'Adil Khan in Goa and incorporated it within his fortification of the city.

161. "Hindi" is an unclear reference. The indigenous language of the Goan region was Maratha; Persian was the administrative and court language of the Bahmani sultanate; and Sanskrit was the sacred and official language of the Hindu majority.

leather.[162] Although the Portuguese gallantly fought him, he was successful, because he had [already] made a pact with some native guards. When it became known in the city that Kamal Khan, which was the name of that captain, had introduced these people on the island, the spirits, desires, and hopes of the Moors and Gentiles rose that they might have their former ruler again. Accordingly, since it was night, they killed all the Portuguese they found on the streets. When the viceroy saw that it was already impossible to stop such a universal revolt, he called his men to the fortress to defend themselves there. The city was immediately seized by the enemy, and Captain Kamal Khan put the fortress under siege. When the king came with 60,000 men, the viceroy could not hope to be able to hold out long. He asked to surrender, but the besiegers did not permit it. Thus he first had all those who were prisoners there killed, and, having opened wide the doors of the fortress, they all courageously came out, their weapons in their hands. They made way to the port on the last day of May and retired to the opening of the canal to pass the winter there. The enemy continued to harass them because they were afraid that they would try to take the city again. In order to spy on them, 'Adil Khan sent some food as a gift to the viceroy, accompanied with the message that knights should wage open war on their enemies, not kill them through hunger. But the viceroy understood the ploy and had two barrels of wine and a table with many biscuits laid out on the deck of the ship and thus surprised the ambassadors. All the men were wearing their armor and had a glass of wine and a biscuit. [The ambassadors] took word back to their king that the Portuguese were men of iron because they ate stones and drank blood, since they did not know what bread and wine were. When the viceroy heard the message of 'Adil Khan, he thanked him for the gift and praised it as one worthy of a prince, but refused to accept it. He said that his soldiers did not lack for food, and besides, they were accustomed to hardship and war and not used to such luxuries; that when they would need food, they were like birds who would rather look for it in freedom than receive it in cages. He added that when they ran out of food, 'Adil Khan would hear from them and have them, whether he wanted it or not, as guests at his table. The ambassadors were sent away with the entire gift and with additional gifts from the viceroy.

162. The "baskets" were probably inflated ox-skins, commonly used as floats for troops fording rivers. The event described took place at Agacaim on May 17, 1510.

They told 'Adil Khan how little account had been paid to his gift, and [the king] resolved to harass them frequently with arms. In several exchanges the Portuguese came out the losers. Because of these external events and the internal turmoil caused by the lack of food on the ships, the viceroy decided to leave the channel of Goa on the first of August. The sand had opened up. As soon as the weather permitted, he spread the sails and took all the wounded and sick to Anjidiv Island.[163] Shortly thereafter, they saw four ships that they thought were the sultan of Cairo's, and they prepared themselves for battle. But when they came near and unfurled their flags, they saw with much relief that they were Portuguese going to Malacca and commanded by General Don Diego Mendez. They went with them to Cananor,[164] where seven other Portuguese ships, commanded by Don Consalvo of Sequieria, soon arrived, on the way to get spices. All of them had been separately sent by the king with different orders. The viceroy thought, however, that with the arrival of these ten ships (one had been lost en route), his forces had been increased and that they could try to retake Goa. He proposed the matter in council. Although at first the two generals were reluctant—one not wanting to delay his return to Portugal, the other wanting to proceed directly to Malacca—yet when they had considered the importance of that endeavor, they promised to follow him. Thus the viceroy immediately ordered Timogia,[165] who was a Gentile captain friend of his and who was a relative of the king, to go on land with 6,000 men to besiege Goa by land. He himself would do the same by sea. He left Cananor without delay with twenty-three well-stocked ships. He arrived in the port of Goa on November 20, 1510. He made a personal oration to the soldiers and gave them such encouragement that, even before finishing, he was interrupted with a courageous "To arms!" from everyone. In that moment, dividing his forces among several captains, even though Timogia had not yet arrived, he ordered the debarkation and the besieging of the city. He resolved to attack on the night of the 25th and commanded that the first assault be made at a gate, later called St. Catherine's, because it was her Feast Day: thus the besieged would all run to that place thinking that all the effort was being placed there. So it happened, and the attackers were able to scale the walls without difficulty in many other places. The Moors were confused

163. Anjidiv Island is 90 km south of Goa.
164. The city of Cananor in the northern part of the Malabar coast.
165. Identified in other sources as Timoja.

at being attacked from the rear and tried to flee. But they were pushed by their commanders to make a desperate sortie through the gate just mentioned, which was the reason for their total loss. Courageously pushed back by the Portuguese, they reentered the city with the attackers. The Portuguese took the gate, and the viceroy himself entered with many troops. They hacked to pieces all those who did not save themselves by fleeing and abandoning the city entirely. The first Portuguese who entered was a certain Dinis Fernando of Mello.

Having taken possession again of the city in this way, [the viceroy] immediately issued an edict extending security to the lives and goods of the Gentiles who had remained in the city and on the island. He made them understand that they could freely go to their houses and work in the countryside, paying only the ordinary tribute of the country, because he was not making war on them but only on the Muslim Moors. So that the government would be more to their liking, he gave authority in litigations and differences among the Gentiles according to their ancient laws to Timogia, who had arrived in the city in the meantime, even if late. With this [ordinance] he quickly and easily reestablished order both inside and outside the city. He then applied himself to make better defenses for it than before. To this effect he erected a new fortress with the name of Emmanuel in honor of the reigning king. He also decided to leave a visible memorial to himself, the captains, and the soldiers who had behaved with valor in that assault. [But] he was not able to do as he wished, because when he had had incised on a stone a succinct account of the capture of the city with his name and the names of those he thought most worthy of that honor, there were many complaints on the part of others whose names had not been placed there. To quiet the complaints, he decided to turn the stone around and put the written part into the wall of the tower, where it is still conspicuously visible. On the other side he had these words cut: *Lapidem, quem reprobaverunt aedificantes, factus est in caput anguli.*[166] All were satisfied to see that everyone had received equal treatment. The nature of the Portuguese is such that praise of a companion bothers them more than lack of praise to themselves.

166. This appropriate quotation comes from the Latin Vulgate Bible, Psalm 118:22: "The stone which the builders rejected has become the chief cornerstone." (*The New English Bible* [Oxford and Cambridge: Oxford University Press and Cambridge University Press, 1970].) It is cited by Christ in Matthew 21:42. I am grateful to Dr. John Osborne for identifying the source.

The viceroy did many other actions worthy of immortality, for which he merited the title of Alfonso de Albuquerque the Great. He established a mint in Goa for making coins that were to serve for commerce in the Indies. To the gold coins he gave the name *emmanuels*, to the silver *speri*, and to those of copper reales. The mint was immediately rented by some Gentiles for 2,000 pardaos. With all these considerations of politics he did not lose sight of the principal goal, which was the growth of the sons of the Catholics, as well as the growth of the [Christian] faith among the Gentiles. Thus he thought of an excellent means to take care of both these objectives. Having already captured the spirits of his new subjects with the mildness of his rule, he ordered that Portuguese marry daughters of the natives, who had first been persuaded to become Christians. He gave each bridegroom fifty *scudi* from the royal treasury and assigned them land on the island for the appropriate support of the wives and the sons who would be born. Although it was at first hard for the Gentiles to have their daughters change religion and leave their houses, they saw that they acquired honor and fortune, and they competed with one another to become related to the Portuguese. They tell of one time when the viceroy had many of these marriages performed together in his house. They were entertained until late at night, when all retired to their rooms. Because of the darkness and because they did not know their wives well yet, they got confused and went to bed with the wives of one another. When they realized their mistake in the morning, each took back his own wife and peacefully settled all questions of honor. The viceroy was so fond of these couples that he called the men "sons-in-law" and the women "daughters." To this day their descendants are the principal nobility of India. Those women, although brown in color, were of Brahmin families, which are the most esteemed among the Gentiles. That same olive color is still preserved today in the mestizos, their sons and descendants. They are called thus by those of Lisbon, because of the mixture of Christian and Gentile blood; however, they do not like this name and consider themselves insulted by it. Between the mestizos and the Portuguese reigns an inborn hate and antipathy, which I believe they got from their Gentile mothers' milk. Often they come to blows, even though the mestizos are not courageous and are of weak physique, perhaps because of the food and water they take. They are of little spirit in everything. They allow themselves to be ruled by women, of whom, however, they are extremely jealous.

When the viceroy had settled the principal matters of the city and of his new dominion, he began to gather 52,000 pardaos revenue annually, 12,000 of which were paid by the island of Goa and 40,000 by the other islands and the mainland subject to it. All these revenues were distributed by order of the king among these initially mixed couples, so as to please everyone in the population. At that time the city was not very large. One can still see it in the moat that began at the church of St. Francis and ended at the church of St. Dominic. As the population increased, it was enlarged considerably by the Portuguese. It embraces the nearby hills. On the side of the river it extends about two miles, from the ammunition dump to the Church of the Reformed Fathers, called the Church of the Mother of God. This church is now outside the city [in an area that is] mostly in ruins, and only some palaces and monasteries remain of importance today. The convents are those mentioned of St. Dominic and of St. Francis, of the Carmelites, and of the Jesuits (called "of the good Jesus"). In their church there is a chapel to the right of the main altar with the body of St. Francis Xavier, called the Apostle of the Indies. It is enclosed in a very rich gold casket with precious stones. The church of the Theatines is in the plaza near the palace of the viceroy and that of the Augustinians is on a hill near the ammunition dump. The Dominicans have another monastery on the sea, where they have their school, named St. Thomas. Another school is that of the Franciscans, named St. Bonaventure, the church of which does not have a door on the street. The Jesuits have two others, a large and noble one called St. Rocco and an old one called St. Paul. The Augustinians have one attached to the monastery and thus occupy a good part of that hill, which is the best location in the city for air. At the foot of that hill there is a convent of nuns, unique in the city, subordinate to the archbishop, but administered in temporal and spiritual affairs by the Augustinians, since it is of the same order. It is quite rich and ample. Usually there are about eighty nuns of the noblest families. They are served by many native women and Moorish women from Africa, who stay there with them. All the monasteries are big and magnificent, and they continue to grow. The clergy buy ruined places near them, or they receive property in inheritance, since the Portuguese want to give much to monasteries when they die. These latter get bigger, and the clerics live splendidly without reflecting about the rest of the city, which is deteriorating, nor about the poor beggars who die of hunger.

The houses that are standing are big and have many ways to take in fresh air. Due to the rains that fall abundantly in winter, the roofs rise pyramidally. The rains are often accompanied by strokes of lightning, which happened more than twenty times while I was there. The streets are mostly long and wide, but nearly deserted because of the absence of shops. Things usually get sold in private houses or in the towns of the banians. This is bothersome. As I have already said, it is necessary to buy a whole piece, even if one only needs a little. Besides, they often want the money even before letting one see the goods. Workers never do anything unless they receive half their pay in advance.

Despite all this, there are Portuguese and Gentile merchants who, besides their ordinary merchandise, have considerable business in jewels and diamonds. They get these [precious stones] especially from Golkonda, which is a city of a vassal king of the Great Mogor, thirty days distant from Goa and near the city of San Thomé.[167] They find the diamonds in some mountains. The merchants buy pieces of land without being sure that they will find anything to dig there. During the excavation an official stands by to be sure that they do not exceed the length, width, and depth of the land they have purchased. Also, they appropriate the largest diamonds for the Great Mughal, who therefore has extraordinary and very valuable ones. Into Goa, too, come [diamonds] in considerable quantity and quality. Anyone who knows about them and who might have cash, gold cloth from Europe, or occidental jewels, especially emeralds and red coral, could make some very good investments. They particularly esteem emeralds.

None of the Gentiles and Portuguese of Goa wears stockings, due to the heat. The merchants, however, currently dress in the French manner, and the Christian natives of the island in the Spanish fashion. All the nobles use the palanquin, which was at first prohibited by the Inquisition. They thought it indecent that Christians should have themselves carried on the shoulders of other men. Besides, only the Gentile kings use them, and they claim divinity. Few Portuguese engage in mechanical arts. As soon as they pass the Cape of Good Hope, they profess nobility, even if lowborn. To encourage his subjects to travel to the Indies, which is difficult, the king has granted the privilege of nobility to whoever goes there. Thus they are

---

167. One of the major fortified cities in the Deccan, Golkonda was ceded by the Hindu state of Warangel to the Bahmani kingdom in 1363. After the dissolution of the Bahmani dynasty it became the capital of the Qutb-Shahi dynasty in 1512 and preserved its nominal independence until 1687, when it became part of Awrangzeb's Mughal Empire. It was a major cultural and commercial center and the most important diamond market in Asia, described by Marco Polo in 1292 and by numerous later travelers. Bembo's geography is off, however, since Golkonda is near Hyderabad, not San Thomé on the Coromandel coast.

all fancy and armed and dress in silk and carry swords, except for the doctors in law and in medicine. By virtue of that privilege they aspire to equal the nobility of the king. Pietro della Valle says in this regard that he thought it ridiculous to see merchants armed and a mechanic dressed as if he were courting. All the arts are thus practiced by the natives of the kingdom of Kanara, whether Christian or pagan. These dress as in Surat and partly go naked, as was described before. This is due to the excessive heat. In Goa the sun is perpendicular two times in the year. In that season, especially at midday, when the sun is highest, there is no house or tower, no matter how tall, that provides any shade. In the whole year there is no more than an hour's difference between the longest and the shortest day. The people of Kanara, although they are Christians, preserve some customs of the pagans, especially that of a person's not changing the family profession and of not taking a wife from a family of a different office.

Besides the people of Kanara, there is another group of people in Goa, called *Kafri.*[168] These are Negroes of Africa. Although most are Christians, they are all slaves. Usually they serve to carry an umbrella behind their masters, whether they are in a palanquin or on foot. They are quick at walking. They are of a proud and bold nature. They are responsible for almost all the homicides and fights in the city. Usually they carry a bamboo in their hand and undertake any task, even if dangerous, given them by their masters. They are very united and faithful among themselves.

Franciscans do not wear the thick woolen habit because of the heat, but instead an ash-colored cloth one. Only sometimes do they wear the woolen mantle. The Augustinians wear a long silk habit with sleeves that reach the ground. The other orders dress as in Europe. Jesuits have only their caps different, as I have said above.

The dress of the Portuguese women is almost like that of the Gentiles of Surat. They wear a short blouse of very fine cotton through which the flesh can be seen. From the waist down they cover themselves with a silk or cotton cloth of various colors that comes from Bengal. They go barefoot and use only velvet slippers that allow part of the foot to be seen. Thus they wash their feet and themselves often. They tie their hair in a white cap, which they wear inside the house. When they go out, they put very fine cloths of many colors on their heads, and they adorn themselves as much as they can with jewels, pendants, and bracelets. The women live in constant laziness,

168. Elsewhere he spells it "cafri."

since they have nothing to do, not even for entertainment. They pass whole days having their slaves move them. They sit on a rope that is attached to beams, and the slaves swing them; or they have themselves massaged to make it easier for them to sleep. The men do the same. It is impossible for them to sleep without these things. Not all do it in the same way. Some have their whole bodies rubbed, others have their joints moved, others have their bodies pinched; and others have themselves tickled and slightly scratched all over. Still others have their feet scratched. Since this is women's work, they pass easily from these to other, greater confidences and freedom. I tried this custom of theirs because they insisted. At first, it kept me from sleeping and bothered me, but after a few times I enjoyed it.

They have another custom practiced by both men and women, which rather resembles the vice of tobacco among us. This is the eating or chewing of betel leaf and betel nut.[169] Betel is a leaf in the shape of a heart and similar to ivy. In fact, it grows like ivy around trees and walls. In the language of the country it is called *pan*. Betel nut is called *foufel*. It is a very hard fruit the size of a chestnut, but red with some white veins. The tree is tall, straight, and thin and produces branches and fruit only at the top. They chew the two together. First they put on the leaf a little lime made from oyster shells. They say that the mixture is good for the stomach. It is of a pleasant smell and spicy hot to the taste. It leaves the teeth and lips colored red, which makes women attractive. The men, however, try to remove it. They use this betel leaf and betel nut in all their conversations and give it to their guests, particularly after eating. The women use it so much that they don't stop chewing it even in church. They do not make exceptions for the days of communion, so that many have been scandalized. Then too, they leave little pools of spittle and water where they have been.[170] They use water to wash their mouths and have it carried after them in little earthenware jars that keep the water rather cool. They also have carried after them a little basket or box with provisions of betel leaf, lime, and betel nut. This mixture is rather exciting and provokes licentiousness. Because of idleness and these things, the women are excessively passionate. They join themselves too easily to others, especially to relatives and religious, because they are not watched carefully and because they know how to keep quiet. Thus from

169. Betel leaf and betel nut or areca.

170. Modern pan preparation and consumption is not significantly different from what Bembo describes.

many houses this mixture is completely banned. They also know how to use witchcraft for reasons of love and hate. And they use poisons that are easy to give people in food, since they all eat in separate dishes. They put [poisons], too, in candied fruits, of which they are very fond.

Since I have just mentioned fruits, to which I have referred elsewhere without describing them, I think it appropriate now to describe the principal ones as well as those that are most appreciated in those parts. The most popular is the pineapple, which I liked best. Its taste is between sweet and sour. In color, shape, and texture it resembles a pinecone. The skin is soft, however, and on top it has a tuft of green and white leaves that are not very long and resemble an artichoke. When these are cut and planted again, they make the fruit grow again, which does not grow above the ground but on it, like melons. It is cleaned like the citron and is similar to it in its solidity, but juicier. In color it is between white and green. Inside, it has some small seeds that are black like those of apples, but these do not serve for planting. The fruit is good for the digestion and would be very delicious if it were eaten cold.

The cashew is ordinarily eaten with soup or fish. Since it is very bitter, they first cut it into pieces and leave it in water with some salt so that the bitterness will come out. I did not like it at all. In form and color it is like a long apple. On the top it has a pit of a green color that is shaped like the horn of our Doge. When it is planted, it makes the fruit again. This, too, is cooked to eat the nut, which tastes like chestnuts. The tree is not very tall, and the flowers give a good smell.

The banana, called "fig of India" by the Portuguese, but *mouz* by the Persians and Arabs, is more popular than the pineapple. It is less esteemed, however, because there are many of them, and they grow all year. I have eaten some of these also in Tripoli. Their size and length is like that of a small cucumber, except for those of Mumbai, which the Portuguese call "for *azar*," that is, for roasting.[171] These [bananas] are longer. In taste they are like ripe pears. They grow from a plant that does not develop as a tree and does not have branches, but rather six or seven large leaves that grow close together. They grow to the height of a man and more. In the middle of these grows a long stalk with sixty or seventy figs that at first are green, then yellow when they are ripe. When the skin is removed, they are white and have

---

171. Evidently a reference to the plantain.

some small seeds about half the size of pear seeds. These are not used to make a new plant. Rather, they use the seeds of the same plant.[172] Before the first figs are ripe, a new plant comes up that produces its own fruit in a short time. Thus they make one plant after another, because one plant does not have fruit more than once. When they have gathered the figs, they cut the plant, which would be useless. It does not produce flowers but rather more plants to make its sweet-smelling fruit. They say that in Egypt one finds this fruit. Those people believe that this was the fig tree whose leaves Adam used to cover himself when he was ashamed to be naked.

The most appreciated fruit in India is the mango. They call it the king of fruit. I did not like it so much, however, because it is so sweet. It resembles the peach in shape, size, and texture, but it is juicier, and the skin is thicker. The pit resembles the heart of a man. The inside of the pit, if eaten, leaves an aromatic smell in the mouth, and it is an aphrodisiac. The tree is rather large and produces much fruit, which flowers in January and matures in May and June.

The papaya is a fruit similar to the melon, except that it grows on trees and is a bit smaller than ordinary melons. In the rest—the form, the green color outside with some marks, the red inside with its seeds, and the taste itself—it resembles the melon. Its seeds, however, are black and look like pepper grains. The taste is sweet and not strong. The tree is not very large, but is straight with a smooth trunk. It produces a few branches all at the top, and the fruit is there also. It produces fruit the same year it is planted, and they are ripe in November and December.

The rose-apple is a rather fine fruit of the size of an apple. It has a sweet smell and leaves a nice smell in the mouth. Its water is sweet smelling, like roses. It is whitish in color, and they say that it cools the temperament and is good for melancholy. There is another fruit called rose-apple of Malacca, so called from the city of this name. It is smaller and of the color of citron with a smooth skin. It is more sweet smelling, less juicy, and sweeter.

The jack fruit is a fruit that grows around the trunk of its tree and on the biggest branches. It is of the size of a pumpkin, which it resembles from the outside, only that its skin is very rough and tender, although it is thick. Inside it has many nuts similar to chestnuts, around which there is a cer-

172. Bananas grow from rhizomes.

tain yellow material, sweet and good to eat; in some it is liquid, and in others it is solid. The tree is rather tall and does not make flowers.

The sweet-sop[173] is a rather good fruit, similar to a green pinecone, with a thick skin that is removed in sections. Inside it has some seeds the size of pine nuts, and around them there is a white stuff that is watery and sweet. The tree is not very large.

Similar in size and quality is the yam, which has an outer skin of a brown color and which is harder.[174] They also have some fig plants, but they produce little fruit. They have been brought from Portugal, like some grape vines. These [vines] are cared for very carefully but do not grow well. Those that produce grapes get them in February. There are other, less important fruits, besides a great abundance of oranges, lemons, and citrons. There are some oranges called *Batavian,* although some say that they were brought from Socotra, an island at the mouth of the Red Sea, where aloe grows. These were brought as gifts by the Commissary General of the Franciscans and are very esteemed. They are of the form and size of large citrons, which they resemble also in their interior color and in their seeds. These, however, are large, like those of our watermelons. Inside, they are of a bright red color. They are of a delicate and sweet taste. I brought some of the seeds to Venice and tried to plant them, but was not successful because the difference between our climate and that very hot climate was too great. They give off no smell, and the plant is of the ordinary size of other orange trees, which are very big there.

Pepper grows on a plant that is similar to ivy and also climbs around trees and on walls. It produces its fruit in bunches, like grapes, first green and then black. They say that before loading it for Europe, they boil it. Cinnamon is the bark of a tree that in the size and shape of its leaves is similar to laurel, except that the leaves of the cinnamon tree are larger and have the same smell as the tree. They put them in water and wash themselves with it. It grows in several places in India, but best on the island of Sri Lanka. During the season they go into the woods, which are full of these trees. Many workmen there open the bark of the trees with knives. This then dries in the sun and drops to the ground. They gather it and cut the nude branches so that it will give new shoots. They do it every year. There are also many sugarcane plants, particularly in Bassein. It is very similar to

173. Bembo calls it the *atas.*
174. Bembo calls it *batatos.*

ours. Inside there is a white material that, when squeezed and purified in fire, leaves sugar, which is then sent to our countries.

I also observed flowers, which are no less different from ours than the fruits. To describe them would be too much of a digression without need, so I will note only one that seemed to me very extravagant. It is called turmeric.[175] It is similar to the jasmine in form, but different in its color, which is yellow. It is also called saffron of India. They use it in many of the ways we use saffron. It has this name of turmeric because it flowers only at night, very profusely. In the morning when the sun comes up, it dries and falls from the tree, which is very large with rather small leaves. Cotton grows everywhere in India in great abundance. They sow fields of it like wheat. It makes a plant about six palms high that produces some smooth chestnut-like fruits inside of which is the cotton with its black seeds, like apple seeds. From it are spun very fine cloths. That should be enough about fruits and flowers and such things of India so that the reader will have enough information about them. I think it is time to return to the narrative of our journal and to other details of more importance.

Counseled by the Carmelites, whose advice I usually followed, I decided to go visit the viceroy. My visit was delayed some days, however, because he had much to do with the arrival of three ships from Lisbon. On the morning of the 12th I went to the palace with the Prior of the Carmelites and with Father Giovanni Seabra. When I had climbed the stairs, I was introduced into some rooms that had no furniture except for some paintings. These served more as a frieze than as decoration. They had painted on them all the ships that had come to India from Portugal up to that time, along with their names, the names of the captains and the directors of convoys, along with information about whether all the ships of a convoy had arrived and the names of those that had been lost. In one of the rooms there was a window that looked into a smaller room that had the silverware of the viceroy on display. This consisted of a good set for the table and some bowls. I did not stop to comment about them for fear that they should think I had not seen things like them in our country, where, in fact, such items would have been ordinary.[176] I stayed in those rooms until Father Giovanni had

175. Bembo gives two names—*malinconico* and *trisoe*.

176. Despite his open-mindedness toward much of what he sees, Bembo retains an understandable pride in Venice and the visible signs of prosperity with which he grew up. There is no evidence that he is personally affected by,

gone inside to advise the viceroy. Shortly afterward, a man came to introduce me into another room that was also unfurnished. There was a door that passed beyond, and in front of it there was a screen a little distance from the door. It was fixed to the floor. They do that to let air pass without at the same time being seen. I saw leaning against it a man of good presence but ordinary dress. I thought he was a person in the viceroy's confidence who was there to introduce me. Therefore I advanced to pass into the other room, where I had seen the man enter who had accompanied me. As I got close to the screen, however, I heard the prior speaking with that person in very reverential and submissive terms, and I realized that he was the viceroy! I made the appropriate greetings, for earlier I had greeted him in a summary fashion due to the false guess I had previously made. He seemed not to understand Italian, so the prior gave him my greetings in Portuguese, and he responded kindly. Then I remembered that it is the custom of those viceroys to receive high-ranking people while standing so as not to give them a seat. When he passed through [Goa] on his way to bring help to the city of San Thomé, the General of the French was received in the same manner, for which he was subsequently very sorry. Since I was leaning against the door screen while I was talking with him, he thought, as I was told later, that I had done it on purpose to put myself on equal terms of rank with him. He was of good appearance and well mannered. In our conversation about various things to do with Europe and Italy, he seemed very informed, and although he pretended the contrary, he spoke Italian well. He was about forty-six years old, and his name was Luis di Mendozza Fruttado d'Albuquerque.[177] He was a partisan of the prince, who had given him the first command of the armada. He had behaved bravely during the war with the Dutch in India, so he had been made viceroy of India. Although this office is not full of pomp and ceremony, it has great authority and esteem in India; and it is very worthwhile financially. In addition [to their office], some engage in commerce, especially in jewels. They get the most precious

---

or even aware of, the extraordinary damage done to Venetian commerce by the success of western European maritime nations (Portugal, the Netherlands, Britain, and France) in wresting control over India Ocean trade from Indian and Arab merchants and shipping.

177. Luiz de Mendonça Furtada de Albuquerque, Conde de Lavardio, served as viceroy of India from 1671 to 1677.

ones. Following their example, the other ministers of the fortress do the same, to the detriment of their subjects.

After some talk I took my leave. He was very courteous and ordered that I be shown through the palace, which is quite large. I saw the royal hall, which is rather vast and majestic but a little dark. There the council meets, and he receives ambassadors. At one end of this hall there is a baldachin of velvet with a companion chair and a small table. There is no other comfortable place to sit nor any other furniture, except for some paintings. These are the height of a man and are the portraits of all the viceroys and governors of India. Excluding the viceroy, there are only three governors.[178] Underneath are written their names and the time of their government and the noteworthy incidents of their rule. The first viceroy was Don Francesco d'Almaida.

Adjoining the hall is the chapel of the viceroy. On going out of the palace I saw some armed banians, the ordinary guard. In the courtyard are the jails; previously, they used to keep the gunpowder there, but because of a fire that greatly damaged the palace, they have moved it outside the city to a powder depot. At the palace begins a rather beautiful street ending at the Church of the Misericordia. It is called Straight Street, since it really is. At one end of this street the merchants gather to do business. Walking along this street, I met some judges, whom they call *desembargadori*. They are sent from Lisbon and are changed every once in a while. They wear long robes with long sleeves and carry a long rod in their hands. The viceroy has no right of life and death over them or over the knights. He can imprison them, however, until the king orders that they be sent to Lisbon to be sentenced. Not far off is a royal hospital under the care of the Jesuits. Only soldiers are taken there, along with knights. Near this hospital there is a vast courtyard full of wood to build ships, and they say that cannons are made there too.

Near the Church of the Misericordia there is the house of the spinsters

178. Portuguese royal authority in India had been vested in viceroys, in governors, and occasionally in commissions of two or more individuals. The first viceroy, Don Francisco de Almeida, had ruled from 1505 to 1509 and had been succeeded by Don Alfonso de Albuquerque (1509–1515). At the time of Bembo's visit the incumbent viceroy was the fifty-third legitimate governor of Goa, as well as the viceroy of India. There were also three governors in charge of the other Portuguese colonies.

who are noble orphan girls. They are kept cloistered until they marry, when they receive a dowry established by the king, at whose expense the whole place is kept. In this same place are women who are separated from their husbands, and women whose husbands are off on some mission, and all are maintained by the king. There is also a house for reformed women, and they have a church dedicated to St. Mary Magdalen. There was a funeral on the 18th in the church of the Carmelites for a rich merchant named Simon Riberro of Lisbon, who had died a few days before my arrival. He had given the fathers a sum of money with the stipulation to use it to complete a portion of the monastery that they had already begun. He had also appointed them executors of the rest of his considerable fortune. His things were sold at auction, as they do there even among nobles. Among the other things some diamonds were sold. They also sell slaves at auction, even if they are baptized. The clerics themselves sell and buy them for their own service. In the funeral the office of the dead was sung very well. The musicians belonged to the Augustinian choir, since all those clerics, except the Carmelites, keep a school where the pupils are dressed and maintained by them and follow their same style of life. Besides science, they teach them music for the solemnities of the churches. The Carmelite church was all decorated in black. In the middle there was a catafalque with many lights and with the heraldic arms of the deceased. With his inheritance they are building a hostelry with a staircase separate from the monastery, so that the clergy and the guests will be less bothered. Many of the guests come from Italy and France and stay there with those clerics, who receive them with great amiability. Since at that time this place was not yet finished, they assigned me, as I said, some of the best cells. They helped me all the time. Since there was not much to do there, I seldom went out of the house. More for the sake of decorum than need, I also had a palanquin that the fathers had found for me, along with the four bearers and the servant with the umbrella. All this cost eighteen pardaos a month without any other obligation.

On the 20th the Superior and other fathers took me to a country place of theirs called the Lagoon, because it is situated in a low place that is flooded all year due to the winter rains. It is a place of recreation for bird hunters, who go there to hunt ducks and other water birds that gather in great numbers in those swamps. Around this lake there are many delightful places belonging to various knights. It is not farther from the city than half an hour's walk, so that many have it as their permanent residence. The house of the fathers there was left to them by a knight along with a piece of land. They are obliged to say Mass for him, so they have built a small church there and keep a priest there all the time who also looks after the house. It is a private place, and they go there to rest. There they send priests who are convalescing and novices who are studying, since the house is large and has many rooms. All the beams are of carved and gilded wood, very hard and long-lasting and called teak. Around the walls of all the rooms at about two arms' height from the floor there is a frieze of majolica in many colors. It is not very fine work and is made in the kingdom of Cambay.[179] It is the only ornament in the whole palace. In the gardens are the remains of many fountains that indicate that this was a very delightful place.

On the morning of the 21st I went to hear mass in a church on a little hill that is the parish church for the houses and nearby workers. It is called the Rectory and is administered by a single cleric who has the title of curate. These rectories are taken care of by clergy, and since those islands and places on the mainland subject to Goa are very rich and depend partly on Franciscans or Dominicans or Augustinians or Jesuits, they are positions much coveted by the clerics. And for this reason there is much rancor and discord among them. Those rectories are not only free from the rule of the cloister, but the curates also keep many servants and palanquins and live in great luxury and comfort. Only the Jesuits with their prudence keep themselves free from these scandals, even though they are by far richer than all the other groups together. It is common knowledge that in the Portuguese lands in India alone they take in annual revenue 12,000 more reales than the king himself. This is known through the careful observations of the viceroy Antonio di Melo di Castro.[180] These fathers also have a printing press, which is unique in Goa, though not good.[181] Some of the rectories are administered by the Canarini Fathers, natives of the country, who are not well thought of because they are brown in color. There are many, however, of great virtue and civility. Instead of a hat, they wear a cap with four

179. An art form particularly favored in Iran, multicolor glazed ceramic tiles were also used in buildings in Sind and Gujarat, the source of this majolica.

180. He was governor of Goa from 1662 to 1663.

181. Christian missionaries had earlier brought both printed books and printing presses to India, as well as to Iran. Despite interest in the products of printing, Indian rulers did not try to adopt the new technology until considerably later.

points. After lunch I went around and looked at things as far as the walls extend. [The walls] were erected at great expense by one of the first viceroys. They are more than twelve miles in circumference and enclose several hills and country houses. [They are of this size] because that viceroy, seeing the prosperity of those early times, when almost all the commerce of India went to that city, thought that it would always increase. He was deceived, however, due to the other ports that were opened in India that have taken much of the traffic. The city has remained of small size, as one can see now. On his return from Goa he had to make his expense account in jail and to pay back the royal treasury out of his own pocket.

On the 26th I went to another resting spot of the same fathers. This is called Mulla, where they have a small but rather pleasant house on a stream of water that comes from the sea. I went in a boat to various quite delightful places that are along the same stream, which comes out on the side of the fortress of Marmagao. In that same place there are many knights' houses that have abundant spring water, coming from the nearby mountains. They make the water play in delightful fountains, and part of it they have enclosed in big stone tanks in a beautiful grotto, so that they can wash themselves several times a day, as is the custom. The countryside is also pleasant, since all year round the trees are green. Although I stayed there only two days on that occasion, I went back several times to enjoy those delights for a longer time.

While I was in Goa, there came to the city an ambassador from the 'Adil Khan.[182] On the day he entered the city, the viceroy ordered that he be met by the entire [viceregal] guard of Kanarini and other native soldiers with flags unfurled. There went [along with them] a great multitude of other people too. As he entered, they preceded him with their weapons in their hands, which they beat one against the other, dancing and making a concert, as is their custom, and adding many festive cries in their own language. This [practice] serves for pomp and majesty [among them], as trumpeters, drums, and other military instruments do among us. The ambassador in a palanquin followed them and was accompanied only by six persons of his retinue on horseback, by a good number of knights, by a captain of the city, and by many ordinary people. When he arrived at the palace, he was intro-

182. Bembo is referring not to the dynasty's founder but rather to the dynastic name for the 'Adil-Shahi monarchs: 'Ali ibn Muhammad ruled from Bijapur from 1656 to 1672; his son Sikandar ibn 'Ali, from 1672 to 1686.

duced into the royal hall, where the viceroy was seated under the baldachin. The ambassador immediately asked about the health of the king. When he saw the portrait of King John IV that was hung on high under the baldachin, he asked the viceroy why he did not have a portrait of the living king. He was told that they were waiting for a portrait to arrive from Portugal any time now. The truth was that the viceroy was very partial to the Prince Don Pietro, who only had the title of governor of the kingdom, since the king Don Alfonso was confined on Terceira Island [in the Azores archipelago]. Thus for political reasons he did not have the portrait of either one or the other. The ambassador's question was not without its motives, since he was very well informed about the happenings of that kingdom, and intelligent men were not lacking among those pagans. When the public audience was finished and they had agreed on a secret one, the ambassador was accompanied by the same retinue to a house designated by the viceroy, where he was kept at royal expense. The ordinary ambassador of the same king is in the same situation. Although he is an ordinary person and of not much importance, he is given a house and three pardaos a day for his expenses by the king. A few days later the beatification of Pius V was celebrated by the Dominicans with music and a procession in which there were many floats like ours in Venice, but without good proportions. In the procession there was a mixture of dancers who danced as Gentiles and Africans and who went in the same way to Church. Then in the evening they made many artificial lights and illuminated the façade of the church and the bell tower with many lights divided in various colors that made a beautiful sight in the whole city, since the church was higher than any of the largest private houses. The other religious do the same thing on holidays.

[NOVEMBER 1673]

On the 21st of November I got a fever that continued and obliged me to call the native doctors. They wanted to begin taking blood from me for every day as long as the fever lasted. But I did not want to allow such drastic measures, so as not to deprive myself of good blood and to have to produce more, which would be weak due to the quality of the food and the continual drinking of water. I thought it would do more harm than good. Then I got the viceroy's doctor, who was Portuguese and whom he had brought with him from Lisbon. Although he was not very good, he stood out in that country! He took care of me in European fashion and ordered some powders for me that would do me wonders. Through them and through a rigorous diet I found myself free of fever in a few days. I spent more than I would have, had I listened to the natives, but I did not want to risk my health, which I have always thought more precious than gold. In spite of the brevity of the sickness, my convalescence was quite long. For two whole months I had a tired feeling, even though I had taken myself to Mulla, mentioned above, for more rest. It is the usual thing in that climate that all foreigners get a dangerous illness. For only four days of fever, there were four days of convalescence. With all this I still got off better than those around me, who were all in danger of their lives. They listened to native doctors. For a sickness the latter take blood thirty or forty times, sometimes up to two or three times a day, until the fever lets up because of weakness. Then they begin to use medicines that leave the patient exhausted. I went to visit Father Giacomo, who was in the sick ward of his convent. There are many sick people and convalescing people there all the time who seem almost dead and just barely moving. All these sicknesses come from the bad and humid air, which, along with the excessive heat of that climate, make it easy for the blood to break down. Once this [blood] has been removed in great quantities, it has to be remade from the veins, and that is why the period of convalescence is so long.

Those doctors know herbs well and how to use them as medicine. They use various stones, among them that of *bezoar*, of which there are many.[183] There is another stone, called the Stone of Gaspar Antonio, which is made in Goa by the Jesuits from various precious ingredients. They claim, according to the label, that it has the same virtues as the bezoar, and that it is for all troubles, especially for poisonings, which, as I had said, are frequently done by women. Besides the ordinary sicknesses, there is a particular one in the country called cholera, which is deadly if not recognized at its inception and cured properly.[184] This illness attacks the head and the vital faculties, causing deafness and pain in the upper part of the body. Its first cure is to burn the heels of the sick person with a well-heated iron until there is

183. Bembo is referring to the *bezoar*, a gastric or intestinal stone from goats, sheep, and other animals, which was considered an antidote to poison, as well as to treat fever and maintain good health. It is described by Chardin, *Travels in Persia* (London, 1927), pp. 149–150.

184. Cholera. "Mordesin" is Bembo's rendering of the Portuguese *mordexim*, from the Mahratti verb *modnen,* meaning "to collapse."

pain, and he cannot stand it any longer. Then they prohibit all sorts of food and drink. They give him only in the morning and the evening a rice soup made in water and without salt.[185] They put some sugar in it. Even some healthy people take this drink in the morning to refresh themselves. In this way they get better in a few days, whereas if nothing is done, they die; particularly if blood is taken, there is nothing more to be done that will be of help. Any other cure done before the scalding of the heels is also useless. As a result, they undertake this treatment as a precaution at the beginning of all illnesses. If the burns are felt immediately by the sick person, they can be sure that he does not have cholera. Some of those who were with me did not escape this treatment, but I did not want to submit to it, because I did not feel a headache. Many told me I should have it in order to be safe, but when the viceroy's doctor came, we omitted such a painful treatment.

On the 27th the rumor spread in Goa that the Dutch and the Moors together had taken the city of San Thomé from the French. This city had been rebuilt by the Portuguese at the beginning of their conquests. This city is located on the shores of the kingdom of Vijayanagara on the Gulf of Bengalla and was originally called Malabar.[186] When the Portuguese took it, they enclosed it with strong walls like those of Daman—of the same size and constructed by the same architect. It was made noble by several buildings, and its name was changed to San Thomé, that is, St. Thomas, in honor of the apostle of that name, since there was in that city a small house where he had lived, which they say was built by his own hands. In a chapel near the principal portal in the cathedral there is his tomb, which is venerated not only by the Christians, but also by the pagans.[187] The Portuguese held the city until 1661 or 1662. When they saw that its scant population would make it impossible to defend in case of attack from the Dutch, with whom they were then at war, they gave it over, like a deposit, to the king of

185. Bembo calls it *cangia,* and it appears to be identical to the Chinese *congee.*

186. San Thomé is just south of Madras, on the Coromandel coast. Here Bembo seems to render Malabar as "Meliopor," though later he names it "Mallavar." Bembo uses the word "narsinga" to refer to the kingdom of Vijayanagara, or Bisnagar, which ruled most of south India in the sixteenth and seventeenth centuries. The Portuguese name is derived from the name of King Narasimha (1490–1508), who was king when the first Portuguese fleets reached south India.

187. Hinduism's capacity to assimilate holy figures from other faiths is well established.

Vijayanagara, who has the title of *Zamorin,* which is an honorific title, as was Caesar among the Romans.[188] When the war with the Dutch was over, they wished they had not transferred it, since they thought that the Zamorin would not give it back. To oblige him [to do so], they seized two rich ships belonging to the king [which were] then in those seas. They kept everything intact. When the Zamorin heard the news, he immediately sent an ambassador to the viceroy complaining of this hostile treatment, since he was a good friend of the Portuguese and ready to return the city given to him. The viceroy accepted these offers and immediately returned the ships and all the merchandise and sent the armada to that port to receive the fortress. The fortress was never handed over, however, and since the Portuguese did not have sufficient forces to take it by arms, they left feeling cheated. The city remained in the hands of that king until there was a war between the French and the Dutch. The French armada stopped in that port to procure supplies, which were denied them, even though they were going to pay for them. The French general was so incensed that he ordered his troops to debark and assault the city, which was taken in twenty-four hours and then sacked in the month of May 1672. Some say that this was only a pretext on the part of the French, whose real motive had been to get a safe port in those parts in order to defend themselves against the Dutch. When the Dutch heard of that city's fall to the French, they immediately sent aid to those natives so that they could take it back. They promised them that they would give them three other, smaller fortresses in exchange for that one, once they won it back. The natives replied that they could not give it to anyone, since they held it in trust for the Portuguese, but that they would welcome the help. Since the Dutch preferred that anyone other than the French possess it, they sent an armada as help from the sea. The Gentiles fought from the land, and the [Dutch] fought from the sea. The five hundred Frenchmen fought bravely against multitudes of natives and a large Dutch fleet. After a siege of more than a year, most of the defenders had died. They had never received any help. Monsieur François Baron,

188. The Hindu lord of Calicut on the Malabar coast was known as the *Zamorin;* in the fourteenth and fifteenth centuries the spice trade had made him the most powerful ruler in southwestern India, so that he controlled an area extending from Cochin to Cananor. Commerce was dominated by resident Muslim merchants. Initially friendly to Vasco da Gama and his successors, the Zamorin subsequently lost control of much of his domain to the Portuguese.

who was at its defense and was one of the directors of the company and who had been consul in Aleppo many years before, surrendered it, since he could not hold it. That loss was noised about in Goa but was not believed. Later I had it confirmed to me by Frenchmen themselves in Persia.

Since on several occasions I have touched on the subject of St. Thomas, I think it well to write more on the qualities and religion of the Christians who call themselves [followers] of St. Thomas. Mostly they live in the mountains and on the Malabar coast.[189] They had their first instructions in the faith from that saint, although now they are almost all infected by the Nestorian heresy. They know, therefore, as was taught to their ancestors by the holy apostle, that after the death of God Our Lord Jesus Christ, the twelve apostles spread throughout the world to preach the Gospel. St. Thomas went with St. Judas Thaddeus, and together they went into Mesopotamia to the city of Edessa, now called Urfa. They traveled with a merchant who was going to the Indies, where all the inhabitants lived in the darkness of paganism. Some say that the holy apostle sold himself to that merchant. Others say that he agreed to serve him for the trip, which is more probable. Having left St. Thaddeus in the above-mentioned city, as is found in the books of the Chaldeans that are preserved in those mountains,[190] the first land that the apostle reached was the island of Socotra at the mouth of the Red Sea.[191] It is sixty miles long and twenty-seven miles wide. There he stopped for some time and converted those people to Christianity. He erected a church where they could adore the one God and left a cross and writings in their language. He knew all languages by gift of the Holy Spirit. The writings were the Ten Commandments and other things necessary for the preservation of Christianity. When the saint left, many errors were introduced, as were precepts different from those he had left, as Tristan of Accugna, General of the Portuguese, saw when he landed on that island with the fleet. [The General] entered the port, which is called Socco, in which was a fortress held by the Moors of Arabia. He took it after a bloody

189. The Malabar coast.

190. That is, the books of the Nestorians of Anatolia.

191. Bembo calls it "Sacatorà" or "Cocotorà." Off the southeast coast of the Arabian Peninsula, Socotra had a long-established Christian community until the seventeenth century. The Mahri sultans of Socotra also ruled the southeastern coast of Arabia from their chief city of Qishn. It came briefly under Portuguese control between 1507 and 1511.

battle. He heard from the natives that they were Christians who had been made subjects twenty-six years before by the king of Qishn, who was ruling in the part of Arabia called Ras Fartak, which was a frontier of the island itself.[192] Since he wanted that island, that king had sent a fleet of ten ships with one thousand soldiers in 1480. When they saw it, the natives were frightened and retired to the mountains, of which the island is full. The Moors took the port and built the fortress there. After some time they came to an agreement with the natives that the latter should pay an annual tribute to the king of Qishn, who kept one hundred men in the fortress and called himself the King of Socotra. When the Portuguese took it, they found an old blind man in a deep well, as Giovanni di Bares tells. When he was taken into the presence of the general and interrogated as to how he had been able to see to save himself in the bottom of that well, he answered that there is nothing that blind men see better than the road to liberty, for which answer he was given it. When the Portuguese took the whole island, those Christians were well received by the General. They said that despite the tyrannies of the Moors, they had kept themselves in the faith. They were, however, infected by the heresy of the Jacobites, since they had mixed their race with that of the Abyssinians, a subject people of Prester John, who lived on the coast of Africa on the shores of the Red Sea. The major part of those Christians bore the names of the Apostles and of the Virgin. They adored the cross, to which they were so devoted that all wore one around their necks. Three times a day they went to pray: early in the morning, at vespers, and in the evening. They said their prayers in Chaldean.[193] Some Portuguese observed, however, that they mixed Alleluias in their prayers. They practiced circumcision and fasted. They took only one wife and gave [to the church] one tenth of their goods, despite the fact that the land is not fertile. Like the land, the inhabitants are rough and not very clever. Their ordinary food is millet, greens of every sort, and milk. They are of fair height and of a brown color. The women are whiter and stronger than the men, since they do the hardest work. When it is time to fight, they go with their husbands to battle. It was the opinion of some that at one time they had lived without men, like the Amazons, and that they had joined themselves for the purpose of procreation with the sailors who passed by. When

192. "Cassen" is Bembo's rendering of Qishn, 50 km to the west of Ras Fartak in southeastern Yemen, near the border with Oman.

193. Syriac.

ships did not come, they would do magic so that ships would be forced by there. This is credible, because of the continuity of their magic and witchcraft by which they do marvelous things.[194] The dress of those people is of heavy cloth made by them. Others use animal skins. They fight with stones and slings, and some with raw iron swords.

When the Apostle had left that island, he went to the coast of Africa in the kingdom of Abyssinia and from there passed to Malinde and then to Mozambique. This was always a port of great commerce, and now it belongs to the Portuguese, who have a fortress with a good port there. It is perhaps the richest land that the king of Portugal has. Not far from there is the River of Quama, whose sands have gold.[195] In Goa they make coins from it. There are great quantities of ivory and ebony there. From the African Moors one can get all sorts of things in exchange for goods, since they do not use coins there. Food itself is used as a means of exchange. Between those coasts and those of Mombasa one finds ambergris, which some say is the vomit, and others say is the sperm, of some whales, but not of all whales. Some [people] more probably say that it grows in the bottom of the sea and that it is uprooted during storms and comes to the surface of the water and is carried ashore, where it is found by chance. But only the Portuguese find it, since other nationalities do not go there. Anyone who finds any [of it] has to give one-fifth to the king. The ministers are very strict about this. If they find any of it in contraband, they confiscate it all for the king. All the Portuguese ships returning to Lisbon stop by that port, where they load on ebony for the king. They say that Solomon's fleets also came here to get ebony and gold for the building of the temple.

When St. Thomas had spread the Gospel in that place, he went to Persia and then returned to Socotra, where he boarded a ship with which he went to the Malabar coast, as is found in a manuscript those people have. Where exactly he landed first is disputed, since it is an honor that many of those places claim. Particularly the Christians of the province of Perumpadappus near Kerala on the Malabar coast say that he debarked in the city of

194. In his discussion of Socotra and its Nestorian Christian community, Marco Polo also refers to their powers of magic (*The Travels of Marco Polo*, trans. R. Latham [Penguin, 1958], pp. 270–273).

195. Bembo uses the term *Ampazza*. The apostle presumably proceeded to Somalia, then south to the city of Malinde in Kenya, and to the port of Mozambique, near which is the Quama River.

Mogodover Patana, which means "city of the Great Idol."[196] That port was frequented by merchants of Arabia and Persia. There he converted to the faith a son of the king of Perumpadappus himself with many of those people, some of whom still preserve the Christian faith. The Chaldean books, however, say that he first touched their coasts at Calicut, where he converted Perimal, the emperor of the entire Malabar coast.[197] He was one of those inscribed on the stone by the saint himself when he wrote down the names of all those he had converted. Nevertheless, it is a more common opinion that he landed in Mogodover Patana, although the chronicles of that city are lost. In them were recorded all the memorable things of the city, and time was numbered from the date of the foundation of the city, as the Romans did *ab urbe condita*. Before then, it was marked according to the course of the planet Jupiter, which is of twelve years, similar to what the Greeks did in marking time according to the Olympiads, which were of five years. In that city also there took place the miracle of the hand, which they related in the following way. That king was celebrating the wedding of a son. A young Jewish girl was dancing and singing in her language the precepts of the laws of God and the miracles of his prophets. (Remember that the Jews remained in those parts with Solomon's fleet, as said above. Others, who are in Cochin, descend from those who fled Jerusalem during the invasion of Titus. After being slaves in Persia for a long time, they passed to India.) Since the apostle, who had been invited, was present, he heard the praises of God. He was so fixed on the contemplation of God that he went out of himself and remained in ecstasy. When a minister saw this, he attributed the external immobility of the saint to sleepiness and bad manners. He gave him a slap in the presence of the king. The saint arose and said to him who had hit him: "Son, so that you will not pay for this injury with eternal punishment in the next life, God in his mercy will punish you only slightly." Before the party was over, that man went to get water from a fountain. A tiger arrived there to drink and attacked that unhappy man, and, biting him in the sacrilegious hand, he took it away completely and let it fall to the earth without doing him further injury. The poor man went all bloody to the group, and while he was telling his story, a dog came with the hand in

196. Bembo uses a short form, "Peru," for Perumpadappus, near Kerala. "Mogodover Patana" is Cranganore.

197. In contemporary Portuguese the king to whom Bembo refers was Cheruman Perimal.

his mouth. The saint was moved to compassion, took the hand from the dog, and attached it to the man's arm, where it remained perfectly healthy as it had been before. Because of this, the holy faith was received by most of the group. This miracle is still celebrated by the people of San Thomé. After having worked many other miracles and having converted many people in the whole state of the Great Mughal and in Hindustan, he passed to China. He worked with profit for the faith in Christ. On his return he stopped again in the kingdom of Vijayanagar and in the said city of San Thomé, which was then in his honor called City of San Thomé.

Among the other miracles he did there was a marvelous one concerning a great tree trunk. It was stuck on the seashore and was bothersome there. The king commanded that it be removed from there, but the efforts of many people were not enough to remove it, nor was the strength of elephants. When the saint saw that the king was really anxious to have it moved, he told him that he would remove it by himself to wherever the king wanted, if only the king would concede him enough land to build a church to the one true God. The king laughed about this, especially since he saw that the man was thin from much fasting. The saint replied that he should trust in the help of God whose power was much greater than that of all creatures together. The king promised him the land. The saint tied that trunk with the cord he had around his waist and dragged it to where the king wanted it. Everyone was infinitely amazed and almost all were converted. When he had received the land that he had been promised, he began the building of the temple. Since it is a custom to this day in that city to give the workers a portion of rice and a small coin called a *fanaon* (one of which I brought with me), and since the saint had neither rice nor money to satisfy those who were working on the building, he gave them a portion of sand, which turned into rice, and a small stone, which changed into the coin. Thus he was very venerated by all and called by the name of *Martamama,* which in their language means "saint." [198] He finished the church in a short time. For the beams he used that same trunk that he had carried, and in that church he had his burial. The king himself had given it four hundred rupees a year. (As I noted elsewhere, four and a half rupees make an ongaro.) That church had enjoyed that revenue to the time of the Portuguese. The doors of that church are a continuous miracle. Many pieces are

198. The word *martama* is presumably derived from *Mar Thomas* (Priest Thomas).

taken from them for devotion by both Gentiles and Christians, yet they are preserved whole, and nothing is missing from them. Finally, when that holy apostle was praying in his oratory, he was pierced with a lance by a Brahmin, a priest of those idols whom the saint's preaching was depriving of their unjust cult.[199] This happened in the 30th year of King Zaga, who had been converted by him. He was buried, as I said, in that church, and his relics were found there by the Portuguese, although some say that Abdia, his disciple, took them to Edessa, then metropolis of Mesopotamia, by some thought to be the ancient Raquis, which was full of Christians converted by the apostle Thaddeus.

A bishop lived there (in Edessa) under [whose authority] was the Bishop of San Thomé, until those of the sect of Nestorius entered. In the ruins of the city was found by the Portuguese a square stone. On one side it had a cross sculpted on it and a bird flying, like the symbol one makes to indicate the Holy Spirit. All around, it had characters that were never understood, and it was covered with drops of blood, so fresh that they seemed to have been shed just then. It was believed that on that stone the saint had ended his martyrdom and his life, and so it was carried in solemn procession to the cathedral. These Christians also lived for a long time under Catholic bishops. When the Nestorians came out of Edessa and Babylon, however, they spread the heresy. Finally, because of the many wars that arose about three hundred years after the death of the saint, almost all those Christians fell into idolatry. Many maintained themselves Christian in the city of Cranganor, which always was the principal one of the Christian land until it was completely destroyed.

In the year 811 a Christian Armenian named Thomas Cananeo came to the city with his wife and many riches, along with other people with wives and sons. He advanced so much in the graces of that king, who was a Christian named Cocuragon, that he received the city itself as a gift for himself and for his people. He was also given another place in Cranganor and an entire forest, where he built various churches, of which the first stones were placed by the king himself. That kingdom grew so much that it was governed by its own hereditary king. When the line died out, they came again under the king of Cochin. From what can be seen in the books of the Chaldeans, this Thomas Cananeo is the same one mentioned by St.

199. Marco Polo recounts that St. Thomas died as the result of a hunting accident.

Anthony, who every year sent the Pope a gift of pepper through European Christians, who in those days frequently visited the tomb of that holy apostle. Because of this and other good works done by the said Armenian, he was placed in the list of saints by the Christians of those parts.

Many years before he had arrived, those people had lived without clergy, and they lived until the year 730 in that faith that was taught to them by their elders. In that year two Nestorian bishops arrived from Babylon.[200] One was called Mar Xabio and the other Mar Prod. They were received with much veneration due to their external sanctity. By those zealous souls they also were included after their deaths in the list of saints, from which they were removed by Archbishop Don Allesio di Menesses, a Portuguese, when he went to visit that church and recognized that they had been heretics sent by the Patriarch of Babylon. When they died, those Christians sent to Babylon again for a bishop, since they had no way to advise Rome. Only an unordained deacon remained among them. He took for himself the title of priest, thinking he could do so legitimately, their ignorance having reached such a degree! The Patriarch of Babylon sent them an archbishop by the name of Mar Joana and two subject bishops. He put his seat in Cranganor. After the death of these three, Mar Giacob was sent from Babylon. At this time in 1502 the Admiral Vasco da Gama arrived in the ports of Calicut and Cochin with a Portuguese fleet. [Mar Giacob] was sent by those Christians as their ambassador to the Portuguese to say that they were Christians and therefore persecuted by those Gentile kings and by the Moslems, by whom they were forcibly kept subject. They asked the King of Portugal, as a Catholic king, to protect them, and they gave themselves to him voluntarily as vassals, and as a sign thereof they sent a scepter to Don Vasco. This was the scepter of their ancient legitimate kings, which is a red rod ornamented with silver and with three bells at both ends. This [scepter] was accepted by Don Vasco in the name of his king, and he promised them help and assistance. With that hope and with various gifts those Christians returned much consoled.

200. Bembo is referring here not to Egypt, often called "Babylon" in contemporary European writings, but to Baghdad, in Iraq. The Nestorian patriarch had his seat in Baghdad. The Christians of St. Thomas had elected to unite with the Roman Catholic Church in 1599; subsequently they split, one part retaining its allegiance to Rome and the other choosing association with the Syrian Orthodox (or Jacobite) patriarch in Antioch.

Mar Joana I succeeded Mar Giacob, and Mar Ianabo and others succeeded him in order until 1556. At that time Pope Paul IV was ruling.[201] Simon Sulacca, bishop of Caeremit, now Diarbichier,[202] and with him two other bishops called Mar Elias and Mar Gioseffe, presented themselves to the Pope and promised him obedience for themselves and for their people. The first was confirmed as patriarch of Mosul, and the other two were established in their bishoprics and made subject to the patriarch of Mosul. Mar Gioseffe, who was bishop of Nineveh, was sent by the Pope to govern the Christians of Malabar, and, as coadjutor, he received Bishop Ambrogio Monticelli, a Dominican, who was to be his successor. When they arrived in Mosul, the patriarch was killed by the heretical patriarch there. Mar Gioseffe and the Dominican Bishop were barely able to escape. They passed to Hormuz and then to India and were well received by those Christians. Don Ambrogio did not like that land, however, and went to Goa, leaving the government to Mar Gioseffe, who was completely infected by heresy and began to spread it. When this reached the ears of the viceroy and the archbishop of Goa, [Mar Gioseffe] was made a prisoner and sent to Portugal. His followers sent to Babylon for a successor of the same sect, and a Mar Abram was sent to them, who arrived there disguised as a sailor. When the ships returned from Portugal, however, Mar Gioseffe returned with them, loaded with honors given him by Cardinal Don Enrico of Portugal and by the queen who was governing at that time. He had been able to hide his malice, and those great personages had got him pardoned by the Pope and had had his bishopric confirmed, since he promised to make all those Christians obedient to the Roman Church. On his return he was received with affection by some of his subjects, but others had become attached to Mar Abram and denied their recognition. Thus there grew up among them a great division and schism. Therefore, by order of the archbishop of Goa and of the viceroy, Mar Abram was taken prisoner and sent to Portugal as a heretic and author of that turbulence. Since the ship had to stop in Mozambique, he fled in a boat and returned to Babylon, where he asked for new authority. He further considered, however, that if he did not get them from Rome, they would not serve him, and so he went on foot to see Pius IV. He expressed his faults and condemned them and asked for forgiveness and professed obedience to the Pope, from whom he got letters and was

201. Paul IV was pope from 1555 to 1556.
202. Amida, now Diyarbakır.

confirmed bishop of that land. Since he had not been legitimately ordained before then, [the Pope] sent him to Venice to the patriarch, from whom he received orders and was consecrated bishop. He was then given letters and went through Persia to Goa. When he presented his letters, they were examined by that bishop and found to have been based on the false information that he had given. He therefore kept him in the Dominican convent until he could inform Rome. Meanwhile, one day, seeing that the clergy were all busy with a feast, he saw the possibility of escaping and went to his bishopric. A little while earlier, Mar Gioseffe had been removed by order of the Holy See and by the cardinal of Portugal, since he had been recognized as an obstinate heretic. Mar Abram entered in the absence of his competitor and was received by all and recognized as prelate. Worried that the archbishop of Goa would try to take him prisoner, however, he tried to be careful. Of all this turn of events the Pope was kept informed, so that in 1578 he sent a letter to Mar Abram to tell him that he had to preach the Catholic faith. He was also told to go to all the councils that would be celebrated in Goa, and he went, in fact, to the one convoked by Archbishop Don Vincente d'Alfonseca, after which he returned to his residence to do everything differently from what he had sworn at the council.

At the same time a Mar Simon came to those Christians who said he was the successor to that bishopric, as established in Babylon. He said he was a favorite and lived in the house of the Queen of Pimento, that is, "of pepper," who then ruled in that state. With her help he put himself in office and began to exercise ecclesiastical authority over those Christians subject to the queen. He had his residence in Cartute.[203] When they found out about this in Goa, they managed to arrest him and to send him to Portugal, whence he was sent to Rome, where it was discovered that he was not only not a bishop, but not even a priest! Thus Mar Abram remained once again in the peaceful possession of his bishopric, where he continued to disseminate errors. When he was called to Goa by Archbishop Matteo in 1590, he did not want to participate in a council. When the Pope found out about it, he sent in 1595 a letter to Archbishop Alessio of Menesses [indicating] that he should inquire into the faults of that bishop. If he should find him in heresy, he should make him prisoner and govern the bishopric. In the

203. The references to the queen of Pimento and Cartute are unclear, but "Cartute" may be his rendering of the important port city of Calicut, south of Goa.

future he was not to allow the coming of bishops from Babylon without permission from Rome. Before the inquiry was finished, Mar Abram, who was already an old man, died, blind in his errors. Thus the direction of that bishopric remained with the archdeacon, who was no less infected in the same heresy, until the archbishop went to visit that land and found it full of 1,000 wrong beliefs. They denied the Incarnation of the Word, the purity of Mary, and the Virgin birth. They admitted only the cross and no other images in their churches. They thought that the souls of the saints would not see God until after the Last Judgment. Of the sacraments they accepted only baptism, orders, and Eucharist, and these with ceremonies and forms that were so different they were invalid. In baptism every *cassanar* was the ordinary minister.[204] These are clerics who marry, and their women are called *catatiaras* or *cassanairas*, and they carry a sign that distinguishes them from other women as more worthy. In baptizing they use different formulas according to their whim. They do not use holy oil, but rather coconut oil or oil of *gergilin,* fruits of that country, without blessing them, however. (It is usually used by those of Malabar, because it has many good qualities for the body.) They do not like confession, although some practice it, because they were in contact with the Portuguese, whom they saw practicing it; to cleanse themselves of sin, they made great fires in the middle of the churches on Sundays and threw into the fires much incense. They take some of that smoke with their hands, and they spread it on themselves, thinking that in this way they cleanse themselves of faults. They receive the Eucharist without any more preparation than some days of fast. Their Masses are full of improprieties and indecencies. Before they got wine from Portugal, they consecrated palm juice, boiled with raisins. Instead of hosts, they used a certain bread of theirs called *bolos,* made with oil and salt. The sacrament of orders was given to every sort of person without regard to age. There were few houses where there was not an ordained person. These did not abstain from secular works. There were priests of seventeen years of age who even after ordination would marry one and more times. Nor did they abstain from their wives before celebrating. One would see in church fathers, sons, and nephews, all priests administering the sacraments. These were sold to those who offered the most [money] without any concern about its being simony. In matrimony there were infinite abuses,

204. *Cassanar* denotes a priest of the Mar Thomas Christians (Syrian Church of Malabar) and is derived from the Malayalam word *kattanar,* or "chief."

because to be married it was [simply] sufficient to say that one was. Others thought themselves married with the taking of a string from around their neck and putting it on the neck of a woman. When the women had children, they abstained from entering church according to the custom of the Jewish law for forty days if it was a boy child and for eighty days if it was a girl child. They blessed water by merely throwing into it some of the earth where the apostle had walked, along with a grain of incense. They paid attention to astrology and to magic arts, the study of which they had in a book called *Paresman,* that is, "Persian Medicine." From it they got good or bad omens for their businesses. In addition to these and very many other abuses, they still had many customs of the pagans in their practices.

I read more than one account made to Pietro Alvares Cabrald by two Christians of Cranganor who said they were true descendants of the first Christians converted by St. Thomas. In all they were about 12,000 who paid tribute to that king, and they had many rites of the Greek and Latin Church. In their temples they only have the cross as an image. They do not use bells. When the priests wanted to call the people to Church, they beat on a piece of iron or wood that is hanging up in the Greek manner to make some noise. They were governed by a Pope, twelve cardinals, two patriarchs, many archbishops, and bishops. The Pope lived in Armenia, where bishops would go to get consecrated, as well as priests, who, instead of a tonsure, have a cross on their heads, while others have a small tuft of hair in the middle of the head, while they shave off the rest. Of the two patriarchs, one lives in India and the other in Catagio.[205] The reason they had for electing that Pope was that at the time that St. Peter lived in Antioch, there was in Rome the schism of Simon Magus, so that the apostle was called there to look after the needs of those Christians. When he left Antioch, so as not to leave the oriental church without a pastor, he left a vicar who should rule in his absence. At his death [this vicar] remained as Pope. Those who were elected afterward remained in Armenia, although [the church] passed under the dominion of various countries. The election was by twelve cardinals. Marco Polo, the Venetian, who traveled at length in those parts, spoke about them and their Pope.[206]

205. The reference here is to the Nestorian hierarchy. The patriarch resided in Baghdad; there were four archdioceses and seven dioceses, one at Zakha, presumably the source for Bembo's reference to Catagio.

206. See *The Travels of Marco Polo,* trans. R. Latham (Penguin, 1958), pp. 20, 247–250.

Although that Pope was Catholic, he was called Jacobite. They consecrated unleavened bread and raisin wine. Children were baptized only after forty days, except for those in danger of dying. They received the sacrament in our way. They buried their dead, and to the sick they gave a blessing, instead of holy oil. After the death of someone, the relatives gathered and banqueted together for eight days; then they buried the deceased. When they entered into church, they sprinkled themselves with holy water. They kept the Advent fast and also the Lenten fast with great devotion. During the entire day of the vigil of Easter they neither ate nor drank anything, and they observed all the principal feasts. Their priests lived in chastity, and those who were found at fault were deprived of their ecclesiastical powers. They also had a monastery for virgins, who were very cloistered. The above-mentioned Alessio di Menesses corrected in those Christians all the things that were consonant with the purity of the faith.[207] He had them all practice the Roman Catholic faith, baptizing many of them again. When the visit was over, he provided them with a legitimate and zealous pastor, who was Father Francesco Roz, a Portuguese Jesuit, who besides all his other qualities knew the languages of Malabar and Chaldea. He was received with universal satisfaction by all those Christians, whom he taught with such charity and diligence that they were well raised with the milk of true Christian piety. After him they have always had bishops of the same order. However, since some were too rigid and not fond of those people, as is often true of the Portuguese, because of their dark color, and since they despised them and mistreated them, they could not support their dominion, even if only spiritual. Many times they sent to Rome complaints and requests that they be sent better pastors. When this news reached Babylon, a heretical prelate came from there who told them that he had the title of Bishop of Jerusalem and that he had been sent by Rome in reply to their requests to the Pope. Those poor Christians, so bothered by the rigorous care of the Jesuits, received him with all submission and joy. The Jesuits managed things so well that they imprisoned the false bishop and sent him prisoner to Portugal. From his prison he found a way to write them a pastoral letter exhorting them to gather together twelve priests and to elect a bishop in his absence. This was done. By twelve, infected with heresy, a bishop was elected. The Jesuits immediately advised Rome, since they could not imprison him. The Pope sent to visit them a Carmelite, Father Joseph, who returned to Rome when he had finished his investigation and brought

207. This is, in fact, Bembo's first reference to Alessio di Menesses.

exact information about that heretical bishop and about the aversion that those people had toward the Jesuits. The Pope sent him back immediately, having made him bishop with ecclesiastical authority to elect another one in due time, if he should not like his stay there. When he arrived there the second time in 1660, he made them once again obedient to the Roman Church. He excommunicated the heretical bishop who persisted in his errors, along with others who followed him, [for he was] protected by some native religious persons through the inducement of money and women. Since the Dutch took the city of Cochin from the Portuguese on January 10, 1663, the new bishop did not want to remain there. He elected in his place one Alessandro of Campos, one of the twelve priests who had elected the heretical bishop and who had since then renounced his heresy and detested his errors. He lived his life as a good Catholic and subject to the Roman Church. His title is bishop of Magara, and he still lives and guides his flock with zeal. When the Carmelite bishop returned to Rome, those people remained with a Catholic bishop and a heretical one: the latter died this year 1673 in the month of April. In his place an older brother of his, who had been the archdeacon, has been elected. The Latin bishop is trying to think of a way to take him prisoner in order to remove that scandal and reduce those people to the unity of the church and to obedience to the Roman Pope. This is what I have been able to find out about the Christian land called San Thomé or of the *Sera,* that is, "of the mountain."

[DECEMBER 1673]

On the 10th of December an extravagant ceremony was held in Goa, called by the Portuguese the Act of Faith. It took place in the cathedral church located in the plaza called Sabaggio's, where is also the house of the Inquisition, which was the palace of the Sabaggio, as I said before. This Inquisition, as I have mentioned elsewhere, is very rigorous in all the lands of Portugal, not less than in Spain, especially in the matter of faith, due to the many secret Jews who once in a while are discovered calling themselves Christians. The reason known to all is that the king of Spain in 1450 obliged all the Jews, under punishment of being burned, either to leave his kingdom in a space of thirty days or to receive baptism. Some received baptism and truly made themselves Christians. Most of those who were baptized, however, did it so as not to leave the houses and goods that they owned. They lived secretly in the Mosaic law, although externally they professed that of Christ. The Inquisition watches over this in all secrecy.

Those who are discovered are condemned to be burned, and all their goods are confiscated by the king. Usually they are important merchants. Similarly, the Inquisition keeps watch over the lands in India, where there are many people who became Christians by force. The Portuguese oblige all orphans under fourteen years old to be baptized. First they put them to be trained with the Jesuits or with the Franciscans. Then they are baptized solemnly in their churches. They do not even allow the pagans and Moslems to use temples or mosques, and thus many of them abandon the country and go to live under the Dutch, who leave them in liberty of conscience and allow them to practice their cults in their temples to which they go in sickness, even after having received baptism. They also practice witchcraft. The Inquisition of Goa conducts investigations to find such delinquents. When they find them a first time, as long as they profess repentance, they are allowed to go free with a simple admonition. The second time they get a slight punishment. But if they persist and are incorrigible, they are condemned to be burned without hope of pardon. This is the same sentence also given on the second instance of sodomy. They also proceed with great rigor against those who swear and against witches. At the ceremony mentioned above, then, they do the following. First of all, when anyone is accused, he is immediately made prisoner and processed by the Inquisition. He is sentenced, although that [sentence] remains a secret until the appointed day, even if he is innocent. That all depends on the judgment of the inquisitors, who act according to the number of defendants. The ceremony [of the *Auto da Fé,* or Act of Faith] is done only once a year, and only on that day are the sentences given out. The night before this day, which the Inquisition many days before makes known in the entire city, a single bell is rung for many hours. This has such a grave sound that it brings universal terror. It is rung again the following morning and during the whole day. In the churches no other bells are rung as signals for Mass or Divine Offices. When the sun rises, all those who have been invited by the Inquisitors to assist at the trials go to the house of the Inquisition. These are primarily the most important knights and clergy or other important persons of the city. They consider themselves honored by such an invitation, because it is a work of much piety and great merit. To each of these invited individuals is assigned a prisoner whose hands are tied, and in procession they go to the cathedral. The prisoners go to the right and the gentlemen to the left. The prisoners that year were one hundred and sixty, and I was told that sometimes there are more than two hundred. All were dressed in penitential robes, and each had a sign that told what his crime was. Those who were to be burned came last without signs, but with their robes all painted with various figures in flames. These were separated from the others by a crucifix carried facing them. When there is no one condemned to death, the crucifix is carried in front and facing forward. In the cathedral, which was very full of people, the viceroy sat on a platform with the inquisitors and with the secular judges. In front of them on a bench were seated all the prisoners. A sermon was made to the people denouncing these errors and exhorting them to stay away from those people and to live in the Catholic religion with the holy fear of God. Then they began to read all the accounts and sentences of each one and the number of times that they had been previously accused. Many were condemned to be whipped, others were sent out of the country, others to work in the powder magazine, others were found innocent and sent home with much applause and with a palm branch in their hands. Five were condemned to be burned, but the sentence was not pronounced by the inquisitors. After the accounts were read, they were turned over to the secular judges and had from them the death sentence. Three of these had been tried many times for idolatry and had never wanted to confess nor to leave their errors. One was a woman who was a witch. Another was a Portuguese priest who had been convicted of sodomy several times; first he was degraded by a bishop who had been called to Goa for the purpose. The Auto da Fé ceremony lasted all day and ended in the evening with the death of those unhappy people. After being strangled, they were thrown in the fire, where they soon were reduced to ashes. Almost all of those tried were natives. The Portuguese rarely reach such extremes, because, when they know that they have committed some act that is a matter for the Inquisition, they prevent through self-humiliation the accusations of others, and this way they receive a slight punishment.[208]

The season was coming when the fleet would be able to go into the Persian Gulf. The viceroy had ordered that some ships and galliots be prepared to go to collect the revenues in that country and to go through the sea under his dominion. He also had the intention of going against the Arabs of Muscat, who were their enemies, and also to escort the ships of

208. For a similar, more detailed account of the Inquisition in Goa between 1673 and 1676, see Martin Collis, *The Land of the Great Image* (New York: Knopf, 1943).

Surat that go to Persian ports. These ships are in danger from the above-mentioned Arabs, who infest those parts. He had already chosen the captains, and the port of Goa had already opened with the end of winter. I, too, was going around thinking about how to return to Aleppo. I was gathering advice and instructions about the road I should take so as to see places I had not seen and which would not make the way too long, since I was being summoned by letters from my uncle. I would have liked to take the way through the Red Sea, at the end of which one arrives in the port of Suez, only three days' distance from the land of Cairo, whence one can go to Jerusalem in a few days, partly through the desert and partly along inhabited coasts. From there one arrives in Aleppo in less than fifteen days. This is a very short trip, and I would have very much liked to have seen Cairo, which is such a famous city, and to visit the holy places and worship at the Holy Sepulchre. Everyone counseled me, however, against that route. They said that the coasts of the Red Sea were full of thieves and assassins. Even letters from our nobleman Giovanni Antonio Soderini advised me against it. He had been to Cairo and told me not to take that route because I would be betrayed and murdered by the guards themselves. He found out about those things when he was in that city. Also, that route was not permitted to Christians by the Sherif, the Muslim lord of Mecca, because of religious zeal since the tomb of their false prophet is there.[209] Then, too, no one in Goa had taken such a trip, so I could not get information. Only Father Giovanni Seabra was without concern for such difficulties, since he wanted to get back to Europe on business for his order and for the viceroy, and was trying to persuade me to take him with me on that route. I would not have refused his company, although up until then he had not been very faithful and had even been less than useful. Nevertheless, when I saw that his best friends were trying to dissuade him with the example of all the Europeans of India—Portuguese, French, English, and Dutch—who had all avoided that short route and returned to Europe by ship or through Persia or Baghdad, I decided to let him document himself with his own experience. That is what happened, because he had to remain in India another winter, as I will tell. I was thinking of returning by sea. However, the difficulties and

209. The Prophet Muhammad was buried in Medina. In 1673 the holy cities of Mecca and Medina were under Ottoman suzerainty, with local power invested in the Sherifs of Mecca.

length of the trip, with much expense and discomfort without ever seeing a country en route, made me abandon the idea. Thus I resolved to embark on the Portuguese fleet and go with them to the Persian Gulf. I had the Carmelites get me passage on a ship and pay the fee, which I would then return to them. The Prior spoke with Pietro Tavera, a friend of his, who was a nobleman of India, like all the captains of the Portuguese ships. Immediately and courteously he not only promised me passage but insisted on having me at his table without charge and offered me, besides, half of his room. I was not able to refuse such kindness and accepted it with the idea of giving him an equivalent gift at the end of the trip.

Through these fathers I also tried to get some money changed for the expenses in that city and for the return trip, as well as for buying some small jewels as souvenirs of the country. I could not believe how difficult this was. Those merchants had no correspondence with the markets of Aleppo or Venice. Nevertheless, with the help of Father Valerio I found a merchant who was said to be secretly a Jew. He would have given me some money with an interest rate of 50%. Before the deal was completed, however, he was dissuaded by Enrico Gary, to whom he had written for information about me. I think that Gary may have written to him unfavorably about me because some letters I had written to him had got lost, which often happens with public and private correspondence in that country. He had always showed himself very benevolent toward me, and I had not given him any reason to think badly of me, except perhaps this innocent lack of civility. Others offered me money, as long as the monastery would accept responsibility, [a requirement] about which the fathers argued a lot. Some claimed that it could not be done, others said it had to be voted on in a chapter meeting, and others were well disposed. Father Feliciano of S. Rocco, who was the prior, thought it best to get me money elsewhere. Since he was the executor for the merchant who had died and whom I mentioned above (the one from whose goods I had hoped to be able to buy a diamond, which he then gave to the general, since he asked for it), the prior had his heirs give me 1,500 pardaos at 20% interest. I suspected that that money really belonged to the monastery, but that, not trusting me, he had given it to me under the name of the heirs. I was very bothered by this affair, and it made me sorry that I had ever set out on my travels and was now finding myself somewhere without knowing people and without the money I needed and in the company of two clerics, one of whom was only out to cheat me and the other, although he had known me in Venice, did not trust me sufficiently and thought I had been traveling without the permission of my uncle, even though he had seen letters from him. However, in the end I was given 1,000 pardaos by the monastery without interest. I insisted, however, that the contract for this be made with an interest of 20%, like the rest of the money. All would have to be paid in Aleppo to the Carmelites. I made four copies [of the agreement]. After a few days, through Father Giacomo and Father Valerio and by means of the provincial of the Osservanti Fathers, I was given 3,057 pardaos that needed to be taken to the Holy Land and that I would pay in Aleppo. This was given me by their commissary, who was to travel with me. He could have given me more, but invested [it instead] in some jewels. He was reprimanded for having given me the money on interest by his general, because it was not proper that the fathers should traffic with alms given by the faithful. They were only to deliver the money in the most convenient way possible. These alms are collected by a lay commissary called Fondon, who is well known in those parts for the many trips he takes to China and the nearby provinces. He gathers much money for the holy places in the Holy Land. The commissary who gave me the money had been a companion to the one who collected. His name was Father Ambrose, and he had been a layman. The main commissary had sent him once to the Holy Land to take alms there, and he had gone on to Rome, where he was ordained, and, forgetting the gratitude he owed to his companion, he had had himself appointed main commissary and superior to the one who had been the author of his fortunes.

[JANUARY 1674]

Half the month of January had already passed, and the fleet was not yet ready to leave the port. In fact, it was said that it would be delayed one more month. With Father Giacomo and others of my companions I thought to go to Mulla to spend carnival time. I often went there for recreation. I was kept from doing so, however, by a sickness known as *zarna* or *cerna*, which is a scab, very familiar in Goa, especially after illnesses.[210] It causes diarrhea and produces scars everywhere on the body. To cure oneself, the only remedy is to wash with warm water many times a day, by

210. Infection by staphylococcus bacteria would cause both diarrhea and skin infections and would also respond to bathing and washing the skin. My thanks to Richard Nuttall, M.D., for this information.

which one quickly gets better. They say that to use any other cures just makes things worse. My case was a bad one, and it lasted a long time, but I got better with only warm water.

[FEBRUARY 1674]

Lent began on the 7th of February. Carnival had not been a time of much fun, and Lent in that city was a time full of devotions, sermons, and processions with all the people attending. One of the principal days was that of the 11th, which was the first Sunday. Every year there is a procession made by the Augustinian fathers called "the way of the footsteps," in memory of the painful trip that our Lord made when he went to Calvary with the cross on his shoulders. There were many floats in that procession, and all were rather well made. Among these the most important was one in which there was a man representing Christ our Lord, who was carrying the cross. There were a great many flagellants dressed in white, and in many places in the city there were altars and tombs where the procession stopped. The man who carried the cross would turn to look behind him in memory of what Jesus had done when he had turned back to look at the women who were crying for him and said to them: "Filie Jerusalem nolite flere super me," etc.[211] When he would turn around, all the people would break into tears. When the procession arrived at the church of Graces, where it ended, the nuns sang something. Then another float came out representing St. Veronica who, while drying the face of the one who was representing our Lord, received his image on the cloth, which was a copy of the one preserved in Rome. They unfolded the cloth so that all would see it in the plaza. All cried out in contrition and implored mercy, and with that the service was over. Every Friday in Lent they make another procession, called [the way] "of the disciplined," going to visit the altars that are in the city during the day and at night, in the same way that they visit the church of St. Peter in Rome on the Fridays in March. They call that visit the *Correr os Passos,* that is, "the Following and Visiting the steps of our Lord." It serves them as a way to pass the time devoutly, especially at night. These services are held by the Portuguese with much seriousness and magnificence by the clergy, who are rather rich. This brings

211. Luke 23:28: "Daughters of Jerusalem, do not weep for me; no, weep for yourselves and your children."

them admiration and serves also as an example to the [other European] nations in India, because, although [the Portuguese] have lost most of the lands they had at the beginning, they maintain completely their former decorum and splendor, especially in religious feasts.

Since I have touched on the point, I do not think it a bad idea to enumerate the kingdoms, provinces, island, and cities of which the Portuguese have been owners in India and how these have passed to other rulers. At the time of King Emmanuel they took Goa, now the metropolis, and Malacca from the Moors; they built the fortresses of Hormuz, Cochin, Calicut, Socotra, Anjidiv, Cananor, Coclan (?), Colombo, Ciaul, Pacen (?); Ternate (Molucca Islands); Cranganor (India); Sofala (East Africa).[212] The kings or rulers of Hormuz, Tidore, Quilon, the Maldives, Coclan, Malinde, Zanzibar, and Batticaloa[213] made themselves vassals of the king of Portugal. Many others asked for peace and for friendship with the Portuguese. At the time of John III they founded many settlements in the lands of friendly kings, and they acquired on the Coromandel coast the city of Meliapor, that is, San Thomé, of Negapatan,[214] and all the coasts and ports of the island of Sri Lanka, although they did not go inland. They also got the fortresses of Galle, Negombo, Batticaloa, Trincomalee, Kalutara, and Jaffna,[215] which for many years was the metropolis of their dominions. On the northern coast they took the cities of Bassein and Daman with many forts and villages along the entire coast along the sea in the kingdom of Cambay. There they built the fortress of Diu. In Malabar they built the fortress of Calle, and in China that of Macao. At the time of Don Sebastian, Don Enrico, and Don Filippo they built the fortresses of Mombasa in Africa and three in Kanara, that is: Onor (Honawar), Barcelor, and Mangalor.[216] They built the

212. Bembo is not presenting these fortresses in any geographic order: Hormuz (Iran); Cochin and Calicut (India); Socotra (Arabia); Anjidiv and Cananor (India); Coclan (?); Colombo (Sri Lanka); Ciaul (India); Pacen (?); Ternate (Molucca Islands); Cranganor (India); Sofala (East Africa).

213. Tidore in the Molucca Islands; Quiloa (Quilon) on the Malabar coast; Batticaloa on Sri Lanka's east coast; Malinde on the East African coast.

214. Meliapor (or San Thomé) just to the south of Madras; Nagappattinam on the southern Coromandel coast.

215. All in Sri Lanka. Bembo spells them as follows: Galle, Negumbo, Batticalà, Triguimalà, Calaturre, and the fortress of Giaffanapatan.

216. These three forts (Bembo's Margalor, Barcellor, and Onor) dominated Kanara from north to south.

fort of Sinan in Pegu.[217] In Africa they built the forts of Sena and Tete on the river they call the river of Kuama.[218] On the Gulf of Bengal they built the city of Golin[219] and took the Moro of Chaul, which was one of the best fortresses in those countries. In Arabia they took about eighty-seven Portuguese leagues of coast, where they took the fortresses of Coriate, Matara, Soar, Cofacan, Libidia, and Doba with the city of Muscat.[220] They became owners of all the shores from the Cape of Ras al-Hadd to that of Musandam and made into their vassals the kings of Pate, Pemba, Quitene, Monomotappa, and many other places.[221] With these conquests they had become powerful and feared in all of India. Into the port of Goa came all the precious and rich things that had been gathered in other places. There one always found many ships full of all the good things found in India. From Japan there came rich fleets with silver; from China, gold, silk, porcelain, and musk; from the Molucca Islands, cloves; from Sunda, nutmeg; from Bengal, fine cotton cloth; from Pegu, rubies; from Sri Lanka, cinnamon; from Mussulapan and Golkonda, diamonds; from Manar and Persia, pearls; from Ajeh, gum benzoin (or benjamin); from Jaffna, elephants; from Cochin, angelins, which is a sweet-smelling wood, and leather; from Malabar, pepper and ginger; from Kanara, rice, which is the only food of the Indians; from Solor, wood; from Borneo, camphor; from Madura, saltpeter; from Cambay, several kinds of merchandise; from Quisn, incense; from Arabia, horses; from Persia, rugs and silks; from Sofala, gold; from Mozambique, ebony, ivory, and amber; from Hormuz, Diu, and Malacca, much money.[222] In this state of grandeur the Portuguese lasted until 1600.

When the English entered India at the time of the viceroy Don Mattias of Albuquerque,[223] they encouraged the Persians to make war against the Portuguese. With their help 'Abbas I, king of Persia, took Hormuz, Bandar 'Abbas, and the islands of Qeshm and Larak from the Portuguese at the time

217. Pegu in Burma.

218. Kuama in Mozambique.

219. Golin remained in Portuguese hands until it fell on September 29, 1633, to a Mughal army sent by Shah Jahan.

220. They thus gained control of the whole Arabian coast on the Gulf of Oman and in the Persian Gulf.

221. All on the East African coast.

222. Sunda, east of Goa; Solor in Indonesia; Madure (Madura) in south India; Qishn on the Arabian Peninsula.

223. Don Mathias de Albuquerque was viceroy from 1591 to 1597.

when the king of Spain was also reigning in Portugal.[224] When the Dutch entered India at the time of the viceroy Ayres de Saldanha under the pretext of doing commerce,[225] the Portuguese lost the fortresses of Amboino, Ternate, and Tidor and the island of Mannar, which is in front of Sri Lanka and was famous for its pearl fisheries, which are now exhausted.[226] They lost the city of Negapatam on the Coromandel coast, the fortresses of Cochin, Cranganur, and Cananor, and the city of Cochin in Malabar, which they lost recently on January 10, 1663. The king of Arakan took the fortress of Sirian in Pegu.[227] The Great Mughal took the city of Golin in Bengal. The king of Vijaynagara recovered San Thomé, which was given to him. They also lost the fortresses of Mangalor, Barcellor, Onor, and Cambolin. The Emir of Arabia took the whole coast from Ras al-Hadd to Ras al-Musandum with all the fortresses and cities. Other kings obliged the Portuguese to abandon the fortresses they had in their kingdoms, among them that of Calicut. Others were destroyed because they could not be maintained. After those losses they had to go to Surat to get spices and cloth to use in their lands, and they had to buy them at very high prices from the Dutch to whom previously they had given what they needed. There they also had to buy European things brought by the French, English, and Dutch, except for those things that their ships brought from Lisbon.

Suddenly on the 17th [of February] the news reached Goa that the Arabs of Muscat were passing the coast in the north with twenty ships and burning the towns of the Portuguese as far as the city of Bassein. The viceroy ordered then under pain of death that all the soldiers had to be ready the next day to embark and that also the captains should be ready. He himself wanted to go with the fleet, which consisted of eighteen galliots and three large ships with many soldiers and many knights who would follow the viceroy as usual. This quick departure obliged me to leave unfinished the preparations that I was making and to embark that same evening. At the 24th hour I left Goa as best I could, but I did not reach the ship until the 18th, since it was at a distance of nine miles from the city. The ship was called the

224. Shah 'Abbas I ruled from 1587 to 1629. Qeshm and Larak are in the Persian (Arabian) Gulf.

225. Ayres de Saldanha was viceroy from 1600 to 1605.

226. Ternate and Tidor are in Indonesia; Mannar is in northern Sri Lanka.

227. The kingdom of Arakan occupied the western coast of Myanmar (Burma).

St. Catherine. On it was the captain to whom I had been entrusted, who welcomed me with every courtesy. He excused himself that the room had been put at the disposal of the Captain General, who was going to embark on this ship. Thus I took a place in the open. That same day, in order to make his trip by way of the Red Sea, Father Giovanni Seabra boarded a merchant ship that had come from Bassein by order of the viceroy. At lunch time I was called by that captain to his table, where nothing but rice cooked in water was served, as well as butter, which everyone served himself as amply as he wished, since there was permission to have milk products during that Lent because there was a lack of oil. Since everyone ate with his hands, but I was not able to, they found me a spoon. After the rice we were offered some cheese and biscuits, with which we ended the meal. The evening meal was the same. To tell the truth, I was disconcerted, thinking about the many times the captain had told me not to make provisions of food, since he wanted me at his table. Then, however, I saw that that is the usual way they treat gentlemen on the fleet. When I saw on the 19th that the viceroy had not embarked, I returned to the city and provided myself with some things to eat on the side. Having remained until midnight with the Theatine fathers, I embarked again on the ship's launch, which was waiting for the sailors, who were natives forcibly removed from their towns and placed on the ships to do the most menial and tiring work.

I arrived aboard on the morning of the 20th, and the viceroy did not arrive that day. Father Feliciano, Prior of the Carmelites, was happy about the opportunity to go to Shiraz,[228] since he had to be present at the chapter to be held there to elect a procurator to go to Rome. He decided to come aboard with a companion, especially since he wanted to be elected to that office, and he was putting confidence in the presence of the viceroy, who was his friend, to support him in his desire. With these thoughts he had already provided himself with some fine things to take to Italy and had taken leave of the gentlemen and ladies in Goa, as if he were already elected. He was disappointed, because the chapter elected a Flemish father named Cornelio di San Cipriano, who had served with merit for twenty years in those parts and who was of advanced age, perhaps too advanced to undertake such a long trip. In fact, he died in Basra, as I learned with great sorrow after my arrival in Venice. He had been very amiable toward me. Father Martino, a Portuguese native of Goa, who had gone as his companion, took

228. Shiraz in southern Iran.

his place. Thus the prior returned not too happily to Goa to continue his work.

[THE ARABIAN SEA AND THE PERSIAN GULF]

Finally on the 24th the viceroy embarked on a ship called *Cardais,* because he had chosen its captain as Captain of the Fleet, even before the news of the Arabs had reached us. He reviewed the whole fleet and army, in which the principal knights were enlisted to accompany the viceroy. They get some pay anyway (about which I spoke earlier in the entry for April 22),[229] since they do not consider it disgraceful to be in the pay of the king. On my ship there were, besides the Captain of the Sea and of War, who has the supreme authority in navigation and in the army,[230] two captains of soldiers: they were both knights and sat at table with the said captain. One was Francisco Pereira and the other Consalvo di Sosa. There were also ninety soldiers who formed two companies that took turns of one day each at the watch. On each company's day its captain had all the authority in the event that the Captain of the Sea and of War is absent. In case both should be missing, authority rests with another official, who also has the title of Sea and War and is chosen by the principal captain. To govern the ship while at sea, there is an official called the Master,[231] although usually the Captains of Sea and War know all about navigation. There were also a pilot, a steersman, and other minor officials, along with twenty Portuguese sailors who serve as cannoneers and helmsmen and who trim the sails in case of fighting. In addition, there are all the native crewmen—many on each ship—who do the hard work, since the Portuguese think it below them. Those poor people are badly treated, as I have said elsewhere. On the same day the Captain General embarked on our ship, along with the Father Prior and a companion of his. The viceroy unfurled the flag on the lead ship.

On the morning of the 26th a sail was seen, and the viceroy sent the Captain General to recognize it, since the ship he was on was the fastest. We took up the anchors quickly and left the port with a good wind but soon

229. Presumably he is referring to the entry for April 22, 1673. In fact, he has not mentioned this point before.

230. The commander in chief of the Portuguese armed forces in Goa.

231. The sailing master.

were becalmed. The Captain General had two launches, each armed with a cannon, as well as many soldiers, and sent them to identify the ship and oblige it to come into port. The wind turned, and the launches remained far from that ship without being able to reach it, so they returned and reported that it had a mast similar to that of the *terrade*. With that we returned to port. After we had dropped anchor, a gentleman by the name of Emmanuel de Andrada came to see the Captain General and brought information from the viceroy that a small ship, recently come into port, had reported that the Arabs had left the shores of Bassein after having burned three churches in the town of Mahim and had destroyed almost the entire place where I had been before arriving in Bassein. In addition, the news had arrived that a fleet guarding Diu had fought with the Arabs and had lost two ships; the fleet's captain had died, and the fleet had burned one enemy ship.

On the 27th at sunrise the viceroy gave orders to lift anchor. The three ships and six smaller vessels left the port but did not advance very far because there was not much east wind. At midday it became a northwest wind and obliged us to remain there until the 22nd hour and finally drop anchor again so as not to make leeway. All along that coast one can drop anchor and be safe while being at the same time a short distance from land. We were in front of Karwar,[232] land of Shivaji, about seven miles from Goa. The Captain General invited to dine with him the captain, some knights, the officials mentioned above, the Carmelites and other clerics, and some civilians.

On the morning of the 28th we lifted anchor, and the northwest wind continued; thus we kept the prow toward the sea[233] in hope of finding another wind and so as to get away from the land and from the currents. There was no change, however, and on the morning of the 1st of March we were out of sight of land. Despite the fact that we were sailing, the chaplain celebrated Mass. Each ship has a salaried chaplain, and they are mostly Augustinians. They say they have a special dispensation [to say Mass under these conditions], and they even say more than one Mass in one day if there are clergy on board. The altar is on the deck and protected from the wind by some curtains, and, as a precaution, the priests help one another during the celebration. At midday the pilot, a Dutchman with much experience, took a reading of the sun and observed that we were to the south of Goa.

232. Bembo uses the word "Chiaporà" here.
233. They are tacking.

The wind continued, and we were being pushed toward the land. During the night the northwest wind became stronger and gave us much trouble.

[MARCH 1674]

Early on the morning of the 2nd, the watch reported that the ship of Captain Mor, who commanded the fleet of small ships that sailed with ours, was without a mast, and that the others were in much trouble. The viceroy decided then to tow the ship of Captain Mor, since the wind was getting stronger. He ordered that the Captain General should tow three ships, and the other ship should tow the other two. We directed ourselves toward land to return to Goa to fix them, since they had suffered considerably, as they were small. During the night we had luck with the wind, and around the third hour the viceroy gave orders that we should turn out to sea. They were always using a sounding line to find the depth of the water we were in. We were in only fifteen arm's lengths. Around midnight the tow line of two of our little vessels broke, and they remained stranded. The same happened to the lines of the two being towed by the third ship. One of the latter came close to us, and they cried out that they were sinking and lit a lamp. The Captain General turned the ship to follow it, although it was not possible to reach it all night. It was going toward land, and we lost sight of the viceroy.

At daybreak of the 3rd, the watch spied five small vessels and a ship. The Captain General dropped anchor and decided to go toward land, when the wind permitted, in order to see if the viceroy had entered the port of Goa. If he should not find him, he would look for him toward Muscat. At midday, according to the astrolabe, we were south one more degree, which is about thirteen Portuguese leagues. Soon thereafter we saw the viceroy, and we took up anchor right away and sailed toward him. At around the 22nd hour the watch spied four small sails, six large ones, and then nine more, which made us suspect that it was the Arab fleet that had been pushed into those waters by the wind or that was coming to those coasts to provide itself with rice. With that supposition we unfurled the flag at the bow and fired a shot to signal that we had seen some sails. Immediately, soldiers were mustered and cannons and munitions and everything were got ready to fight. In truth, those soldiers showed such courage and joy that one would think that they were about to sack a ship that had already fallen to them. Shortly thereafter, the viceroy fired two shots, and the other ship was going toward those sails and was the closest to them. The Captain General, observing that the small vessels were dispersed, judged it best to stay close to them, even though by so doing so he was leaving himself exposed. At such times grave disorders occasionally arise among the Portuguese, since they do not communicate enough with one another and since each one wants to be the first to attack the enemy. I don't know whether it is because they want glory or because they want booty, but many times they expose themselves to certain danger. As the nineteen vessels advanced, we observed that they came in good order, and from that it was reasoned that they were Europeans and not Arabs, who go in groups without any order. At the 23rd hour we saw the flag of the Dutch admiral, and then we raised that of our admiral on the bow. When the Dutch recognized it, they immediately dropped anchor, even though they were far from land. No greetings or messages passed between the two groups, due to the pretensions that each nationality has of being the more important. At night we anchored not far from the Dutch in front of the island of Anjidiv.[234]

They lifted anchor at the same hour as we did on the morning of the 4th to take advantage of a little bit of wind. We all kept our prows toward the north, which was useful for them too because they were going to Surat. The wind began to come from the northwest at around the 23rd hour, so we lowered the anchors in order not to make leeway.

On the morning of the 5th we set sail again with a slight wind. In the evening we anchored again because of a current. We did the same on the 6th. We should have been able to reach Goa in two days, but we were only able to drop anchor near the Rock of Marmagao, a rock at the mouth of the port beside the fortress of the same name.[235] From there we set sail on the morning of the 7th after being becalmed for some hours; the wind came from the west, and we entered the port. We dropped anchor, and the Captain General immediately went aboard the viceroy's ship, where they consulted about what should be done. They decided that the viceroy should debark and send to Persia the normal fleet, since it seemed difficult to find the Arabs at sea. They wanted to try to gain some victory over them on land. Besides, some disorders had arisen in Goa during the viceroy's absence that called for his attention so that they would not cause more trouble. I was told by those gentlemen that every time a viceroy goes to sea with a fleet on

234. The Dutch and the Portuguese were not then at war. Anjidiv Island is about 70 km south of Goa.

235. Marmagao is about 10 km south of Goa.

some important mission, everything goes wrong, either because the viceroy dies or because troubles start up in Goa or because there are storms or other grave matters. Many attribute this to witchcraft practiced by the wives and lady friends of those gentlemen who only leave when the viceroy does. I don't know how believable this is.

For whatever reason it was, on the morning of the 8th the viceroy debarked and was saluted not by the firing of cannons but by the shouts of the sailors and soldiers, regulated by the whistle of the steersman. He answered many times with a "Bon Voyage!" in a loud voice. They introduced this custom when they first came to India to save ammunition, and, finding it a good idea, they practice it to this day. That same day the Captain General also debarked and was similarly saluted. They said that [his debarkation] was because he might distinguish himself in some exploit and because there had been competition between [the general and the viceroy] even in Portugal. The Captain General's name was Giovanni Corea di Sà, and it was a worthy family; he was young and full of spirit, with a noble, generous, and confident spirit, [qualities] not common to that nationality. I had made friends with him, and very courteously he would invite me to spend the days aboard ship with him.

On the 9th the wind became strong again and continued all night. At the fourth hour our ship's anchor cable broke, and we were in danger of colliding with the others or of running aground. Although we immediately dropped two anchors, the ship kept on going toward shallow water, so we were already getting ready the launches to go ashore. However, we dropped the third anchor, and it held, so that we were saved, thank God.

The wind died down, and on the 10th we got some provisions on land, and around midnight the signal was given to lift anchor. Almost immediately, the sails filled, and we went out of the port with very little wind. On the morning of the 11th we were three ships under sail, and, since another ship had been readied during our absence from Goa, the viceroy ordered that it join the three of us, along with five small vessels, since Captain Mor's ship, which had suffered more than the others, could not be repaired in time. The captain of the fleet was on the ship *Cardais,* and his name was Emmanuel Mendes. Around the second hour of sunlight there was a signal from the port that we should return. The small vessels paid attention, but the ships pretended not to notice and continued on their way. The signal had been sent by Captain Mor, but the captains of the ships were not fond of him because he had his position through the viceroy's partiality, not because he was of the profession. Around midday the wind came from the northwest, so we dropped anchor so as not to drift back. We were in front of Karwar, from where we could see the port of Goa. The other two ships did the same. After the Captain General had got off the ship, the captain had taken into his quarters the captains of the troops and Emmanuel Tesseira Franco, a cleric who was brother of the Inquisitor of Goa and who had come aboard as a friend of the Captain General. The viceroy wanted him, as well as the many others who had signed up and been paid, to go with the fleet, even though their only reason for doing so [in the first place] had been his own departure [with the fleet]. Since I saw that I would not have a room, I made a bargain with the pilot, who was Dutch. He courteously let me have his little room, where I stayed with all my things, and thus I was freer. When I debarked, I gave him ten reales. I continued the trip with the full friendship and confidence of all those gentlemen, who really would have given me their quarters if I wanted them.

On the 12th around midday we saw a sail and recognized it as the captain's ship, which was coming toward us with good wind. Night came before it reached us, and since the wind came from the east, we lifted our anchors around midnight to follow it. But on the morning of the 13th we saw that it was near the port of Goa with its prow toward the sea, despite the fact that it could have reached us. Then the ship called the *Madonna of Remedy* and the other ship followed us. Shortly thereafter, we saw a sail that, when it came close, was seen to be a merchant ship of some Gentiles of Surat. It had landed on the coast of Daman the past winter and was being handed over to the king of Portugal according to the agreements mentioned above. It was being led to the viceroy by some Portuguese. As an extra security measure, we accompanied it to the port. Because of the wind, we dropped anchor around the 23rd hour in front of the beach of Barde.[236] The small ships had returned to the port, and the head ship was anchored also. We stayed there the whole day of the 14th because the northwest wind continued strong. Although the same wind continued the morning of the 15th, the lead ship set sail, and so did we, along with the *Madonna of Remedy* and the five small ships. The *Madonna d'Oliviera* remained in the port to await its launch. Around midday the *Madonna of Remedy* fired a shot, followed by another, so we went close to her and were told that she was leaking and was going to return to port. We turned to follow the lead ship, which was way ahead. Around the 23rd hour she furled her sails to await the small ships.

236. Bembo's "Bordese," formerly an island, to the north of Goa.

On the morning of the 16th we found ourselves so far to the south that we could barely see the Rock of Marmagao. We had lost sight of the small ships, which we judged were even farther south. We decided to anchor in front of the beach of Salsette, not far from land. At midday we saw the smaller ships, which joined us before nightfall.

On the 17th before daylight we all set sail together, since there was a slight favorable wind from the southwest. The lead ship was towing three of the small ships, and we were ordered to tow the other two, so that we could all travel together faster. However, the wind changed to northwest, and we were not able to go beyond the Rock of Marmagao. We dropped anchor. Toward evening the ship *Madonna d'Oliviera,* which had remained behind, came out of port and anchored near the lead ship. With this unhappy situation of setting out in the morning and anchoring at night, we continued until the 24th, which was Holy Saturday.[237] We went into port then to await a favorable wind. Meanwhile, I observed that on Holy Thursday all the soldiers and sailors went to confession and took communion to fulfill the precepts of the church, except those who could show that they had made their devotions during Lent. Since one sailor on our ship could not demonstrate this and did not satisfy the precepts like the others, he was excommunicated and put into solitary confinement, until the chaplain asked for his pardon and said that he would make his devotions as he should. Yet with all this piety, nothing of all that had been stolen on board was returned. Holy Saturday was solemnized with the firing of shots for the Gloria. Just when I was thinking that I would not be able to go with the fleet to Persia that year because of the adverse winds and because the officials had little desire to set sail, we finally left on the 24th. We traveled all night with a good north wind and headed west. At the fourth hour of sunlight on the 25th we were again obliged to heave to, because the wind changed to the south. Thus we celebrated Mass on the holy day of Easter. We passed that day gaily seated around a rug in the captain's room and eating fresh meat and salt pork from Portugal. We traveled then for many days, losing sight of land that evening of the 25th [of March] and not seeing it again until the 17th of April. Nothing of particular note happened in that time. We saw many flying fish, which I de-

237. In the week before Easter, Holy Thursday commemorates Judas's betrayal and the institution of the Eucharist, and Holy Saturday the burial of Christ.

scribed during my trip to Goa. Two soldiers died during that period and were buried at sea.

[APRIL 1674]

On the morning of the 17th [of April] the fog was so thick that we could see nothing from one end of the ship to the other and could not take a sighting of the sun. We almost collided with the lead ship and worked to get a good distance from it when we could hear voices from it on our ship. At around the 21st hour the fog lifted, and to our fright we found that we were only one league from land. We thanked God that the wind had stopped; otherwise we would surely have run aground in that fog. It was the land of Arabia, which lies between the Red Sea and Persia. [It is] a happy land[238] due to its fertility, since it produces in abundance all that is necessary for food; there is also coffee. It is rather populated and has many ports. Its principal city is Medina al-Nabi, which means "City of the Prophet" because Mohammed is buried there.[239] The second city is Mecca, famous because he was born there. Every year many people from Turkey and India go there, and a very rich fair is held.[240] The port nearest to this city is on the Red Sea and is called al-Mukha.[241] These places are dominated by a Prince Sherif who is a descendant of the prophet, as are most of his subjects.[242] He is called the "Zealous Protector" of the sect and is a vassal of the great lord of Constantinople. Around the 23rd hour the wind came from the southeast, and since we were not able to pass that point of land, the lead ship decided to drop anchor near land. Our ship did the same, despite the fact that some did not like stopping like this in

238. Bembo is making a play on the Latin name for the Yemen, Arabia Felix.

239. The Arabic *Medina al-Nabi* is now usually shortened simply to Medina.

240. He is referring to the annual *hajj,* or pilgrimage, which brought Muslims from all over the Islamic world, not just India and the Ottoman Empire. To Muslims Mecca is the holiest spot on earth not because Muhammad was born there (as Bembo suggests) but because it contains the Ka'ba, first constructed by Ibrahim (Abraham) as a temple to one God.

241. Mocha (al-Mukha) is on the South Yemen coast; the nearest Red Sea port to Mecca is Jiddah.

242. The Sherifs of Mecca were descended from 'Ali, the Prophet's cousin and son-in-law, had ruled the city since the tenth century, and were nominally under Ottoman rule in the seventeenth century.

enemy territory. If we were recognized, the news could be sent to the Arabs of Muscat in four days, and a fleet could be sent to meet us. Thus we did not unfurl the flags and hoped that anyone on land would think we were ships from Surat.

On the morning of the 18th we set sail, and by the sun we judged that we were more than four or five leagues distant from Ras al-Hadd. Since the wind calmed down around evening, we once again anchored near land and set sail again before dawn on the 29th with a slight wind from the east. Before midday we saw a terrada that was traveling toward the lead ship, since it thought it was a Moorish ship. When it recognized her, it turned and went toward land. The lead ship sent a launch after her with two small cannons and many soldiers, but they were not able to reach her or make her give herself up. At around the 22nd hour we dropped anchor near Ras al-Hadd, which is located at 22°30".

On the day of the 20th we did not sail, since Captain Mor had brought orders from the viceroy to wait there ten days for reinforcements. If they did not come, then we should proceed with the voyage, and the small vessels had the same orders. While Captain Mor was getting ready two launches to send ashore to see whether they could bring back water, or hunt some animals, or steal some from some flock—since we had seen fires during the night that indicated someone lived there—we saw a large sail. Due to the light breeze, it did not come close before sunset and left us in doubt about whether it was the *Madonna d'Oliviera* or a Moorish merchant ship. Thus at one hour after nightfall we set sail in the direction where we had seen her, with the lead ship heading toward land to stop her. Since the moon was out, we saw the sail again at the second hour of the night, and she was traveling forward with the wind at her bow. Since she saw us, she turned to get away. At that point the lead ship fired a cannon at her. Since she gave no sign of stopping, we fired two more shots after her, at which she lowered her sails and came toward us, saying that it was a ship of Gentiles from Tanur,[243] full of rice and going to Kong and that it had the permission of the viceroy of Goa. It was sent to the lead ship to be recognized. Meanwhile, we put away our weapons, which had been prepared with great courage, and set our path toward land with the merchant ship in front of us. It was then allowed to leave by the lead ship, but we were not able to anchor until the third hour

---

243. Tanur is about 40 km south of Calicut.

of daylight on the 21st in the same place we had been before. All the nights that we spent near those enemy shores we kept a strict watch. On the 25th we saw two small sails near the lead ship and heard a shot. The morning of the 26th a terrada entered port. In a launch that came from it some Portuguese brought us the news that it had been taken by the lead ship the night before and that it was in the company of another ship, as we had seen without knowing what ships they were. While the lead ship took this one, the other had tried to get away and run aground. All the Arabs were saved, and a poor Gentile remained in it, who said that the Arabs had permission to go to the coasts of Sind and Diu, but since they were heading to Muscat they had tried to escape punishment by going ashore. The captains resolved to set sail without going far from that Cape in order to take some other ship, since that was a point of great traffic from Persia to Arabia and from there to Sind and India. Many terrade go without permission or without a legitimate permit (a *cartaz*). We kept watch the whole day of the 27th, and at sunset we saw another terrada, but because of the contrary wind we were unable to recognize it. We continued the watch, and on the 28th at the hour of compline we saw land. At around the second hour of the night the lead ship signaled us with flares and shots to lower the sails and not to move, which we did, replying with similar signals. On the morning of the 29th it came near to us towing a terrada and gave us the first to tow, which was full of rice from the Arabs of Cochin to Muscat. We found other ships and terrade, but all were set free, because they had legitimate permits, and we continued our trip toward Kong.

On the morning of the 30th we found ourselves near land. At the second hour of sunlight we saw two sails that were traveling with a good wind. In order to be able to go after them quickly, the lead ship left the terrada with instructions to stay where it was. As we got close to those sails, we saw that they were two ships, one bigger than the other, and some thought they were merchant ships, and others [thought they were] Arabian ships. The latter seemed impossible, however, to the more experienced men, since the ships were approaching full sail, something that the Arabs would not have dared to do even had they been a great number. They would remember General Girolamo Emmanuele, who with only four ships destroyed seventeen of theirs near their [own] coasts. Reasoning about this, I was the first to suggest that it was the *Madonna d'Oliviera,* and soon all agreed. At midday it was recognized that it was, and we unfurled our flag and greeted her with many shots, and she answered. There was great friendship between our captain and hers, a man called Vasco Luis Cotigno, a gentleman and native of Portugal.[244] He was a worthy man and of noble manner and my good friend; passing by her bow, we greeted their arrival with a thousand cries of joy. He sent his launch to tell us that he had only left Goa on April 1st and that just that morning he had sighted the land of Arabia. He had come across the merchant ship that we had found several days previously and that had been set free by Captain Mor. He had detained her, because the permit seemed to him problematic. Besides, they found Gentile women and holy men on the vessel, and it was absolutely forbidden to carry such persons under punishment of having the ship confiscated. He understood from some of those Gentiles that they had been set free by the lead ship for a fee of four hundred *fardi* of rice, a common standard of measurement. This could cause some confusion, because Don Vasco was an honest gentleman. He also informed us that the rowing fleet had left the same day and was staying close to land.

[MAY 1674]

The morning of the 1st of May we joined with the lead ship. It had wanted to go after one terrada and had lost the one that it had been towing. Since we remained becalmed, Don Vasco came aboard to visit. He told me that Father Giovanni Seabra embarked in Bassein on a galliot for the Red Sea. Halfway along in the trip, it had returned to Bassein. From there he had gone to Surat to find passage into Persia. Since he had not succeeded, he had to remain that winter in India. He also told us that the viceroy had had some men hanged who had attempted to desert the fleet.

On the morning of the 2nd we found ourselves near land in front of the city of Muscat. It is held by an Imam or Arab prince.[245] To take it back, the Portuguese have a continuous war with him. The city is rather strong and

244. The reference is probably to the Coutinho family, prominent in Goan affairs since the establishment of the colony. Dom Vasco Luiz Coutinho subsequently served as field-colonel of infantry in Portugal's Indian territories and from 1701 to 1703 was one of Goa's two ruling commissioners.

245. The Portuguese had seized Muscat in 1507–1508 and had held it until 1649–1650, when they were driven out by the Ya'rubid dynasty, which subsequently set about attacking Portuguese shipping in the Arabian Sea and harassing Portuguese settlements on the west coast of India. From their control over Muscat and Oman they eventually extended their power along

was built in 1588 by Melchior Calazza by order of the Viceroy Emmanuel de Soza Cotigno.[246] It is situated on the northern coast of Arabia on the Persian Sea at 23°4". It was left to the Portuguese by the last king of Hormuz. With it they became lords of the sea, since it has a very good port, and around it on the coast are many fortresses. These were taken with the city by the Arabs when the Portuguese were at war with Spain.

On the 3rd we made good headway with a good wind. However, on the 4th it calmed down but then returned that night. It continued on the day of the 5th, and we found ourselves at 24°37". On the 6th, since we were becalmed, we went aboard Don Vasco's ship and passed happily some hours with wine and sweets. When we left, we were heaped with many wishes for a good trip, which our sailors answered. On the 7th we had a contrary wind from the southeast. After midday we saw the prow of a ship that was following our same route at a great distance. We did not try very hard to identify it, because we saw another one to the south of us that was coming toward us. We turned toward it and got everything ready to fight. At the 22nd hour, since the *Oliviera* was closer to it, it fired two shots, and the ship lowered its sails and displayed a red flag. Since the wind had calmed down, it followed our same route. On the morning of the 8th Don Vasco questioned the captain of that ship, who was a Persian identified as *nakatkhuda,* which in the Indian language means ship master, and his name was Mahmud.[247] He was traveling for merchants of Surat and had goods for Kong and Basra. On the ship were a European pilot and four Flemish ammunition men. He learned from that ship master that the other ship was Dutch and going to Muscat. They had left Surat in a group of six, although two had gone ahead. They had been deceived into thinking that we were the first two ships of their group. Although it had a permit, Don Vasco would not let it go until he had found the lead ship, since the permit had been made for another ship master the year before, 1673. The permit was still good, but there was the problem that it was for a return trip that had already been made. He resolved to keep the ship master on his ship and bring him to Captain Mor. The ship's master was very displeased at not being able to offer his prayers, about which [this prohibition of Muslim prayers] the Portu-

the eastern Arabian coast and down the East African coast. Bembo's comments about contemporary Arab maritime power refer to the Ya'rubids.

246. Manoel de Sousa Coutinho was governor of Goa from 1588 to 1591.

247. *Nakatkhuda* is the Persian word for "pilot or ship master."

guese are very strict. After having taken a reading of the sun, we found ourselves at 25°17", and we saw the land of Arabia at Khawr Fakkan.[248] At nighttime the wind became stronger and continued all day on the 9th. On the 9th at midday we saw Cape of Musandum in Arabia in front of the Cape of Jask.[249] These form the mouth of the Persian Gulf. That Cape of Musandum is full of irregular mountains that look like an organ. Near that cape there are some small islands called the Saleme. Passing by them is dangerous because of the storms caused by the winds coming from those mountains. In sight of this Cape Mahmud's ship turned its prow to the sea, and, according to the superstitious custom of the Moors and Gentiles, they threw into the water a small boat, six to seven palms in length and two palms wide, all furnished with flags, sails, ships [lifeboats and launches], and everything necessary for a big ship, and with inside it a note listing all the merchandise that everyone had aboard the boat. Also they loaded the little boat with cow's tripe and the innards of other animals, dates, and other food provisions. When they throw it into the sea, they all look overboard and accompany it with singing and sounds of drums, and they watch it until it loses itself in the water. This is a tribute that they pay so that their passing will not lead to storms, and they believe as certain that if they do not perform that ceremony on coming from India, they will be lost on their return. A Moor who was on our ship told me that the calms we had experienced in those parts were due to the fact that no tribute had been paid at the Cape. At sunset we saw land on both sides, Arabia and Persia. At the second hour of the night we were becalmed.

On the morning of the 10th the wind was from the west, and we saw Henqam Island before noon. We had gone there to get water with the galliot when I had gone to India. As we approached the port, we saw a vessel and signaled it to find out whether it was the lead ship. If it had been another ship, we were thinking to go for water at another island called Ra's-e Dastakan, even though the wind would be contrary.[250] Since the vessel was

248. Khawr Fakkan is on the Musandam Peninsula.

249. The Musandam Peninsula, the northeastern part of the Arabian Peninsula. The Jask Cape is identified by Bembo as Giasque. The Saleme to which Bembo refers are not actually islands but the extreme projection of the Musandam Peninsula.

250. Bembo's ship has progressed slowly, having sailed only about 50 km since passing through the Strait of Hormuz. Bembo refers to Henqam Island

giving no response, we decided to go see what it was, supposing that it might be a ship from Surat. However, it was the lead ship after all, with the merchant vessel with the rice. Since it was late, we dropped anchor.

We did not begin to fetch water until the next morning, the 11th. After three hours of sunlight an officer with a message written by Captain Mor came aboard to tell us that we had to leave immediately, since they had received word that in Kong there were various ships with merchandise from Surat, and it was thought that they were cheating on fees. He offered to divide equally with us the water that they had taken aboard. A similar letter was sent to Don Vasco, who sent the ship master of the Surat ship to Bernabé di Barres, captain of the ship on which Captain Mor was. He was sent away with his permit approved, although it was rumored that it had cost him something for a gift for Captain Mor. Mor was saluted by the ship master's ship with three shots, and he answered with one. We quickly left the port. During the whole day we were unable to get past the Point of Henqam, and we were obliged to drop anchor near it, where we stayed all day on the 12th.

At midnight on the following night a frigate passed us that anchored in that port. They told us that they came from Kong. In the morning its captain came to visit our captain, telling him that his ship was full and going to Sindh[251] and showing him the permit given him by the superintendent of Kong. The latter had had news of the proximity of the fleet from a terrada that had passed by those shores. He had thought that this year the fleet would not go to Persia, since it was later than usual. After having received that news, the captain was sent aboard the lead ship, where he also said that some boats were about to leave Kong on their way back to Sindh and that they had not wanted to get permits because of the expense: they were hoping not to meet the fleet. We set sail without any delay, although the wind was against us, in order to intercept these ships that had wanted to leave. That day, Pentecost, was solemnized with fresh meat, which we had not had for a long time. The captain of the frigate gave us almonds and melons. They were not of good quality, but we were grateful for them, because they were fresh. Usually those soldiers only had rice and, rarely, biscuits, and their water was strictly rationed. That night we got beyond the point with

---

as Angon Island, and he names Ra's-e Dastakan as Rasa, a point on the southwestern side of Qeshm Island.

251. The province of Sindh in southern Pakistan.

great effort, and the wind continued against us on the 14th. At sunset a galliot of Gentiles passed near us. It was going from Kong to Sindh, and its captain was a Frenchman. After he showed us his permit, he continued on his voyage. Then we saw Ra's-e Dastakan Island. That night we remained anchored near Arabia and set sail again on the morning of the 15th. We could see land on both sides (of the Gulf). We traveled all day and all night.

On the morning of the 16th at sunrise we dropped anchor at Ra's-e Dastakan Island. The other ships had not been able to get past the point of the island, which is only six leagues away from Kong. It is not inhabited, and it is full of gazelles, wild animals similar to goats. In that solitude the captain gave permission to debark to many soldiers and sailors, who came aboard ship that night with oysters and other shellfish. They also brought two poor Arabs they had found on the island, thinking that they might be from the coast of Arabia and their enemies. When they were interrogated, it was recognized that they were fishermen of Kong who had their boat and their companions on the other side of the island and that they had come to get drinking water at a small well almost in the center of the island. Around midnight we set sail, since we saw the lead ship go by. As we remained becalmed at around the third hour of the 17th, we dropped anchor so as not to be carried back by the current. At a distance we could see the ships anchored along the shores of Kong. The wind from the southwest started up again around midday, and we set sail again, but we did not try to move fast, because it seemed that the *Oliviera*, which had remained behind, was anchored. In fact, at sunset we dropped anchor not far from port.

On the 18th the *Oliviera* came close to us with a west wind, and the lead ship anchored at the 22nd hour in the port. It saluted the fort with three shots and was answered by an equal number. It was then greeted by the ships in port, four from Sindh, one from Surat, and the merchant boat with rice. We could also have dropped anchor, since we were so close to land that we could see the houses. But since our captain had the office of admiral, we turned toward the sea to await the *Oliviera*, which was still far away. Together with her, we dropped anchor in port [at Bander-e Kong] at sunset. We greeted the lead ship with five shots, which she answered with three. Some important Persians went aboard the lead ship and were greeted by several shots in salute.

FOUR

Iran

ON THE MORNING OF THE 19th [of May, 1674] I debarked with all my things after having taken leave of that captain and thanked him as was proper. As I left, he had me saluted by all his men. When I got to land [at Kong], I immediately found the commissary of the Holy Land who had come in company with Captain Mor. He decided to make the trip to Aleppo with me, and I agreed, although later I regretted I had ever met him, because he was a man of little virtue and less civility and not inclined to devotion. As soon as I debarked, I wanted to visit the Superintendent, Gaspar de Souza, my friend, to whom I was very grateful for all he had done for me, when I had passed through on my way to India. But he had closed himself in his house and was admitting only his closest friends, because the fleet had brought him news of the death of his wife in Goa. This is the Portuguese custom for several days. Meanwhile, in order to have shelter and freedom until my departure, I asked that the Augustinian Father Vicar, whom I had already met, find me a house. There I retired with my company and my things. Since I thought I would not be there long, I asked one of the Portuguese women there to take care of the household. I would have nothing to do except tell her how many people were coming to dinner. She behaved very well and politely. Nevertheless, it is true that in the few days I was there I spent more than two hundred reales, because I had continually with me ten or twelve officers of the fleet, who would come without having been invited. They would also invite others; they passed the time pleasantly, and many of them even stayed to sleep. When I went out of the house, they came with me and demonstrated their gratitude for the liberty and openness with which I treated them. I had gained their esteem and affection to such a degree that they behaved with all candor, acting as if I were one of their oldest and best friends. In the evenings they would take me to parties and to dinners with women, to whom they are much inclined, even though there is not one there who is worth it. Some soldiers sell their clothes and all they have in order to satisfy themselves, nor are they ashamed to ask alms to have a shirt washed, and all enjoy a worldly life. Those who are not sensual are players of dice and reduce themselves to the same poverty as the others. Those of our ship especially importuned me so much that I had to give some money to all of them. Since the captain had not wanted to receive any fee for my passage, I gave him, the day after I debarked, refreshments of fruit, vegetables, veal, hens, and wine of Shiraz, for which he was very grateful. Another day I went to visit Don Vasco in his ship, and he gave me a letter for a brother of his who is a knight of Malta and lives on that island. When I left, he gave me a walking stick made of turtle shell that was quite beautiful and that I brought with me to Venice. With a ship from Surat came four Franciscans who confirmed the news that Father Giovanni would remain that winter in Surat, because he had not found a passage out of India. In fact, he did not reach Aleppo until the next year; from there he went to Livorno and then to Rome, although he had wanted to go to Venice.

In that warm season they wanted to take me with them to bathe in the Persian bath. These baths are vaulted, with a cupola of glass made in Shiraz that serves to give the place light without letting in air. In one of these rooms there was a paste with which to clean oneself; everyone helped himself to it, since the people who worked there do not soap [the customers]. A greater inconvenience is that everyone keeps his drawers on. In the same room there are many faucets out of which comes water to wash away the soap. After that they have one lie down on the floor, and the employees of the bathhouse wash one in a very improper way. They climb on one and rub the whole body indiscreetly; as a result, during the whole time I was in Persia, I did not want to go into their baths anymore.

In Kong there are, as I have already said, many Gentile merchants who enjoy various privileges in exchange for the large tribute that they pay. They pay it in a curious ceremony on the day the commander enters the town. On that day the commander's servants and officials set up a butchery of many bovine animals along the road on which he will pass. They adorn [the butchery] with branches, wreaths, and other strange things. Nearby, he is attended by the Gentiles, who present him with the usual tribute, but in the manner of a donation: they beg him to free those animals from their impending deaths and [to assure] that during his whole period of government he will not permit any animals of that kind to be killed. The commander swears that he will do as they wish.[1]

On the 28th I prepared all my things for my departure. Especially, I prepared the necessary provisions of food, and I found animals to ride and carry things and a muleteer who would guide me on my trip. Since there was a scarcity of horses, I took donkeys and mules, as is the custom in all those caravans. Mules are used in Persia, even in the cities, since they are of a rather beautiful and fast race and are richly furnished with saddles and other trappings in Turkish fashion. For myself I bought a horse from the Father Vicar. As a sign of friendship and favor, he gave me the trappings, and through his advice I took into service a *chapar*, who is like a foot guide, very experienced about the roads.[2] With one of those, one can go safely alone through all of Persia without a caravan. That is what I did, traveling and stopping at my pleasure without fear of thieves and assassins. The governors of the city and of the provinces must pay for any damage that may be done to travelers, and the king pays the governors for a competent number of mounted soldiers who are to guard their lands and keep them free of criminals. They must be ready, even in times of war. In paying back any damages, the word of the traveler holds.

On the 29th, while the last bargains were being made and the mounts were being readied, I went to take leave of Don Vasco, Don Pietro Tavera, and other captains; and after that I went to see Don Gaspar de Souza, who was beginning to admit visits. He insisted on having me to lunch. He had lodging with him the Carmelites, who, like all religious, were at the best hostel. At the 22nd hour I mounted on horseback. I could not prevent Don Vasco and Don Pietro from accompanying me outside the city. They came in palanquins, along with twenty other gentlemen and officers from the ship on horseback, as well as the Augustinians. Everyone insisted on accompanying me in such a noble and decorous way until sunset. Then they all got off their horses, and we toasted with good wine and pistachios brought by the Father Vicar. Finally I took leave, embracing all of them, as is their custom. I accompanied that act with expressions of my affection, since I realized that I had been treated with affectionate and cordial partiality and with

1. This ingenious method of exacting tribute exploits the Hindu aversion to killing cows.

2. "Sater" is Bembo's rendering of the Persian word *chapar*, a man who rode with the mail bags.

honors the like of which not many can boast to have received from people of that nationality. When we mounted again, they returned to the city, and I followed on my journey.

I was in the company of Father Ambrose, the commissary [of the Franciscan Fathers] of the Holy Land, and the usual people, except for a servant named Ludovico, who remained in the service of the Portuguese as a soldier. To replace him, I took a Persian who, besides his own language, also knew Portuguese, and his job was to buy provisions and to cook. The Father wore his habit, which is respected in all of Persia. I dressed in the European manner. Our fashions are not strange there. The others dressed as natives. After having briefly traveled through some small hills until the second hour of the night, we stopped in a town called Barshah.[3] For the comfort of travelers there is a walled enclosure for taking shelter without any expense, as is the case with the caravanserais that I will mention many times in this Persian trip. We dined rather well, since we were able to buy hens and other things, and there was good water to drink.

On the 30th we did not leave until after the heat of the day had passed. The wind was so hot that it seemed to be coming out of a furnace, and it took one's breath away. Much of this trip was made at night or in the late part of the day. I climbed on horseback after the 20th hour, and after four hours' travel we found a cistern of fresh water in a plain. I stopped until the animals came with the things, and we continued to travel until one and a half hours after nightfall. We lodged in a caravanserai called Chiambar, the name of the town itself. These caravanserais are the same as the khans in Turkey. They are for sheltering caravans, and many along the roads are of good architecture, although this one in Chiambar was not much, since it was in a deserted place where there is not much travel.[4]

On the 31st we likewise got on our mounts after the 20th hour and went with difficulty up a mountain. More difficult and dangerous was the descent,

3. Bembo and his companions are following the mountain road from Bandar-i Kong to Bar Shah and then from there through Lar to Shiraz.

4. During the reign of Shah 'Abbas I Iran undertook a vast building program, of which one of the most notable components was the construction of caravan inns (caravanserais) along all the country's trade routes. As well as enabling greater military and police security along the routes themselves, this commercial policy helped Iran delay for many decades some of the deleterious effects of Europe's domination of the sea routes from Southeast Asia and India.

which I did on foot, particularly because it was night and because the way down could not be seen. These mountains that surround all of Persia are its frontiers and its security, since a few people in the passes can keep out armies. We traveled in this difficult way until after midnight. One of my feet was swollen, so I stayed in an earthen house near a good water cistern until the 21st hour of the 1st of June.

[JUNE 1674]

The mountains continued with frequent ups and downs. We met a chapar, that is, a letter carrier, on foot. Around his belt he had many little bells that serve to keep him awake, since he walks day and night.[5] Usually I would go ahead of the others with my chapar and then stop to wait for them at some cistern. This was quite a relief for me, for in this way I could take rests several times a day. That time I stopped at a place called Chahar Cheshmah, which means "four fountains."[6] There were, in fact, four cisterns of rather fresh water there. When the others arrived, I continued the trip. At the foot of a mountain I saw some salt pools that were very beautiful, and the water was half salt and half sweet. At the second hour of night we dismounted by an earthen house near a cistern called Basse.

On the morning of the 2nd we started up again early, and after three hours' travel through a rocky plain I arrived at Cogar, a rather large town, and lodged in a caravanserai, or *caramusera,* of good construction.[7] One entered through a stone portal, and the whole building was stone, divided all around by arches, half of which were walled from the bottom and formed niches for several people and much luggage. Above these there is a terrace for sleeping in the fresh air. I stayed there all day and part of the next day, since that was what the muleteer wanted, as he came from that town. I found good watermelons and cantaloupes there for refreshment.

At the 21st hour of the 3rd of June I went on my way and journeyed from mountain to mountain. At night I stopped in a caravanserai similar to the past one, which was called Bastae.[8] After the 24th hour of the 4th of June

---

5. The bells also served to identify and hence protect the chapar as a royal official.

6. Bembo's "Chiaburchia."

7. Caravanserai is the common term. *Caramusera* is an unusual transcription.

8. Bastae Qalat.

I went down into a plain. I had started traveling at the 22nd hour. At the 3rd hour of night I stopped in a caravanserai called Parao, which was beautiful like the others. From there at the 21st hour of the 5th I left, and we traveled until the second hour of the night, when we arrived at a beautiful caravanserai in Anveh, a large town.[9]

After the 20th hour of the 6th I got back on my horse, and after a little traveling in a plain I began to go up a very difficult mountain on a spiraling road that was so narrow that on its outer side they have built a waist-high wall. At the time of the Angelus we stopped to eat at a caravanserai called Sarapascan and immediately mounted again and continued our trip to the town of Hormud-e Bagh.[10] We arrived there at the 5th hour of the night in a caravanserai that was not better than the past ones. In fact, its arches were narrower, and behind them for the whole length of the place there were covered stalls for the animals. One should know that besides the caravanserais where we took lodging, there are many others we found every day, two or not more than three miles from one another. This is very convenient for travelers. There are many fountains or cisterns and, even more frequently, earthen houses.

The day of the 7th we left at the 20th hour and traveled until the Angelus. We rested in a caravanserai called Misidarga and left two hours before daylight on the 8th. At the second hour of sunlight we arrived in the city of Lara, or Lar, located in a plain but surrounded by small mountains.[11] On one of them there is a fortress overlooking the city. It is not very important, however, because there are two nearby mountains that overlook it. In ancient times this city was the capital of a kingdom whose lord was independent. In 1600, however, while Ibrahim Khan was reigning there, it fell into the hands of Shah 'Abbas, king of Iran. Ibrahim died while he had him in prison, and thus this kingdom was made a province.[12] It is governed by

9. Bembo's "Anaui," a town south of Lar in southern Iran.

10. Bembo calls it "Cormu." The town is just to the south of Lar.

11. Lar is situated more than 900 m above sea level on a plain separated by mountains from the Gulf.

12. First mentioned in Islamic sources in the fourteenth century, Lar was a flourishing and prosperous trading center; its geographic isolation permitted it substantial independence from central authority. It was subdued by the principal general of Shah 'Abbas I, Allahverdi Khan, who sent its local monarch, Ibrahim Khan, to 'Abbas's court in Isfahan.

a Persian minister with the title of Khan,[13] which is like a viceroy. He lives there when he wants to, and usually leaves [as his deputy] a *sabandar,* that is, an agent.[14]

The city is without walls and not very large. The houses are low and made of earth, except for some bazaars, constructed of stone with high, polished arches.[15] Inside and outside the city are many cisterns where they keep water for their needs for the rest of the year, since there are no springs. Thus they suffer in those years of scarce rainfall. These cisterns are, however, so numerous and so large that they are sufficient to supply water for several years. The inhabitants are not more than 3,000 people—Persians, Armenians, Hebrews, and Gentiles.[16] The natives are of a dark color because of the heat, which is especially strong when the wind comes out of the west, which they call *causin.* Its blowing seems like a flame, and at that time almost all of them retreat into their houses and close themselves in as best they can. Our lodging was in a new caravanserai outside the city, although it was not well built. There were many gardens all around, and there I found melons and watermelons that did not seem to us to be very good and not better than the ones in Kong. The natives, however, seemed to me to be polite and open with foreigners. The coins in use in Lar are ongari, zecchini, reales, and some of their own, which I collected carefully in all places and brought back with me to Venice. Among these I was able to get an old one

13. Bembo spells it "Chan." In order to differentiate between identical spellings, I capitalize *Khan* to refer to a person or authority but use lowercase *khan* to indicate a caravanserai.

14. In his discussion of Aleppo, Bembo defined a *sabandar* as an official appointed as head of the merchants.

15. The *Qaisarieh* bazaar, a large trading emporium built under the auspices of Shah ʿAbbas I, is still the most impressive structure in Lar.

16. In order to further his commercial policies, Shah ʿAbbas I forcibly transferred entire Christian Armenian communities (whose merchants were known for their international ties, particularly with Europe) from northwestern Iran to commercial centers, such as Isfahan, elsewhere in Iran. There were long-established Jewish communities throughout Iran. The presence of non-Muslim Indian merchants in Isfahan is well known, but it is surprising that they were also prominent in smaller towns such as Lar. The ethnic diversity of the population is presumably a result of the importance of the town for international commerce.

called by the name of the city, Larì, of good silver and of a strange form. It is like a bent little rod. On top of the bent part it has some characters. The two points are rounded. Its value was one-fifth real, but they are very rare.[17] On the 9th we did not leave because we wanted to rest a little, but we were disturbed by extreme heat and by many flies, the most insolent and biting I have ever experienced. At the 22nd hour I mounted on horseback; on leaving the city, I noticed the tombs of the Persians. They are similar to those of the Europeans of Aleppo. In addition, they have decorations and intaglio with colors and gold. There is a hole in the middle of the stone where they put food for the dead.[18]

We took the road behind the fortress through dry and arid mountains, similar to the ones we had passed. There was not a single tree because of the excessive heat from the sun. Around the second hour of the night, I stopped in a little plain at a cistern that is close to a caravanserai called Ostami. There I waited until the arrival of the others, and together we continued the trip. The night was pleasant because of the moon. At the seventh hour of the night we all rested in a caravanserai named Dehkuyeh, which was round in the shape of a theater. Inside it had arches like the others, and it also had two rather cool rooms on top of the portal.[19]

On the 11th we traveled from the 22nd hour until the 2nd hour of the night and lodged in the caravanserai Beriz, bigger than the others, with several little towers around it. The arches inside were open from top to bottom, and each arch corresponded to a room. There were staircases in the four corners to go up to the terrace.[20]

We left there at the 22nd hour of the 12th. At sunset we stopped to eat at the top of another mountain, from which we enjoyed a very beautiful view. We continued traveling through level parts and mountains. In the mountains we enjoyed fresher air, and at the fourth hour of the night we

17. There is a marginal note in the text: "Others say of Basra and Arabia; it has on it the name of the prince who minted it."

18. Bembo describes the tombstones of Europeans buried in Aleppo as large marble slabs with inscriptions in Latin and in the deceased's native language. The Lar tombstones apparently have colored inlays that could be of ceramic or stone.

19. Dehkuyeh is 36 km north of Lar. More likely, the caravanserai was octagonal.

20. Bembo calls it "Biri." Beriz is 19 km northwest of Lar.

arrived at a caravanserai named Borun, on a mountain.[21] We ran out of biscuits because those muleteers had eaten them without discretion since they were not used to having them. We had made abundant provisions of biscuits, but during the rest of the trip it was more convenient for me to buy bread. This was a flat cake of barley and not well cooked, which I found difficult to get used to and ate only out of necessity.

Coming down from the mountain on the 13th, we entered a beautiful plain. We stopped to eat in a caravanserai that is called Deadumbae, like the town. Then, always in a plain, we continued the trip until the 8th hour of the night. We took shelter in a caravanserai called Mauser, where the jurisdiction of Shiraz begins.[22] It is located near a stream and some palms that produce dates. Since it is not a town, and there are no other houses, some men stay there who sell bread of the kind described, rice, meat, hens, and every other thing for people and animals to eat. I saw that they give animals flour with water to refresh them. At night those people close the doors of the caravanserai for greater security.

Having mounted at the 22nd hour of the 14th, we traveled through mountains where we began to find woods and thorn trees. At the 24th hour we ate on another mountain near a stream and continued until midnight, when we took shelter in a half-destroyed caravanserai called Chiatal, inside which they sold food, as in the last one.

The morning of the 15th, while Father Giacomo and the Father Commissary were fooling around, they began to argue, and the latter took hold of a knife, although he protested he had done it in jest. I showed my extreme displeasure, and they no longer were polite with one another after that; in fact, there were always more problems. Since we had to travel that day through difficult mountains, I sent the whole company ahead at the 20th hour and remained behind with the chapar until the 22nd hour so as to protect myself from the sun as long as possible. The sun often caused blood to come from my nose, and this was very uncomfortable, especially while riding. I traveled around six continuous hours through difficult and dangerous mountains, where I found flocks of partridges, ten or twelve in a group. They are tame, since they are not hunted by the Persians, and

21. Borun (Bembo's "Benaru") is 6 km from Beriz.
22. I have not been able to identify the present-day name of Bembo's "Deadumbae." "Mauser" may be Mansurabad.

barely got out of the way of the horses. When the mountains ended, I rested a little by a cistern, and after another one and a half hours I arrived at the caravanserai where they were. This was not a nice one, and it was located a pistol shot away from the city of Jahrom.[23]

On the morning of the 16th I entered the city. It is located in a rather beautiful plain. It is larger than Lar and is surrounded by many palms, instead of walls. The houses are all of earth, and the bazaars are not good. It is governed by a sabandar appointed by the Khan of Shiraz. Here I renewed my provisions and found many fruits at a cheap price, especially apricots, apples, and grapes, which I had not seen since I had left Aleppo. To let the animals rest, I put off our departure from there until the 21st hour of the 17th. We traveled through beautiful and fully cultivated countryside. There were many villages and gardens all around, which made a beautiful view. I observed that they were cutting wheat at that time and that it was very abundant. The climate is not very different from ours. We also passed several pleasant hills, and at the 6th hour of the night we stopped in a small caravanserai called Mokhaq.[24] There, since there is no nearby town, some people live and sell foodstuffs.

On the 18th the journey was through countryside full of barley and rice. The ground was low, and there was plenty of water. Along the road I saw some tombs here and there with the remains of destroyed towns. At the 9th hour of the night we stopped in a caravanserai called Shahr-e Khafr.[25] A Frenchman arrived there after midday on the 19th. He was on horseback and dressed in European fashion and had with him a chapar and a Persian servant with two pieces of luggage. He came to greet me and told me that he was coming from Bandar 'Abbas, where he had been on business for his company and that he was going to Shiraz and from there to Isfahan. He wanted to continue the journey with me, and I was glad of it. Meanwhile, we went together to see the town. We entered a garden full of fruit and ate to our satisfaction. When we left, the gardener was happy with a small remuneration. As we went through the town, we were asked to enter the houses of those natives to visit their sick, as happens in Turkey. Certainly he who knows medicine and the language would be of great use there and could also enjoy the trip. At suppertime I invited the Frenchman to eat with

23. Jahrom (Bembo's "Giron") was a major center of textile production.
24. Bembo's "Mocach."
25. Bembo's "Cafrè."

me. He seemed to be a polite and discreet person, and his name was Monsieur Pierre Monferé. He wanted to pay for his portion, but I did not allow it. I saw that he then gave money to the servants for food. At midnight we set out, and we began to feel fresh air. I covered myself more. Our whole journey there was through a great cultivated valley, full of gardens.

The morning of the 20th at the first hour after sunrise we stopped in the caravanserai Barayian near a stream.[26] Since a town was nearby, we sent one of the servants to buy fruit. At the second hour we started out again, and the trip became more and more pleasant, because the countryside was beautiful, and the air was ever more temperate. After we had passed some stony hills at the 24th hour, we dismounted to eat. Then we continued until the fourth hour of the night when we stopped at the caravanserai Muzaffari, which is rather large.[27] We could get no fruit because the town was far away.

On the 21st at the usual hour we began traveling again in a very beautiful plain, in the middle of which we ate at the 24th hour. At the 6th hour of the night we stopped in the caravanserai Baghan[28] after having passed two or three small mountains which are at one end of that plain.

On the 22nd we left at midday so as not to give anyone a chance to tell the French in Shiraz of our arrival and also so as to arrive in the city before sunset. We entered a large stretch of cultivated countryside. We could see the city in the distance. It is in a plain beyond some small hills and between two great mountains. At the 23rd hour we stopped to eat some fruit in a town that is a Persian league distant from the city, that is, four miles. They call this [league] a *farsang* or *parasang*.[29] We remounted and entered the city. The chapar did not know which was the house of Giovanni Belli, an Armenian with whom I was to lodge. He led us a little this way and a little that way. While passing in front of the house of the French, Monferé went in there with such alacrity that he did not even say good-bye to me.

26. Bembo identifies it as "Para." Barayian is a present-day village on the site.

27. Bembo gives the name "Mozaferì." He and his companions are approaching Shiraz from the southeast, and his route is taking him between the ruins of two great Sasanian (c. A.D. 250–651) palaces, Sarvestan and Firuzabad, neither of which he mentions.

28. Bembo's "Baagì."

29. Bembo calls it a *fersegna* or *parasanghe*. The farsang corresponds to approximately 6 km. Bembo has made the journey of approximately 500 km in twenty-three days.

Finally, after having gone through nearly the whole city, we found the house of that Armenian. I had met him two times in Kong and was recommended to him by the Portuguese. He spoke Italian very well. He greeted me courteously and assigned me the best rooms in his house. I let him take care of providing me with all that I needed during the time that I stayed in that city. I was treated very well and with all cordiality. He said he was a Catholic and had made various trips to Venice, Florence, England, Portugal, and Rome, where he had taken the Jesuit habit for a year. He left it when he returned to his own country.

Shiraz is held by some to be the ancient Persepolis, the city of Darius, and to have been built on the ruins of that city in the same place. Those that believe this [story] deceive themselves, for that city was located in a very great plain at the foot of a mountain where there are still ruins near a town called Zargan, about ten farsangs distant from this city.[30] The Persians themselves say that Shiraz was famous in the days of Darius, but that it was situated a little farther down, two or three miles more toward the plain, where I saw many ruins. At present Shiraz is three leagues long and three leagues wide. It is surrounded by many cypress trees and gardens that serve it as walls. It is all open, except toward Isfahan. There it has a wall for a little stretch that is a little higher than the height of a man and three arm's lengths wide. It has been newly made to protect the nearby houses from the overflowing of a stream that, getting swollen with the rains and with water from the nearby mountains, had destroyed some buildings a few years ago.[31] Now it runs delightfully through the city and through the middle of some bazaars. Most of the bazaars are large, beautiful, and majestic, covered by vaults of baked bricks. The houses are low, and from the outside they seem to be poor, because they have earthen walls and no windows along the road. But inside they are of baked bricks and are similar in structure to those of Turkey and Europe. In addition, they are decorated and ornamented with

30. Bembo gives three spellings for Shiraz: "Siràs or Xiràs or Sciraz." Persepolis is 80 km north of Shiraz. The plain to which Bembo refers is Marv Dasht, and he gives the name "Mircascun" to the town of Zargan.

31. Extraordinarily heavy rains caused the Khushk River to overflow and flood Shiraz in 1630 and 1668. The latter flooding was notably severe and was followed by an epidemic of plague. The city had not yet fully recovered when Bembo was there, and many of the ruins he describes were the result of those disasters.

various works in low relief on colored and gilt plaster. The beams, too, are sculptured and painted with much gold. Some also have the walls covered with porcelains.[32] The principal doors giving onto the streets are closed with wooden locks. To knock, they use a stone that is kept for that purpose in a hole near the door. There are many mosques, but only four minarets, which are beautiful and tall. For the lodging of foreigners there are many caravanserais, and many of them serve as warehouses where even Armenians sell their goods. There are several of these [Armenian merchants], and none is married. There are also several Nestorian Christians. Of native Persians there are about 40,000 houses, 500 to Jews, and 100 to Gentile men without women. The Gentiles are allowed to have their own temple. Due to the [religious] liberty permitted there by the king, so that one can be Christian,[33] there are also many apostate Moslems. The only obligation is that they must go to the mufti and say that they cannot observe the laws of Mohammed. He notes their name in a book, and they are called faithless.

The Persian dress is not very different from that of the Turks of Europe. In fact, it is richer and more expensive. This dress is allowed everyone without regard to color—Mohammedans, Christians, Jews, and every other nationality. All can even wear green shoes.[34] They make these of leather in the form of slippers with a rather high and strange heel. Europeans dress in their own style and are well accepted. In fact, all the officials of the various countries dress in their own style in Persia. The women go dressed a bit differently from the men. As is the custom in all the Orient, they cover their heads and faces with a large white cloth that hangs behind them almost to the ground. The jurisdiction of this city begins at Mauser,[35] three days' distance from Lar, and ends not far from Isfahan. It is the head of a province. When the Empire was divided following the ancient Persian kings, this province had its own king.[36] In 1502 it was taken by Shah Isma'il Safavi

32. Glazed polychrome ceramic tiles.

33. That is, so that one may be Christian and that missionaries may proselytize. It is also unusual that Hindus and Jains would be allowed to have their own temple.

34. Green is the color of the Prophet's family and the wearing of it is usually reserved only for his descendants.

35. The village of Mansurabad is halfway between Lar and Jahrom and may be Bembo's town of "Mauser."

36. Bembo's historical reference is to the pre-Islamic Achaemenid dynasty.

(1501–1524). He placed a Khan to govern it. This continued until Allahverdi Khan, who they say was the son of an apostate Armenian.[37] Because of his valor, he had ascended to that dignity. He was so well placed in the favor of Shah 'Abbas, who was then reigning, that he gave him as wife a sister of his and made him Captain General of his army. With it he conquered the kingdom of Lar and that of Hormuz with the help of the English. At that time Hormuz was in the hands of Castilians under Philip II.[38] However, after many years Imam Quli Khan was suspected of wanting to be crowned king of Shiraz. At the same time, a brother of his fled to the [Great] Mughal with part of the army under his command. Shah Safi [1629–1642],[39] the successor to Shah 'Abbas, had his head cut off, along with the heads of all of his relatives, except for his sons. Since they were of royal blood on their mother's side, he spared their lives, but he had their eyes put out, and all their goods, which were of infinite value, were taken away. I was told that three of these blinded sons still lived in Shiraz. At present the king sends someone from his court to Shiraz with the title of governor, with an income of 3,000 tomans annually. A *toman* is worth fifty 'abbasi, which are fifteen reales.[40] He collects the revenues of the province for the king, and they say that these amount to 60,000 tomans a year.

On the 24th I went to see the Carmelite fathers. They had first come to see me, as soon as they had heard of my arrival. There were three priests— Father Girolamo of Jesus Maria, a Pole and the Provincial who had been

37. Shah 'Abbas I (1587–1629) created an elite military corps from captured Georgian Christians. From their ranks Allahverdi Khan rose to become the shah's most effective general, as well as governor of the province of Fars. He died in 1613. His son, Imam Quli Khan (whom Bembo calls Imam Pulican or Culican) succeeded him in that year as the province's governor and exerted wide influence on affairs of state, most notably in gaining the cooperation of the English in seizing Hormuz from the Portuguese in 1622. His power apparently threatened 'Abbas's grandson and successor, Safi (1629–1642), who ordered the executions Bembo describes. Bembo's source of information was almost certainly the Carmelite mission in Isfahan, whose records are one of the most important sources for Safavi history.

38. Spain and Portugal were united under the Spanish monarchy between 1580 and 1640.

39. "Sa Soffi or Seffir" in Bembo's transcription.

40. In modern Iran a *toman* equals ten rials. A rial was a unit of Iranian money.

Superior in Basra when I had passed through there; Father Felice from Naples, who was rather old and had been in the missions for thirty years; and Father Anastasio, a Frenchman. Not far from the house of Giovanni Belli they have a rather pleasant house with many rooms, a good guesthouse, and a small church with only one altar, where the Armenians also have their services, since they do not have their own church. As I said, none of them except Belli is married. There I heard Mass, and four Frenchmen also came. They were in the city to sell some merchandise. Their chief was Monsieur Perot. Afterward I went through the city and saw several bazaars. Besides the beauty of their architecture and their shops, they are rather delightful places because of the above-mentioned water that runs through them. Over the water are some boards, and on these are some platforms that lead into the coffee shops where the Persians go to talk and to amuse themselves drinking coffee and smoking tobacco. Many of them, however, are very fond of studying the sciences and the fine arts. Although they do not know modern authors, on the basis of their ancient ones they learn astrology, mathematics, philosophy, their theology, and poetics, which greatly delights them.[41] They say that some young men send verses to the women they love. As a sign of love, they say they are wounded, and they receive from their ladies cloths to heal the wounds.[42]

Among all the bazaars the best organized was the bazaar of sweets. They make many of these, and they are of good quality, the equal of our Italian ones. I walked through the bazaar of foods, where they sell all sorts of cooked foods. Because of all those heavy smells, it gives a person nausea, but it is very convenient for the artisans and for ordinary people always to find ready their pilaf, their usual rice soup, meat, and every other thing to eat.

41. Since the thirteenth century Shiraz has been famed as the center of poetry in Iran.

42. The same custom was reported more than seven decades earlier by Ulugh Bek, sent in 1599 as a member of a diplomatic mission to Europe. He converted to Christianity and before his death in 1604 completed a memoir (*Don Juan of Persia,* trans. G. Le Strange [New York and London: Routledge, 1926], pp. 54–55). For a representation of this practice, painted twenty-eight years before Bembo describes it, see Anthony Welch and Stuart C. Welch, *Arts of the Islamic Book* (Ithaca and London: Cornell University Press, 1982), no. 36; a broader discussion of the imagery of love can be found in A. Welch, "Worldly and Otherworldly Love in Safavi Painting," in Robert Hillenbrand, ed., *Persian Painting from the Mongols to the Qajars* (London: I. B. Tauris, 2000) pp. 301–317.

Then, too, they bring food to sell throughout the city in ovens covered with copper for the convenience of the shopkeepers who usually eat in their shops. The bread is rather good and white. They make it in large flat cakes with fennel. The wine is the best in all of Persia. They make a lot of it. Even the present king drinks a lot of it, although it is strictly forbidden to his subjects. All the countries provide themselves with wine for their armies here. They ship it to India. Thus the French, Dutch, English, and Portuguese have a license to buy what they need, as well as an agent who keeps it, and every country has a house where he lives; they keep it well furnished so that it also serves for the lodging of [members of] their company when they happen to be in that city. The Armenian Giovanni Belli had the commission for the Portuguese. At the proper time he takes the wine to Kong at his expense in cases of ten flasks, each one of which contains a pound and a quarter of wine. The superintendent pays him twenty-five 'abbasi per case. He then sells it for double that price to the fleet, and the earnings are for him. However, when the Armenian brings him more, the superintendent is obliged to sell it at fifty 'abbasi to anyone, and the earnings from that go to the Armenians.

There are six furnaces, which are large, and they can have seven workers each. They work sitting down, as is their custom, since the furnaces are low. They use *pietra viva*,[43] and the glass is thin and white. They are the best I have seen made outside of Venice. I think it has to do with the air. To be as good as ours, they only lack the inventiveness and mastery in working it. They also make steel mirrors in the city.

On the morning of the 26th I mounted on horseback with Giovanni Belli and went to see the garden of the king, called in Persian _____.[44]

43. *Aiyar*, or new, raw glass, was made from stone and soda. Iran had an ancient history of glassmaking, revitalized by Shah 'Abbas with the assistance of Venetian artisans. Bembo's contemporary Chardin, however, cites glass as one of the arts that the Iranians did not understand, though he singles out Shiraz glass as Iran's finest and refers caustically to a "beggarly and covetous Italian" who taught the art in the city (J. Chardin, *Travels in Persia* [London: Argonaut Press, 1927], p. 275). Fourteen years before Bembo's visit, the Capuchin father Raphaël du Mans reported that the better standard of Shiraz glass was due to their use of new glass, instead of remelted old glass, possible in Shiraz because of the abundance of wood for heating the glass kilns (Raphaël du Mans, *Estat de la Perse en 1660* [Paris: Leroux, 1890], p. 198).

44. Bembo left a blank here and never filled it in, perhaps because he for-

It is immediately outside the city. On going out (of the city), one enters a great avenue, two-thirds of a mile long and ample enough for seven or more carriages to travel abreast. On one side and the other there are the earthen walls of some gardens that border the avenue. In the middle of the avenue are six marble columns that are not very large. They are placed two-by-two and in all occupy a third of the length of that avenue. Among these the Persians have horse races when they play at jerida. At the end of the avenue there is a large palace, half ruined. Running water flows out at its gate. On entering this door one sees on the other side of the palace a garden more than two miles around and divided by an avenue half a mile long. It has large, tall cypresses on both sides. It is crossed by other avenues, also bordered by cypresses.[45] But they are not well kept, and neither is the whole garden. In part, it has barley and vegetables that can be sold, and the rest is full of grasses. Since the king rents it at 150 *tomans* a year, the person who keeps it is only out to make money from it. There is delicious fruit everywhere. At that season it had apricots, apples, cherries, blackberries, plums, and almonds. All were especially delicious. There is plenty of water that runs along the avenues and through the whole garden in some man-made canals. At the end of the principal avenue there is another palace of baked bricks, also in ruins. It is of a round shape with several arches, and around it there are many stone fountains that were all broken. The waters from them run together. Behind this second palace there is another garden, and this was made by Imam Quli Khan, who was mentioned above. Afterward I went to another garden farther from the city. Because of its beauty, it is called Firdaus, which means "earthly paradise."[46] At its entrance there are two rooms, one on either side of the door; and there are also two rooms above. Beyond, one sees a long avenue of cypresses at the end of which there is a stony hill and

---

got the Persian words when he came to write in his journal after returning to Venice. The Persian words were surely *Bagh-i Shah* (Garden of the King). This now-destroyed garden was located to the northwest of the city and is also described in detail by John Ogilby, *Asia, the first part being an accurate description of Persia and the several provinces thereof* (London: Published by author, 1673); and Charles Le Bruyn, *Travels into Muscovy, Persia, and Part of the East Indies* (London, 1737). See also Donald N. Wilber, *Persian Gardens and Garden Pavilions* (Rutland and Tokyo: Tuttle, 1962), p. 205.

45. The description conforms to the classic Safavi garden.

46. The Bagh-i Firdaus (Garden of Paradise) no longer exists but was also described by Chardin (cited by Wilber, *Persian Gardens,* p. 175.)

on that a ruined palace. It is a very delightful place, since from it one sees much of the countryside and the entire city, even though very many houses are hidden because of the quantity of cypress trees that fill the gardens. They are so thick and tall that they make a wood. The same is true in Isfahan. If there are some large trees, only a few, very small trees can grow near them. There used to run some water everywhere around the palace that went to many fountains made in the hill. At the hill's base the fountains ended in a very large tank, or open cistern, of square form and of the height of a man. One would go there in a boat for amusement, and in the middle of it there was a fountain that sent water so high that it reached the height of the palace. However, as I said, now everything is ruined. One sees remains of many columns and very fine sculptures. It was built by the penultimate king of Shiraz, who was a Moor Kafir of Africa.[47] By his ingenuity he rose from being a slave of the king to being his successor. They say that his tomb is in the nearby mountain. The palace was destroyed by the Khans, who took the columns and stones to the city to use them to build mosques and private palaces. The first floor of this palace with all its architecture, which can still be recognized among the ruins, was made by Imam Quli Khan. It has many rooms around a large hall with a fountain in the middle. There I stayed to eat with my company. We enjoyed a view of the whole hill, which was full of fruit trees. This place, too, is rented to a vegetable grower by the king. At the proper season there are very many flowers, particularly roses, from which they make a very sweet water and the most agreeable scent that I have ever known. I took some to Venice, and, after comparing it with others, everyone agreed that it was so.

On the 27th I was visited by Monsieur Monferé, with whom I had many drinks. In those parts it is the custom that the owner of the wine be the first to drink and then to invite the others, so as to reassure them that the wine is good and not poisoned. They also have the custom of putting snow in wine, which makes it cooler and tempers it, since it is rather strong. Moslems put it in water and in sherbets, and it does no harm. That same day I had the opportunity of meeting and talking with an old woman by the name of Perikhan,[48] a sister of the lady Mahani, who was the wife of

---

47. This is apparently a reference to the eleventh-century Seljuq Atabek Qaracheh, said to have been responsible for the construction of the Bagh-i Takht (Garden of the Throne) on the north side of the Khushk River.

48. Bembo calls her "Ismichan."

Pietro della Valle. When her brother-in-law left from Baghdad, she was a small girl of only five years old. Now she was an [elderly] woman of great spirit and vivacity. She was going with her whole family to Isfahan in the company of some Frenchmen with the intention of marrying one of her daughters-in-law to Monsieur Perot. This daughter had been married to one of her sons and had 6,000 reales as a dowry.

On the 29th the Carmelite Fathers Feliciano, Celso, and two others came from Isfahan. These others were Fra Angelo, a Frenchman who was the prior in that city, and Fra Aurelio, a German who was his companion. They came to Shiraz for a chapter meeting to elect a procurator to send to Rome to vote for the election of the new general of the order. Walking through the city, I had occasion to see the courtyards of the mosques, through which one can pass freely. I saw through some low balconies in a mosque that there were no ornaments inside, only many oil lamps hung by twine. They do not let any Christians go inside. I passed through the court-yard of the governor's house. Not a very large patio, it is surrounded by walls, and there were many good horses and mules with their saddles and with rich trappings. The mules walk better than the horses and even cost more. Those animals all belonged to Persians who had come to court to take care of their affairs, since there are days set aside to hear cases and decide litigations. These days are Saturdays and two other days during the week.

[JULY 1674]

I had agreed with the muleteer to leave on the evening of the 2nd of July, since I had finished getting my provisions. But since the animals were rather tired and not good for continuing the trip, I decided to change them. Therefore we did not leave until the following day.

Thus on the morning of the 3rd, since I had the time, I went by horse-back outside the city to see a ruined palace, which nevertheless still preserves much majesty in the ruins. It is rather famous because of the many tombs there of important people.[49] There they still keep in good condition a fishpond that is made in the form of a well with a staircase of stone by which one descends to the water. There, if one throws some bread, many fish come out to eat it without fear. The people venerate them and hold

49. Bembo is describing the area around the modern tombs of the poets Hafiz and Sa'di.

them to be holy. Many dervishes are there guarding them so that no one will take them. The Persians drink that water for devotion, and sick people wash themselves with it. Nevertheless, if a foreigner gives a tip to those dervishes, they can take the fish, but in hiding during the night. When I had taken care of my bills with Giovanni Belli at around the 22nd hour, I had the things loaded. I went to take leave of the Carmelites. There I found the agent of the English from Bandar 'Abbas with several others. They had arrived the day before in order to go to Isfahan, as everyone does. They leave that port during times of great heat and take the occasion to sell their merchandise that has come by ship from India. They also buy other things to send them to India when winter is over.

As I went out of the city, I entered a straight road that was about one and a half miles long and wide enough to take four carriages abreast. There were walls on one side and the other with many houses and palaces, most of them destroyed by time. In the middle of the road is a very large rectangular fountain that is as long as the road. It is full of water and was made, as were all those buildings, by Imam Quli Khan. The road ends between two mountains that rise up these like the sides of a gate. At the foot of the mountains there is a portal or great arch from which the whole street can be seen. On the mountains there are several houses with terraces toward the road. The Persians stay there to enjoy the fresh air in the evening, drinking coffee and smoking tobacco, and they enjoy that beautiful view of many surrounding gardens and of a stream that falls down the mountain behind that gate that always remains open. Through that gate one goes on the road to Isfahan.[50] On my taking leave of Giovanni Belli there, one of the muleteers decided that he did not want to set out on the trip. When the Armenian saw this unreasonable impropriety, he first insulted him and then beat him. This is a considerable liberty that Christians in Persia have over their servants, even when the latter are Moslems. In the Ottoman states, even if one had every reason, it would be a grave crime to punish one's Moslem servants. After three hours of traveling through rather difficult mountains, we stopped at the caravanserai Bagiga, which is large but all ruined. Near it there is a stream of rather good and fresh water. From that point on, one keeps finding better and more beautiful caravanserai with all that one needs

50. This is the Qur'an Gate, a Safavi guesthouse that has since been replaced by a twentieth-century gate. The arch over the road contains a copy of the Holy Qur'an so that travelers leaving Shiraz pass under it.

for traveling. A person alone on horseback can travel in complete safety, as in our countries.

On the day of the 4th we left only at sunset, since the road was through easy mountains and through plains. At midnight we arrived at a town at the foot of a mountain; the town, called Zarqan, is rather big, with houses of earth, since ordinary people live there.[51] This town is off the road that goes straight to Isfahan, but I wanted to go there to see an ancient and very extraordinary ruin that is commonly called the Palace of Darius. I had arranged this with the muleteers before leaving Shiraz, as I was told I needed to, otherwise they would take the straight road. Since there was no caravanserai in the town, I lodged in the house of the muleteer who came from the place, and stayed there all day on the 5th. At midnight I mounted my horse and traveled through a vast plain.

At sunrise on the 6th I crossed a stone bridge with three arches, called Quli Khan from the name of the Khan of Shiraz who had it made. Underneath it runs a river called Bendamir, although Pietro della Valle calls it Kur and attributes the name of Bendamir to the bridge. That river runs through the countryside and then disappears. We continued the journey through that immense plain, which was all cultivated with wheat. At the 4th hour of sunlight I arrived at the town of Marvdasht, located in that same plain.[52] Although it is large and has many bazaars, it has only one caravanserai, and that a small one. It was all filled with the merchandise of some individuals, so I lodged in the garden of some dervishes. With one of them I went at around the 22nd hour to see the antiquities that are at the foot of a mountain and a cannon shot's distance from that town. They are called by the Persians Chehel Minar, which means Forty Columns.[53] To the west of the ruins is the plain, mentioned above. Going toward the east, one first

51. "Zergun or Zercon" in Bembo's transcription. Zarqan is about 25 km northeast of Shiraz.

52. Pul-i Khan (Bridge of the Khan) is the name of the bridge Bembo crossed. Della Valle was correct in identifying the river as the Kor; the Kor River runs southeast from the Zagros mountains and crosses the Shiraz-Isfahan road between Zarqan and Kenareh south of Persepolis. The Band-i Amir (*band-i* [dam of] *amir* [the lord]) is a dam, not a bridge, and was constructed in the tenth century; it is 18 km to the east of the Pul-i Khan. In Bembo's text "Marv Dasht" is the town of Mircascun.

53. The term *chehel minar* really means "forty towers." In Farsi "forty" is synonymous with "many" in this usage.

sees the walls of the marble foundations, about 6 meters high.[54] They follow in the same way on three sides—the western that is on the front, the southern, and the northern; the mountain is to the east. In the façade are two stairways to go up, one from the south and one from the north.[55] They end on a small, square level area that is the width of the same stairs. At that point both stairways continue to climb in the opposite direction: the one that first faced south now faces north, and the other, vice versa. I think the height of these stairways was about fifty steps, but they are low (steps), about one third of a palm. On the northern side, near the mountain, the ground rises so much that one can go up, as I did, on horseback without needing to go up the stairs. When I got to the top, I found a great plaza, all spread out evenly. Where the stairways end, there are two great stones, twenty-eight feet high, at a well-proportioned distance from each other, which makes it seem as if they served as a gate. On each of them there is sculpted a great winged centaur. It has the body of a horse furnished with the trappings of war. Its head is that of a bearded man with long hair and with great wings. They are turned with their faces to the main part of the building. Farther inside there are two columns of the same height, maybe even higher, placed the same distance from each other, and still farther ahead there are two more, but these are broken and lying on the ground. Finally, there are two more stones exactly like the first. These figures are turned toward the east, that is, toward the mountain. Between these figures and the first there is the whole length of this building from west to east.[56] The rest of the construction is all to the south.

Going in that direction, one first finds another area of plaza and then a small stairway in two orders, like the first ones just described. The first level goes toward the east, and the second toward the west. It is in the middle of the façade that looks toward the south, and it stretches from east to west.[57]

54. "Three *picche*" in Bembo's text.

55. Bembo is describing the only formal entrance to Persepolis, the terrace stairway in the northwest. Persepolis was the religious and a political center of Iran under the Achaemenid kings and was constructed over a period of more than two centuries from about 521 B.C. to about 330 B.C., when it was burned on the orders of Alexander of Macedon. Its several different buildings occupy a roughly rectangular site measuring approximately 270 m by 450 m and were built for the most part of a highly polished gray stone.

56. This is a good description of the Xerxes Gate.

57. The north staircase of the apadana.

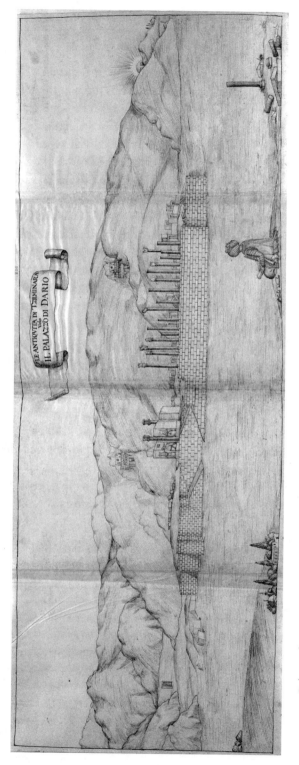

FIGURE 19. Palace of Darius at Persepolis.

The entire wall is not taken up by the stairway. In fact, in those spaces that advance from one side and from the other are sculpted many figures in low relief. They are in order, as if in procession, all turned in the direction of the stairway which is in the center. All the empty space of that façade is carved with similar figures. All are in the same order, which is thought to represent a sacrificial procession, since that building is thought to be a temple, perhaps; or it could be a triumphal procession, or one for accompanying the king when he went out. At the extreme ends, where the figures end, there are some unknown characters. They are unknown not only to the natives but also to all the travelers who have seen them and have brought copies to Europe, as I also did, with a complete drawing of that ruin, as can be seen [figure 19].[58] The dress of those figures is with long trousers that serve as drawers, like those of the *schiavoni*.[59] They have a tight little jacket that goes to the belt where it is tied by a sash, and it reaches to the middle of the thigh. The figures have hair and beards. Some have their heads bare, others have crowns, others have caps like those of the Greek *calogeri*,[60] or hats like our generals, and these latter have beards, long hair, and long robes that reach the ground, as well as long sleeves like the Arabs. Most of these figures have musical instruments in their hands; some have round balls or baskets full of things; and others are leading animals like lambs, rams, camels, or others; some have their weapons drawn; others pull two-wheeled carts; and others carry amphoras and vases. In the same clothing there are some who are larger, who seem to have more authority or higher rank.[61]

Once having gone up this stairway and facing toward the south, one finds a space with the scattered remains of very large columns that three men together can barely encircle with their arms.[62] The number of these, they say, was four hundred, although one does not see the remains of that many. From the many bases that are in their well-ordered places one can see that they could be somewhat fewer. Now there are only nineteen standing,

---

58. The trilingual inscriptions are in neo-Elamite, neo-Babylonian, and Old Persian.

59. Slavic soldiers who served in the Venetian armed forces.

60. Greek Orthodox monks.

61. Bembo has described the images of the representatives of subject nations bearing tribute to the Achaemenid king and demonstrated an impressive understanding of their meaning.

62. The apadana of Darius and Xerxes.

including the first two. Storks make their nests on top of them. From their height one cannot say that something else was on top of them.[63] On continuing to walk toward the south, one finds two small rooms. One is to the right toward the plain, and the other is toward the mountain.[64] These are nothing more than two uncovered squares, surrounded by many great pieces of marble that form various doors and windows. All are carved with large figures, similar to the ones already described, in the act of fighting with beasts. Farther ahead, one finds another enclosed place that is larger and has the same openings and marbles.[65] Behind this there is an open space with the remains of another order of columns, but of lesser size.[66]

One cannot understand any more clearly what all this was. This is not only because time has removed the shape of that great construction and has confused the order of its original construction, but also because it has been destroyed by the villainous barbarity of one of the Khans of Shiraz at the time of Shah 'Abbas I, as I was told by the Capuchins of Isfahan. Since it was the generous custom of the kings of Persia to pay the expenses of foreigners so that they could go to see those and other antiquities that are in their state, they ordered that the Khans of the provinces pay the expenses of Europeans who would go there. Imam Quli Khan, son of Allahverdi Khan, then Khan of Shiraz, on seeing that the number of foreigners was growing because of the ease of seeing those things without expense, swore to remove such an expense and to destroy those ruins entirely. He began to do so. When the king was immediately informed, he sent out an absolute command to suspend that barbarous undertaking that had only been carried out in part.

In the mountain face abutting the plain and in the middle of the natural crevices there are two structures at some distance from one another. It would be hard to go up to them even with a ladder.[67] These are all carved in low relief in the mountain itself, as can be seen from the drawing, and

63. The columns supported capitals on which rested the beams holding up the roof.
64. The building to the west is presumably the Hall of Mirrors, or Palace of Darius; that to the east is the main room of the central palace.
65. The courtyard of the Palace of Darius (521–485 B.C.).
66. Unfinished palace of Artaxerxes III (361–338 B.C.).
67. To the north is the rock tomb of Artaxerxes II (405–361 B.C.), and to the south the tomb of Artaxerxes III, along with a well.

FIGURE 20. Achaemenid tomb at Persepolis.

in the middle there is a hole through which one enters; they say that there are some arches with various tombs that are commonly called the tombs of Darius. I was not able to enter because they were full of water then. At the foot of the whole complex on the south side there is a column with many pieces of others nearby.[68] On the north side not far from the mountain there

68. The Hall of a Hundred Columns.

is a gate of stone that is not very large, and there is no wall nor any ruins nearby.[69] Not far away there are rather beautiful towns scattered in the countryside, as well as ruined houses and considerable ruins of [other] buildings, which lead one to believe that this could be the famous Persepolis.

About the builder of that ancient complex there are many opinions. Most of them conclude that it is older than Darius and the Persian monarchs of those times. The characters one sees there do not resemble those that the Persians used at the time of Darius.[70] These are still preserved by some families, who to this day worship the sun and who write and speak in the ancient Persian way.[71] They are few and scattered here and there through Persia. To the Persians of today the language and the characters of these people are completely unknown. This has come about because the natural language of Persia has been corrupted, since Persia was invaded in part by the Turks and in part by the Arabs. Through exchanges with them the language that they now use was formed, which is a third language, although they pronounce Arabic words without hardness, like the Turks. In writing they use the Arabic alphabet except for some letters, as do the Turks. This leads one to believe that the founder of that place was more ancient than Darius. In Isfahan many Persian authors who are worthy of being believed think that it was built by one of the first four kings of Persia, called in their language Haquumarus, Huchaiug, Talmoure, and Gemseid.[72] The first of these could have been at the time of Bello, or could have been Bello himself, thus called in Persian because in ancient times they were called by various names. Pietro della Valle says that it could be Gemseid, who was a magician and who, because of his beauty, was called Chorseid, which means "sun."[73] He

69. The unfinished monumental gateway in the northeast.

70. There were three Achaemenid kings named Darius, but Bembo is presumably referring to the founder of Persepolis, Darius I (521–485 B.C.). The inscriptions at Persepolis were written in cuneiform, not in the Pahlavi script to which Bembo is referring (see figure 21).

71. Zoroastrian communities in Iran preserved both their faith and its liturgical language, Avestan.

72. Bembo has given the names of the mythical first four kings from Iran's great epic, the *Shahnama* (Epic of the Kings), composed by the poet Firdausi between A.D. 980 and 1020: Gayumars, Hushang, Tahmuras, and Jamshid. His subsequent reference to *Bello* is unclear.

73. The modern Persian word is *khurshid*. Pietro della Valle and Bembo are giving us the pre-Islamic Persian *Khursha*.

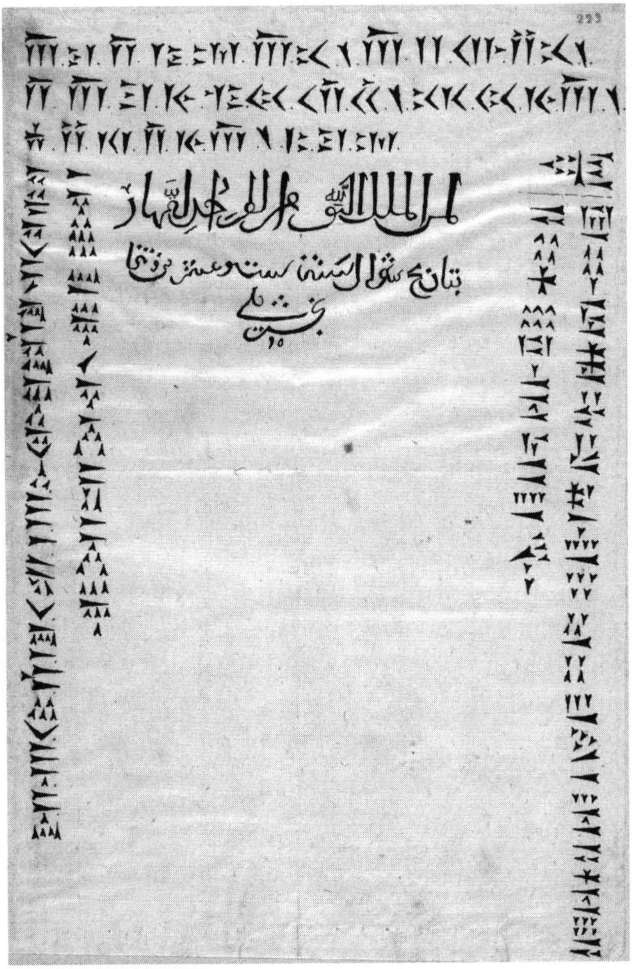

FIGURE 21. Inscription at Persepolis.

sent statues of himself to many places so that they could be adored, so that he is thought to be Nabuccodonosor,[74] if Gemseid is not before then. Other Persian learned men believe that it was built by Artaserse Assuero,[75] whose name was also Darius and who lived in Susa, and that he came to that temple of Persepolis for recreation. However, there is no certainty at all about

74. Nebuchadnezzar.
75. Artaxerxes Sevvom (Artaxerxes III).

any of these opinions, and meanwhile foreigners call it the Palace of Darius, since they do not know what older name to call it. By the Persians it is called Chehel Minar, that is, Forty Columns, because of the many columns, since they consider 40 to mean a rather large and uncertain number.

That night I remained to sleep in the house of those dervishes; it was rather delightful because of the abundance of water and fruit. On leaving I left them a present, because they had treated me with much courtesy. On the morning of the 7th I mounted on horseback. One of those young dervishes came with me. He made me understand that he wanted to go to Europe and become a Christian. However, he repented after a few days and suddenly remained behind.

I continued my journey through the same plain. I passed a stream called Pelvaosuè, or Pellevaosiù. Pietro della Valle believes that it is a branch of the Avasse. It is crossed by a bridge made of three baked brick arches, which is called Giacubehan.[76] At the third hour of sunlight I stopped in the town Zangiabad[77] from which one could see Persepolis very clearly in the distance. I left the things in the custody of the muleteers, and I went with some of the others to see some mountains that are two miles away. There are some very ancient sculptures there called Naqsh-i Rustam by the Persians, that is, sculptures or exploits of Rustam.[78] They say that these sculptures represent the doings of a certain Rustam, a famous man among the Persians in ancient times. They tell fabulous things about him and attribute to him all sorts of deeds and ancient events about which the truth is not known. When we arrived there, I saw those mountains sculptured all around with various figures. The stone was polished from top to

76. The bridge spans the Shadkam River.

77. Bembo's "Zaengiabà."

78. The Achaemenid necropolis of Naqsh-i Rustam is 7 km from Persepolis. It contains four tombs (Darius II, Darius I, Xerxes, and Artaxerxes I) with cruciform façades, three facing north and one facing west. In front of the tomb of Artaxerxes I there is a large fire-temple, which Bembo oddly does not mention. Bembo has mistakenly identified long hair and long, flowing garments with women: there are, however, no female figures on horseback. All but one of the relief sculptures are Sasanian (c. A.D. 224–651), and, despite the name given to the site, the relief carvings show not Rustam but instead historical kings: Bahram IV (388–399); Shahpur I (241–272) defeating the Roman emperor Valerian at the Battle of Edessa in 260; Bahram II (276–293); and Ardashir I (224–241) at his investiture.

bottom. At the base of the mountain, which is divided in large squares, one sees full-relief figures of women on horseback, of women, of kings, and others. The figures wear clothing similar to those shown on figures in Persepolis. However, their movements and gestures are different. They say that they represent the exploits and loves of the said Rustam. Farther up above these squares, where, even climbing with ropes, it would be difficult to get to, there are three façades like those described at Persepolis, which cannot be considered to be anything other than tombs. Those kings of Persia would have themselves buried in mountains and in grottoes carved on high around Persepolis. They would carry the bodies in machines made for this purpose. The doors that are carved in these tombs have nothing more than a small hole through which one enters stooped. These were made by the Muslims, who thought they would find gold and jewels inside, since they knew that it was the custom of those kings to be buried richly clothed. However, they were disappointed, since they found nothing more than some arches under which there were stones for burial with many figures around. This was told me by many who had been to see them. Even if they have not expressed it, one can say that they found the same answer as Darius when he opened the tomb of Semiramide, over which she had had carved that any king who should need money should open it and take all he desired. Thus when Darius seized the city of Babylon, he had that great stone lifted, and behind it he found written: "If you were not a bad man and thirsty for money beyond measure, you would not be looking in the purses of the dead." All around those mountains, above and below, one sees figures, niches, and tombs. A Frenchman who had been inside told me that there are many underground passages through which it is believed those tombs communicated with one another, and not just with the tombs at this site but also with those at Persepolis, which are not farther than two miles from there. There is no other way to enter except for the hole made there by the Muslims, so that one has to believe that they passed through those hidden passages from one place to the other. In fact, in the plain itself there were many similar underground passages that linked those places with each other and also linked one mountain with another. Now they are not used, since the passages have been closed by time and by ruins. One can judge that the city was close to those mountains and that from it they passed underground to the nearby mountains and from one mountain to the other. On the same mountain I saw a column, but I was unable to get any explanation about it. It seems to me that it was a wise idea of those ancient kings to impress their memory on the mountains. These monuments last long after the destruction of many other things, since they are not so subject to the injuries of time.

Having satisfied my curiosity, I returned to the said town of Zangiabad from where I took up my journey again at the first hour of night. Since I had left the main road, we had to take a man from the town to help us find it again. The muleteer himself did not know how to get around there because of the many pools, swamps, and little water canals that form a labyrinth in that plain. When we got a little distant from the town, the unfaithful guide fled with the tip that had been given him, leaving us confused in the darkness of the night without knowing which road we should take. Thus we went wandering for a long time through those narrow strips of land between one body of water and another. Often we would come back to the same place. While crossing those pools, the animals fell down several times with the luggage, so that it was necessary, with discomfort, to unload them and load them again. We continued this way until midnight, without having advanced more than six miles, and our troubles increased because there was no moon. However, when it pleased God, we found ourselves without realizing it on the right road again. Since it was a good and easy road, I went ahead with several of the company and left behind the things with the muleteer. In a short time I arrived at the town of Jarmabaq,[79] where I got onto the main road to wait for the others. There was a very large beam lying on the ground there near a stream. To rest better, I dismounted, and, holding the horse's bridle, sat down on that beam, as did the others of the company. Won over by fatigue, I went to sleep. I had thought that when the muleteer passed, I would wake up. But he passed with the animals on another road, so I did not wake up until the day of the 8th, without knowing what had happened to the others with the luggage. I thought that if they had stopped earlier, they would have sent some servant to advise me; so I concluded that they had gone ahead, which turned out to be true. There was still a good stretch of road ahead before we would reach the town of Mahin,[80] where we had arranged to lodge, and it was already an hour after sunrise; so I had the horses fed. They had traveled much of the previous day and almost the whole night without eating. I had the idea to set off then for Mahin in order to join my companions or to wait for them there if they had not arrived yet. Meanwhile, I sat down again on that beam and took

79. Bembo's "Germavà."
80. Bembo writes it as "Mayn."

another little rest. I was awakened by the noise of people whom I had heard confusedly in my sleep. I found myself surrounded by the whole town, some of them mounted on horses or donkeys and others on foot. Some had come to sell us fruit and other food, and others were attracted by the curiosity of seeing foreign people and their strange clothes. After we had eaten those fruits and given straw to the horses, it was an elaborate struggle to pay them. First, I gave them some 'abbasi, which is the coin of Persia, but they did not want any, telling me through the interpreter that these coins were scarce. They did not know reales. There was no way to change a zecchino in the town. Meanwhile they shouted that they wanted to be paid. Having got angry, I mounted my horse and threw a real apiece to those who had brought the fruits and another to the person who had carried the straw. Thus I paid dearly not only for the food, which was worth very little, but also for the night's lodging on a public road and on a hard bed, which was the beam. Having got on the road that they told us was the way to Mahin, we arrived at a mountain where there were two houses. I was worried that we had taken the wrong road, and I asked two children who were there. They answered in Persian and with gestures, which I understood better than the language, that it was necessary to go down the mountain and then on a road that they pointed out to us. Since that road was not very traveled, as we could tell by the thorns and stones that filled it, I thought we might be entirely lost. I wanted to continue, however, hoping to find either someone who could indicate the way to us or a more traveled road that would lead us to some town where we could hire a guide to take us to Mahin. In fact, after some traveling, I found a more traveled road in the middle of a great plain. After two hours we saw some towns in the distance, and a little beyond that point another road that joined the one we were on. That road was the right one from which we had deviated without realizing it. Some persons we met pointed out to us that Mahin was behind some mountains that we could see not far off. Finally, one of the muleteers who was looking for us found us. He had left the others in Mahin with the luggage: they had arrived there only two hours before midday after having traveled all night because the muleteer himself had taken the wrong road. He had kept to the right of the mountain before arriving in Germava, so that it had been easier to him to go down to the plain and there take the same road we had taken. After going around some mountains, I arrived at Mahin, a large town. I went into the caravanserai located in the midst of the houses; the English had arrived in three days of direct travel. They were the ones I had seen in Shiraz. My good religious companions had made friends with them and had remained with them to eat. They told me that they had even waited a long time for me. However, since I was quite tired, I went to rest where my luggage was, without letting myself be seen by those Englishmen. Nevertheless, their chief, whose name was Master Flor, sent me a gift of some smoked fish. They had been given to him by the aga of that town. They left immediately with six good horses and several men on foot, taking with them all that they needed. In truth, they always travel in decorous fashion, as do all the Europeans, for which they are much respected. Many of them would not receive in their own countries half the esteem they get here.

To let the animals rest, we stayed there the entire day of the 9th until sunset, when I mounted and, as usual, went with the interpreter ahead of the others. We went over several mountains. At the foot of one of them I sat under a tree and rested awhile. Then I climbed up another mountain. The descent in the night was so hard and dangerous, on a very narrow road with precipices on both sides, that I decided to walk. After that I found the muleteer with the luggage. They had lost a mule with its load.

It was dawn of the 10th, and we were unable to find [the mule] until after we had arrived at the town of Ogia or Ugian, two hours after sunrise. There I had some fresh fish. It was rather good, but it was expensive, even though Pietro della Valle says that he had had his expenses paid in that town through a fund that a son of Shah Safi's, who is buried there, had left. He had ordered that in his memory all foreigners passing through there should have their expenses paid. I saw nothing of that, nor did I hear any news of it. I took lodging in the caravanserai, which was not a good one. At midday the dragoman of the Dutch came with four servants and a horse. They had left Shiraz two days after the English to go to Isfahan. When the sun went down, I began to travel again in a very beautiful plain. The dragoman came after us, but then he went over a mountain to make the road shorter, since he wanted to catch up with the English. Thus he was traveling all night, and when there was no moon, he lit some lanterns. We followed along the plain and found many streams.

At the second hour after sunrise on the 11th we arrived at the caravanserai Aupaz or Asbas, where we stayed until the second hour of the night, since a slight illness had overtaken my dragoman. When he got up, we set out on our trip again through a long stretch of mountains and then descended into a swampy plain. We kept to the left at the foot of the mountain and often passed streams that were coming down from the mountain. At an hour after sunrise on the 12th we stopped in the town of Kuskh-i Zar[81] in a caravanserai that was rather large, with many rooms and covered places for the winter.

There were good stalls and good terraces. At the 23rd hour we remounted and, traveling in a plain, we passed many streams and a larger one called Pulisacunsuì, which was crossed by a bridge called Pulisacun. That night we covered a great deal of road, and we also passed a mountain where we began to see a little snow, which we had not seen since leaving Persia.[82] Thus the nights were cool.

We traveled along a plain, and on the 13th, one hour after sunset, we arrived at the town of Deh Gerdu[83] and entered into a caravanserai that had some water in the center surrounded by trees. After the 23rd hour we took up our trip again, and after an hour's travel in a plain we went up a mountain by an easy road. Two hours before day on the 14th we went down to the foot of other mountains and stopped in a town called Yazd-i Khvast,[84] which because of the narrowness of the place has houses one on top of the other. We left from there at the 24th hour, and we traveled all night in a vast plain on a straight and quite worn road. It is wide enough for eight or ten carriages traveling abreast. At midnight we passed the town of Aminabad, which means "colony of the faithful." In front of it there is a small brick castle where an aga lives.

At the break of dawn on the 15th we stopped in a caravanserai called Maxubet, where I had more disagreements with Father Ambrose, and I stayed there until midnight, letting the others go ahead with the things.

After having traveled in a plain until the first hour after sunrise on the 16th, I arrived at the town of Qumisheh, which can be called a city because of its size.[85] It was, in effect, a city in ancient times. There are vestiges of many tombs in the form of towers, where one sees many stone lions. There are also remains of many bazaars and caravanserais, of which ten still stand. I went to most of them before finding where my party was. I found many

---

81. Bembo's "Coschiser or Cuxchizer."
82. That is, since leaving Basra on the outbound journey.
83. Bembo's "Gergerdun or Delighirdà."
84. Bembo's "Gesdacàs or Izdchást."
85. The monuments Bembo describes in Qumisheh (Cosmizá or Comzè) are no longer extant.

kinds of fruit, particularly some very good melons. I saw many ruins of ancient houses and buildings.

At the 24th hour I started off again and traveled all night through a plain. At daybreak on the 17th I stopped in a good caravanserai in the town of Mahyar, where some servants of the aga came to demand a fee that they said foreigners usually paid.[86] I refused to pay, since I knew that foreigners enjoy more exemptions than Persians. They quieted down but asked me for something as a courtesy, and I gave them what I thought appropriate. I left there at the 23rd hour and met some Dutchmen on the road who were going to Bandar 'Abbas with much silk bought in Isfahan. Around midnight I crossed another difficult mountain. It was very hard to go down, since there was a single path, wide enough for only one person at a time. This serves as a great protection and makes a fort unnecessary. A few people are sufficient to prevent the passage of great armies. Here the muleteers told me a curious fable that they believe to be true. In that mountain there were once a father and a son who did not allow caravans or people to go through if they did not first pay them a fee. They appeared on huge black horses and fought alone against four hundred people. Thus the caravans were obliged to take another road. A few years ago they had finally been killed, and the pass had become safe. That night I saw a lunar eclipse that darkened the moon almost completely except for a very small part. It lasted almost an hour. It had begun to get dark after the second hour and only regained its full light in the third hour before daybreak.

On the morning of the 18th I passed a mountain divided in many delightful hills, after which I entered a very great plain and saw Isfahan at a distance. It seems rather a delightful wood because of the multitude of trees that obstruct the view of the buildings, as can be seen in the drawing. Before entering the city, I passed a large and very long street, similar to that of Shiraz, but inferior in the number and quality of palaces. Along its sides, however, are the walls of the orchards, and along the road itself many trees are distributed in an orderly manner. Water flows on both sides and makes

86. One of the largest Safavi caravanserais, the Mahyar (Bembo's "Mehiár") caravan inn was built during the reign of Shah Isma'il I (1502–1524) and repaired under Shah Sulayman (1666–1692). The town is 51 km south of Isfahan. For a plan, photograph, and discussion, see Maxime Siroux, "Les Caravanserais Routiers Safavids," in *Studies on Isfahan, Iranian Studies,* ed. R. Holod (Boston: Boston College, 1974), vol. 7, p. 356 and figs. 1, 2.

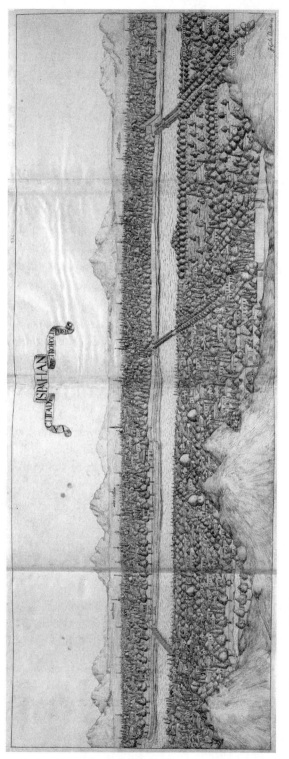

FIGURE 22. Panorama of Isfahan.

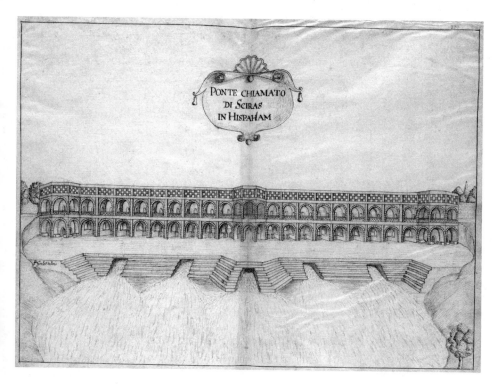

FIGURE 23. Khwaju Bridge in Isfahan.

that passage delightful. At the end of this street I crossed a bridge that the Europeans call the Bridge of Shiraz because it is on the road that leads to that city. It is all made of fine bricks with twenty-seven small arches, under which there is a platform, also of fine bricks, where the water, which is scarce, runs through several holes.[87] Around it there are steps. When the water rises due to the melting of the snow, it rises above that platform and flows through the above-mentioned arches, which are double. Between them there is a wide, covered space, above which is the bridge that people

87. The Khwaju Bridge was relatively new when Bembo saw it. Begun on the orders of Shah 'Abbas II in 1650 to replace an earlier bridge, it was originally linked to the southeast corner of the *maydan-i shah* (royal square) by a street and a covered bazaar. The bridge was also a dam and provided a sheltered walkway over the river for strollers who wished to get a cooling respite from summer heat.

walk across. Beneath it, however, there are also various passageways between the arches. One can pass from one side of the bridge to the other; the covered roadway is in the middle. Above the arches there is the same order and number of arches and passageways with a wide street in the middle. Outside these arches on both sides of the bridge there is a colonnade, or railing, so that one can lean on it while looking at the water. Above the arches there is a very beautiful cornice of porcelain of various designs in very fine work, as can all be seen in the drawing.

After crossing the bridge, I entered the city and continued on a rather wide, straight street with many shops along it, although the houses were rather low. After that I was led through various bazaars before arriving at the convent of the Discalced Carmelite fathers who lived in that part of the city called Mirdan Mir. When I arrived there, I presented to Father Vladislao the letters from his Provincial that instructed him to give me lodging, as he did. He assigned me several rooms in the lower cloister, where we could all comfortably fit, and provided us also with a separate kitchen, which gave us more liberty and left the Father freer. He was of Polish nationality and spoke Italian with great difficulty. I wished that he could always have honored my table with his presence, but he rarely came because of his many fasts. He had the title of Vicar, although he was alone, since the others had gone to a chapter meeting in Shiraz, as I said. The convent is rather comfortable, with a lower cloister with twelve rooms and with a good dormitory above. Usually there were twelve religious there. When Hormuz belonged to the Portuguese, these fathers had their novitiate in Isfahan, but first they took the habit in Hormuz. There is a room that served as a printing shop. It was unique in those parts and had been introduced to please Shah 'Abbas, who had wanted it. They gave him a printed book of the Four Gospels and an Arabic alphabet, but at present the press is all ruined.[88]

They have a church dedicated to the name of Jesus and Mary that is as big as a nice hall. It has several altars kept with much devotion and cleanliness. They have good gardens, in the second of which there is a house that is separate from the convent and furnished entirely as a hostelry, particu-

88. Despite the shah's interest in European printed books and in the printing press, the technology was not adopted. Manuscripts continued to be copied by hand and illustrated by paintings, though a number of the artists were significantly influenced by the styles, techniques, and motifs of European prints they had seen.

larly for the Europeans who continually come there. At that time there was a French guest, named Monsieur Chardin, a very worthy merchant with much capital, who had often gone through those parts.[89] He was in the company of another Frenchman named Racine, who had been in Surat. Chardin was a studious man and knew Persian and Turkish. He has composed a book about the coronation of the living king of Persia, and he was going about making an itinerary of Persia with drawings of all the cities and most important things. For this purpose he had with him a French draftsman who was the one that I would take with me and who made my drawings for this work, as I will tell. The land on which the Fathers had built the convent had been given them by Shah 'Abbas when they came to Persia in 1605, sent there by Pope Clement VIII as his nuncio and bringing a letter from him. As such, they were received by that most gracious king, who called them *Papalino* because they had been sent by the Pope. The first were Father Paolo di Jesus Maria of Genova, Father Giovanni di S. Eliseo, and some others who made the journey by way of Moscovy and Poland. They were so well considered by that king that he would often have them with him, and he would have the Psalms translated into Persian and have them explain to him Italian and Latin letters. Thus he gave them many things and privileges, besides the land I just mentioned. The investiture of the property and all the other exemptions and prerogatives were confirmed by the other kings, his successors, at their coronations. When that Father learned that three days after my leaving Shiraz, Father Cornelio had been elected Procurator for Rome and Father Martino as his companion, he expected the return of the religious of that convent soon, as indeed took place. They arrived a few days after the Father Provincial, the new prior Father Anastasio, Father Angelo, and Father Aurelio. As soon as I had arrived in the city, I was visited by the Father Vicar of the Augustinians. He came on horseback with his syce on foot to make way for him in the road. He had received letters from his Prior, Father Emmanuel, saying that I should be received in the convent, so he courteously insisted that I should go live there. I declined in the proper manner, even though Father Ambrose, as a Portuguese, counseled me to go there, telling me that their convent was

89. Jean Chardin's two books on Iran—*Le Couronnement de Soleiman Troisième* (Paris: C. Barbin, 1671) and *Journal du Voyage de Chardin en Perse et aux Indes Orientales* (London: Muses Pitt, 1686)—are among the most valuable sources for seventeenth-century Iranian and Indian history.

more comfortable and that I would have more liberty since their rule was not so strict, as well as other reasons that were not sufficient to make me change my mind. Besides, I had taken lodging everywhere with the Carmelites, with whom I got along better because many of them were Italian. In the conversation with that Father he told me that news had arrived that some Portuguese knights had been able to restore to his throne King Alphonsus IV, who had been confined on Terceira Island [in the Azores]. They had taken the government from Prince Peter, and among their number there were two brothers of the then viceroy of Goa. Since there had not been confirmation of things, they were believed to be rumors spread by interested people. This proved to be the case, for the news soon vanished, and no one knew where it had come from.

The next day, the 19th, the Prior of the French Capuchins came to visit me. His name was Raphaël, a friar of much virtue and a good mathematician, for which he was greatly esteemed and venerated by the Persians, who take much delight in that science.[90] He discussed it with them, since he had perfect knowledge of Persian. He had been in that city for many years. The other clerics also speak Persian. On meeting other Europeans I got a great deal of news and stories from those parts. If they were not all true, at least they conformed to the taste of those who told them! They told me that the king of France was fighting against the Empire with 200,000 men; that Spain had taken the Franche-Comté; that England had made peace with the Dutch to its advantage and that Spain was the mediator and was obliged to make the Dutch observe the peace; that the king of England consented because in Parliament they spoke against his very person as one who was inclined to the Catholic party; that the Poles, united with the Muscovites, had gained several victories over the Turks and had recovered Chemnitz; that the king of Poland had died a natural death. I had much other news and was surprised at the differences in the news coming from Europe. The news comes through the Capuchin fathers, the Jesuits, and others, besides through letters of various individuals that include printed sheets from

90. Father Raphaël du Mans was one of the most learned Europeans to reside in Iran, and, unknown to Bembo or to any of the other travelers of the period, he had already composed one of the most useful studies on seventeenth-century Iran. His *Estat de la Perse en 1660* was written at the request of Louis XIV's government and remained a private document until 1890, when it was first published by Charles Schefer in Paris.

France. To the Augustinians and Carmelites comes all the news from the East Indies and from Portugal. The Carmelites also get news from Turkey, which arrives from their missions in those parts; they also get the reports and accounts of the councils of Venice. All the way over there, I was able to know about the election of Francesco Foscari as consul of Aleppo to succeed my uncle, and to hear of the exile of seven noblemen for some inappropriate behavior with nuns. These things got communicated from one to another, and many of the Persians themselves, curious about happenings in Europe, go to interrogate those fathers in their convents. The fathers explain everything to them in Persian, and in return the Persians tell them what is new in the country. Thus, although late and with some alterations, European accounts reach Isfahan, as does news of all the world. The Jesuit fathers also came to see me and gave me a message: I don't know if it was affectionate or affected. They excused themselves that they were the last to come, saying that they lived in Julfa outside the city. They had with them some Frenchmen, and others came after they had left, who are all in the king's pay. They live in Julfa and practice the arts of goldsmiths and watchmakers and other similar things. They have their shops near the royal palace. They are much esteemed by the king and well treated. Besides giving them houses and money, he provides them with monthly provisions of every sort of food of the country. The provisions are very abundant, and he also gives them more for every new piece of work they do. They are at liberty to work for other individuals, whom they charge considerably, when they are not doing work for the king. The king is not too inclined to the Europeans, since he is too much of a ladies' man and very different from his great-grandfather, Shah 'Abbas. This latter very much honored and loved all Europeans. To all, according to their station, he gave lodging and spending money, and he called them his guests. Those of them who wanted to stay in Persia he would make rich and often invite them to his public and private feasts. He liked to drink wine in their company, rather than with Persians, and he said that [Europeans] drank wine like men while his people drank like beasts. Pietro della Valle tells about himself that during the reign of that amiable prince, he had the honor to receive the name of "guest" from the king. From him he had many favors and the usual provisions, enough for all his family, which, including the women, numbered twelve people, and for six horses and eight camels. These are the same provisions that every day are given to the above-mentioned Frenchmen according to how many they are in the family. They are double what they need, as they themselves told me, even though some little things that were given to Pietro della Valle are no longer provided. The provisions for one month are the following: 250 patman of flour, and a *patman* is a measure that corresponds to a little less than nine Venetian pounds;[91] 150 of rice and 37 of butter; 80 hens; 19 steers; 17 lambs; 600 eggs; 15 patman of chickpeas with which they flavor pilaf; 12 patman of salt, which is enough even for the horses; 3 patman of spices in general, 10 of dried pomegranate seeds that are boiled in water, which they serve to flavor food, 27 of onions, 20 of wine; 50 wax candles of three pounds each; 12 patman of tallow, 5 of raisins to flavor pilaf, 5 of prunes, 5 of vinegar, 10 of cheese, 20 of sour milk, 3 of sugar; a flask of candied sugar; 5 large carafes of rose water; 5 patman of honey; 1,000 oranges; 100 patman of barley for the animals for which he also assigned 15 *chilè* of land planted with barley, and in every *chilè* they cut 10 measures of grass for a horse, which they give them as pasture in the months of April and May. With greater generosity are treated all the ambassadors of princes. The provisions are given them from the first day they enter the state until the day they leave, and they are different according to the title and position they hold. When they are received, they are not permitted to speak with other ambassadors or with nobles of the country until they have first delivered their message to the king. They can only speak to some of his subjects who are assigned to them for this purpose; and they permit Europeans to talk with religious. Before the Jesuits with the Frenchmen took leave of me, I gave them, as is the custom here, a *bandegia,* which is a bowl of thin wood painted in various colors and full of every kind of fruit that was found in that season, since there were many of all kinds and of the same sorts as in Italy.[92] It is a false accusation to say that peaches were brought to Europe to poison us and that they are deadly, because I ate many most delicious ones.[93] That climate and that fertile and good land do not merit such a false idea among us. Similarly, there are many kinds of grapes, each better than the next, and pistachios as good as in Aleppo. They also have the custom of drinking wine with fruits. The first to drink is the one who receives

91. The *batman,* or *patman,* was the most common measurement of weight in Safavi Iran. Jean Chardin also provides valuable information on weights and measures in his *Travels in Persia* (London: Argonaut Press, 1927), pp. 284–285. I have not been able to determine the meaning of the measurement *chilè.*

92. Bembo's word *bandegia* (Persian *bandagi,* a compliment, a service) apparently refers not to the bowl itself but to the courtesy of giving.

93. The same accusation was made about tomatoes from South America.

the visit and gives thanks for it, as the Persians do. They do not drink wine, however, except on the sly, but rather drink water or fruit drinks. Spahan, or Span, or Isfahan (since it is difficult to write this name in the manner that the Persians pronounce it) is the metropolitan city of the kingdom of Parthia and royal city of the king of Persia's empire, within which there are many kingdoms and provinces. Shah 'Abbas the Great brought his capital there from Qazvin,[94] a city about ten days' distance, also in Parthia, or as others say, in Media. He moved the capital because of the bad air there and also because he was told by an astrologer of his that he would die there or run the risk of treason.

This city is large in itself and also very big due to the three citadels, or suburbs, that are about a mile from the city and can really be called contiguous and united, because they continue the gardens of the city itself. One is called Julfa, inhabited by Armenian Christians; one is inhabited by ancient Persians (of the ancient Persian religion); and the other, by people from Tabriz.[95] Thus it is very large, as can be seen from the drawing, and very populated, not only by natives but also by foreigners there for commerce with the Indies and other places, which makes the city very rich. Besides the Persian natives of the city, there are many from subject countries, and there are 12,000 Indians, partly Moslems and partly Gentiles, all rich merchants. There are many Jews, but [they are] poor and of bad repute, being inferior to the Indians in astuteness and cheating, their chief quality; they live mostly as rental agents and by means of other vile offices. The Armenians of Julfa also are mostly merchants. The ancient Persians are few and rather poor. In addition to these [groups], Arabs and Turks from many places are engaged in business there. Also from Europe there are Muscovites, Poles, French, English, Portuguese, and Dutch.

The houses are high and mostly built of earth, and the walls along the streets have no windows, except for the large palaces. Instead of [sloping] tiled [roofs], they have terraces, which are comfortable and delightful. Much of the city can be seen from them, when the trees are not in the way: there are an infinite number of very large trees. In the summer the terraces

94. Bembo spells it "Casbin." It was the capital from 1548 to 1598.
95. By "ancient Persians" Bembo is referring to Zoroastrians, who lived in a particular suburb of their own. Tabriz, which Bembo calls "Tauris," is the major urban center of Azerbaijan in northwestern Iran and was capital from 1501 to 1548.

serve as places to sleep in the open and stay cool, even though the air is not so very hot, but instead temperate and rather light. Similarly, in winter it is not very cold, especially during the day, though at night it gets colder. In winter [the Isfahanis] make blocks of ice by pouring water into special stone conduits made for that purpose. They keep it for the summer to put in wine and other beverages, as I said elsewhere. There is not much rain, since it falls only five or six times during the winter. If it were more frequent, it would destroy the city, since it is all of unbaked earth, although the houses are rather good and clean inside, with walls painted in various colors and in gold, as is their custom, as are also the beams and the ceilings. There are, however, many buildings of good architecture, among which are the caravanserais, which are many, and three hundred baths and quantities of bazaars with large stone arches, arranged in good order. Some of them are open, and all are full of shops abundant in everything. Their main streets are long and beautiful to look at, but the other streets are terrible, since they are not only narrow but also full of refuse and sewage because the latrines of the houses are there.

Food is not expensive, especially in the absence of the king and the court, who make the price of everything rise. The wine is delicious and mostly white. It is made in Julfa by the Armenians, who drink quantities of it. The Persians do the same surreptitiously, even though it is forbidden by the Qur'an and even more strictly by the laws of the king, which command that Moslems who are found drunk shall be disemboweled alive. Nevertheless, the king himself openly drinks quite a bit and often gets drunk. This fact, however, is not a source of scandal to his subjects, because they hold the king in such veneration that he is almost worshipped, and they believe him to be free to do what he wants, even in matters of law, so that, as a consequence, he is not accountable to God for his life after he dies. The bread is good, well cooked, and made in the form of flat cakes, often with fennel. I liked it when it was fresh, but not when it was more than a few days old. The other foods could be found already cooked by artisans in the bazaars, since they have stores where all kinds of cooked things are sold, as I have already said about Shiraz.

After having rested from the trip for a few days, I began to visit the clergy. First I went to see the Augustinians. I dressed in the Persian manner. The Father Vicar took me to see the whole mission, which is very large and dark, painted in various colors and gold in Persian fashion. They had bought it at the time of Shah 'Abbas, who permitted them to have the place and to construct the church and mission in their own way. Before then, they had lived in the king's house as his guests. They had come to Isfahan several years before the Carmelites as nuncios of the king of Spain, who at that time dominated Portugal and parts of the Indies. The church is in the middle of the mission, all painted gold and in many colors. Over the door there is the choir with a small organ, since the church itself is small. But all is so well kept and clean that everything seems new, although it is many years old. In the sacristy I saw some very fine and rich ornaments, made in China. The refectory is big enough for many religious, although there are only two priests: one native of India with twelve years' time in that mission, who was not able to be prior because he was born an Indian, and the Father Vicar, who was Portuguese, came from that kingdom, and had four years' time there. They have no lay brothers to serve them but instead they use the services of Armenian Christians of Julfa, who work like mules there and keep the mission neat and clean, as can be seen. In the garden there is a separate apartment for visitors, and it had been all set up for me with very good beds in Italian fashion. In a corridor with a beautiful view over the garden there was a table set with many sweet jellies in Venetian crystal plates. We exchanged toasts, and then I took my leave of that courteous cleric. Outside the convent I met the other Augustinian, who was on horseback and wearing an aba and a hat in Persian fashion, so that I thought he was a native, but he recognized me as a European and greeted me kindly.

I then went to visit the Capuchins, who had come to Persia some years after the Carmelites as nuncios of the most Christian King and are therefore all French—two priests and a layman. They have a comfortable house without ornaments, as is their rule, and a small church. Altogether there are three Catholic churches in Isfahan in which more masses are celebrated than there are people to hear them, since there are no other Catholics except the priests' servants and a few European Catholics who chance to pass through. Those few Armenians who are Catholics can hear mass with more ease in the church of the Jesuits in Julfa. Master Flor, an Englishman, was lodged with the Capuchins, who have contact with all nationalities. He sent a greeting to me in the name of his agent, because he was confined to bed. They took me to see the refectory, where they had prepared some fruit, and then I took my leave and went immediately to the house with a bit of fever, which lasted some time and during which I took care of myself with a rigorous diet and without doctors. I ate only cangia, as I did in Goa, which is something they do also in Persia, putting some pepper in the rice soup instead of sugar. During the hours that I had fever, I confined myself to bed, which was on the floor without sheets, the same way I had slept during my traveling. When the fevers passed, I would go out and see the most interesting things in the city. During those days I took only one liberty, which was to eat melons, since they are delicious and of many different types with a firmer body than our melons and a rather thin skin. The sickness of my dragoman and of Father Giuliano and Father Giacomo was more serious. They were taken care of by Father Angelo, a French Carmelite who had practiced medicine and who liked *spargirica*[96] and practiced it with the Persians themselves, since he had perfect command of the language. There are, however, many doctors, who with great dignity stay in their own houses or in the bazaars, as in Shiraz, seated on carpets with an inkwell and paper. The sick go to receive orders for their sicknesses. Those who, because of the gravity of their diseases, cannot visit the doctor, send information about their condition; using the information he hears, he makes a prescription that often serves the sick person as a passport to the next world.

After lunch one day while I still had fever, I was visited by Master Flor, with whom I wanted to act the gentleman and so had more than one drink in his company, despite the fact that I was fasting; I did it because I did not want him to be offended if I did not drink with him, since the English are wont to be offended and not to give heed to excuses, even legitimate ones. I did not eat any fruit, however, which I had ready in ice for such situations. After he left me, however, my fever rose, and I had an attack of vomiting that was very troublesome. It was not until three days had gone by that I got better, and then I went to visit him in the house of his agent. He led me to a delightful apartment, where he entertained me first in talk of news from Europe, telling me, among other things, that the Poles were about to elect as their king the son of the Grand Duke of Muscovy. Shortly afterward, a sumptuous refreshment of fruit and cakes was brought in with various kinds of wines and brandies. After I had done my part, I took leave, and the agent accompanied me to the door. On the way home I observed in a small square not far from the Carmelites' mission a tall and very strange column or minaret all covered from top to bottom with the skulls and horns of wild animals, arranged in good order, as can be seen in the drawing. It is commonly called the Kielle Minaret,[97] and its construction was ordered

96. Pharmaceutical treatment.

97. A two-storied hexagonal or octagonal building had been constructed around the minar's base: the second story was used for the call to prayer. The minar was in the middle of an enclosed square whose sides were also lined with shops. The illustration here is also found in the 1723 edition of Chardin's *Voyages*.

FIGURE 24. Tower of Skulls in Isfahan.

by Shah 'Abbas or, as some others say, by a relative of his, from the catch of a single general hunt that lasted many days, as is still the custom of the present kings, who employ in [such hunts] thousands of people. Around the base of this minaret there are a number of shops, as around the campanile of San Marco in Venice, and above them, where the skulls begin, there is a wooden raised platform from which the people are called to prayer at the usual hours.

I passed through the bazaars of silk, which are quite rich in that kind of cloth in many colors with gold and silver.[98] They have so much silk that they use silk thread to sew woolen and cotton things. The best comes from the kingdoms of Gilan and of Khorasan and from the city of Kashan, where they also make the best rugs of raw silk and with gold.[99] They usually make them in twos, so that it is rare to be able to buy only one. They charge good prices, and they sell them at so much the cubit, measuring their length and width. When they measure many cubits, however, the price rises. Also very beautiful to see is the bazaar of the dealers in sweets. They have many of their wares on display, and they are varied in design and similar to ours in Venice. In the bazaar of those who sell ice, I saw pieces that were two palms and more in width and more than three arm's lengths long. For sale in earthenware bowls on the ice, they have milk that is mixed with something similar to our rose sweets.[100] The bowl leaves the imprint of its shape on the ice. In passing through these and other bazaars I observed that in the fruit season all the artisans and most of the Persians eat a lot of fruit in the middle of the morning without leaving their shops and work or businesses. They eat bread and cheese with the fruit, since they say that it cannot be harmful if eaten separately from the main food. In the evening they have their big meal, which is of pilaf and good meat. They eat seated on the ground, as everyone does in all the Orient.

Another day I went to see the maydan of the Shah (*Sà*, or *Xà*, as I've written elsewhere, or *Scià*, since this word depends on a pronunciation which cannot be expressed in our characters).[101] This maydan is the King's Plaza, and it is the principal one in the whole city. For its size and beauty it surpasses many of the most beautiful in Europe, and I think it is itself surpassed by few indeed. Pietro della Valle, who measured it, says that it is 690 paces long and 230 paces wide. All around, it is surrounded by a building of equal arches in a double order, one above the other.[102] The arches of the upper level

98. He is speaking of finished textiles woven either with silk and gold or with threads around which silver or gold has been wrapped.

99. Bembo spells them "Ghillon, Korasson, and Cassan."

100. The Italian word is *rosate*.

101. In Bembo's time it was known as the maydan-i shah, or royal square. The name *Maydan-i Shah* was changed after the 1979 Iranian Revolution to the *Maydan-i Naqsh-i Jahan*, or Design of the World Square. Likewise, the Royal Mosque *(Masjid-i Shah)* became the *Masjid-i Imam.*

102. Note in the margin: "Built by Sà Abbas the Great; others say it is 700 paces long and 250 wide, its length, that is, from south to north."

have very beautiful openings with imaginative ornaments of the same material.[103] The arches serve as dwelling places for merchants, and the lower arches as porticoes under which are bazaars with shops on one side and the other. All around the plaza is this [one] building, always uniform, with every so often a double-arch of half the normal width remaining open to give light to the bazaars. Near these porticoes runs a stream of water that surrounds the entire plaza. It always stays within its limits, which are traced out in a straight line on all four sides of the plaza. It is crossed by many small bridges of stone in one piece. Between this stream and the porticoes there is a continuous row of very tall plane trees, planted equidistant from each other. One cannot sufficiently express how beautiful and pleasant is such a sight, as one can imagine from the drawing. About two-thirds of the way along one of the long sides there is a façade with a gate to the palace of the king, which is not too big in its perimeter, being a little more than a mile, including separate apartments and various gardens.[104] It makes a majestic sight, however, and is decorated with ornaments in porcelain and gold.[105] On top of the whole construction there is a very large hall or loggia, open on three sides, supported by diverse wooden columns, completely gilded and painted in colors. It can be enclosed with curtains, and in it the king gives public audiences to ambassadors and other people, and he banquets there publicly. In front of the palace gate there are several cannons, half on one side and half on the other. Six of them are of extraordinary size; Shah 'Abbas had them brought from Hormuz, when he took that island from the Spaniards. Their transport was remarkable, since they had to come through those rough and inhospitable mountains of Lar.[106] Some say, however, that they were brought in pieces and then put back together and that they are kept more for the memory than for any need, since the Persians do not use cannons except on battle-

103. Bembo is jumping ahead of himself. Polychrome glazed tiles (the "same material" to which he refers) cover almost all the surfaces of the buildings enclosing the maydan.

104. Bembo's reference is to the 'Ali Qapu, an elaborate structure on the maydan's west side that served both as a public palace, fronting on the maydan, and as a gatehouse to the king's private palace (the Chehel Sutun) and its extensive gardens, which spread into a vast rectangle to the west.

105. The 'Ali Qapu's façade, like the maydan and the buildings in it, was faced with polychrome ceramic tiles, and its wooden surfaces were brilliantly painted.

106. This is a route that Bembo knew well, since he had followed it himself very recently.

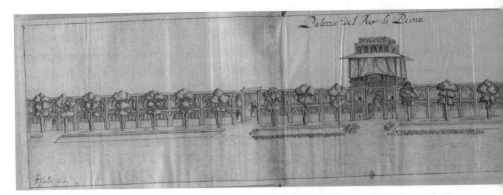

FIGURE 25. 'Ali Qapu Palace in Isfahan.

fields, since their strength is in their cavalry, not in their firearms or sword fighting or arrows. On the other side of the plaza and facing the palace of the king there is a mosque with dome and façade in fine polychrome porcelain.[107] At both ends of the Square there is a beautiful fountain, and at the side that is closest to the palace there is the royal mosque with two minars decorated with porcelains.[108] On the other side there is a large and majestic arch through which one passes to other bazaars.[109] It has two loggia in which at sunset there is a concert of Persian instruments that can be heard throughout the whole maydan. Underneath those loggia is the mint or house where they cast coins. Anyone who pays a certain fee can have coins cast there. At the sides of this gate are several stands of jewelers with many jewels in small boxes covered with silk nets. I observed that most of the rings were of silver, and when I asked the reason, I was told that gold leaves stains on the fingers, which prevents them from going to their prayers if they do not cleanse themselves, so they prefer to use silver, as the king himself does. Next to these stands there is a whole bazaar of jewels where one can find many turquoise and lapis lazuli stones that are gathered in the nearby provinces. In the may-

107. The masjid-i Shaykh Lotfallah on the east side of the maydan was begun in 1601 and completed in 1628.

108. On the south side of the maydan, the masjid-i Imam was begun in 1612 and completed in 1638.

109. This portal on the north side led into the royal bazaar, the largest of Isfahan's bazaars, which extended from the maydan-i shah to the old maydan adjacent to Isfahan's great jami' mosque.

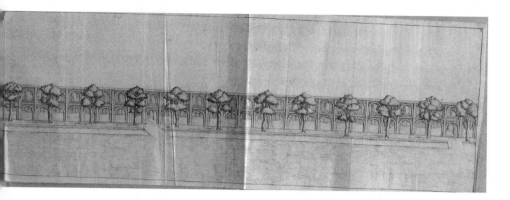

dan it is like a continuous fair, for it is full of shops and stands where they sell all kinds of things. There are also some stands of magicians who sell secrets, dance on ropes, and present theater pieces, as in the plazas of Italy. In the middle of the maydan there are twenty small platforms with chairs on them, one [platform] in front of the other, where the money changers, who are called *saraffi*,[110] conduct their business. This is of great convenience for ordinary people and for foreigners, since they accept all kinds of coins in gold and silver that are not in use and change them for current coins for a small fee. I bought some gold coins from them that were not used in the city, and I could not spend them.

I was only able to see the lower part of the king's palace where the humbler servants live, since the people in charge of it were not present at that time and since the king himself had been absent from the city for months, having gone with the whole court to Qazvin, which means "punishment."[111] That city is so called because those who merited punishment were exiled there. Since it had been the city of his ancestors and thus full of famous memories, the king could not allow it to be deserted and aban-

110. The modern Persian word for money changer is *saraf.* As usual, Bembo tries to render words phonetically.

111. Bembo offers two spellings: "Casbin or Casuin." Isfahanis were and still are fond of jokes at the expense of Qazvinis, the inhabitants of the former royal capital. This is apparently one of them, though Bembo did not understand it. *Qazvini* was also a word for "fool" or "catamite," and the verb *qazvini shudan* (to become a Qazvini) means "to fly into a passion."

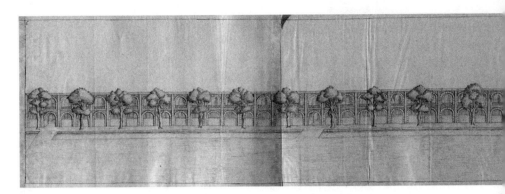

FIGURE 26. Mosque of Shaykh Lutfallah in Isfahan.

doned. Protesting that they had had no money ever since the king had taken his capital to Isfahan, the citizens wanted to leave it. At least partially to repair the damage done to those worthy people, the king usually resides there with his court for several months each year; therefore he brings with him considerable business activity [for the city], for which they praise his name, which is Shah Sulaiman, son of Shah 'Abbas II. He was previously called Shah Safi II, since his grandfather had been the first of that name, but he abandoned that name during a grave illness on the advice of his astrologers, without whose opinion the shahs usually do not undertake anything.[112] They always have several astrologers with them. The Persians, and particularly the nobility, take great delight in astrology and magic. There are public masters of astrology paid by the city. When Shah Safi II was told by his astrologer that he would never get better if he did not change his name, he went publicly to the mosque along with all the nobility and almost all the people, and there in their presence he left behind the name of Safi and took that of Sulaiman with which he has happily reigned for nine years. He is about thirty-six years old.[113] His reign is absolute and monarchical and independent. He has a prime minister

112. Shah Safi (1629–1642) was the grandson of Shah 'Abbas I and the father of Shah 'Abbas II (1642–1666), whose son Sulaiman (1666–1694) is referred to here.

113. Another marginal note in the same hand as for footnote 102: "The coins have characters on both sides: on one side the name of the king who orders the

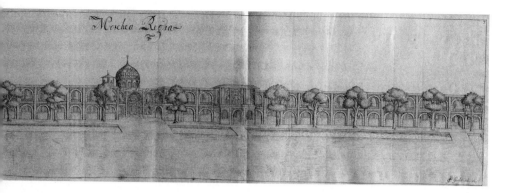

(just as the Ottomans have a first vizier) called *I'timad al-daulat*,[114] who has all the power in the king's absence. He resides in Isfahan, where the Chief Qadi lives who is the vicar general of the law, and where there are also some mufti who are like bishops, as well as some clerics who are called dervishes and *qalandars*.[115] After the prime minister in authority are the Khans, who live in the provinces as viceroys. They collect revenues and have the obligation to maintain at their own expense a set number of cavalry, according to the size of the province where they rule as long as the king wants. In this manner the king always has ready an army of 40,000 horsemen or more, even in peacetime. The Khan of Shiraz is the principal one, and he maintains 25,000 cavalry. After the Khans are the darugha, who are magistrates, and then there are other high offices, which are usually given to nobles who serve the king. Many of these titles and honors are inherited, since there are many families who have titles similar to our counts, marquises, and dukes in Christendom.

The king lives with much splendor and greatness. All his dinnerware is of very fine gold. He has a harem, that is, a house of women, in which there are four hundred women served and guarded by eunuchs, some of whom

minting [of the coin], and on the other the name of the city where they are minted."

114. *I'timad al-daulat*, or "pillar of the state," was a title also used in Mughal India. Bembo spells it "Atmaudolet."

115. *Qalandars* were itinerant holy men.

FIGURE 26a. Detail of Shaykh Lutfallah Mosque.

are made important officials. These women are daughters of nobles and of great men of the country; they can also be Christian slaves. Once in a while he gives some in marriage to prime ministers or other important Persians and endows them with appropriate dowries. Some he marries off while they are still virgins. By religion he is a Muslim, although he and all the Persians are considered schismatics by the Ottomans. The principal difference between them, from which many other differences have derived, is that the Ottomans venerate Abu Bakr, 'Umar, 'Uthman, and then 'Ali as the true successors of Muhammad, and the Persians consider the first three as impostors and tyrants and say that after Muhammad the kingdom belonged by right of heredity to 'Ali, of whom they are followers. They say that the kingdom was taken from him through treachery, and in their prayers they curse them and all those of their sect and pray first to Muhammad and then to 'Ali, whose tomb is in Najaf and is very venerated by the Persians.[116] There

116. Bembo's explanation of some of the principal doctrinal differences between Sunni and Shi'i Muslims is essentially correct. Sunnis accept the legitimacy of the first four caliphs (successors to Muhammad): Abu Bakr (632–634), 'Umar (634–644), 'Uthman (644–656), and 'Ali (656–661). Shi'is hold that 'Ali, Muhammad's cousin and son-in-law, should have been the first caliph and that subsequent lead-

the kings of Persia used to be crowned, and every year many go there on pilgrimage. The tomb was kept hidden for many years by a few, until [the time of] Shaykh Junayd Safavi of Arabic nationality and of the line of 'Ali. He was called to religious life and from him descend the kings of Persia of today.[117] With his way of life he acquired much fame and a great reputation so that all came to see him. He lived in the city of Ardabil, three days' journey from Tabriz, which is noteworthy for being the homeland of Shaykh Haidar, restorer of the monarchy of the Persians, as well as for being the place of burial of all the kings. Wherever they died, they are taken there and buried in the temple with their predecessors. When Shaykh Junayd Safavi died, he was held to be a saint, and his successors had the same office in life and acquired an ever-growing following by revealing his convictions.[118] These were Shaykh Sadr al-Din, Shaykh Junayd II, or Junayd, who had such a [great] reputation that he became sultan and absolute lord of his homeland of Ardabil. He made himself a relative of the royal house, which was then of Ottoman race, and took as wife a sister of King Uzun Hasan's.[119] Shaykh

---

ership of Islam should have remained in the Prophet's family. Accordingly, many Shi'is cursed the first three caliphs as usurpers. 'Ali died in battle against the 'Umayyads in 661 and is entombed at Najaf. Along with Kerbala (where his son Husain was buried), Najaf is one of the most important Shi'i pilgrimage sites.

117. Bembo's history of the rise of the Safavi dynasty is truncated and somewhat muddled. The founder of the Safavi religious order, based in Ardabil in northwestern Iran, was Shaykh Safi al-Din, who lived from 1252/53 to 1334. His great-great-grandson was Shaykh Junayd, who directed the community from 1447 to 1460 and transformed it into a military-religious order, an essential step toward the Safavis' eventual assumption of temporal power in Iran. Junayd died in battle in 1460. He was succeeded by his son Haydar (r. 1460–1488), who also died in battle. Haydar's son 'Ali directed the order from 1488 to 1494 and was succeeded by his seven-year-old brother Isma'il, who was crowned shah of Iran in the city of Tabriz in the summer of 1501.

118. This statement is apparently a reference to the fact that Junayd was the first of the Safavi line to apply to himself the temporal title "sultan" and that Shi'ism, evident as a tendency among earlier Safavis, became decidedly militant under his leadership.

119. By the term "of Ottoman race" Bembo is referring to the Aq Quyunlu, who were Turks but not Ottomans: they were a Turcoman tribal federation whose ruler, Uzun Hasan, was based in Diyarbakır in eastern Turkey. Shaykh Junayd spent three years at the Aq Quyunlu court in Diyarbakır (1456–59) and married Uzun Hasan's sister, Khadija Begum.

FIGURE 27. Mosque of the Imam (formerly Royal Mosque) in Isfahan.

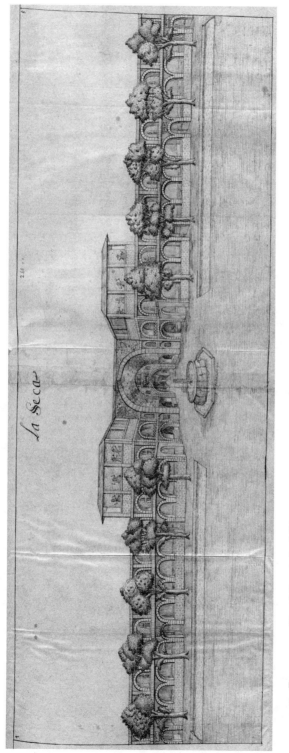

FIGURE 28. Entrance to Royal Bazaar in Isfahan.

Haydar, his son, had for wife a niece, others say a daughter, of the same Uzun Hasan, named Marta, a Christian born of Despina, daughter of Johannes, emperor of Trebizond and the Black Sea, so that Isma'il Safavi, son of Haydar, was of the line of 'Ali on his father's side and of the imperial line of Trebizond on his mother's.[120] When Uzun Hasan died and his successors spurned their relationship to Haydar, they so persecuted him that they had him killed. Nor did they restrain themselves from trying to kill his son Isma'il Safavi, from whom the other kings took the name of Safavi and the Persians the name of Safavis. Finally, forced by the harassment of his enemies, although he professed the religious life as had his ancestors, Isma'il took heart with the help of Turks who were tired of that government and who were bound to him by religion. He made himself felt in arms, and with such a fine following of people he not only retook his previous position but he also extinguished little by little all the heirs of Uzun Hasan and took possession of the whole Turkish empire, where his direct descendants now rule.[121] He was the first to give himself the title of Shah, which means king, in the year of our salvation 1500.[122] So that his soldiers would be different from others, he gave them the order to wear a high, round, and red baton in their turbans, as a sign of the new religion. This baton has twelve folds. He wanted them to be called Qizilbash (*Cheselbas* or *Quizilbassi,* that is, "Red Heads"). Now, they are of two kinds: those who are descendants of those first ones, who passed the title on to their sons, and those who are created by the king, who gives this honor to his slaves and to other people, who remain in the militia and in the nobility with that name. They are much more esteemed than the janissaries of Turkey. The king himself, as head of the militia, wears that same turban on some solemn occasions. The descendants of 'Ali wear the same turban, and when one of them has to be beaten, they first remove his turban, in reverence to 'Ali.[123]

120. Shaykh Haydar married Uzun Hasan's daughter 'Alamshah Begum (who was also known as Halima Begum Agha and Marta); her mother was Despina Khatun, the daughter of Calo Johannes, emperor of Trebizond.

121. Bembo's historical account is accurate, though his expression "Turkish empire" should be understood as the Aq Quyunlu "Turcoman state," essentially consisting of western Iran from Azerbaijan to the Gulf, and not the Ottoman Turkish empire.

122. Bembo offers three spellings: "Sa, or Xa, or Scia."

123. The distinctive scarlet baton (or *taj*) for the Turcoman military wing of the Safavi order was developed by Shaykh Haydar, not by Shah Isma'il I. The

On returning home I observed many writing shops, since they do not have printing presses. Their *mulla,* who are doctors, usually write many books and distribute various copies here and there.[124]

I saw several coffee houses, large and well built, where they gather to drink coffee and take tobacco. I saw a way of smoking tobacco that is very different from that of the Turks and that they also use in India. They have a glass vase or a coconut full of water with two small holes in the upper part: in the upper part of one hole they put the tube with the pipe and the tobacco, and in the other hole there is a shorter little tube through which they inhale the smoke. They say that it comes out tasting fresh, probably because it passes through water. I never took part in such entertainment, but I brought one of these pipes with me to Venice for curiosity.

Not far from the maydan, I passed through the bazaar of the Indians, which is very rich with all sorts of colored cotton textiles from India. They use them to make pavilions, coverlets, cushions, and other things. The Armenians, too, although they live in Julfa, have shops in Isfahan, where they stay during the day. The Indians' principal business is with things from Europe, that is, textiles, mirrors, and glass beads, of which I saw whole warehouses full, since selling them in India has been prohibited. When I wanted to buy anything, I admired the honesty of the Persians: if a buyer has bought something and two or three days later finds that it is of a lesser quality than its price or for some other reason regrets having bought it, the buyer can return to the shop and, once the purchase has been recognized by the merchant, return it to him and immediately receive back the purchase price without any difficulty. This is a very worthy custom, especially with regard to purchasing jewels, since one can easily be deceived in this area.

[AUGUST 1674]

On the 8th of August around evening Father Ambrose, along with Monsieur Chardin, left with a caravan for Tabriz. Many days previously

---

turban wrapped around it was divided into twelve folds in commemoration of Shi'ism's Twelve Imams. The Ottomans derisively called them *Qizilbash* (Red Heads), and the Iranians adopted the Turkish term as a point of pride.

124. By "doctors" Bembo means learned scholars producing texts. His observation, however, is probably not accurate, since the copying of handwritten books would generally have been the job of professional copyists.

he had gone to have meals with that gentleman, and he had paid his portion. He left my company on the pretext that the Frenchman wanted him at his table due to the friendship they had contracted on trips they had made together. The truth was that many times during the trip I had let him know that I was disgusted by his presence; the last time I had done so was in Isfahan, because he had tried to cheat me when he sold certain things that he had with him as merchandise. He thought he would displease me by separating himself from me. In addition, he convinced Father Giuliano to go with them by offering him money at a very reasonable exchange, although in truth Giuliano went [with them] because he was in a hurry to see about some business of his in Aleppo and to get some rest as soon as possible, since he had a fever. I was not in the least displeased, especially since Giuliano had such just reasons. But, although they left a month earlier from Isfahan than I did, they arrived in Aleppo only a few days before my company, since I took the shortest road. I did not take their road, not just because it was longer, but also because I was short of money. In all that time in Isfahan I had not been able to obtain funds, even though I sent the dragoman to Julfa to get some from the Armenian merchants who always kept me hopeful but never, ever reached any conclusion. Thus I had been obliged to pay back a loan that that Father had made me in Shiraz: I had had to borrow the money from Monsieur Chardin and to give him as security some jewels for three hundred Iranian 'abbasi, which accrued an interest of ¾ real during the month that I had them. On that and other occasions I found him to be a very greedy man. He offered me the sum that I needed if I wanted to wait in Isfahan until the return of some letters of exchange that were paid in Aleppo to his correspondent Monsieur Forestier, whom I knew very well. But the arrangement was not practical, due to the long delay, and I realized that they had left suddenly in order to make me sell them some jewels in haste. The attempt was useless, since I had got the money I needed from a Turk.

I went one morning to see the enclosure of the lions and the dogs, which are very fierce and of extraordinary size. They serve as night guards for the king, as is the custom here. In another half-destroyed place I saw two elephants, rather old and very tame. While I was present, I had the pleasure of seeing them take food with their trunks with which they also defend themselves and eat everything. In the same place there was a rhinoceros tied with a heavy chain on his feet. It is a very fierce and ugly animal, as can be

FIGURE 29. Rhinoceros in Royal Zoo, Isfahan.

seen in the drawing.[125] It is taller than a buffalo and twice as broad, and it has short, thick legs with three nails on each foot. In the head it is little different from a buffalo, but on its nose it has a horn similar to a sugar cake, with which it fights, particularly with elephants, toward which it has great antipathy. It vanquishes them when it can wound them in their lower parts with its horn. Its skin is very thick and resists the shots from arquebusses. It is scaly and bumpy, and in some places it is doubled, so that the head and the feet seem to come out of it like a turtle's. It was given to the king by the Great Khan of the Tartars.[126]

I went to the mission of the Capuchins to visit a Frenchman who was residing there in order to learn the Persian language. He had got sick.

125. Grélot's drawing relies very heavily on Albrecht Dürer's famous rhinoceros print, even though his inscription states it was drawn from life (*ad vivum*).

126. Probably the king of the Uzbek khanate.

Before that he had been with the Capuchins in Aleppo, where I had seen him many times. At that time he was learning Arabic and Turkish with the intention of being hired by his king in the office of translator. He had traveled from Aleppo to Diyarbakır, and from there he had traveled in a kalak along the river to Baghdad, where he had encountered a great deal of suspicion that the Persians were about to attack the city. Thus they did not permit through passage to any caravan or person, so he had had to continue his trip along the Tigris to Basra. From there he had gone by terrada to Bander-e Rig, on the [Gulf] coast of the king of Persia.[127] He mounted on horseback there and came to Isfahan. As a result of this information, I made plans to take the Tabriz road on my return, since the Turks do not have such fears there and thus let everyone pass through freely.

A few days later a Roman, named Domenico Santi, arrived at the mission of those same fathers. He came to visit me many times and went around the city with me, and I also saw him after my return to Venice. He was a man of ordinary circumstances and had happened to come to Isfahan on an overland trip. He had left from Venice and passed through Vienna, Constantinople, Georgia, and Armenia in eight or ten months of travel. He had with him glass and crystal merchandise that was not as valuable as he thought it would be. He had sold two rather large crystal vases at the court in Qazvin, but for much less than he would have liked.

On the 28th I went to see a very beautiful apartment of the king's that is called Bab-i Bulbul [the Nightingale's Gate]. It is to the left of the palace on a very beautiful broad street that leads to Julfa. It joins the big palace on the maydan through its interior gardens.[128] At first they made it difficult for me to enter, since I was dressed in Turkish fashion, but when they recognized me as a European Christian they led me everywhere with very great courtesy. When I went out, I gave them a tip of some 'abbasi. This apart-

127. Fifty kilometers northwest of Bushehr.

128. The Nightingale's Gate. Bembo subsequently refers to it as the Palace of Mirrors (Ayineh Khaneh), the name that also appears in the illustration. According to Bembo's description, this palace was on the Chahar-Bagh avenue and thus to the west of the Chehel Sutun Palace. Since the 'Ali Qapu Palace, fronting on the maydan, was the eastern gate to this walled, rectangular garden-palace complex, the Bab-i Bulbul was probably the western gate, providing access from Isfahan's principal, ceremonial thoroughfare. Thus the shah could move from this public avenue through the Bab-i Bulbul into the private royal garden and from there through the 'Ali Qapu into the public royal maydan. Somewhat

ment or palace is square in plan, as can be seen from the drawing. It is open on three sides with arches and colonnades that are covered with sheets of Venetian mirrors. The archways lead out to the [surrounding] veranda. On each of these three sides there are two rooms; on the fourth side there are more rooms. All the rooms have doors from one to the other. Their walls and ceilings are covered with similar sheets [of Venetian mirrors], some big, some small, and all of the mirrors are enclosed by gilt borders and are carefully arranged. The main hall in the center of the palace has a gilt cupola, and in some places there are several paintings by Persians that represent the exploits of the kings, such as the siege of Qandahar and Van under Shah Safi and others.[129] Under several sheets of glass that did not have silver behind them, I saw many images of saints made on gypsum and on parchment that are indecently sold by the Armenians, who offer them publicly in the bazaars along with medals and papal Agnuses,[130] not only to Christians but also to Muslims, who buy them as curiosities. This is truly a scandalous thing and done by the Armenians as a sign of disrespect, because when they are in Europe they pretend to be Catholics and, by demonstrating superficial devotion, gather good collections of such things. When they go back to their own countries, they reveal themselves as schismatics and make fun of our religiosity. There are also some paintings of European men brought both by the Armenians and by others from Europe. On some stone pedestals are flowers painted with imaginative colors. They are made by the natives, who give them a very beautiful varnish. They use this varnish to make various very fine things.[131] In the same central hall there are many fountains, including a very noble one in the middle. All the arches of this room can be closed from top to bottom by silk curtains. The arch in the center of the fourth side has a silk curtain with many gold flowers.

---

farther to the south of the Bab-i Bulbul on the Chahar Bagh is the Hasht Behesht Palace, one of the best preserved of extant Safavi palaces. See Donald N. Wilber, *Persian Gardens and Garden Pavilions* (Rutland and Tokyo: Tuttle, 1962), p. 115, for a different analysis of the palace's location based on other sources.

129. This is a valuable reference to mural paintings that are now lost. Still-extant murals in the Chehel Sutun Palace also depict historical events important to the Safavi dynasty.

130. A wax medal with a representation of the Lamb of God.

131. Bembo is referring to the production of lacquer works.

FIGURE 30. Ayineh Khaneh (Palace of Mirrors) in Isfahan.

The upper story is as large as the lower and has the same arrangement of rooms, although the rooms on the sides also provide access to the balconies that look down into the central hall. All the rooms are gilt and mirrored and have some European paintings, among which is an image of a nude woman that they esteem very much.[132] In some of the rooms I observed some prints that represented the life of man and the life of courtesans, things that they like very much. In all the rooms there are some cabinets full of fine Chinese porcelain, Venetian glass and crystal, and various fine German things. In one of the upper rooms there is the king's bed, which is made up of two large silk mattresses on very fine silk rugs. The floors of all the rooms are covered with carpets, in the first- as well as in the

132. Paintings of men and women in European dress, as well as representations of seminude women, are still preserved on the walls of the Chehel Sutun Palace.

second-floor apartment. All the cushions are also of gold brocade made in [Persia]. In another room on the second floor there is a chased silver fountain that is rather large. The construction and furnishing of the whole palace was ordered by a principal minister at his own expense, who then gave it to the king.[133]

One can believe that these people are very rich and generous, because they show every magnificence in the number of servants they have and in the clothes they wear. Their clothes are of silk and gold with turbans of the same very expensive material. The common dress is long, as is the custom in the whole Orient, but it is unlike that of the Turks and the Indians in its cut and in the fact that the Persian robe is a little shorter. They bind the robe with very rich scarves. Similarly, the pants are also shorter, and their slippers have a rather elegant heel. These slippers are made in various colors of leather, including green, which they allow even the Christians to wear.[134] The men have large moustaches and a beard not longer than about an inch, and they cut their hair short, an ancient custom in the Orient. They tie their headdresses differently from the Turks. The rich have gold turbans that are very valuable. In addition, they wear various kinds of caps. Some of them are long and expensive. They are made of lambskins from Khorasan, which have thin, curly hair, mostly black with some white and grey.[135] These lambs are raised with great care in the kingdom. The shepherds keep them covered and wash them often. This kind of lamb cannot be raised anywhere else; hence their hides are very expensive. Sometimes even the king himself wears one of those caps. I bought one, though it was of mediocre quality, and took it with me to Venice. From the same skins they also line robes, which are likewise held in high esteem.

The clothing of the women is more expensive. It is long and not too

133. This description of the Nightingale Gate Palace indicates that its ground plan was similar to that of the extant Hasht Behesht Palace (see A. U. Pope and P. Ackerman, *A Survey of Persian Art, from Prehistoric Times to the Present* [London and New York: Oxford University Press, 1939], p. 1196). Similar mirrored surfaces can be found in the throne niche of the Chehel Sutun Palace. The more elaborate hanging on the fourth side would have designated the area where the king sat.

134. Since green was the color generally reserved for sayyids and sherifs, descendants of the Prophet, non-Muslims in Islamic countries generally either avoided or were not permitted to wear it.

135. Khorasan was a large, productive province in northeastern Iran.

FIGURE 31. Iranians.

different from that of the men. As Justin the Historian tells us, this costume was introduced by Semiramis, who was the first woman to cover her arms, legs, and head.[136] She commanded that all of her subjects dress this same way, so that her wickedness would not be recognizable in her clothes, which were not different from her son's. She was also the first woman to wear pants, and that item of dress was subsequently worn by women and men in the whole Orient. On their heads they do not wear anything, as the women of Syria do, but they have attached to their heads a thin white cloth that falls down their backs and covers almost all their clothing, as can be seen in the drawing. They cover their faces with a similar white cloth that

136. Marcus Junianus Justinus was a third-century A.D. Roman historian whose epitome of Pompeius Trogus' late first-century B.C. *Historiae Philippicae* was widely read in medieval Europe and was considered a major source for the history of the Near East and Iran. He reports the Greek tradition that the legendary Babylonian queen Semiramis secretly married her son Ninyas and tried to conceal the fact through altered clothing fashions.

falls to their necks. It is attached to another cloth that conceals their foreheads and leaves their eyes uncovered. Sometimes one sees women of rank
in the street. When they go out, they ride a horse and sit like men and have
walking in front of them one or more syces, according to their condition.

The Persians are very jealous of their women, even though they can have
as many wives as they please and can repudiate them easily. Like the Turks,
they give a certain amount of money to the father of the bride, rather than
take a dowry from her, though the women do bring, according to their
wealth, many goods, especially clothes. There are a good number of public courtesans. In Isfahan alone they are 12,000. They pay a certain tax to
the king. In addition to them, it is said that there may be just as large a
number of unofficial courtesans who pay no tax. Nevertheless, they do not
transmit the diseases that European prostitutes do. I was also told that
there are women and virgins who go into marriages with a written contract
in which the pair promise to live united for a specified time and pledge that
any sons who are born [from this union] are legitimate.[137] When the time
is up, they separate or renew the contract, which they can do as many times
as they wish. It often happens, however, that in this manner they become
true wives. Thus young women generally go to men of their own social level
and not necessarily their own age in the hope of becoming their wives. This
way of keeping company is particularly prevalent in Shiraz, and it is very
convenient. Rumor has it that the women of that city are very frivolous, and
the following story is told. Two women friends met. One of them asked
the other how long she had been with her husband. The other answered
that it had been two months: the first woman commiserated with her and
asked her how it had been possible for her to put up with one man for so
long!

I was able to get information about Persian weddings, even though I was
not able to see one. These are curious ceremonies. First the family and
friends of the bridegroom gather in his house; they are all dressed in his colors, especially his sponsors. Meanwhile, the wife comes out of her house on
horseback. She is accompanied by her family and friends, who are also on
horseback and all dressed in the same colors and as richly as possible. The

---

137. *Sighe* (Arabic *mut'a*) is a Persian term for a time-limited marriage that
may be for a contractual number of hours, day, weeks, months, or years. This
Iranian practice was noted by two other seventeenth-century travelers, Adam
Olearius in 1637 and Jean Chardin in 1673.

wife has her face covered with a woven cloth on which the sun and moon are painted in gold.[138] With the whole company and with many musicians carrying their instruments, they all go to meet the groom. With his own retinue he also goes toward her. When they come together, they all return to the bride's house. There the men stay to dance in a richly decorated hall in the middle of which is a light. The women, too, go to dance with music and singing in another room. While they dance, they let many coins fall that they have attached to their foreheads and that are payment for the musicians, who gather them at the end of the feast. The men, too, throw money on the ground for the same purpose. When the feast is over, everyone stays to eat in the house of the bride. The next day the entire company goes to the house of the groom, where there is a sumptuous banquet, after which two old women appear and take the groom into a room to which the bride is led by another passageway. The friends and relatives continue to dance until around midnight, when the two old women come out again and unfold in everyone's presence a little cloth stained with blood. Thus the feast is over, and everyone leaves very happily. This is a custom that is also practiced in Aleppo by the Jews. If there is no blood, the two old women take away the bride, and the groom repudiates her publicly and goes off with his whole party and pays a certain sum of money.

All those women and some of the men dye their hands black and their nails red. Some pierce their noses and attach a ring there.

[SEPTEMBER 1674]

On the 16th of September I went to see the citadel or suburb of Julfa. On going out of the city I entered the great road called Chahar Bagh, where there is the Palace of Mirrors described above. This road is more than a mile long; where it starts (that is, as one leaves the city), there is another apartment of the king's, which adjoins the grounds of the palace on the maydan.[139]

138. Bembo uses the word "taftà." The Persian *taftah* is the past participle of the verb "to weave" (*taftan*) and is the source of the textile term *taffeta*.

139. The Chahar Bagh (Four Gardens) avenue extended on a north-south axis from Shah 'Abbas's New Isfahan across the Zayendeh River to New Julfa. The palace to which Bembo refers is the Hasht Behesht (Seven Paradises) Palace, noted above and located about midway between the Nightingale's Gate and the bridge over the Zayendeh River.

It is all full of windows to permit the enjoyment of viewing the great street, on both sides of which are walled gardens. Once in a while there are palaces of various architectural types that are located face-to-face. Some belong to the king, and others belong to other individuals. Near the walls there is a line of plane trees equidistant from one another. There are also three very large pools or open cisterns with various water jets that take up almost the whole length of the avenue. There is only a little bit of space to pass on either side. Both sides are made of stone for the avenue's whole length. In the middle of the avenue is a similar passageway, set with some flower beds that were full of dried grass then but which in springtime are full of flowers that must make the whole avenue much more delightful. On both sides of the street there is a little stone canal where water flows. It is connected to the pools, the last of which on the approach to the bridge to Julfa has two straight rows of trees between which the stream of water runs, about an arm's length wide. Water flows from this pool to [watercourses] in other large streets.[140]

The broad street ends in a beautiful bridge, commonly called the Bridge of Julfa, because it goes there.[141] It is made of bricks, is straight, and rests on thirty-three double arches on both sides, as can be seen in the drawing. The arches are linked with one another through some openings. In the middle of each arch at river level there is a large marble stone that allows people to cross from one archway to the other. In the summer when the water is low, one can take walks there and, being protected from the sun, keep cool. On the bridge itself, besides the central broad street, which is uncovered, there are two additional passageways, flanking the street on each side, that are covered by vaults and porticoes whose arches, although they are closed, are connected with each other by some small doors or large windows made for that purpose. The first vaults at either side of the bridge are made to look like towers. The ones in the center are in arch form and are a little broader, and there are some rooms in them with lascivious paintings; it is said that rich Persians go there to enjoy the cool temperature. From the many windows there they enjoy the river, which is called the Zayendeh Rud (that is, "Living River"), which originates at the foot of a mountain three days' journey from Isfahan.[142] Some say that two more days' journey beyond

140. A marginal note offers the avenue's dimensions as 1,500 paces in length and 70 paces in width.

141. This is the Allahverdi Khan Bridge, or Thirty-Three-Arch Bridge. Bembo renders Julfa as "Giulfa."

that it surfaces again even greater than before. The river is almost dry during the summer and can be forded on horseback or on foot, since the greater part of the water is taken up through the conduits that convey it to many houses, streets, coffee houses, and gardens. During the winter, however, it is such a vast and precipitous torrent that it often destroys houses in Julfa and Isfahan. Once one is over the bridge, the broad street continues with the same walls, trees, and houses, but of lesser quality. It ends in the great garden of the king, also called Chahar Bagh, beyond which is a mountain. Situated on the banks of the river, Julfa is a suburb. Its perimeter is large, for almost all the houses have immense gardens with outside walls that are earthen and not too high, even though they are well made and clean on the inside. The streets are narrow and long with a little stream of water running through them and with many regularly planted plane trees. Since the Armenian and Christian subjects live there, Julfa is governed by a Christian Armenian mayor named the *kalantar*.[143] This magistrate is appointed by the king or by the prime minister, and his authority is very limited, since all matters of importance are reserved for the judgment of the officials in Isfahan. Thus the position is more honorific than substantial. Perhaps it is given because of ancient privilege, although the Armenians do not consider it a princely office.

In this regard I remember that a young Armenian came to Venice at one time. He said that he was a son of the Prince of the Armenians, and maybe he was the son of one of the Julfa chiefs. Nevertheless, as Father Filippo, the Discalced Carmelite writes, it is believed that they secretly keep a king of the ancient family of Armenian kings who are consecrated in proper succession by their patriarch, operating with every secret precaution.

There are some rich Armenians, at least rich in appearance, who go about in much splendor. It is thought, however, that they overspend. They keep their houses well furnished with a good number of servants who, however, do not cost them very much, since they provide them simply with

142. Bembo spells it "Zendeh Rud or Sendeh Ruk." The words *Zayendeh Rud* convey the sense of "life-giving river." There is a marginal note saying that the bridge was built by Allahverdi Khan and that it is 20 paces wide and 350 paces long.

143. A marginal note states that Julfa acquired its name from the original city of Julfa in Armenia, whose inhabitants were brought to Isfahan by Shah 'Abbas. The Ottomans also adhered to the practice of allowing restricted internal self-governance to the different religious communities.

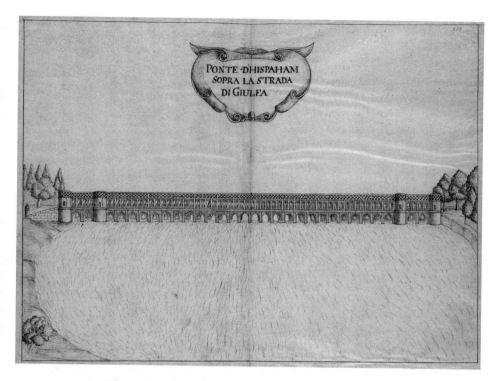

FIGURE 32. Thirty-three-Arch (or Allahverdi Khan) Bridge in Isfahan.

food and clothing. They spend a lot on horses, but even more on clothing for their women and themselves. Due to the freedom I mentioned that the Persians give to all nationalities with regard to clothing, the Armenians want to compete in pomp with the clothing of the wealthiest lords of Isfahan. When they go on horseback, they have walking in front of them a syce, who is the person guiding the horse. All cultivated people do this. Taking advantage of the goodness and sweet dispositions of the Persians, many Armenians are rather proud and are boasters, as I learned from experience. Among many things that happened to me, this is one. I was visited by the brother of an Armenian merchant of Venice, named Gregorio. He pretended that he was very wealthy: this was false. He confessed to me, and others then confirmed it, that all the business he did for his brother in Venice amounted to six *proni,* and that only a portion of that was for him. He added that he was being summoned to Isfahan to present his accounts and to give a report on his management. Similarly, I talked at some length with another Armenian, who had been in Venice for many years as a rental agent. While

I was in Aleppo [on my way back to Venice], he came there from Venice clothed in black and wearing a collar and a cloak, really dressed up as if he were going out on the town in Italy. He told me that he was returning to his country to divide the inheritance of his deceased father with his two younger brothers. Despite the fact that he was aware that I knew something about the country, he told me that he was noble and rich by birth, because his father had been the chief of Julfa; he referred to him as a prince. Other Armenians then swore to me that all his wealth had consisted of a small villa with a value of 6,000–7,000 reales, a house, and little else, all of which had to be divided into three parts. He was dressed in the Persian manner. He had his hair under his turban and said he would return to Venice to get his wife, who was the daughter of an Armenian Paulin.[144]

In Julfa there are two convents of Armenian nuns, where bells are rung. In the other churches they use certain little tablets of silver with many rattles all around. There is also the church of the Jesuit fathers, who have the title of missionaries. I went there to pay them a visit, but only one of them was there, whose name was Lamasia, a Frenchman. A few days before that, the superior had died, being a rather old man named Father Mercé. They have a good house with a large garden. It serves the Armenian Catholics, as most claim to be, and those French in the pay of the king, all of whom live in Julfa. There is also a house for the head of the company of Bander 'Abbas for those times when he comes to these parts. The good Jesuit father received me courteously and, as is the custom in the country, gave me fruit and wine, but he proved himself very poor, since the fruits were very ordinary and the wine tasted like vinegar. He told me that, even when there are more fathers, they have only ninety reales to live on: that sum is sent to them from France. It is convenient for them to keep a school for young Armenian boys to whom they teach reading and writing in Persian, since they know that language and Arabic very well. Having taken leave of the father, I went to visit Monsieur Louis Elettual, a Frenchman, who had visited me many days earlier. He had been born there of an Armenian mother and had served as dragoman for the French company. He had three other

144. This is a puzzling reference. The Paulicians were believers in a dualistic form of Christianity; they first appeared in Armenia in the middle of the seventh century and gained substantial support, but they seem to have been vastly reduced in numbers by the end of the eleventh century, although their doctrines became popular in the Balkans.

brothers, one of whom was named Giacomo, who dresses in the French manner and who had been in Venice for seven years at the Rialto with Pietro Calderari, a watchmaker or jeweler. Another served the king in Qazvin,[145] and the third had gone to France. Except for him, all were married in Julfa and lived together in a rather comfortable and beautiful house, decorated as is the custom of the country with various decorations and gold. It has only one story, as do all the houses in the Orient, but it is divided into several apartments for the women, who do not let themselves be seen. Their garden was the cleanest I saw in those parts, and it was arranged in the European manner. Next to the garden was the house of the leader of the French, and one could pass from one to the other. That house also belonged to Monsieur Elettual. He gave me very delicious fruit, which they always have ready on ice, and after several toasts with perfect wine, I took my leave.

According to what I was told, the women of the king sometimes go to this suburb of Julfa for recreation. They also go to the other suburbs. When they arrive, all the local men, with no exceptions, leave the place. Announcements are made to this effect a few days ahead of time. If a man should accidentally be found, he would be killed by those women themselves. In return for the royal visit, the women of the suburb beautify their houses and set out food and various refreshments everywhere. As they wish, the king's women go from one house to the other and are served everything and are courted by those Christian women. Sometimes the king himself goes in their company. If he sees a beautiful girl, he takes her for himself and puts her with the others in his harem, though only if she is neither engaged nor married. Thus the Armenians contract marriages for their daughters when they are seven or eight years old: that also allows more affection to grow between husband and wife.

Not far from Julfa there is another suburb inhabited by Persians of the ancient religion of Darius's time. They adore fire and keep it with great veneration; they also worship the sun, the moon, and the stars. They detest the laws of Muhammad and maintain their ancient language and writing of Persia. They are poor people. In some cities they have temples and schools. Their dress is rough and similar in cut to that of the others, but all of one color. They neither cut their beards nor their hair, which they let grow down to their shoulders. They wear turbans on their heads. Their women walk the streets with their faces uncovered, contrary to the custom of the country.

145. Bembo writes "Casbia."

Among their rites is this one: they do not burn or bury their dead, but they keep them on certain terraces made for this purpose in a walled place like a castle. They put them there standing with their eyes open and leave them there forever, where they are devoured by birds and consumed by the sun and the air.[146]

Back at the house of the Carmelites, I had the opportunity to speak many times with the draftsman of the already-mentioned Monsieur Chardin, whose name was Monsieur Joseph Grélot. He confided to Father Giacomo, who was with me, that he wanted to return to Europe and complained of the bad treatment given him by Chardin that had caused him so much desperation that he was resolved to abandon him and go with Domenico Santi, the Roman mentioned above. Advised of this and thinking that through him I would be able to make a good number of drawings of the curious things that I had seen and that I would see (which I had always wanted to do, since it is very appropriate for an itinerary to be illustrated), I proposed my companionship to him with the promise to take him to Europe with me. He accepted the arrangement and told Monsieur Chardin that he would leave his service if he did not take care of some differences they had and promise to treat him better. Knowing that the poor youth had no money and no way to set out on such a long and expensive trip, Chardin did not pay any attention to his request. When he found out about the agreement that Grélot had with me, he was displeased and tried to win him back, but was not successful; so he refused him his pay for twenty months, when he left. It was the pay for the drawings, for copying out his itinerary, and for many other services. When many French and English friends of Chardin remonstrated with him about giving Grélot what he owed him (I always pretended to be ignorant about this), he replied that he was not held to it by the initial agreement established between them, according to which he would pay him in France at the end of the journey and would in addition give him a substantial bonus, which he would determine. If Grélot made extra copies for anyone of a drawing or gave drawings as a gift, or if he left his service on any pre-

146. The Zoroastrians were also known as Gabrs; hence, this part of greater Isfahan was known as Gabristan. Shah 'Abbas II had built a royal palace there known as Sa'adatabad. Believing that flesh is a corrupt element that must not pollute the purities of earth, fire, and water, Zoroastrians expose their dead in Towers of Silence; when the bones have been stripped of all flesh, they are buried.

text before the end of the trip, Chardin was no longer obligated to give him his salary or to give him the bonus. With this kind of reasoning he would often mistreat Grélot, heaping injuries upon him without reason, so that the poor man had often requested permission to leave. Chardin did not deny permission but always said that if he left of his own will without being dismissed, he was under no obligation to give him anything; and that is what transpired, most unjustly. Yet this Grélot was a very discreet young man of great goodness and modesty. In addition to his own French, he also understood many languages, such as Latin, Spanish, literary Greek, Arabic, and Persian, if not perfectly, then at least well enough to be able to get along. During the trip he applied himself to everything with great amiability and without ulterior motives. Often he would have us enjoy very good food that he had prepared. Since he and I had still fresh in our memories some of the things we had seen, he made various drawings before we left Isfahan with the help of some sketches that he had, most particularly of the city and important places in it. Finally, after much trouble and with the help of the Carmelite Father Provincial, I got the money I needed from a janissary of Baghdad, named Jacob, son of an Armenian Catholic priest, who had left his religion, as also had a female cousin of his with whom he had amorous relations. The Capuchins of that city had denied them permission to marry, but they got married anyway after making themselves Turks.[147] Twenty days passed, however, before my contract with this man could be firmly settled, since he kept on confusing issues in order to earn more. Out of necessity I was compelled to agree to give him an interest rate of 29% until we reached Aleppo. He himself was to come in my company. When we had closed the deal, a caravan from Baghdad arrived. As the problems with that city had blown over, another caravan for that city was prepared and was soon ready to depart.

Thus on the 21st of September, the feast of St. Matthew, having acquired all the requisite provisions, I took leave of all the religious with many embraces. From the Capuchins I had many letters. Since Monsieur Chardin was in their house, as I have said, I attempted to take my leave of him as well, but he sent a message that he was resting and told the same thing to Grélot. I found out that this was due to his displeasure at my having taken the latter into my service. Around the 21st hour, then, I mounted on horse-

147. The couple must have become Sunni Muslim, and the young Armenian joined the Ottoman janissary corps.

back, along with Father Giacomo, Monsieur Grélot, the dragoman, an Armenian servant, and the above-mentioned janissary. We rode out of the city through a gate that, like all the others, is always open. When I entered the suburbs, I observed some dovecotes of a rather strange form.[148] The doors of the local houses were made of a single slab of stone, rather than being made of boards, since wood is scarce. The closing mechanism is wood, however. They are all like that in many towns that are near the city. After an hour's travel we stopped with the caravan that I had chosen to join at a caravanserai called Muhammad 'Ali Bek. There was much merchandise and many men and women. The women travel completely covered and seated in a kind of covered place on top of camels or mules.[149] Seeing that the whole caravan was not yet assembled and therefore would not leave until the following evening, the janissary returned to the city that night. Meanwhile, a great confusion arose among them, because a rumor was spread that a caravan with many wounded had just arrived.

According to the rumor, this caravan had fought with two hundred Kurds, who are subjects of the Persians and live in the mountains. They had rebelled and were violently overrunning the countryside. They were refusing to obey a chief appointed over them by the king whose vassals they were. When he then sent a new chief with troops, they calmed down. Due to all this disorder with the Kurds, the rumor disconcerted everyone, even though it proved false. Some persons were so afraid that they did not know which road to take: some suggested one way, and others another.

The next morning, the 22nd, at the third hour of sunlight, most of the caravan left and went to another caravanserai some three leagues distant to wait there for the others. The size of the caravan increased with the arrival of other men and women. I remained with the smaller group to await the janissary, who came late in the day with his things. As soon as he arrived, he caused yet another confusion, since he claimed to be the caravan leader,

148. The pigeon towers in Isfahan's environs may have numbered several hundred in the seventeenth century. Designed as a means of collecting droppings for subsequent use as fertilizer, the bastionlike towers could be as large as 12 m in height and 9 m in diameter; they were often domed and had polychrome decoration.

149. A *haudaj* was a litter of cloth wrapped around a rectangular or circular frame.

a position that I have defined elsewhere. When these difficulties were taken care of, the caravan set off just as the moon was rising. After four hours' travel, at first through beautiful gardens and then in a beautiful plain, we arrived around midnight at caravanserai Ascaba. There we joined up with the first part of the caravan. We stayed only long enough for them to begin the trip with us. The janissary wanted to go ahead, but the muleteer opposed it. He was worried about the safety of his mounts. He said that he had heard that there were in the countryside fifty Kurds—thirty of whom were on horseback and armed with arquebusses, while the other twenty were on foot—even though another caravan had passed without having suffered any attack. The muleteer was of Arab nationality and was called Hajji Muhammad.[150] Unlike the typical member of that insolent race, he was a rather discreet man and was also faithful. I thus respected him and always invited him to eat with me, even though I was not obliged to do it. When we were all on the road, I counted the members of the caravan, which consisted of 170 loaded animals, mules, horses, and donkeys; and about 100 armed men, some with arquebusses or swords, and some with bows and arrows. There were also some other animals, including two camels with women on them, and other, poorer people on horseback.

At the third hour of sunlight on the 23rd, after having passed some small hills, we stopped in the caravanserai Shah 'Ali Shah, which was rather small.[151] Space was taken over by those who got there first, and the rest of the caravan had to make do with the open air, since there was no other lodging except for another caravanserai that was in such a ruinous state that it was useless. Some tents were set up near a well of rather good water, not far from which there were two or three small houses where bread, wood, and barley were for sale, in addition to similar things necessary for travelers. After midnight, when the moon came out, we set out again on a plain. At daybreak on the 24th we journeyed along a good road between several mountains and stopped at midday at the caravanserai Cusini, but just to eat. Then we continued the trip to the town of Deheq, where we spent the night.[152] The place was large and situated among delightful hills. We found

150. The title *hajji* indicates that he had made the *hajj* or pilgrimage to Mecca and Medina.

151. Bembo transcribes it as "Sciarxià or Cialisihà." I have not been able to identify it or its location.

a lot of fruit and good meat. The caravanserai was in the town itself but was half ruined. We left from there two hours before daybreak on the 25th and traveled among mountains and hills, though on an easy and level road. At midday we arrived at a town made up of tents that is called Dar 'Arban,[153] that is, "town of the Arabs," which gives its name to the nearest caravanserai, where we lodged that night. We kept a good guard because of the nearby Kurds. At daybreak on the 26th we remounted and continued our trip through mountains on roads that are as level and good as if they were in a plain. This is true of this part of Persia. The roads in the part near Gara are disastrous, as we have said. At midday we stopped at the town of Covgà, or Cogà, in a rather good caravanserai, where all the goods were weighed by the royal weighers and a fee had to be paid for each *qintar*, which is a weight of 120 pounds. One must also pay so much a head, but it is a slight sum. We rested there the whole next day, the 27th.

I went about two miles away to see the city of Gulpayegan, which is rather large and has many towns and gardens around it, abundant in fruit and cotton.[154] It is situated in a very vast plain at the foot of some mountains. The houses are low and of earth with many gardens full of trees. The roads are narrow, and the bazaars are roofed with boards and dry leaves from palm trees. It is governed by a Khan, although the inhabitants are ordinary people who dress poorly. Most of them wear large caps on their heads. The peasants wear some tall hats with small rims like those of Flemish soldiers. They tie small ribbons of various colors on them. I saw in the city several richly decorated camels with men going on foot who were holding unfurled flags and who were saying something in loud voices. I did not understand them, and I was told that they were inviting people to go on pilgrimage to Mecca, since it was the day of *Kurban Bairam*, that is, the Great Feast, which is seventy days after the feast of Ramadan.[155] Because of the great distance, people had begun to assemble three months earlier.

At dawn on the 28th we continued our journey and traveled in a plain.

152. "Cusini" is Bembo's transcription. The town of Deheq is about 75 km northwest of Isfahan. Bembo transcribes it as "Dià or Delà or Dehè."

153. Bembo's transcription is "Dur Arabùm."

154. An ancient town, Gulpayegan (Bembo writes it "Culpeichan or Ghiulpaigan") has a celebrated jami' mosque (generally, the principal mosque in a city) dating to the Seljuq period.

155. Bembo gives the Turkish name (Kurban Bairam) for what is known in Arabic as 'Id al-Adha, the sacrificial feast on the tenth day of the pilgrimage

FIGURE 33. Caravanserai at Missian.

I observed there the difficulty that Persians have in cultivating the earth, especially where rain is scarce. They first break the earth, and then they water it so that it will give way to the plow. Nature has provided them with many springs, and they make the water run through some small canals in the countryside, in orchards, and in gardens. They alternate in giving the plants much and then little water, so that the fruits do not all have the same flavor. When the sun came up, we went through the middle of a town called Abu Qassem Bek.[156] On coming out of there, we crossed over a poorly made stone bridge. It consisted of only one arch; the stream flows under it and has the same name as the town. Thereafter, we found hills and mountains

---

month of Dhu'l-Hijja. His explanation is a bit muddled, however. He saw this event on September 27, 1674, or, in the Muslim calendar, 26 Jumada al-ukra 1085, sixty-two days before the beginning of the month of fasting, Ramadan, and 151 days before the beginning of Dhu'l-Hijja.

156. Bembo's transcription is "Pucasembegh."

with an excellent road.[157] At midday we rested in the caravanserai Mazayen,[158] which is quite beautiful, as can be seen in the drawing.

We left there at dawn on the 29th. The trip that day was partly on a plain full of towns and partly through mountains. We did not stop until the 22nd hour in the caravanserai Bagh-i Mulla[159] at the foot of a mountain. That night we began to feel cold, although during the day the air remained rather warm. At that time I had a terrible pain in my belly that would begin when I mounted on horseback and would continue all day. Three hours before the last day of September we awoke and traveled through mountains and then through a beautiful plain where there were many tent towns and some swamps. After midday we took lodging in a caravanserai outside the town called Mesèt.

[OCTOBER 1674]

We left there three hours before daylight on the 1st of October. We continued in the same plain, and at sunrise we dismounted in the town of Sarù at a caravanserai called Sciaersarù. We stayed there all day and the next so as to let the animals rest. There was food there at good prices, and wine in particular, and I stocked up on it and stored it in goatskins. The janissary, who always ate with me, consumed a lot of it. When we would arrive at a caravanserai, he would get me a good place and would then go to buy the best there was without paying [much of] anything. What with getting up before daylight and sleeping at around the ninth hour, there was not enough time for two meals. Thus I had become accustomed to do as the Persians do and have a breakfast of fruits, which are to be found in abundance, as soon as we arrived at a caravanserai. After having rested during the day, I ate well and heartily in the evening.

On the morning of the 3rd about three hours before daylight we began to travel through mountains. We descended from a rather difficult mountain and came into a great plain full of villages. Before midday we stopped in the town of Isabat, or Dizabad, or Dizavà in a rather dirty and ruined caravanserai. Since the city of Hamadan was only a day's journey from there,

---

157. They are entering the Zagros mountain range.

158. Bembo's "Muscian." The drawing is identified as the caravanserai at "Missian."

159. Bembo's "Bagzamulà."

the janissary with others on good horses went there on business.[160] They intended to reunite themselves with us after a few days. Before leaving, he gave me what I had given him, as well as some other things of his, since they were few, for fear that they might be taken from him. He asked me to lend him 300 'abbasi, which I did out of politeness. On our arrival in Baghdad he wanted to avoid paying me, and I had to go through some trouble to get my money back.

Three hours before daybreak on the 4th we mounted and traveled through easy mountains and hills. At dawn we passed a half-ruined bridge under which runs a river called Isabet, like the town.[161] After four more hours of similar terrain, we stopped in a town called Usùbassi, which had few houses and was almost entirely ruined. Since there was no caravanserai, we pitched our tents during the hours of sunlight. At night we slept in the open in order to be ready to leave again.

We left three hours before day on the 5th of October, and around midday we came into a great plain, where the caravan split up. One part went behind a mountain on a road that led to Hamadan, since they had some merchandise for that city. The two parts of the caravan were reunited after a few days, since it is almost the same road. Our muleteer wanted to continue in the plain in order to avoid a fee that had to be paid [in Hamadan]. They concealed all this from me and told me that some women with many Persians were going on a pilgrimage to visit some tombs, particularly that of 'Ali in Najaf, a small city, anciently Kufa, which is near Baghdad and is inhabited by Turks, who call it *Mashhad 'Ali*. By the Arabs it is called *Ba 'Ali*. Many Persians go there for devotion, especially on the 21st day of the month of Ramadan, the anniversary of ['Ali's] death.[162] In that place the

160. Known in Achaemenid times as Ecbatana, Hamadan was one of the major cities of northwestern Iran.

161. Perhaps this is the site of the modern town of Estuh on the Duab River.

162. The cousin and son-in-law of the Prophet Muhammad, 'Ali was the fourth caliph of Islam and the first Imam of the Shi'is. He was murdered on January 27, 661 (21 Ramadhan 40). For Shi'is, his tomb at Najaf (Bembo's "Caffe"; his term "Maxd Ali" renders the Arabic *mashhad 'Ali*, or "'Ali's shrine"; the other name that he reports, "Ba Ali," is presumably a rendering of *bayt 'Ali*, or "House of 'Ali") is a pilgrimage site of central importance. Najaf was near the early Muslim garrison town and capital city, al-Kufah, about 150 km south of Baghdad. Brought into the Safavi state by Shah 'Abbas I in 1623, it reverted to Ottoman control fifteen years later.

Persian kings would be crowned and take the sword, since their great caliph lived there, who has the first place among their priests. But since that city is too small and close to Baghdad, it was judged better to have the coronation and other royal ceremonies in the city of Baghdad itself. In this regard the Moslems of that caravan told me a curious fable (a crazy superstition of theirs). In the plaza of Najaf near the mosque, they keep a horse completely ready and saddled day and night for the arrival of the Mahdi, nephew of 'Ali, who, according to the opinion of the Persians, did not die.[163] He must come to resolve the differences that the Persians, Arabs, and Turks have and convert the whole world to their perfidious sect. Thus they keep that horse ready. Each time they light lamps in that mosque, they bring the horse in and offer it to 'Ali, beseeching him to send his nephew quickly. It is true that the Persians have as much veneration for that place as the Turks have for Mecca. However, since Najaf is now owned by the Ottoman [sultan], he keeps officials there who exact a fee from all those who go there on pilgrimage. Having taken the road in the plain with the portion of the caravan that remained (which was no more than twenty-four men on horseback and twenty-six men on foot with only thirty pack animals, among which were some carrying women), we stopped after midday on a mountain in the town of Amilapà. Since there was no caravanserai, we set up the tent near a running stream. We found much fruit, especially melons and watermelons, all rather good.

We left at dawn of the 6th by a good road and at the fourth hour of sunlight we stopped in the town of Respè, which is on a delightful hill. We rested there very comfortably in a caravanserai of the same name, which has very comfortable rooms for the winter. Because of its beauty, I had it drawn, as can be seen.

Two hours before daybreak on the 7th, we remounted and traveled through mountains until the third hour of sunlight. We traveled two more hours in a plain and lodged in the town of Kangavar at the foot of a mountain in a caravanserai of little note and half destroyed. It was in the middle of the town and had its gate toward the bazaar of foodstuffs. We

163. According to Ithna 'Ashara Shi'ism, the twelfth Iman, Muhammad al-Muntazar ('Ali's direct descendant but not his nephew), disappeared from earth around 873, when he was taken to heaven, and will return to earth as the Mahdi (or Guided One) to instate perfect government.

FIGURE 34. Caravanserai and landscape at Respè.

found there quantities of fruit, too, among them some pears of rare quality. This town was formerly a city of importance, as its ruins demonstrate. Among them are remains of large columns and other ancient works. Since we stayed there all of the following day to rest, I was able to go all around it. In the part that is in the plain there is a great expanse, perhaps even greater than that of Persepolis, that is all covered with pieces of smooth columns that are seven of my palms in diameter. There are many capitals of various types that can still be seen at proper distances from one another. Since many houses have been built among those ruins, I was unable to have a drawing made. However, a large marble wall that is on one side of the plain can be conjectured to have been a temple or some rich palace, not too different from that of Persepolis. I was unable to get more information from the ignorant people there, since all of them told stories at their pleasure that were far from the truth. However, I was told by some who were more studious and who spoke with more sense that that city had been very large. Those ruins were the remains of a castle that was called Takt-i Giaour,[164] whose name is preserved, since it was built by a Christian king to whom they give the insulting name of *Giaour,* which means "faithless." They use the same term for the ancient Persians who adore fire.[165] I would believe instead that it was a temple of theirs and the work of ancient Persian monarchs of around the time of Darius.[166] They added that the city and the castle had been destroyed by a king called Murtaza 'Ali, who they say was not a Turk, while he was making war on a Moslem king called Sulaiman, who was the master of the place.[167] That day the janissary returned with the rest of the caravan, and we left together once again.

On the morning of the 9th at dawn we left and traveled most of the day through mountains. At sunrise we crossed a stream over a bridge of many arches, after which we found many other small streams. That night we lodged in the town of Sahneh, located in those mountains.[168] Near the caravanserai there was a little stream of spring water that was rather good. That caravanserai had been built by a nobleman of Isfahan who also had eleven others put up on different roads.

Two hours before day on the 10th, we remounted, and two hundred donkeys loaded with cotton joined us. They were passing from Hamadan to another city. Persia is full of those animals, and almost daily we met large caravans of them. (With much reason Pliny writes that Nealco, the painter of great skill, painted a donkey as the symbol of Persia in his painting of a naval battle. Wanting to express the fact that this battle between the Persians

---

164. Or Place of the Infidels.

165. *Gaur* is a Persian term for infidel, derived from the Persian *gebr* (or fire worshipper).

166. Bembo is not far off when he attributes the ruins at Kangavar to the Achaemenid period. The town is the site of a large Seleucid or Parthian temple dating to the third to second century B.C. In the 1840s Sir Henry Layard found eight standing columns and the foundations of a temple dedicated to Anahita. Bembo's reference from 170 years earlier is particularly valuable, since Kangavar is one of the very few major sites of this period in Iran and apparently much more of it was extant than when Layard came. It is truly regrettable that Grélot was unable to draw it.

167. The local historians are probably referring to one of the four campaigns of the Ottoman sultan Sulayman (1520–1566) against the Safavi shah of Iran Tahmasp (1524–1576).

168. Bembo's "Sahani or Sehenè" is 15 km west of Kangavar.

and Egyptians had taken place on the Nile, he painted a donkey drinking in a river in which there was a crocodile lying in wait for him.) At sunrise we arrived at a river called *Qara Su,* that is, "Black Water,"[169] which goes through that whole countryside and floods almost all of it. Guided by one of the natives, who showed us the easiest crossings, we traversed twelve flowing, muddy streams. Over the last one we found a bridge of bricks with four arches. All that countryside is called *Rut Canà,* that is, "Dwelling Place of the Kurds."[170] There are many Kurdish tent towns there. At the end of that plain we found a very high mountain, and, after going some way around it, stopped at its foot in a Kurdish tent village called Bisitun Bagh.[171] Although there were two caravanserais, we lodged in the countryside because one of them was completely ruined, and the other, though new, was not yet finished. It was being built on the orders of a nobleman named Shaykh Ali Khan Zanganeh,[172] and the caravanserai is named after him, since the town receives its name from the mountain, which is called Bisitun.

In a cavity of the mountain I observed some figures in relief not very different from those of Persepolis in quality and in costumes. I had them drawn, as can be seen, as well as they could be done. They were rather high up and corroded by time or ruined by the Moslems, who are enemies of such glorious memories. Over the first figures, which are not so far up, as can be seen from the drawing, there are some Greek letters, half obliterated by time. I copied them as they were, having gone up to where they were with much effort. The figures represent things similar to those already described, that is, sacrifice or triumph. One among the figures has in one hand a little figurine that resembles the figure of Fame, with large wings and a trumpet at its mouth. In the other hand it has a circle or ring. Over the other figures there is a similar figure in the act of flying.[173] Nine figures of men are sculpted

169. A tributary of the Qara Su (Turkish for "Black Water") runs just to the east of Bisitun and joins the main river to the southeast of Kermanshah.

170. Kurdistan.

171. Bisitun garden.

172. The caravanserai of Shaykh 'Ali Khan Zanganeh was completed in 1685 and was still in use in the 1970s.

173. Bembo's interpretation of the reliefs' meaning is impressively accurate. There are two Parthian reliefs near the bottom of the Mt. Bisitun rock face. In the first, four satraps are making obeisance to the shah, Mithridates II (188–123 B.C.); this relief is partially damaged by an eighteenth-century inscription. In the second, four mounted warriors are fighting; the two foreground figures are

in low relief in a great composition farther up the same mountain. They stand behind each other in a row: their arms are tied behind their backs, and their heads are uncovered, except for the last one, who is wearing a tall conical cap, like a clown's hat. All nine of them are looking toward the figure of a large man in front of them who has one foot resting on a step and holds a bow in his hands. Behind this figure there are two smaller male figures, one of whom also holds a bow, and the other, a lance. Above all these figures—in the middle and as if suspended in the air—is the upper part of a man who has wings instead of feet and who holds a ring in one hand. Below all the figures are many letters, some of which I had copied by looking through a telescope. These characters are of the same type as at Persepolis, but they are intact, since they are not exposed to the winds or rains and are safe from any other kind of damage, due to their high location.[174]

At the foot of the mountain beneath the first figures is a rather abundant spring that flows into many small streams throughout the countryside and subsequently into the river mentioned above. Not far from these figures was a site from which the local people were taking stones for the construction of the caravanserai, and there were remains of many ruined buildings and sculptures there. In the middle of the tombs in the town I saw four pieces of very fine marble column, and near the caravanserai there were some capitals with figures and floral forms in low relief. I thought at the time, and think so still, how surprising it is that Pietro della Valle makes no mention

---

Gotarzes II (A.D. 40–51) and his rival, Meherdates, who battled for the monarchy in A.D. 50; a small winged victory brings the crown to the king.

174. This low relief is more than 60 m above the ground, and it represents the victory of the Achaemenid shah Darius I (521–485 B.C.) over the insurrection of Gaumatas. The crucial battle of Kundurush took place near Bisitun and is commemorated in this relief: the tallest of the three figures at the left (the other two represent his loyal followers), Darius holds a bow in his left hand, raises his right hand in judgment, and pins his rival Gaumatas under his left foot; the nine submissive figures to the right represent rebellious satraps, whose clothing identifies their region. (The man with the conical hat is a Scythian.) The famous trilingual inscription in Old Persian, neo-Babylonian, and neo-Elamite records the details of the victory. One hundred sixty-five years later, in 1839, the great British scholar Henry Rawlinson had himself lowered by ropes from the top of the Bisitun cliff so that he could accurately copy the inscriptions on the face: this exploit and his subsequent analysis of the inscriptions provided the keys for deciphering the Old Persian and Elamite languages.

FIGURE 35. Rock relief sculpture at Bisitun.

FIGURE 35. Rock relief sculpture at Bisitun.

at all of this place and that he also does not mention Kangavar and another place that I will describe later, which is the most important of all. It is surprising, since these antiquities are noteworthy in themselves and are in places that are conspicuous to travelers, that is, at the foot of mountains that border on vast plains and are near springs and close to roads traveled by caravans. Besides, Pietro della Valle diligently traveled in Persia and wrote about it in much detail, and he also passed through these same places. I think the only explanation can be that he passed by them at nighttime and that his caravan stopped in different towns, since resting places vary according to the season and some caravans make longer stops and some shorter stops.

FIGURE 36. Panorama of Taq-i Bustan.

That night we remained in the open air, since the only person who had a tent was the janissary, who, as we got closer to Turkey, became more impertinent with each passing day and displeased me in a number of ways, not that I could expect anything else from a renegade. It was just our luck that night that there was some rain, as well as the cold, which we had to endure without shelter; thus we slept little. Then, too, we were keeping more careful guard because of the Kurds, who are quick to steal when they have the chance. We got up at midnight and traveled through those small hills and that plain; we always stayed to the right of the above-mentioned mountain, but this way takes a long time because the perimeter is great.

At daybreak on the 11th we passed a small bridge and then, a bit later, a large one of stone with seven arches.[175] On it is built part of the town of

175. The bridge is still extant and is 3 km from Taq-i Bustan, which Bembo describes below.

Pulsà, or Pulischiah, which means "bridge of the king,"[176] which in Turkish would be Schià Chiopresi. The river that runs under the bridge is the same Qara Su of the preceding day. It flows into the Euphrates at the place of the two castles where we debarked while passing [down the river] with the terrada, and I was told that it is navigable to this town.

There we lodged for four days in a caravanserai that was not very good. This time made it possible, however, for me to go a league's distance to see another mountain with many ancient sculptures, of which I had a complete drawing made, as can be seen, as well as separate drawings of each grotto for greater clarity and understanding.[177] Before arriving there, I found many gardens, and at the foot of the mountain there is a spring that makes a nice pool, bounded by stones. Over it there is a stone bridge, as can be seen from the drawing; it leads to the larger grotto. The water flows from under two arches that support the town's mosque, located to the right of the sculptures; subsequently, it divides into several smaller streams, which are filled with many fish. In the small stream [at the far right] there is a large marble statue eroded by time and weather. It stands upright in the middle of the stream, but it has no feet, nor could I discover whether it had been originally made in this way or whether it had been damaged before it was put there; it did not appear to be an appropriate place for it, since there were no other stones or remains in the area that might have belonged to it.[178]

Above the grottoes in the mountainside has been cut a very convenient flight of steps [beginning from behind the mosque]. I ascended it the whole way, but it did not seem to me as though it had been completed, since it led simply to a rugged mountain. One can see from it, however, an extensive plain below, which makes me think it was never finished.

176. Pul-i Shah.

177. Bembo is visiting Taq-i Bustan, one of the most remarkable of pre-Islamic Iranian sites. Nowadays, a large pool of water stretches in front of the mountain face in which deep, arched grottoes were cut and decorated with elaborate low-relief sculptural programs. They date from the reigns of several Sasanian (ca. A.D. 250–651) shahs: Shahpur II (310–378), Ardashir II (379–383), Shahpur III (383–388), and Khusrau II (590–628). Located on one of the great east-west trade routes and provided with an abundant water supply, Taq-i Bustan was a resting place for travelers, caravans, and armies, and the sculptural program was intended as visual propaganda for the dynasty.

178. This sculpture, as well as several other architectural fragments, are the remains of Sasanian structures formerly in the area.

In a small plain to the left of the sculptures [in the grottoes] and before one crosses the [main] stream there are two wooden railings, one larger than the other, which are rebuilt each year by the Khan of the city of Kermanshah in whose jurisdiction it [Taq-i Bustan] is located.[179] He is under orders to do so, and [these structures] commemorate Shah 'Abbas I, who, when he marched to attack Baghdad, pitched his tents within these enclosures.[180] Above the river there are some other gardens, nicely laid out, where the Persians of the neighborhood come to enjoy the cool air and amuse themselves, as may be seen in the drawing.

I shall now describe those antiquities which, not having ever been able to discover any name for them, I shall call the *Antiquities of Kermanshah,* since the mountain is within the jurisdiction of that city, which is a little more than a league's distance away. The largest grotto is cut into the mountain itself, is vaulted with precise proportions, and is about the length of . . . paces.[181] Two pilasters have been carved in the front of the cliff face, and above, on each side of the arch, are carved two winged women holding in one hand a circle and in the other hand a cornucopia. Inside the grotto on the wall opposite the entrance is a square surface on which is represented an armed man on horseback, [carved] in such high relief that it seems to have been cut from a distinct stone, although, in fact, like all the other figures that I have mentioned before and will discuss shortly, it is cut out of the rock face. His weapons consist of a bow and [a quiver of] arrows, a shield and a very long spear, all of the same stone. His face is covered with mail, as it were, with which he is also clothed down to the waist, and upon his head he has a kind of globe tied with bands. The horse is likewise covered with armor and with tassel ornaments. Some of the sculpture is broken, however, particularly a leg of the horse, as may be seen in the drawing, which is a faithful copy of it in every respect. The size of this figure on horseback, which is exactly proportioned in every part, makes it take up almost the entire space of the square, which on either side has a pilaster that supports a large carved cornice cut also from the rock face.[182] In the curved

179. "Chermonsac" is Bembo's transcription of *Kermanshah.*

180. Shah 'Abbas I besieged and captured Baghdad in 1623.

181. Bembo omitted this measurement. The site is now known simply as Taq-i Bustan.

182. The figure on horseback is Shah Khusrau II, mounted on his favorite horse, Shabdiz.

FIGURE 37. Shah Khusrau at Taq-i Bustan.

surface above the cornice [and beneath the vault] are three figures in high
relief, the middle one larger than the others, but all of them larger than life,
strangely dressed, and with many bands hanging down. The middle image
represents a man with a long beard. Upon his head there is a crown with
two wings, between which is a half moon enclosing a globe. His right hand
rests upon a sword, which he holds with its point down in front of him;
with his left hand he either touches or indicates his refusal of a banded circle or ring, which with an attitude of respect is being offered to him by the
figure standing to his left. This figure is a man with a beard who has a helmet on his head that has a banded globe on it and [who wears] a long man-

tle that hangs from his shoulders. On the right is a woman with a long dress and hair like the others, who wears on her head another form of cap with a globe fastened with bands. With her right hand she is similarly offering a circle to the figure in the middle, and in her left hand she holds a vase, from which she is pouring water.[183]

The square spaces on the [grotto's two other] sides are all full of figures in low relief. On the left side is shown a wild boar hunt, [including] enclosure palings, a marshy spot, trees, fish, and water fowl, as may be seen in the drawing, in which even the number of the animals is exactly set down, and the same precision is evident in the other drawings, as I made a point of going to the spot the very day after [they were drawn]. The boars are numerous and are also hunted by the elephants, some of which are seizing the boars with their trunks and throwing them up to the men who are riding them. Other elephants, laden with dead animals, remain outside the palings. There are also men loading other [boars], killing them first or catching them while they are attempting to get out of the palings. Inside the palings there are five small boats of a rude shape; three of them seem to be filled with performers on different instruments, with two rowers with very roughly shaped oars in each [boat]. In one of the two other boats, in addition to the two rowers, there are two other men of the same size, one playing the harp and the other holding an arrow. Between them there is another man standing up who is of larger size, has a beard and hair, and wears on his head a cap that is shaped like a crown. In his hand he holds a bow bent toward the boars. The other boat contains five figures arranged in the same way, except that the one in the middle, larger than the others, has nothing on his hair, but around his head there is a diadem, like those we give to holy pictures of saints. In one hand he holds a bow and in the other an arrow.[184]

On the right side, opposite this hunting party, there is a similar kind of low relief with a hunt after stags and similar animals. They are also pursued by numerous elephants and camels, some of which are laden with the prey, placed upon them by men who remain outside the palings. Inside the palings on one side there is a large stage with many performers on various instruments, and on the other a smaller [stage] with singers. In the middle there are various horsemen, [racing at] full speed and shooting arrows at the

183. The upper relief shows the investiture of Shah Khusrau II; the god Hormizd is to the king's left, and the water goddess, Anahita, is to his right.
184. Grélot's drawing is not as accurate as Bembo asserts.

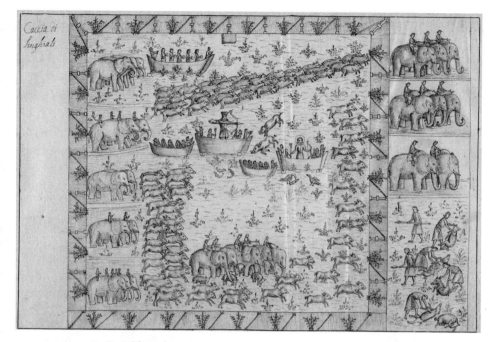

FIGURE 38. Royal boar hunt.

stags, which are numerous and are pursued by dogs, as is shown in the drawing. Among them is a man on horseback larger than the others, who has a beard and hair and a diadem similar to the one [of the man] in the boat. Across his shoulders he is carrying a bow, with one hand he guides his horse, and with the other hand he holds the pommel of his sword. Behind him is a man carrying an umbrella, who is followed by three others, who appear to be pages.

At a little distance to the right of this aforesaid cavern there is another, smaller one, within which there is only one sculpture in the rock face. It is located on the back wall facing the entrance and occupies only the curved surface beneath the vault. [It shows] two high-relief figures of men in strange dress. They are wearing long and tight breeches that seem to be made of skins, and they have various bands, as well as beards and hair. One of them has on his head a helmet with a half moon engraved on it and [on top of the helmet] is a globe with two wings. The other has likewise a diadem, and within it is the helmet, upon which there is also a winged globe. In their hands, which are raised as high as their breasts, each of them holds a staff that does not reach down to his feet. To the sides of these figures there

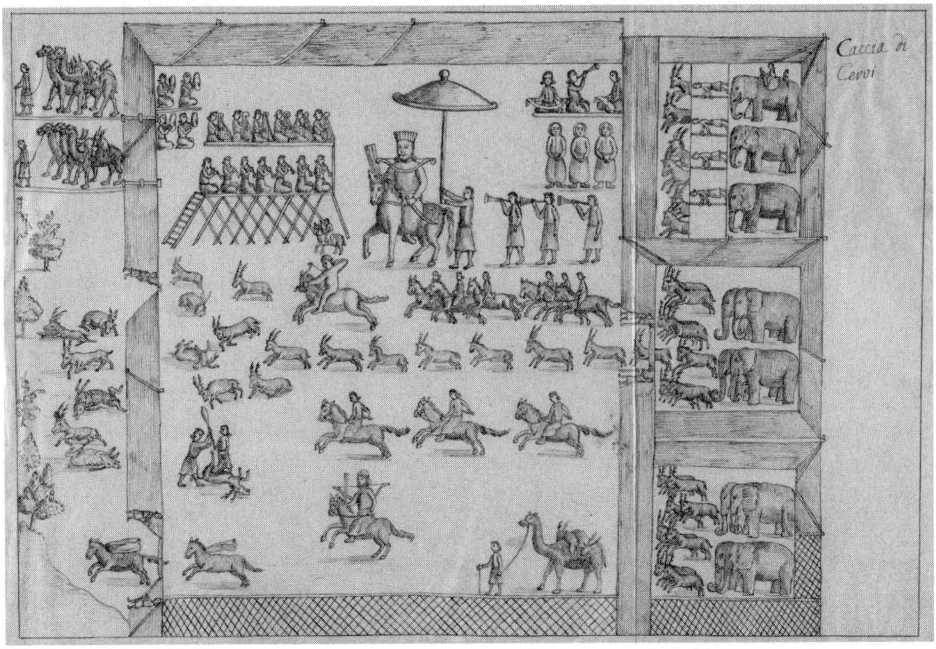

FIGURE 39. Royal deer hunt.

are several entire letters, which I had copied exactly as they are, and I think they are Coptic, which, if it please God, I will endeavor to get translated into Italian, hoping to gain from them perhaps the whole history of these antiquities.[185] I was put to some considerable expense to copy them, since I was obliged to send as far as to the town to get ladders to get up to them and to clear away the dust and cobwebs with which they were completely covered. Without this it would have been impossible to have them exactly rendered from below. While [we were] performing this [work], the Persians looked at me with astonishment, for they courteously grant every liberty to Europeans, which is not the case in Turkey, where such curiosity might leave one open to considerable trouble and perhaps even to the loss of one's life.

185. On the right is Shah Shahpur II (310–378); on the left is Shahpur III (383–388). Bembo's descriptions are in some points more accurate than Grélot's drawings. For instance, Grélot makes Shahpur II's helmet far taller than it actually is and puts the hands of both kings lower. The inscription on the left has fallen away, and Grélot's rendering of it may permit a reading of what was originally there.

FIGURE 40. Shahpur II and Shahpur III at Taq-i Bustan.

In the space beneath these figures there is nothing other than a large crack in the rock face, which I also had put into the drawing.

Also, to the right of this second grotto, in the same cliff face and closer to the river, there is a kind of square [surface] with four figures in relief that are not much dissimilar in their dress from the two mentioned above, [for they have] many bands, and all of them have beards and hair. One of them lies stretched upon the ground, like a sleeping or dead man, nor has he anything upon his head. Standing upright upon him are two of the remaining three figures. The one on the right has a crown on his head on which is a winged globe, and he is offering a crown or banded circle to the other figure, who is in the middle. [This middle figure] is placing his right

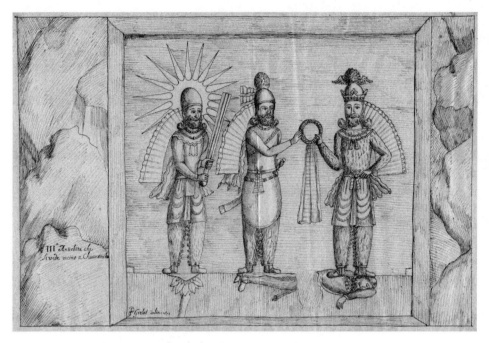

FIGURE 41. Investiture of Ardashir II.

hand on the [banded circle], as if he is refusing it, while his left hand rests upon a sword at his side. On his head is a small helmet with a globe attached to it by bands. On his right there is a fourth figure, whose feet are not on the dead man, but he is raising with both his hands a sword and is in the act of threatening or wounding the figure who stands in the middle. [This fourth figure] has on his head a helmet surrounded by large rays, like the sun.[186]

I was not a little amused on hearing from these countrymen, through my dragoman, many ridiculous stories that they attach to these figures, referring everything to the deeds of one of their ancient kings called Rustam, respecting whom not only the country people and the ignorant, but even

186. This low relief depicts the investiture of Shah Ardashir II. The god Hormizd (Ahura Mazda) stands at the right and hands the symbol of royal power, the ribboned diadem, to Ardashir. Beneath their feet is a conquered Roman soldier. To the king's right is Mithras, the god of light and of the sun and the protector against evil, who is standing on a lotus flower and is holding a bundle of sacred branches, known as the *barsom*.

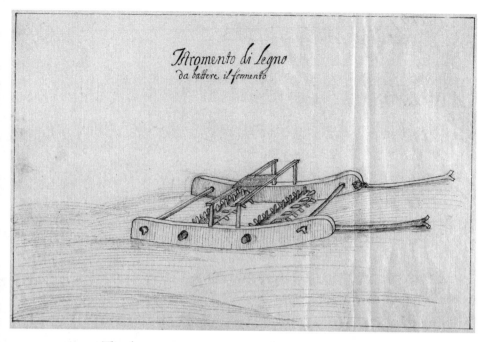

FIGURE 42. Thresher.

the most learned, invent the most silly fables; but I am inclined to think that they are all mistaken, as Rustam in good Persian signifies "antiquities."[187] They assert, therefore, that of the figures in the first grotto, the one on horseback represents Rustam, the other two above [him], one Khusrau, the other Shahpur, and the lady is Shirin, which means "mild," a lady of rank strangely beloved by Khusrau, respecting whose amours the Persians recite many verses and songs. And thus they go on with regard to the rest, some inventing one story and others another.[188]

When we returned to our lodging, I observed a wooden instrument in the fields that they use to beat wheat, and I had it drawn, as can be seen, as a curiosity. A horse pulls it around the mound of wheat. With its two

187. Bembo's etymology is incorrect; his mistake may have been based on mishearing the first word of *rasum bastani* or "antiquities."

188. The local belief that Bembo reports is that the mounted warrior is Rustam, famed in Iran's great epic, the *Shahnamah,* as the great champion in service of Iran's kings. Rendered by several Persian poets, the story of Khusrau and Shirin is one of Iran's great love stories: the shah Khusrau had fallen in love

wheels that have wooden spikes, it separates the wheat from the chaff and also cuts the straw, which is then given to the horses to eat.

On the 13th I was able to finish the drawings as I liked. That day we had some freshwater fish, but it had many bones. I also had an argument with the janissary because he wanted me to bear the greater part of the expense of buying a *taub*[189] and some coffee to give as a present to the scribe of the Khan, who lives in the town, to keep track of the caravans that pass into Turkey. I got out of this expense, however, because of the exemption that all Franks enjoy in Persia. He nevertheless cheated me into paying five 'abbasi for something else. On the 14th the scribe came to take down everyone's name and the amount of merchandise in the caravan. His account was then signed by the Khan of Kermanshah,[190] who is one of the principal ministers of the court. That city is large and near the border and about three miles from the town. The signed account is then taken to an official who resides at the border, and he checks everything again, particularly the number of weapons, so that no one brings armaments to Baghdad under the pretext of using them, and he checks the number of men who go out of the country. That janissary noted all of us down as Armenians with assumed names. After the scribe had left, however, his agent came back and said he wanted to erase the names of the four Armenians from the document, since he had since discovered that they were Franks who should not leave until everything had been straightened out with the Khan. So I went with my interpreter to the scribe and complained. From the answers he gave me I came to understand that the janissary had confused things; but the scribe took care of everything easily. Thus I felt obligated to show him my gratitude, especially since he had

---

with the Christian princess Shirin (Bembo's Sciria) when he had come across her by chance while she was bathing, and they subsequently married. Her name means "sweet," "gentle," "delicate," or "mild." The hapless stonecutter and sculptor Farhad also loved her. This folk explanation of the sculpture at Taq-i Bustan may be derived from the great romantic poem *Khusrau and Shirin* of the poet Nizami, in which Farhad carves into the side of Mt. Bisitun a relief sculpture of Shirin and of Khusrau on his horse Shabdiz. Bembo, however, says that the third person in the group is Shahpur, a Sasanian shah.

189. A *taub* (Bembo's "tobé") is a robe. Giving someone an outer garment was a traditional expression of respect and honor in Islam.

190. From 1665 to 1698 the Khan of Kermanshah, the last major Iranian city on this caravan road to Baghdad, was Shaykh 'Ali Khan Zangana, who also served as one of the major officials at the court of Shah Sulayman.

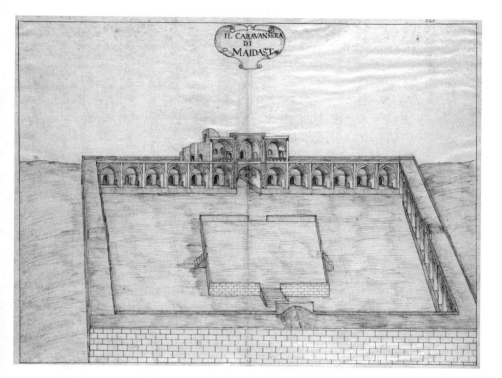

FIGURE 43. Caravanserai at Maidast.

to take care of the confusion with the commander. I gave him five 'abbasi worth of coffee, since he did not want to accept any money, since he could be severely punished if the Khan found out. I was told this by some Persians who had been very kind to me all those days and had even invited me to eat in their homes. I had not accepted, because I had no way of repaying them. If I had gone into the city, I certainly could have got the Khan to punish both the scribe and the janissary, but there was not sufficient time for me to go to the city, so I had to be patient, and the janissary went unpunished.

At dawn on the 15th the caravan set out. Four Arabs on horses and four dervishes on foot had joined us. The trip was in good part through small mountains, after which we descended to a plain, until about noontime, when we stopped at a caravanserai called Maidast or Mahideset; it was built near a stream and was one of the most comfortable and beautiful that I saw.[191]

191. Mahidasht (Maidast) is 26 km to the southwest of Kermanshah on the road to Shahabad.

Over the gate it has several beautiful rooms for the winter, and they have many shaded windows both on the inside and outside. Thus I had it drawn so that one can see how it looks inside. We found everything we needed there, especially much fruit, including watermelons and other melons.

We got on our mounts again on the 16th at three hours before daybreak. We crossed a stone bridge under which runs the stream that begins near the caravanserai that I have just mentioned. The trip was through difficult mountains. At dawn we ascended one of them, and on the top I was amazed to see the whole caravan eating acorns, which they took from the oak trees with great satisfaction, as if they were the best fruit in the world. One of the Arabs came to me and offered me a fistful, which I had to accept so as not to offend the giver, but I let them fall to the ground without anyone seeing me.[192] When we had come down the mountain, we found several Kurdish towns in a small plain. From time to time these settlements, along with the families, baggage, and furniture, are loaded on donkeys and other animals and are moved to another location, changing place according to the season. At midday we stopped in a caravanserai called Arnebat, near a stream on whose shores was one of those portable towns of the Kurds.[193] Near this caravanserai there was another new, large, and beautiful one, but it was not yet finished. These were the last ones I saw, because in the country of the Ottomans there are no such delightful lodgings. In fact, it is only with difficulty that one finds even a miserable roof.

On the morning of the 17th, an hour before dawn, we began to travel again. We crossed that stream on a stone bridge, and then we passed another. After traveling in a plain for an hour we arrived at some high mountains full of trees. In going up and down these mountains, we had spent several days, as can be seen in reading this journal. These mountains divide the Persian from the Ottoman Empire.[194] On them we began to feel the cold and to see some ice. Around midday we dismounted near a stream where there were also some ten or twelve Kurdish tents at a distance. That place is called Gesmet Cambar, and there the whole caravan made a stop in the open.[195]

192. Obviously, the acorns were an edible variety about which Bembo was unaware.

193. Harunabad (Arnebat) is now known as Shahabad and is 44 km to the southwest of Mahidasht.

194. The Zagros mountain range.

195. This is apparently a reference to the town of Cheshme Zarneh to the

Those who had tents opened them up here. I took advantage of a tent belonging to a muleteer named Malik Shah,[196] who offered it to me very courteously, as he always behaved toward me, as I did to him. I tried to be very courteous with everyone and gave them coffee and other things, which pleased the Persians and the Turks. In that place we found nothing but melons, and not very good ones at that.

At dawn on the 18th we arose and continued the journey through those mountains full of oaks. I observed many tombs along the road, as I had seen during the trip from Shiraz. I thought they were the remains of destroyed towns, but then I saw that the towns themselves have tombs along the roads. This is either to avoid contagion or, more likely, to encourage those who pass by to pray for the dead, unless it is for some superstition of theirs. At the 4th hour we stopped on a mountain near a stream where there were no dwellings around. That place is called the Mansur Spring.[197] On a hill not far away there is a large town of Kurds, and, as is their custom, they came immediately, bringing milk, goat kids, chickens, bread, and pomegranates. Since the place was not suitable for putting up tents, I stayed in the shade of a tree with my group and my things. That day another caravan, which had left from Hamadan, happened to come there. It was going, as we were, to Baghdad and was large, having forty mules and one hundred donkeys, all loaded, and twenty men on horseback. Along with this caravan, we arose three hours before day on the 19th. The trip was so difficult that I was often obliged to dismount and walk, ascending and descending the mountain. Having climbed on one of these mountains, I saw a very beautiful view of many delightful hills, so orderly and so alike one to the other that they seemed a plain. As we passed through them, we saw quantities of partridges that were so tame that they hopped right up to the horses. They were in groups numbering between twelve and twenty. If one has weapons, one can have good hunting while traveling, since the Persians permit it and also delight in game. In the same hills I saw many wild pistachio trees. On the outside the fruit looks like beans, but inside one sees that they are of the color of good pistachios. They salt them, and then people in both Persia and Turkey eat them with great satisfaction. After midday we stopped in the town Chierèn. It was half made up of tents

---

southwest of Shahabad. Bembo refers to this stop as the "Conae," perhaps his understanding of the Persian word *kunna,* meaning "shade."

196. Bembo spells his name as "Malemxà."

197. Cheshme Mansur.

and half of earthen houses. In the vicinity there is an abundant spring where I stayed in comfort with my group and my things. Here we rested also the next day, which was the 20th. Still, we suffered from the scarcity of food, especially since it was Friday and Saturday. Worst of all, the bread was so black and so bad that I think it must have been made of barley. But from that spring I got some fish that had very few bones and was similar in taste to the fish from the Tigris that I had eaten in Baghdad. During a trip through Persia it would be both frugal and entertaining to carry along a fishing net. There are many opportunities to use one, and the Franks are given complete freedom. That night there was terrible weather with thunder, lightning, and rain, but fortunately it stopped soon, since I had no covering except for the sky.

Five hours before sunrise on the 21st, we arose and began our travel with a difficult and dangerous ascent of a high, harsh mountain. We continued until sunrise, when we began to descend through such a steep, narrow pass that only one person could go through at a time. Although I was on foot, I was constantly in fear that I would fall down one side or the other, where there were terrible, frightening precipices. Here, as elsewhere, I admired the strong defenses that the Persians have, surrounded by such mountains. It is not hard to believe that just these mountains have been sufficient to keep back the Ottomans, who, since taking Baghdad, have not been victorious against the Persians. After a difficult descent we stopped in a town called Sampsur, composed of tents and earthen houses.[198] Near it there is a small spring, but it is of poor quality. There are no trees, not even a place to put up tents, so we stayed in the open air and left from the spot even before midnight. After having crossed two or three rivulets, we arrived at a river called the Caghir Sui, or Ganghir Sui, which means "Water of the Deep."[199] It runs for a long stretch among those mountains and finally comes out in the Tigris. Its course is swift and steep. It strikes the stones with strength, as it does the remains of bridges over which caravans passed long ago. All that night we traveled along its banks without losing sight of it. In fact, we crossed it by fording and recrossed it, due to the turns it takes. At that time of year it had little water, but it becomes large and dangerous when the snows melt, and then it has to be crossed by boat.

At the second hour of sunlight on the 22nd we entered a small plain near the river and stopped in the town of Sumbar, a drawing of which can be

198. About 50 km west of Zarneh, Sampsur is near the Iran-Iraq border.
199. The Kangir River descends from the Manisht Kuh, one of the highest mountains in western Iran.

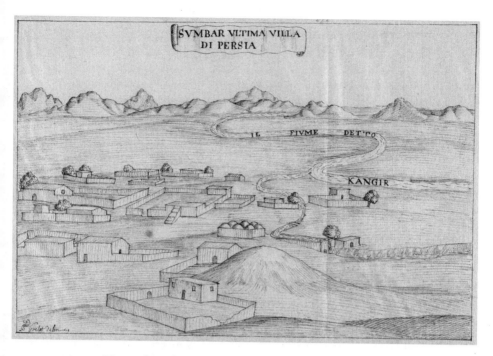

FIGURE 44. Town of Sumbar.

seen.[200] It is the last town of the Persians and is inhabited also by Turks and Arabs. An aga lives there who has been appointed by the Khan of Kermanshah. He checks all the caravans going out of Persia and receives the notes sealed by that Khan. Having been given our list, along with a gift of three 'abbasi, he checked it at sunset but did not check the names and the weapons, because it was dark. The caravan stayed all together in the middle of the town, as if in a plaza. In order to see the caravan, all the inhabitants were on the terraces on top of their houses. They particularly watched us when we were eating, since they are used to eating only one thing, roasted or boiled meat and pilaf, which they eat with their hands. Thus they observed us very carefully and saw that each of us had his set of knives, forks, and spoons and much variety of food, which the ingenious Frenchman Grélot prepared from the few things we could get. He did not let himself lose spirit from the lack of things. At the least, he would add spices to eggs and onions so that they became delicious. The Persians asked us if all the Europeans ate like that.

200. Sumbar, the modern town of Sumar.

FIVE

From Iran to Venice

[OCTOBER 1674–APRIL 1675]

WE GOT UP TWO HOURS BEFORE DAWN on the morning of the 23rd. I had
the town drawn at sunrise, along with the plain that divides the two countries. Our trip was through a plain, and we crossed the river two times.
The first time was in the jurisdiction of Baghdad and thus in Ottoman
territory. With those high mountains we had left behind the kingdom of
the Sofi, 'Ajam, Persians, and Qizilbash, all of which are names for the
Persian kingdom, as well as the civility of its inhabitants and the freedom
for foreigners.[1] After having crossed other small streams that, due to the
aridity of the country, flow through irrigation canals to bring water to
[fields and] gardens, we began to see Arabs with sunburned faces and long
lances, and at the third hour we arrived at the first Turkish town. Before
entering it, I observed the innate hate, which is [quite] unjust, that the
Turks have against the Persians, who treat them courteously. Many boys
and girls ran to see the caravan and shouted insults at the Persians, repeat-
ing often some words that they considered very insulting: *Babà Agiàm
Candilcès; Sà Babà Agiàm Ercansis*—which means "O Father Persian
without a turban," in other words, "without faith."[2] This made me laugh
because they also came to shout it in my face, since they saw me with a
Persian-style fur cloak.

The place is large and called "Mendali."[3] It is in the middle of many
palm gardens, a sign of the territory of Baghdad. I ate those fresh and deli-

1. Bembo's transcriptions are "Soffi, Agiami, Farsi, and Cheselbes."
2. The Turkish would be *Acem Baba sarıksınız* or *Acem Baba destarsınız*.
Neither word makes a lot of sense.
3. The Iraqi town of Mandali.

cious dates, although the right time for harvesting them is in November and December. There is an ancient castle surrounded by a moat. One enters it over a single-arched bridge made of bricks. The city walls are of earth, and it has eight towers. At the time of the Persians it was all covered with colored stones,[4] and it was built by them, since Mandali was a large city where a khan lived. At present an aga lives in the castle; he also commands the town and is superior to a qadi, an aga of the customs house, and an aga of janissaries with some soldiers, since it is a border town. Our lodging was in a *khan*, which is the same in appearance as a caravanserai in Persia, but very different in the reality of things, because it was nothing other than a very large space, roofed and with an enclosing earthen wall. The caravan stayed there to rest almost three days. I went to see the town, where many Turks of some civility live. There is a good coffee house and, unlike in most Turkish places, good bread and good meat. Nevertheless, that entry into Turkey seemed very strange to me after having been in Persia, where I had been courteously welcomed and treated with every civility, where I had found good lodging and abundant food at very good price everywhere, and where I had been safe from robbers and murderers, as well as exempt from tolls and fees, except for the very reasonable ones paid for merchandise. But in Turkey I found the countryside bare and arid, and, even though it presents the constant danger of thieves, it is this countryside that is still the most frequent lodging place for the traveler; in the towns there are thousands of insolences, injuries, and discourtesies that one has to endure even though they are done by the lowliest people; the food is barely adequate; and there are tolls, fees, and extortion at every step of the way. Since it is the Turks' country, we began by paying to the Great Aga one *mahmudi* per horse, which is ½ an 'abbasi, and a sum for every pack or saddle animal. To the owner of the khan, who was a janissary and obliged to watch all the animals entrusted to him—a sign in itself that Persian security was lost—we gave a *gazi* a day per animal, which is the 20th part of a mahmudi, all Persian coins. The aga of the customs house came to take careful note of all things of the caravan and sent a list to the aga of the customs house in Baghdad. He also demanded his fee on all the goods. With much villainy and indiscretion he wanted to look in my *alforges*,[5] which are certain small saddle-bags of the Persians that go on either side of a horse. I had in them my per-

4. Polychrome, glazed ceramic tiles.
5. *Alforges* is Portuguese for saddlebags.

sonal things, and he made a mess of everything, making me remember the civility and liberty of Persia, which I will never be able to praise enough.

On the morning of the 25th a caravan from Baghdad arrived. It was going to Hamadan with much merchandise and several Armenians, who told us that the road was safe from Arabs. It had been cleared by soldiers of the pasha of Baghdad. After such good news we got up with greater courage at the third hour before dawn on the 26th. The cold temperature was also not as troublesome as it had been in the Persian mountains. In fact, once the sun was up, the weather even got somewhat hot. Our journey was in a vast plain that stretched as far as the eye could see. Only off in the distance to the right could we see the mountains of Persia. Up until the 5th hour, the country through which we traveled was bare and uncultivated, and we did not see any water other than a small rivulet that was muddy. We stopped in the town of Imam 'Asgar, named after a prophet of theirs who is buried there.[6] There are a few houses and some gardens, but since there were no facilities to set up tents, we had to stay uncomfortably in the sun. The caravan rested near a stream called Morrusx by the inhabitants and called Diyala by others.[7] Most probably it was a branch of the river that it joins after two days' journey; together they then enter the Tigris. There I saw some small European copper coins. On them are the arms of Sweden, which is a sheaf of wheat. They are worth four to the aspri there, and they call them *fuli*.[8] I brought some with me.

On the morning of the 27th we took with us a man of the town because the mud made the road difficult to follow. We left two hours before sunlight and continued our trip in that great plain, all desert and nothing green except for some palm gardens. At midday we saw at a distance about twenty horsemen with lances. We thought they were Arab thieves, but they turned in another direction when they saw the caravan. At sunset we stopped in the town of Buhriz,[9] in the middle of which runs a small stream that they call *Cherisan*. It is, however, a branch of the Diyala. We crossed the Diyala the

6. With his transcription of "Aman Mascar" Bembo would appear to be rendering the name Imam 'Asgar. This name does not, however, refer to the eleventh Shi'i imam, Hasan al-'Askari, who was buried in Samarra.

7. The Diyala River, a tributary of the Tigris.

8. The Safavis had a copper coin known as a *fulus,* issued not by royal mints but by local municipal mints. The Swedish coins that Bembo describes apparently circulated under the same name.

9. Bembo calls it "Beherus," which should probably be understood as Balad Ruz, midway between Mandai and the Diyala.

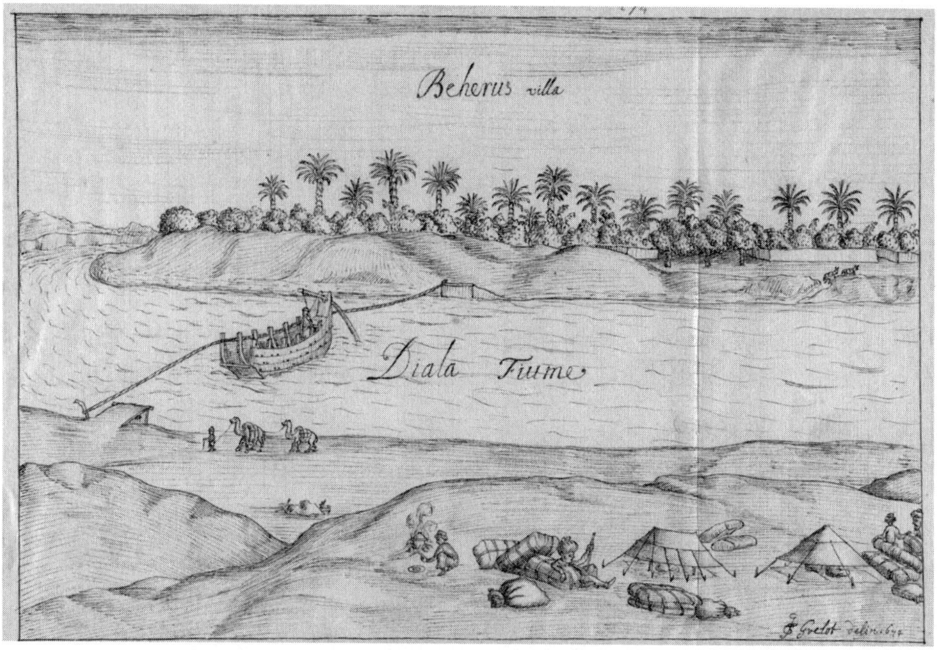

FIGURE 45. Beherus and ferry across the Diyala.

next day on the 28th. It is just outside that town and is rather wide. It runs through the countryside and enters the Tigris below Baghdad, as I had observed when I left that city for Basra. We spent almost the whole day crossing that river, since there was only one boat that could take but six animals at a time. It is pulled with little effort by ropes from one side to the other. As can be seen in the drawing that I had made, it is a very awkward affair and quite similar to those that I described in Birecik. For this ferry passage the Turk there receives a mahmudi per animal, while two gazi go to the ferrymen.

We spent the rest of the day on the riverbanks in front of the town. Some of those in the caravan who only had horses proceeded on to Baghdad. From Baghdad in the evening came four Turks from the customs house. They would not let us leave until the 29th, after they had looked through the luggage and disordered it in their usual manner. They threw all of my things around, including my kitchen utensils. They opened every little package, even though it would have to be opened again in the customs house in the city. They practiced the same insolence on the Persians and on their women, even going so far as to look into their bedrolls. They went about this business with even greater zeal because they thought that this caravan was carrying many things, since none had come from Persia for some time. I saw a trick that some Persians do to avoid the duty on jewels coming from India by way of Persia. They put some jewels inside a hen that they kill for this purpose. This time, though, when they were told that the Turks would not bodily search them, they preferred to hide the jewels on their persons, since they were afraid that the hen might be stolen or that the customs official might want it as a gratuity, and they knew full well that if they refused to give up the hen, the officials would want it even more. In addition, the punishment for contraband is nothing more than a doubled duty. After the visit was finished, we departed at an hour after sunrise. We continued our journey in that plain, which ends with the city visible in the distance. There are neither towns nor trees impeding the view. We saw it when we were three hours away from it, since the day was cloudy, thus shielding us from the burning sun. At the halfway point on the road, there is a large brick caravanserai built by the Persians but ruined since then by the Turks.

At sunset we finally arrived at the walls of Baghdad. These walls are not very large, and from a distance we were easily able to see their whole extent. Here there were several tents with some of the pasha's people who had come to govern the place, and some of his soldiers were in tents below the citadel. After having waited more than an hour for permission from the aga of the customs house, we entered through the gate adjacent to the citadel. Since it was late, he had wanted us to wait until the next day. On entering the city, I saw hanging on the door a great ball of stone, a *murione*,[10] and another of iron. This gate is guarded by some janissaries to whom one pays half an 'abbasi a head and a whole 'abbasi for every four pack animals. They took us all to the customs house, which is next to the river. It is an ancient building made of good stone, built by the Persians, as are the best bazaars, which now are half-ruined and very crudely patched by the Turks with boards. However, sometime after I left they built a new bazaar for dealing in textiles imported from India. It was of stone. After having unloaded my things, I went to the house of the Capuchins. It was already the first hour of the night, the same hour at which I had arrived the first time. I could have gone there as soon as I entered the city, but for greater security I had wanted to accompany my things to the customs house myself. The Capuchin fathers welcomed me with the same courtesy as before, and they told me that the

10. Morion, a variety of black, smoky quartz.

pasha, who had just completed his term of government, and the aga of the janissaries had gone that very day with a large caravan to Aleppo. I could surely have gone with them quickly and safely, if I had only arrived earlier. Persians are treated very strictly in Baghdad. They have their very own khan so that they can be watched. Father Giacomo did not know this, and he received some blows for his ignorance: he had been dressed as a Persian, and when a janissary saw him not going along with the other Persians but rather looking for the house of the Capuchins, he beat him with a rod and demanded why he was not going with the others. A nearby Christian, however, recognized him as a Frank and led him to the Capuchins.

The next day I went with those fathers to the customs house. Since they were friends of the aga, the scribe, and the other officials, my things were inspected courteously. Nevertheless, the customs officials wanted their duty, which was 5% on all the goods. They have an official who estimates the value of everything. The estimate was, however, not strict, since it turned out to be for 360 piasters, that is, reales, and the goods were certainly worth more than that. Besides, he took only ten piasters in all, plus two more for the scribe and the others, including four or five Jews who serve there in the most vile offices. They are quite poor and have no authority.

[NOVEMBER 1674]

On the morning of November 1, after [I had] heard a Mass sung at the mission, a messenger arrived from my uncle in Aleppo requesting that I return at once, because he was expecting his successor at any moment and had set his departure for the first days of November. Nevertheless, I thought that I would be able to reach him in time (as it, in fact, occurred), since, due to the weather, sea voyages cannot be scheduled precisely. I decided to leave behind all the goods and travel only with people through the desert, this being the shortest way. There was no hope of being able to make that journey with a caravan unless I were to wait three months, and I could not. Thus I arranged with that same Arab who had brought the message that he should guide me to Aleppo in a trip of fifteen days through the desert. His name was Hajji Osman,[11] and I promised to pay him thirty reales. I left everything with the Capuchin fathers, [requesting them] to send it to Aleppo when they could. In fact, everything arrived in Venice a year after I did.

11. Bembo writes the name as "Agì Ozem."

The following morning, the 4th, I went to the plaza at the citadel to buy some horses. I was assisted by some Armenians who were friends of the Fathers. That same day I was taken to a wealthy Armenian merchant's house: it was richly decorated. He gave me various delicacies to eat, as well as much wine and brandy. I learned their custom of making toasts. They give the guest some wine. He does not drink it all but leaves some in the glass, which he then gives back to the host. At this point the host gives the guest some bread. The guest eats the bread, and the host fills the glass and returns it to the guest. At the conclusion of my visit he gave me some rose water for my beard, which by now was so full that people thought I was forty years old.

On the morning of the 5th I got together my provisions for the trip: biscuits, salted meat, dried fruit, and so forth. I also got provisions for the horses, as well as water carried in goatskins that were tied under the horses' bellies. I left around the 22nd hour, having taken leave of the fathers, who accompanied me to the other side of the river. That evening I stayed in the house of my guide, who gave me my supper—pilaf and some meat—which we all ate together out of one plate.

On the morning of the 6th, having equally divided all the provisions, some clothing, a coat for each person, and the water, we got on our horses. Two Turks accompanied us. One was qadi of a small town near the city of Anah, and the other served in the citadel of Hit.[12] We went toward the desert, leaving on our right the ruined tower commonly called [the Tower] "of Babel"; although it is very famous, many say that it is more modern, as is evident from the rather tall remains.[13] Not far away are the ruins of a destroyed city. Around noontime we experienced some terrible weather, with rain, wind, darkness, thunder, and lightning. The horses did not want to walk and turned their backs to the wind. Although the storm was soon over, it created a lot of mud and tired out the horses. Thus we arrived that night at our destination much later than we had anticipated, even though we traveled fairly

12. Both Hit and 'Anah are on the Euphrates to the northwest of Baghdad.

13. Thirty-three km north of Baghdad on the Damascus road, Aqar Quf is also known as Aqar-i Babil and as Qasr Nimrud. It is the site of the Kassite city of Dur Kurigalzu, founded in the fifteenth century B.C. The ziggurat is still well preserved and is over 57 m high. To the southeast of the ziggurat was a temple precinct, and the Kassite palaces, to which Bembo refers in the following sentence, are a kilometer to the southwest.

fast, since the horses were ours and since we were not held back by an entire caravan. The plain where we were traveling was so vast that the eye saw nothing else. Our first stop was in an Arab town called Fergu, which means "a little hen."[14] It is located on the banks of the Euphrates and is called Murat Sui by the Turks.[15] Everyone, including me, had to take care of his own horse, because the Arab was old and barely able to take care of his own, and my interpreter had never learned how to put on the bridle. We stayed in a badly built house reserved for travelers. People came to bring straw for the horses and some poor food for us, a custom they have with all travelers. Anyone who wants anything else, as I did, has to pay for it.

On the morning of the 7th we crossed the Euphrates in some boats. Then we found ourselves in the desert without seeing anything but sky, flat, arid earth, and sometimes a thicket near the river, where wild animals lived. At midday we came back to the shores of the river; we ate some bread and garlic, since some cats had eaten all of the cooked meat we had had with us the night before. We filled the goatskins with fresh water and continued our trip. I saw some dunes of gypsum that shone in the sun. At the 23rd hour we reached an Arab tent village near the river. We did not stop there and traveled until the night, when we stopped in a wood that was very dense. In the middle of it there was a town called Beni Amer Arabi Giamus, that is, "Arabs of the Buffaloes," since in it live Arabs who have a great quantity of buffalo, from whose meat and milk they live.[16] Their houses are of straw, and the heads of the town brought a rug for us to sit on and gave us a supper of a large flat bread that seemed to be of sand and a great basin of wood full of warm buffalo milk with several wooden spoons. Hunger made everything seem delicious. We rested in the open air and heard some lions during the night. Since there are many of them, the villagers always keep fires burning around their houses and their animals.

On the 8th at daybreak when we took the horses to water at the river, which is not far, we saw many lions' paw prints in the earth. That day we saw more gypsum hills, and then we met the river again, which was always on our right. It was flowing very swiftly and was rather wider than the Tigris. It makes many turns and provides water to many parts of the desert, where

14. *Farruj* in Arabic.

15. About 55 km or a day's journey from Baghdad, Al-Falluja was an important stop on the caravan route and for river traffic on the Euphrates.

16. Bembo's "giamus" is *jamus* (buffalo) in Arabic.

there is no other source of water. We rode all day until the 24th hour, when we arrived at a castle called Hit, which is on a hill near the river.[17] Around it there are the remains of good cisterns and numerous other ruins that indicate that it was an important place at one time, but not built by the Turks, who occupy the castle, which is half-ruined and built of rough stones, as are the houses, which are quite low. That night I lodged in the house of the Turk who was a member of our company. The room he assigned us was well furnished with rugs and cushions. He courteously set a table for us (although with my money), and he brought us a *sofrà* of straw,[18] which is like the end of a barrel that serves as a table. He brought us many flat breads that also served as plates, a pilaf with chicken, and another type of soup with meat in it. Although they brought some wooden spoons, the Turks eat with their hands, most notably the qadi, who, like a pig without any care or manners, took most of the chicken and devoured it, which was what he did during the rest of the trip, always eating at my expense.

At an early hour on the morning of the 9th the aga of the place, who had heard that we were Franks, sent some officials, appointed by the pasha of Baghdad, to see what we had and to ask for a zecchino from each of us. We offered him three piasters, saying that we were poor travelers and that the interpreter was not a Frank but a Maronite. It was not possible to convince him. The Arab of the house went to the aga, and after a long talk we had to put out eight reales if we wanted to leave, even though there was no obligation to pay anything at all, since the Porte had not authorized it. It was already the second hour of sunlight when we left. For a great stretch of road we saw ruined buildings near the river and kept seeing them almost all day. On the river banks on both sides there are many palm gardens and some small, tall houses in the form of towers, mostly broken, and some inhabited by Arabs who cultivate some small pieces of land near the river. I also saw some small boats and kalaks sailing by, similar to that on which I traveled

17. About 145 km from Baghdad, Hit is the site of ancient Eitha (Asiopolis) and was well known for its asphalt and sulfur springs. The fourteenth-century Arab geographer Mustawfi reports that it was a flourishing agricultural center but was marred by the overwhelming odor of the bitumen springs. It is surprising that Bembo does not mention either the prosperous farming or the stench.

18. The Arabic *sufra* (Bembo's "sofrà") is a flat surface or a cloth on which food is served.

from Diyarbakır to Baghdad. In some places where the river is rather wide and low, it runs into some stones and makes a loud and raucous noise that gives a person fright and melancholy at the same time. At around the 24th hour we stopped at the town of Giuba. The houses are of stone, but rough, and they have no windows; instead, they have many small holes in the walls to let in air and light. The inhabitants are all poor Arabs. We lodged in one of the houses, where there was not even enough barley for the horses. After eating, the muleteer ordered us back to the horses in case the inhabitants of a larger town on the other side of the river should find out about the arrival of Franks and come over to demand money. We rode all that night and took only a rest around dawn in a low place between two mountains. We set off again soon after sunrise and traveled all day through desert places. We stopped only so that the horses could feed and we could eat a little bread. We continued traveling with great effort and arrived at a point overlooking the river and Ana an hour after nightfall.[19] The whole road on both sides of the river is lined with ruins of ancient palaces and buildings that indicate that it was once a large and beautiful city, both because of its buildings and its location. Although now it is no greater than a mile in length, it was some five miles long before. It is divided by the river into two parts, so that one half is in Arabia and the other in Mesopotamia, and they are connected by some little boats.[20] In the middle of the river there is a little island with many houses and a half-ruined castle on it, which is not defensible, since some small hills overlook it on one side of the city. These hills prevent any access to the city except by way of the river. The city is long and narrow with only one road on either side. The houses are almost all along the river and are of rough stones, joined by earth and ashes. Almost all are of the same size with several floors and rooms. Instead of tiled [courtyards], they have terraces on the roofs, but these are surrounded by high walls. The houses are without windows but with many holes. Behind them there are rather well-kept gardens. I was not able to have the place drawn because the muleteer insisted that we stay inside all the time in order to avoid the insults of the prince of the Arabs' people, who was in town. The city is subject to the pasha of Baghdad, who sends there a müsellim, an aga, a qadi, and a subaşı. The

19. The ancient city of Bethuna (Anatho), ʿAnah is 142 kilometers to the northwest of Hit and is located at the bend where the Euphrates turns west.

20. Mustawfi also notes that ʿAnah marks the natural division between the Jazirah and Iraq.

inhabitants are all Arabs, native to the place and not very numerous, and there are also about forty Jews who act as spies. We lodged in the house of an Arab friend of the muleteer, who received us with courtesy. Since it was Saturday, we did not eat well, but we did rest well.

As soon as we arose on the morning of the 11th, the aga's people came to demand five zecchini, but we told him that the interpreter was a Christian from Aleppo and did not have to pay, so we got away with it. That same day the muleteer took me to meet the amir, something I had wanted to do out of curiosity, since he was the same person who had fought near Aleppo. His name was Mehemed Shadid,[21] that is, "Mehmet the Strong," who is Lord of the desert and nearby places. He lives in tents in the country, now in one place and now in another. He is an absolute ruler and independent of the Ottomans, but now he was on good terms with them, as he was not allowing his subjects to engage in robbery, since the caravans that passed through the desert paid him a fee. When I arrived outside his lodging, I saw in the ground a very long lance, something which I had seen in all the Arab villages outside the houses of their chiefs. There were also many soldiers there as his bodyguard. I went into a large, ground-floor room that was rather dark, and there were many Arabs standing near the door. Farther in, but on a higher level, there were several others sitting on their haunches and leaning against the wall. They had weapons, because they were captains, but they were miserably dressed and had their heads wrapped in some black scarves that also went around their necks and fell down behind their shoulders. Their faces were harsh and dry, and they had long, rough beards. Their eyes were frightening, and there in the dark they seemed like the Furies. At the end of that same room to the left of the entrance was seated the amir on some silk cloths with silk cushions, but he was dressed in an ordinary manner. He was of handsome appearance, tall and dark with noble features and a pleasant face. He had a long, black beard. His head and neck were covered by a black scarf. He was wearing only a long white shirt and long white pants. Near him was a fire. They wanted various fees from us. After much discussion I had to pay too much, and we were allowed to leave.

We left before sunrise on the 13th in a thick fog. We traveled all day and rested only at the fourth hour of the night. We continued to pay much attention to avoiding the [bedouin] Arabs, and we were not able to find

21. Bembo spells his name as "Mehemet Sidit or Chiedit." Much more briefly, Bembo mentions him in his discussion of Aleppo and its politics.

much to eat. We passed near a castle called al-'Ashara and another called Rahaba, where the jurisdiction of the amir Mehemed Shadid ends and that of the amir 'Abd al-'Aziz begins.[22]

On the 18th after midday we began to find many ruins of stone, along with the remains of a castle and a tower. The Turks, who are enemies of memories, take stones from them and make them even more ruined. From the good architecture one can surmise that they were the works of Christians, as the Arabs and the Turks themselves concede. However, I was not able to find out anything about them, although Pietro della Valle says that this place is called by the Arabs El-Mer and that perhaps it was built by the Jews.[23] At the 21st hour we arrived in a castle called Taiba, located on a small hill. It is not large, and the houses serve as its walls. The houses are made of earth and have no exterior walls. Inside the castle one sees many columns and the remains of ancient buildings and a whole stone tower of good construction and made by Christians. One can see that it was an important place in ancient times. Outside the castle there is a spring.[24] Here I had to pay a fee of a zecchino apiece to the subaşi of the castle of Taiba.

On the 21st we saw many ruins and many stones on the road where they say that old Aleppo had been, anciently called Ieropoli.[25] Not far away is the

22. The fortress of al-'Ashara (Asara) lies between Bustan and Rahaba, perhaps the source of Bembo's "Rabel Deir."

23. These remarks are less than precise, and I am not sure how to identify "El-Mer." But they most likely refer to Queen Zenobia's empire of Palmyra, conquered by the Romans in A.D. 273. If so, then Bembo is viewing the ruins of Halebiye. Unlike Pietro della Valle, who took a route across the Syrian desert, Bembo is following the course of the Euphrates on his way back to Aleppo. The ruins of Halebiye were noted also by Abbé Carré, who was told by his guides that it "dated from the time of Alexander the Great." Abbé Carré, *The Travels of Abbé Carré in India and the Near East 1672 to 1674*, trans. Lady Fawcett, 3 vols. (London: Hakluyt Society, 1947–1948), vol. 3, 870–871.

24. Taiba, apparently to be identified with 'Ayn Tabus, about a day's journey from Deir al-Zor, was also visited by Abbé Carré in 1672 and 1674, who gives a somewhat lengthier description of the town and mentions that its mosque had a minar that also functioned as a watchtower. Carré makes no reference to ancient ruins. Bembo refers to the castle's spring.

25. Between 301 and 281 B.C., Alexander's general Seleucus Nicator founded at Aleppo a city called Beroia. But the ruins that Bembo is seeing in the vicinity of "Jabbul" are probably those of Neirab.

salt marsh called Jabbul, taking its name from a town nearby.[26] Not being able to arrive at the town before night, we stayed among those stones at the foot of a mountain.

On the 22nd before dawn we remounted, and in two hours we arrived at Villa Malvà or Melluha.[27] There the houses are all of earth, and the roofs are pointed, which makes a nice view from a distance. We stopped there to eat a bit, and then we mounted again right away. We found a beautiful countryside with ruins of stone and pieces of columns, pedestals, and other remains of an ancient city. I think it was part of the same ruins we had seen the previous evening. After midday we entered the gardens of the pistachios near Aleppo, and then we saw the battlements of the city, which we then entered through the Gate of the Prisons (Kireç Kapısı). Since I did not know whether my uncle had left or not, I was not as happy as I might have been. The first person I met inside the gate was a janissary I knew who made perfect my joy with the news that my uncle had not left and that his replacement had not even arrived. Soon afterward with great joy I met my uncle.

On the 28th of November after sunset there were two cannon shots from the castle to advise the city that the new moon of Ramadan had been seen. This is when the Moslems begin their fast that was commanded them by their false prophet, who orders them that after six months, they must venerate the next three [months]. During those [three months] they must abstain from sin, from scandalous acts, and from drinking wine, which is always forbidden. They must perform this devotion during the first of the three moons for their prophet, during the second for the good of their souls, and during the third, which is Ramadan, for the love of God. They observe this latter [month] more than the other two. When the signal is given to the city, the fasting begins. The same signal is given when the next moon comes, and the fast is over. Thus it lasts a whole moon and sometimes a few days more. This fast consists in their abstaining from all food and drink and even from tobacco, all day long from dawn to sunset. During this time they abstain from vice and even from their wives, as long as the daylight lasts.

26. The salt lake of Jabbul is 37 km southeast of Aleppo. Salt from it was one of the main items of trade that the nomadic Arabs of northern Syria brought to Aleppo.

27. According to Abbé Carré, the nearest village to Aleppo was Jibrin (Giberim), some 14 km away. Pietro della Valle also refers to a town named Melluha in the vicinity of Aleppo.

They make alms and read the Qur'an. In the evening, when the first star appears, they begin to eat and drink (but not wine). The first food they take is what they call *ruci,* which serves to excite the appetite.[28] It is made of sweets and cold things. They eat many times during the night and sleep very little. They enjoy themselves with tobacco, coffee, and with their wives and women, whom they are expressly commanded to enjoy at this time. In those nights the nobles and rich people give many alms and often give food to the poor. For the whole period of the fast the bazaars are open at night, particularly those bazaars where food is sold. At that time everyone is permitted to walk through the city, and it becomes an entertainment with much noise, since people pass time in the coffee houses, where there are clowns putting on performances. Other actors read the deeds of their nation and of the sultans; others dance and play instruments. The nobility invite one another and spend time in the coffee houses. Others wander through the city, since the bazaars are lit with many oil lamps and since the shops are decorated with their goods. The shops of those who sell food display a mixture that they make with flour, honey, and other things, which they call candy.[29] Although they are nauseating to eat, they are pretty to look at under the many oil lamps, as they are painted in various colors. So that those who live in the suburbs can enjoy the city, the gates of Bab Enars and Bab Ancusa are left open all that time, and both Turks and Christians go through them freely. The Franks, too, have the opportunity to go about freely, although dressed in the Turkish manner so as to avoid insolence. I went out and had fun several evenings.

During Ramadan, when the first star appears, they light up all the minarets of the mosques with many lamps placed in rows and with colored paper around them.[30] It is a pleasant sight, and, in addition, it is convenient for those who are going about the city. The children set off firecrackers. At the break of day the nobility and the rich go to sleep, but for the poor the days are hard. They have to continue in their work without taking either tobacco or water; and they observe the fast very strictly. The fast is even harder for them when it occurs during the summer. This sometimes hap-

28. The Turkish and Arabic word for these hors d'oeuvres is *iftar.* Presumably Bembo's word *ruci* is purely local.

29. Turkish delight.

30. Bembo is referring to *mahya,* lights that during Ramadan are strung between minarets of a mosque to form words or pictures.

pens, because the Turks, like the Jews, have a year of twelve months, which is eleven days shorter than our year, so that every year the fast comes earlier. The twelve months are called Muharram, Safar, Rabi' al-Awwal, Rabi' al-Thani, Jumada'l-Ula, Jumada'l-Akhira, Rajab, Sha'ban, Ramadan, Shawwal, Dhu'l-Qa'da, Dhu'l-Hijja.[31]

[DECEMBER 1674]

On the 28th of December around nightfall, the new moon, called Shawwal, arose. All the lamps of the minarets were extinguished, and the castle gave a signal with two cannon shots, and thus the fast was over. On the following morning, the 29th, the castle shot off all its cannons as a sign of joy. Thus began the feast called Ramadan Bayramı, that is, the Feast of Ramadan.[32] It lasts three days, during which most people wear their best clothes, go to the mosques and to garden parties and to recreation outside the city, where they dance on a rope. There are games of chance with wheels that are turned by boys. These [games] are set up by the janissaries of the various gates, and they get money from it, because everyone passing through plays something. That year, however, there were few games, because the janissaries were at war. During this feast the consuls of the countries send their interpreters to pay their compliments to the captains and usually give them a present of sweets. The present is always the same, and every time one gives something to a Turk, it is a curious fact that one has to give presents to his entire entourage. During this same feast the consuls are visited by many janissaries with musicians, and to everyone who visits one gives a small present.

Seventy days after this feast there is another, more solemn one called Kurban Bayramı, that is, Feast of the Sacrifice, in commemoration of the sacrifice of Abraham, and others say of Isma'il.[33] On that day from every part of Turkey people of both sexes go in great numbers on pilgrimage to the

31. Bembo's spellings are "Mouren, Sefer, Rabiel Euel, Rabiel Etani, Gemeselauel, Gemas Etani, Rageb, Seban, Ramasan, Sauel, Zelcaide, Zelage."

32. Bembo is referring to the 'Id al-Fitr (in Turkish the Kücük Bairam or Seker-bairami), which begins on the first of Shawwal and celebrates the end of the fast of Ramadan.

33. The 'Id al-Adha or 'Id al-Kabir, celebrated on the tenth day of Dhu'l-Hijja, commemorates God's calling on Abraham to sacrifice his son Ismael.

tomb of their false prophet. There they sacrifice, according to their means, one or more animals. These are eaten that same day, and the meat is shared with the poor. All those who visit the tomb take the name of Hajji, which means "Pilgrim."[34] For example, one who had the name Ibrahim will be called Hajji Ibrahim. After their pilgrimage they observe the whole law rigorously and abstain entirely from wine and other forbidden things. All those who are born during the journey to visit the tomb of the Prophet have the privilege of calling themselves relatives of the Prophet, that is, sherif, and they wear the green sash. Thus many women go on the pilgrimage when they are pregnant or else try to get pregnant during the trip, since, to be a sherif, it is enough to have been conceived during the trip. Here I want to repeat what I said elsewhere, that the tomb of the Prophet is not in Mecca but in another city of Arabia called Medinat al-Nabi. He was born where the Fair is held. Many go to the Fair for business, not devotion, as do our merchants in Europe in similar circumstances. Besides, I was told by many Arabs that what many Turks say is false. They say that the tomb is suspended in the air. The Christians who believe this assertion attribute it to a magnet. However, it rests on its base, is four palms high, and is covered with golden cloth and blue silk. Three thousand gold and silver lamps burn there continuously, donations by kings, princes, and great lords of that impious sect.[35]

[JANUARY 1675]

On the 3rd of January news came from Iskenderun that Francesco Foscari, the new consul, had arrived on the ship *S. Giustina* in a convoy of four warships under the command of Captain Lorenzo Venier. He had first escorted the consul Orazio Bembo to Alexandria in Egypt.

On the 9th the new consul entered Aleppo, met by the parties of the nationalities with the formalities already described. Nevertheless, a difference arose between the French and the English, because the English chancellor tried to go ahead of the French chancellor at a narrow point in the road. Later this was to cause more bitterness between the two countries' [emissaries]. The captain of the warships also came with the consul, but he stayed in the back

34. A hajji (Bembo offers the transcriptions of "Chagi or Agi") is someone who has completed the hajj (pilgrimage) to the Hijaz.

35. Bembo would not have been permitted entry to either Mecca or Medina. He does not state his source for this information about the two holy cities.

of the arriving party so as to avoid the compliments and greetings of those two countries' [emissaries], who, when they had heard of his arrival, had received orders from their respective consuls to try to gain his favor.

On the one hand the French wanted him to protect a ship of theirs that was in the port of Iskenderun from the Barbary and Majorcan pirates. They were especially anxious about it because these latter had seized two French ships in that same port two months earlier. This had happened despite the fact that there were two English ships in the port at the same time that made no attempt to protect the French, even though the kings of the two countries were at peace with one another at the time. The [English ships] tried to make various, though lame, excuses.

On the other hand the English wanted the captain to accept two of their ships in his convoy. The ships were in port at that time, and they wanted them escorted to Zante. They had express orders to serve and honor the captain. Thus a few of them left the consul and insisted on accompanying him to the city. I, too, had the honor of accompanying him, since he had been my friend, fellow student, and older companion in the School of the Somaschi Fathers.[36] We had also been together in the last years of the war of Candia, he with the title of Admiral and I with [the title] of Governor of a ship. After we had arrived in the city, the new consul and the captain were given a banquet by the former consul, who gave up his command and left the palace after the meal. That same day the new consul occupied the palace, but then he ceded it to the captain. The former consul retired with all his court to the house of Antonio Caminada, who was a close friend, even though on some occasions the former consul would remain in the palace until his departure from the city.

The captain remained with the new consul, and I always went with him when he went out. He was assisted by several merchants and by two janissaries and one interpreter. He was invited by many English merchants, and we went several times through the city on horseback and saw the most curious things. We went to see the most beautiful of the gardens, particularly that of Sultan Murad, who had a good house built there when he passed through Aleppo on his way to conquer Baghdad.[37] We saw the three

36. The Ordine Religioso Somasco (the Somaschi Fathers) was a religious order founded at the town of Somasca in the Italian province of Bergamo by Girolamo Emiliani in the year 1528.

37. Baghdad was seized from the Safavis in 1638 by an Ottoman army under the personal command of Sultan Murad IV (1623–1640).

monasteries of the dervishes, who are like monks.[38] They live in community and are obedient to their chief. Only he is permitted to marry, although the others do not take a vow of chastity. They have nice cells and live from their incomes. In the city we went to see some of the houses of the nobility. Although these [houses] seem rough and poorly made from the outside, they are pleasant inside with their gardens and fountains. As is their custom, they have only one floor. The furnishings are nothing more than rugs on the ground, as well as beautiful and rich cushions for sitting on and leaning against, as is the custom in the entire Orient. The best one of these houses turned out to be that of Saban Aga Muhassil, located on the walls toward the Gate of St. George. Among other things it had a stable for fifty Arab horses, each one better than the next. As we were leaving, we met him as he was returning home, and he insisted on taking us to his room, where he very graciously gave us conserves, coffee, and sherbet. He also presented to me and to the captain a silk scarf. And as we took leave of him, he rose to his feet and made a few steps, an honor that is not given to many.

From there we went to see a dervish monastery inside the city. It was being built by the said muhassil with his mosque. He had assigned a sufficient income to support the poor dervishes for whom he had built it.[39] It is in the form of a very large cloister, provided with dervish cells on all sides, and it has a very beautiful fountain in the middle and a terrace above it.

Another day we went to the churches of those Christians in the suburb of Jedeideh[40] where they live. We stayed there to see the ceremonies of their Mass. At the churches of the Maronites we heard Mass said by our clergy. [The Maronites] celebrate [Mass] according to the rite of the Roman Church, except that they used Chaldean instead of Latin. In the event that our clergy should want to celebrate [Mass] in other churches, they have to bring all their vestments, since theirs are different, as their ceremonies are also different; and perhaps some articles of faith are also different. Since that

38. Several travelers (Thévenot, Tavernier, and Abbé Carré) report visiting the gardens and *tekyah* (religious house) of the dervishes outside the city.

39. Bembo is describing the Islamic institution of the *waqf*, or pious foundation. A *waqf* was intended to be an endowment in perpetuity and was usually the principal form of financial support for mosques, theological colleges, dervish centers, schools, hospitals, orphanages, and other social and religious institutions.

40. Borgo Giudaida.

day was a feast day, we met many women who, out of curiosity to see our clothes, lifted the black veils that they wear over their eyes. We observed that they had very beautiful complexions, and many were bold; some can even be found who want a little adventure, but only with those of their own nationality, not with Europeans, since they are afraid of being fined.

When the French and English consuls learned of the captain's arrival, they wanted to honor him, even though he had come incognito. They consulted among themselves, though, and decided not to pay him any special honors. The English, however, were going to have their usual large hunt, and they invited him privately, although only in the name of the head of the hunt. On the appointed day, however, it snowed, so it was put off for a while. At dawn on the new date, almost all the Englishmen of the city went to fetch the captain. I went with him, as did many other Italians. Having turned a corner, we found the English consul, who had come to meet us. He took the captain on his right, and we proceeded into the country. There were few hares, and so there was little sport, since it was the end of the season. Nevertheless, we kept at it until the hour for the meal, when we went to the usual hill, two hours distant from the city, where the meal was set out on rugs on the ground under a pavilion. The meal was abundant and made up of English food. After the meal we passed two hours drinking to one another's health and eating pistachios. Then we got on horseback again and, sometimes racing, went gaily back to the city. When we had entered the city, we passed in front of the English consul's house and tried to take our leave. It was useless, however, because we were obliged to enter the palace and sit down to a delicious snack of candied fruits and other good things that obliged everybody to make more toasts. After many toasts we took our leave, and the consul accompanied us to the staircase, while the other merchants honored us by accompanying us to our consul's house, where the captain lived.

That same evening, the 23rd of January, our consul received the visit of the French consul. The pasha was not there, as he was engaged in a campaign, and the qadi [was also not there], as he had just been dismissed. In such instances one does not make visits to lesser officials. When the pasha is there, both the old and the new consul go to visit him, and the old one presents his successor to the pasha. The new one makes a gift of a gold robe, if it is for the pasha, as well as sherbet, coffee, and perfume. If it is for the qadi, one does not give him the robe. Returning to the house, the new consul goes first and invites the former consul and all of the nationality to a banquet, after which he receives the visits of the other countries. At the 24th hour the

French consul arrived, and he was received with the usual formalities, except that in the audience hall there was a table set for seven, that is, for the three consuls (one French and two Venetian), the captain, the brother of the French consul (M. La Feure, a nobleman), and myself. Those visits proceeded in customary fashion, and we spent various meals in gaiety and friendship. Particularly on the night before our departure, we received from Consul Foscari a splendid meal, during which we happily and pleasantly passed many hours exchanging toasts. Having made the visits due to the consuls and to the others and having arranged everything for the caravan, we left the city on the 30th of January. We were accompanied out of the city by our countrymen and by our consul, the other Europeans having presented their excuses, since it was the custom for everyone to accompany those departing the city as far as the broken-down khan. They offered all sorts of excuses, but the truth was that they did not want to find themselves together, because of the differences between them that I mentioned earlier. In fact, when we got outside the city, we found the English consul with his party on horseback coming back toward us. They wished us a good journey. It was probably a stratagem to deceive the French. They accompanied us for an hour and then turned back. We continued our journey with our countrymen and with some French and Englishmen who were particular friends up to the broken-down khan. There we had a brief meal provided by our consul, and there followed many toasts with precious liquors; then we separated. The consul returned to the city, and we went on to Urum al-Sughra, a town half a day's journey from Aleppo.[41] From the roofs of its houses we could spot the towers of the citadel of Aleppo. We stayed in the house of the muleteer, Haji Rustam, who was good and civil, though a country person. The beds were excellent. Not far from there is another town, or rather the ruins of one, which are in a huge and very deep gully, as can be seen. The inhabitants of Urum al-Sughra say that [its destruction] was a punishment from God, because those people had been so evil that they had refused water to the poor people passing through there. In many places in Turkey I have seen little canals that bring water to the roadside where there is a cup chained to the place so that those who pass may drink.

Four hours before daybreak on the 31st, we started out with two litters,

41. Modern Urum al-Sughra is 23 km to the west of Aleppo on the road leading to Antioch and Iskenderun. The ruins Bembo describes below are probably those at 'Ain Dilfeh.

one for my uncle and the other for an elderly merchant named Lorenzo Carrara, his business associate. The captain and I and twenty other people were on horseback. In addition, there were the pack animals with merchandise and luggage and food, since the only sustenance available along the road was the ordinary Turkish fare. That day's journey was through rough and stony mountains. We saw many ruins of ancient buildings, and around midday we passed a river called Lafoia by the Turks.[42] It is not wide, but the water of it was quite good. At the 23rd hour we took lodging in a town called Maraiana which consisted of a few little straw houses, all rather small.[43] It was inhabited by about a hundred Kurds. They speak a language that is rather different from the languages of both Turks and Arabs, and only the muleteers understand them, due to the practice that they have had in their journeys. We spent that night in one of those houses. Since they have only one room, it served as kitchen and stable, and we made bedding with our saddles and did not sleep well. For such fine quarters we paid ten reales.

[FEBRUARY 1675]

On the 1st of February we got back on horseback early. After some traveling we found a countryside irrigated by a stream named Giacne, which springs from a mountain that we later climbed. We passed by on our left the lake of Antioch, which empties into the sea.[44] We passed the bridge called Qara Pon, that is, "Black Bridge." Then we passed another called "White Bridge."[45] This latter had three arches that were high and two lower ones. Then we arrived at the place called Caffaro, where one has to pay a real [in duty] for every thirty-five pack animals. Around evening we began to climb the very high mountains at Belen that take their name from the Amanus Mountains.[46] They were full of snow, and we had difficulty in arriving at the town named Belen by the second hour of the night. We were

42. Probably the Orontes River (Asi Nehri).

43. I have not been able to identify the humble Kurdish town of Maraiana between the Lafoia River and Antioch.

44. Lake Amik, north of Antioch.

45. Bembo curiously mixes Turkish and Latin in his names for the bridges: *kara* and *aq* (Turkish, black and white) and Latin *pons* (bridge), The Turkish names should be *Kara Köprü* (Black Bridge) and *Aq Köprü* (White Bridge). Both bridges must have crossed the Karasu River, which empties into Lake Amik.

46. Bembo's "Caffaro" is probably the modern Kerikhan. Referring to the

lodged in the same house of the English vice-consul, where we had stayed on our way to Aleppo. The night was terrible with thunder, lightning, wind, rain, and snow, and we were unable to leave until after the midday meal on the 2nd. We arrived in Iskenderun toward evening. There we found all the officials of the ships, and we embarked immediately so as not to remain in the foul air of that place. My uncle went on the ship *S. Giustina*, on which the merchandise was loaded, much of which was his. He was accompanied by the captain and was saluted by the other ship, the French *Biasio Marin*, as well as by his own. I stayed with the captain until it was time to part. Besides the two merchant ships just mentioned, there were the four warships, *Giove Fulminante* (the flagship), *Costanza Guerriera, Fama Volante, Drago Volante*, and two English merchant ships.

On the 3rd the French ship set sail and saluted the flagship with seven cannon shots, and the flagship responded with three. While we stayed there, my uncle went to visit the captain and was received with seven salutes. When the captain repaid the visit, he was received with nine.

Finally, on the morning of the 10th, as I thanked God for delivering me from the hands of such barbarous people, we set sail with a little wind from the north. The two English ships joined us. A good part of the day and the entire night were spent becalmed. However, on the morning of the 11th, the wind started up so suddenly that it tore part of the mainsail. On the morning of the 12th we saw Cyprus. That whole day we remained becalmed. That night a contrary wind arose, and it became very dark, but after midnight the wind came from the east and continued all day on the 13th. We sailed along the coast all that time, but not too near, and at night we dropped anchor in twenty depths of water in front of the Salina. The two English ships stayed farther out. On the morning of the 14th we lifted the anchor and went close to the citadel. We let the anchor down in twelve depths of water. There we found the ship *Biasio Marin* again, as well as another small ship that was also French. They saluted seven times, and we responded with three shots. Shortly afterward, the English ships arrived and saluted five times. To them also we responded with three shots. These also saluted my uncle with three, and he replied with one. Meanwhile, as the ships took on provisions, we

---

spot as "Caffard," Abbé Carré also reports that one had to halt there to pay a tax (Carré, *Travels:* vol. 1, 39). The town of Belen (Bembo calls it "Beilan") is at the pass through the Amanus Mountains, which lie between Aleppo and the Mediterranean Sea.

entertained ourselves and were assisted by the consul Santonini, in whose house we stayed several nights. He had a chair on wheels, unique in the place, that was pulled by a very good female mule. With that and on horseback we often went hunting with falcons, which was much fun.

Messages had come from Alexandria at this time, but without any news from the consul Alvise Cornaro, who was supposed to return with us after the new consul, Orazio Bembo, took over. He was to come to the Salina of Cyprus with the ship *S. Marco Vittorioso,* where we would have awaited him on a certain day that had already gone by a month before. It was therefore resolved to continue our journey, since we supposed that Cornaro had either already gone toward home or had decided to wait for spring in order to have better weather on the sea. On the morning of the 20th we set sail. The English ships went with us. They had gone to see the captain and had asked to be escorted to Zante. He had very courteously acceded to their request, even though they were very slow vessels. One was called *Fregata dal Zante* and the other *Mercante di Soria.* One of the captains was the son of one of the first four commanders of the English Royal army. The *Biasio Marin,* too, set sail to go to Limiso. They were unhappy that they were unable to take advantage of the same escort to *Zante.* We left Cyprus with a favorable east wind. We would have traveled far if we had not had to wait for the English ships. In the evening we had to lower our sails altogether because we were leaving them too far behind. When the *Fregata del Zante* came close, she fired three shots, and we answered with one. We kept the sails almost completely lowered that night, and in the morning we found ourselves by Capo Bianco. On the 21st we remained becalmed, so we were able to celebrate Fat Thursday on board with masks and dances. In the evening and on the 22nd the wind became contrary. Since we had to go on to Suda, the captain went close to the *Mercante di Soria* and told them that we would set out and then wait for them there to go on to Zante. There was no danger in those waters anyway. They were pleased and saluted with five shots, and we answered with one and set out, soon losing them from view. During the night the wind ceased again, and we were becalmed the whole day of the 23rd and part of the next night. Then the wind came up, and we went fifty miles from Cyprus. A rainstorm came on us suddenly, however, and we had to lower our sails. The storm continued all night and also the next day, and we had difficulty keeping the ship under control. The storm would stop for a while and then start up again. Seeing that by the 26th it had not ended, we decided to go back to Cyprus to take on more water and go into port at Baffo. We were only thirty miles from land, and by the end of the day we were near the fort and could see the city among many cultivated and pleasant hills. Since the other ships were still a way off, we decided to wait to cast anchor. On the morning of the 27th, being all together, we turned the prows toward Limiso. Around midday we were almost past the Capo della Gatte, and we could easily see the *Biasio Marin* and the city itself. The wind prevented us from entering the port, and since it was strong, the captain decided to take advantage of it and set out to sea again. A guard was set over the drinking water, and it was rationed. We still had enough for fifteen days. But the wind had deceived us, because the following night we were again becalmed and found ourselves in front of the Capo Bianco on the 28th.

[MARCH 1675]

The wind then rose again, and we made some headway until the 4th of March. On the 5th we saw land toward evening, and some thought it was Scarpante, while others thought it was Rhodes. We remained in doubt all night, and on the morning of the 6th we recognized that it was the kingdom of Candia. We had already passed Cape Salamon, and we were twenty-five miles from Girapetra. Only the captains of the ships *Costanza* and *S. Giustina* recognized our error. That whole day we were unable to go beyond the point called La Cristiana. That night we were becalmed, and also for part of the day of the 7th. Since we were low on water, we decided to go into port in the archipelago or in the kingdom.

At midday on the 8th we entered the port of Paliocastro, which means "ancient castle." It is behind the point called Capo S. Sidero, which means "Iron."[47] The port is not very big, but it is convenient for getting water, and it is safe. They say that the Knights of Malta gathered here after they lost Rhodes. From the natives they obtained the right to reside in the area from the mountains to the port, but the Republic did not go along with this arrangement, and thus they retired to Malta. One can still see, however, some walls that they started to make to fortify themselves there. There are no houses at the shore, and only in the mountains is there a monastery of Greek monks,[48] called the Madonna of Acrotiriagnis, as can be seen in the

---

47. Palaiokastro is about 12 km to the south of Cape Sidheros, the northeastern-most point in Crete. Sitia, which Bembo cites below, is on the coast to the west.

48. Calogeri.

FIGURE 46. Greek Orthodox monastery in Paliocastro, Crete.

drawing. Forty religious, both priests and laypersons, live there. They support themselves with some herds and by working the land around the convent. They pay 300 reales a year in taxes. I had it drawn as a curiosity, since I went to see it myself. It is rather large with many rooms and two churches. One is called the Madonna, the other the Holy Cross. The abbot is selected by the Turks. Among them was a priest who was eighteen years old, and they said that he was the son of a noble Venetian who lived in Sittia and who was a descendant of the four families that had been sent there to colonize. He had remained in those parts in order not to lose his properties, and they said that he had a house and family in Spinalonga. Among the Turks, however, he was just regarded as an ordinary Greek. As soon as they see a sail enter the port, the monks are obliged to give news of it to Sittia, which is twenty miles away. Since corsairs often stop off there to make ransom deals, some one hundred Turks [usually] come. But they had recognized our ship as Venetian, and only four Turks came to collect some taxes from those poor monks for the things they had sold us. The abbot came to visit the Captain and gave him some refreshments. There are good fish in the place, and fishermen from Mirabello and Spinalonga go there overland. From there

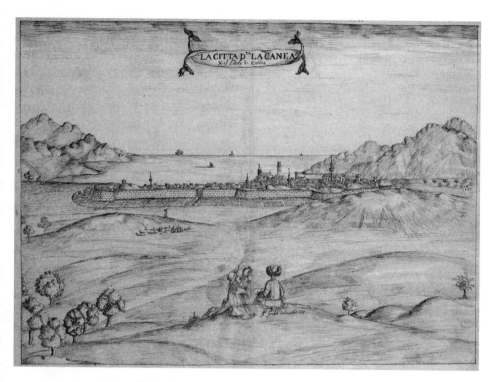

FIGURE 47. City of Khania.

one arrives in Iraklion in two days and in Khania in four days.[49] There is a rocky island there with many wild goats.

On the morning of the 12th we set sail with a slight north wind, which left us after noon. During the night an east wind arose that lasted until after noon of the 13th, leaving us becalmed in front of Standia. That night the wind was erratic and became a west wind on the morning of the 14th. We went toward the archipelago, and on the night of the 15th we entered the port of Argentiera by the light of the moon. There were five corsairs there and two French ships and three Maltese ships. There was also a Venetian ship on its way to Izmir. These had all gone to arms when they had seen us in the distance, but as soon as they recognized us, they immediately went to pay their respects to the captain. We heard from them that many ships had been lost due to the rough weather this season

49. Iraklion and Canae.

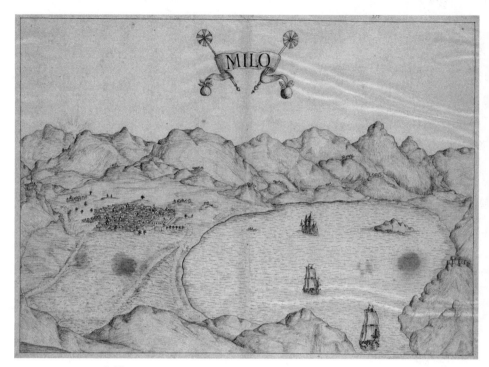

FIGURE 48. Milo.

and that many had been taken by Barbary pirates, who had five ships in the area. We also learned that Consul Alvise Cornaro had remained in Cairo on business. The ship *S. Marco* had left and was in Cerigo, and the ship *Ombra di Moisè* had also left Cairo and was in Suda waiting for the public ships.

On the morning of the 15th we dropped anchor in Polonia, and the corsairs, out of respect, left the port. Three others were in the Gulf of Milo, and they had built a small port with ten cannons and a hundred men. Since most of the sailors of our ships, as well as the captain himself, named Nicolo Armeni, were natives of Argentiera, the captain gave them permission to visit their families. Thus we set sail again only on the evening of the 16th. We traveled slowly because of the lack of wind all the day of the 17th until noon on the 18th. Then the wind came from the north, and we arrived at the fortress of Suda, where we dropped anchor at the 23rd hour. There we found the ship *Ombra di Moisè,* full of oil for Venice. There was also a ship from Messina.

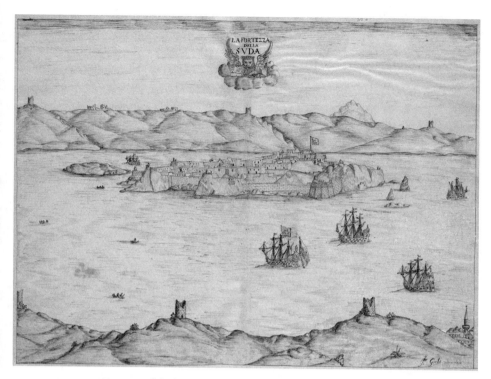

FIGURE 49. Fortress of Suda.

Shortly after us another small Venetian ship came to the port. It was called *S. Francesco di Paola,* and it, too, was going to Venice. All these ships saluted the captain, and to all of them we replied as was appropriate. When we arrived, the Provider General came, who was Benedetto Barbarigo of the *Colonia,* and with him came Giorgio di Mezzo, called Palmetta, who was there to render accounts to the Purveyor Extraordinary, who was Vicenzo Vendramino. I had met both of them in Iraklion, where the first [of these gentlemen] had been governor of a ship.

On the day of the 19th we went ashore and went to pay our respects to Vendramino. The captain, my uncle, and I stayed with him all the time we remained there. In truth, he was most courteous in receiving us and was generous in giving us splendid meals and entertainment in the form of some plays put on by his staff and another [play] put on by the officers of the fortress. He did this even though it was Lent, because he had prepared the entertainment for the Carnival time, which had just passed, thinking that

FIGURE 50. Coron.

the captain, who was an intimate friend of his, would have come by earlier. On the night of the 20th there arose a terrific storm, and the *Costanza, Drago,* and *S. Francesco di Paola* were in danger, and there was little that could be done about it because most of the officers and crew were ashore. However, it pleased God that the storm should die down after midnight without having done great damage.

On the 24th we went to see the castle of Lampicorno, all in ruins. On the morning of the 25th we left the port with the help of the oars, because the wind was calm. We would have left earlier if we could have. We had taken formal leave of the Purveyor on the 23rd. We unfurled the sails in an east wind and went off all together. But the *Drago* was sent to Cerigo to receive the things of Giorgia di Mezzo, mentioned above. The wind became contrary, and we had a difficult time getting beyond the island of Cerigo. After midday on the 29th we got close to the fortress, which greeted us with seven shots, and we responded with five, and they then answered with three, as is the custom when a Captain of the Ships goes by.

Having sent off the *Drago*, we continued our trip, and around noon of the 30th we found ourselves in front of Cape Matapan.[50] We were unable to go forward because the wind grew contrary, and so we dropped anchor in front of Coron at midday on the 31st.

[APRIL 1675]

The wind continued contrary the whole of April 1st. Meanwhile, we got water from a small stream and heard from some Turks that the five Barbary ships had left eight days earlier from Navarino.

Before day on the 2nd we were able to set sail again with a good wind. In a short time we saw the fortresses of Modon and Navarino. We arrived before nightfall at Zante, where we anchored and saluted with various shots the miraculous Madonna of Scopo, kept by Greek monks. There were many of our ships there. The *S. Antonio*, a tender going to Syria, and the *Iride*, going to Izmir, were ours. They saluted the Captain's ship, and to each one it answered. Then the six English ships there saluted, and we answered them one by one. Two of them were the ships that had left Cyprus with us. After a bad storm they had run into Barbary pirates but had been able to escape because it was night. They had arrived ten days earlier. There were also several French vessels, and they all saluted and were answered. The officials of the Board of Health came on ship and gave us and a few of the crew permission to go ashore.

On the 3rd after lunch we went to the house of Giovanni Antonio Celini, who was not yet enrolled in the nobility. There we received the visit of Bernardo Navager, purveyor, and Bertucci Soranzo, counselor, while the other counselor, Marc'Antonio Contarini, had remained in the fortress. On the morning of the 6th several French ships full of foodstuffs stopped in the port. They were headed for Messina. There were also two other French vessels: one was commanded by M. La Bertecchia, and the other had been taken from the Spaniards. He saluted five times and was answered five times. Then he saluted the fortress five times, and after a little delay they answered with three cannon shots. They wanted to take on wine for Messina, but it seems they were not permitted to take on any wine beyond what was needed for table use on the ship.

On the morning of the 7th we lifted anchor and went through the strait

50. Cape Tainaron in the southern Peloponnesos.

FIGURE 51. Old ships, new ships at Modon.

of Cefalonia.[51] At midday on the 9th we saw Paxo, and there I took leave of the Captain and went with my uncle on the *S. Giustina*. He assured me that he would accompany us to Sasino, and his secretary, Andrea Capellasi, assured me of the same. That whole day we traveled together.

On the morning of the 10th we saw that the Captain was close to Corfu. Since we were too far from him (we were at Fano), we continued our journey without being able to salute him with the cannon. On the morning of the 11th we found that we were past Sasino. Near there we saw a sail and were a bit worried, but it turned out to be Venetian. The wind continued to favor us, and on the morning of the 12th we could see the mouth of Cattaro and very soon thereafter the island of Meleda. On the morning of the 13th we had left behind the Pomo. On the morning of the 14th, which was Easter Sunday,

51. The Porthmos Ithakis, the Ithaca Strait between the islands of Kefallinha and Ithaca.

FIGURE 52. Storm-wrecked warship.

we approached Ossero quite early in the day, and after noontime we saw the towers of Rovigno and Parenzo. At sunset we were in front of the Gulf of Trieste. Finally, to my unspeakable relief, at dawn on the 15th I saw the campanile of San Marco and my dear homeland, Venice, which I had missed during all that time. Before midday we were taken into the Castelli. Many friends and relatives came aboard to greet us. Few recognized me at first because of my long beard and my Turkish clothing. On the 16th we passed into the Lazaretto Vecchio, where a citizen named Giacomo Negri was prior. We had to stay in quarantine for twenty-two days. During that time we were visited daily by friends. After we had finally gone on land, I made many visits to friends with my beard. Then I cut if off to appear in the Public Assembly.[52] It was my first time, and I took with me, as is the custom, six of my dearest

52. Broglio.

friends to assist me on that day. They were Girolamo Morosini, son of Tadio; Pietro Pisani, son of Maffio; Antonio Capello, son of Antonio; Giovanni Dolfino, son of Andrea; Giovanni Battista Mora, son of Giovanni Battista; and Alessandro Basadonna, son of Antonio.

EXPENSES MADE IN THE ABOVE-DESCRIBED TRIP FOR FEES AND TOLLS AND RENTAL OF TRANSPORTATION FROM ONE PLACE TO ANOTHER

For the horses from Aleppo to Diyarbakır, 6 reales each	48.
For the passage of the Euphrates, 8 saie per horse at Birecik	2.13
In Birecik a fee of 1 zecchino per European (at that time the zecchino was worth 20 lira)	20.
In the town of Mullasarai where there is no fixed fee, but there is no way out of paying something, I gave 3 reales	24.
In the town of Severec, the same situation, I gave 1 real	8.
For the kalek from Diyarbakır to Baghdad, which I bought for 29 reales so as to travel comfortably and more quickly, although it's possible, if one is lucky, to find a large one and go in the company of others, paying a little apiece	232.
For the fee in the castle of Hasankeyf, 3 reales apiece	24.
For the fee in the castle of Cizre, at 5½ reales apiece	44.
For a fee in the city of Mosul, 3 reales apiece	24.
For a boat from Baghdad to Basra, I paid 30 reales, but one can wait for a big one and go uncomfortably mixed in with lots of Turks for 2 reales apiece	240.
For the rent of a terrada, that is, "boat," which took us from Basra to Bandar-i Kong, at 5 'abbasi apiece	12.
For a cart from Daman to Surat, 4½ rupees	20.
For 3 palanchinos from Daman to Bassein, that is 12 men, with their pay and food, and the tool to cross some rivers, 43 pardaos	105.
For a small boat that took us from Bassein to Tana, 1½ pardaos	4.10

Another boat from Tana to Mumbai, 5 pardaos   15.

Salary for 4 men of the palanchino per month and of 1 to
carry an umbrella, in Goa, in all 18 pardaos   51.

For the room of the pilot on the Portuguese ship from Goa
to Bandar-i Kong, given by him who was a Dutchman,
12 reales   96.

For the rent of mules from Kong to Shiraz, 24 'abbasi each   70.

For rent of donkeys from Kong to Shiraz, at 15 'abbasi each   43.

For rent of horses or mules from Shiraz to Isfahan, 12½ 'abbasi   35.

In the town of Mandole a fee for each person   2.

To pass the Diyala river in a boat, apiece   2.

On entering Baghdad to the janissaries of the gate,
each European   2.

The fee in the castle of Hit, a zecchino apiece   20.

To the Subaşı of the city of Ana, a zecchino apiece   20.

To the Subaşı of the castle of Taiba, a zecchino apiece   20.

One pays the same for all the castles and inhabited places in
the desert through which one passes. Besides, there is the
present to the Emir for the passage of the desert. I cannot
remember what I spent there because, as can be seen in the
account, we gave them clothing rather than money.

EXPENSES MADE BY ME FROM LEAVING ALEPPO FOR INDIA
UNTIL THE RETURN TO ALEPPO*

In fees, lodging, and tolls (zecchini)	173.18.60
In gifts	83.14.13
In food	129.17.10
In clothing	60.19

*This section is in a different hand, clearly not that of a professional scribe,
and probably Bembo's own.

Various expenses along the way   42.12

Trinkets brought to Venice   40.18

Diamonds, large and small, rough and cut (23), 29 small
    round pearls, 2 silk carpets, 2 large bezoar stones, 1 large
    snake stone, gold and silver coins of various places and
    cities   688.11

To change money in various places for these expenses,
    paid as interest in Aleppo   251.04

Total (They were worth at the time 220 each)   1469.08.09

GLOSSARY

ABA	A cloak
'ABBASI	Most frequently used Iranian coin
AGA	Ottoman official
AKÇE	A coin
ALFORGES	Saddlebags
ALMAIDA	A small boat made out of a single tree trunk
ANDOR	A carrier simpler than and similar to a palanquin
ARAQ	Aquavit
ASPRO (ASPER), *plural* ASPRI	A coin of modest value
BAB	Gate
BANIAN	Indian merchant
BARA	Mouth of a river
BAWWAB	Gatekeeper
BAZARCUCHI	A coin of modest value
BEY	An Ottoman district commander
BEZOAR	A stone with healing properties
BOI	A palanquin carrier
CAFRO *or* KAFRO	An African
CALOGERI	Greek Orthodox monk
CANGIA	Rice gruel
CARACHER	A thief
CASSANAIRAS	The wife of a St. Thomas priest

CASSANAR	A St. Thomas priest who had the right to marry
CAUSIN	West wind
ÇAVUŞ	A military herald
CERNA	An illness
CHAPAR	In Safavi Iran an official messenger and letter carrier who rode with the mail bags (Bembo renders the term "Sater")
CIBAR	A small boat used on the west coast of India
DARUGHA	Magistrate
DEVER AGA	An official in charge of a village
DRAGOMAN	A translator
FANAON	A coin
FANTE	Italian term for footman
FARSANG	A unit of distance
FOUFEL	Betel nut
FULUS, *plural* FULI	A copper coin
GAZI	A low-denomination Persian coin
GIBELLINI	Zibellino (sable hat)
HAUDAJ	A litter of cloth wrapped around a rectangular or circular frame and mounted on a camel, elephant, or other draft animal
I'TIMAD AL-DAULAT	Literally, "the pillar of the state," a title for prime minister in Iran and India
JAMI'	The main mosque in a town or city
JANISSARY	Ottoman foot soldier
JERIDA	A game played on horseback
KALAK	A river raft resting on inflated goatskins
KALAKGI	A kalak operator
KALANTAR	Mayor
KANUN	Law decreed by the sultan
KAPI	Gate
KHAN	Caravanserai (khan); title of a Persian minister (Khan)
KOS	A unit of distance

MAHMUDI	Coin with a value of ½ an 'abbasi
MAHYA	Lights strung up during Ramadan
MARCILIANE	A type of ship
MATARA	A canteen
MAYDAN	Plaza
MAZUL	Dismissed from office
MOUZ	Banana
MUASSIL	Official in charge of a customs house
MUFTI	A Sunni judge who interprets Islamic law
MUKARIN	Muleteer
MUSSALEM	Deputy official
NAKATKHUDA	Master of a ship
NAVILII	A type of galleon
ODA PASHA	A captain of a hundred janissaries
ONGARO	A coin worth four and a half rupees
PAISA	A coin in India worth four bazarcuchi
PARDAOS	A coin in India worth forty-five paisa
PICCA	A unit of measurement corresponding to about two meters
QADI	A specialist in shari'a (Islamic law)
QALANDAR	A holy man
QINTAR	720 Venetian pounds of weight
RAMARI	A Goa crocodile
RAQIYA	Woman's headgear
RA'S-E DASTAKAN	A point off Qeshm Island
REAL, *plural* REALES	Portuguese coin
RETI	In India a carrier consisting of a hammock hung from a straight rod
SABANDAR	Chief of merchants
SAIE	Turkish coin corresponding to two Venetian pounds (twenty-four saie equaled one real)
SARPAGI	Small bells attached to a raqiya
SEPET	Basket
SHERIF	Descendant of the Prophet

SOLDO, *plural* SOLDI	A Venetian coin of small value
SPAHI	Cavalry soldier
SUFRA	A round piece of leather with a cord strung along its edge that can be spread like a tablecloth and pulled together to keep leftovers
SUR PASHA	A commander of five hundred janissaries
SUBAŞI	An Ottoman constable
TAFTA	A type of cloth
TAMARA	Food made from dates
TENCERE	Saucepan
TERRADA	A low, fast ship with two masts and a lateen sail
TERRANCHINI	A type of jolly boat
TITABANNO	Market police
TOMAN	A large unit of money in Iran
TRAGHETTI	Venetian ferryboats
'ULEMA	Scholars trained in Islam and Islamic law
VOYVODA	Governor
WAQF	A charitable endowment
ZAGO, *plural* ZAGHI	An Italian term equivalent to the Turkish çavuş (military herald)
ZECCHINO, *plural* ZECCHINI	A gold coin of the Venetian Republic
ZINA	Festival

SUGGESTIONS FOR FURTHER READING

Boxer, C. R. *Portuguese India in the Mid-Seventeenth Century.* Delhi: Oxford University Press, 1980.

Brancaforte, Elio. *Visions of Persia: Mapping the Travel of Adam Olearius.* Cambridge: Harvard University, Dept. of Comparative Literature, 2004.

Chardin, John. *Voyages en Perse.* Amsterdam, 1711. A ten-volume publication in French (Paris: Le Normant, 1811) was the first complete edition of Chardin's travels and included a volume of plates. Partially translated into English in Sir John Chardin, *Travels in Persia* (London: Argonaut, 1927).

Della Valle, Pietro. *Viaggi di Pietro della Valle il Pellegrino.* 4 vols. Rome: Vitale Mascardo, 1650, 1658, 1663. The *Viaggi* have never been completely translated into English. Della Valle's travels in India were published in 1892 by the Hakluyt Society. A highly readable account of his travels is Wilfrid Blunt, *Pietro's Pilgrimage* (London: James Barrie, 1953). A recent study is Antonio Invernizzi, ed., "Pietro della Valle," in *Viaggio per l'Oriente* (Torino: Edizioni dell'Orso, 2001). For a presentation of key documents for the study of relations between Iran and Venice, see Maria Francesca Tiepolo (ed.), *La Persia e la Repubblica di Venezia* (Tehran: Central Library of the University of Tehran, 1973).

Du Mans, Raphael. *Estat de la Perse en 1660.* Paris: Leroux, 1890.

Dunn, Ross E. *The Adventures of Ibn Battuta, a Muslim Traveler of the 14th Century.* Berkeley: University of California Press, 1986.

Ferrier, Ronald, trans., ed. *A Journey to Persia: Jean Chardin's Portrait of a Seventeenth-Century Empire.* London and New York: J. B. Tauris, 1996.

Fryer, John. *A New Account of East India and Persia. Being Nine Years' Travels, 1672–1681.* Edited and annotated and with an introduction by William Crooke, 2nd series, nos. 19, 20, 39. London: Hakluyt Society, 1909, 1912, 1915.

Grélot, Joseph Guillaume. *Relation nouvelle d'un voyage de Constantinople.* Paris: Damien Foucault, 1680.

Herbert, Thomas. *Travels in Persia: 1627–1629,* abridged and edited by William Foster. London: Broadway Travellers, 2004.

Invernizzi, Antonio. "Ambrogio Bembo e Guilllaume Grelot alle Porte dell'Asia." In *Ancient Iran and Its Neighbours. Studies in Honour of Prof. Józef Wolski on Occasion of His 95th Birthday,* ed. Edward Dabrowa (Electrum, 10). Krakow: Jagiellonian University Press, 2005, 111–121.

——. *Viaggio e Giornale per Parte Dell'Asia di Quattro Anni Incirca Fatto da Me Ambrosio Bembo Nobile Veneto,* ed. Antonio Invernizzi. Turin: CESMEO, 2005.

Le Brun, Corneile de. *A Voyage to the Levant: Or Travels in the Principal Parts of Asia Minor.* London, 1702.

Le Strange, Guy, trans., ed. *Don Juan of Persia. A Shi'ah Catholic 1560–1604.* London: Routledge, 1926.

Morelli, Iacopo. "Ambrogio Bembo." In *Dissertazione intorno ad alcuni viaggiatori eruditi veneziani poco noti.* Venice: Antonio Zatta, 1803, 50–79.

Ogilby, John. *Asia, the First Part being an Accurate Description of Persia and the Several Provinces thereof.* London: John Ogilby, 1803.

Pacifique de Provins. *Relation du Voyage de Perse.* Paris: De la Coste, 1631.

Penzer, N. M., ed. *Sir John Chardin's Travels in Persia.* London: Argonaut, 1928.

Polo, Marco. *The Travels of Marco Polo,* translated and with an introduction by Ronald Latham. London: Penguin, 1958.

Richard, Francis. *Raphaël du Mans missionnaire en Perse au XVIIe siècle.* Paris: Editions L'Harmattan, 1995.

Roe, Thomas. *The Embassy of Sir T. Roe,* ed. William Foster. London: Hakluyt Society, 1922.

Stevens, Roger. "European Visitors to the Safavid Court." *Studies on Isfahan, Iranian Studies,* 7 (1974), 421–457.

Tavernier, Jean-Baptiste. *Travels in India,* trans. V. Ball. London: Oxford University Press, 1925.

——. *Les Six Voyages de Turquie et de Perse.* Introduction et notes de Stéphane Yerasimos. Paris: F. Maspéro, 1981.

Thévenot, Jean de. *Relation d'un voyage fait au Levant.* Paris: Thomas Jolly, 1665. (Volume 1 of Thévenot's travels. Three additional volumes published posthumously in 1674 and 1689 by Charles Angot, Paris.)

Welch, Anthony. *Shah 'Abbas and the Arts of Isfahan.* New York: Asia Society, 1973.

——. "Safavi Iran as Seen through Venetian Eyes." In *Society and Culture in the Early Modern Middle East, Studies on Iran in the Safavid Period,* ed. Andrew Newman. Leiden & Boston: Brill, 2003, 97–121.

Calazza, Melchior, 283
Calicut, 222, 252, 257n, 268; Gama voyage
  to, 155n, 248n, 255; Portuguese forced to
  abandon, 270; Zamorin, 248n
Calle, 268
call to prayer, mosque, 64–66
calogeri, 310, 425
Cambay, 6, 152, 154, 193, 208, 268; animals
  cared for, 178, 179; exports, 269
Cambolin, 270
camels, 46, 77, 362, 363, 364, 378
Caminada, Antonio, 47, 406
camphor, 269
Campos, Alessandro of, 261
Cananeo, Thomas, 254–55
Canarini Fathers, Goa, 243–44
Candia, 413; War of, 4, 16, 33, 213, 216
cangia, 247n, 425
Cananor, 229n, 268, 270
cannoneers, Surat, 171–72
Capellasi, Andrea, 420
Capello, Antonio, 422
Cape Matapan, 419
Cape Musandum, 150, 269, 270, 284
Capo Bianco, 412, 413
Capo S. Sidero, 413
Capuchins, 5, 18; Aleppo, 70, 348; Bagh-
  dad, 6, 24, 117–18, 120–22, 124–25,
  394–95; Cyprus, 40, 41; Diyarbakır, 93–
  94, 97; India, 83; Isfahan, 9–10, 19, 311,
  326, 331, 347–48, 361; Nineveh, 112, 113;
  Surat/Father Ambrose, 176, 186, 187, 189,
  191; Tripoli, 43. *See also* du Mans, Father
  Raphaël
carachers, 110, 425. *See also* thieves
caravan, traveling by, 11–12, 86–87, 92,
  289, 362–68, 385–94
caravanserais, 20, 25, 171; Birecik, 89–90;
  Diyarbakır, 98; Isfahan, 11, 330; *khan*
  compared, 391; Maidast, 29, 32, 385–86,
  385*fig;* Messaterà, 93; Missian, 29, 30,
  365*fig,* 366; Persia to Baghdad, 290–99,
  306–8, 318–21, 362–75, 385–86, 394;
  Qumisheh, 9, 320; Respè, 368, 369*fig*
Carmelites, 5, 6, 9, 19; Father Celso, 305;
  Father Felice, 301; Father Feliciano, 305;
  Father Giacomo, 26; Father Girolamo

of Jesus Maria, 300–301; India, 6, 83;
  Isfahan, 9–10, 19, 26, 300n, 324–26,
  327, 360; Kong, 22, 289; Shiraz, 300–
  301, 306. *See also* Discalced Carmelites
Carnival, 59, 78, 266, 267, 417–18
Caron, Monsieur, 102–3
Carrara, Lorenzo, 410
Carré, Abbé, 103n, 401n, 402n, 411n
carriages, French-style, 187–88, 213–14
carrier pigeons, 81
carts, 167–69, 193–94, 201–4
cashew, 236
cassanairas, 258, 425
cassanar, 258, 426
Catherine of Braganza, 209, 216n
cats: Aleppo, 80; lions, 397; Tripoli, 43, 80
causin, 293, 426
çavuş, 47–48, 47n, 426
Celini, Giovanni Antonio, 419
Celotti, Abbé, 15–16
Cerigo, 38, 39*fig,* 418
cerna, 266–67, 426
Ceylon. *See* Sri Lanka
Chahar Cheshmah, 291
Chaldeans, 22, 96n; books, 249, 252, 254–
  55; language, 250, 407
chapar, 289, 291, 426
Chardin, Jean/John, 1, 10, 16, 26, 32;
  books, 10, 28, 325n; Grélot and, 10, 26,
  28, 30n, 35n, 325, 360–62; Hormuz,
  143n; illustrations, 10, 26, 28, 30n; Ira-
  nian glass making, 302n; Isfahan, 10, 26,
  325, 345–46; Shiraz gardens, 303n;
  weights and measures, 327n
Charles II, 209, 216n
Chaul, 156–58, 194, 199, 208–11, 218, 269;
  battle of, 155n; Franciscans, 195–96,
  208–9, 215
Chehel Minar, 307, 315
Chehel Sutun Palace, Isfahan, 335, 348n,
  349n, 350n, 351n
Chialtucsui (River Water), 92
Chiambar, 290
Chierèn, 387–88
China, 148, 268, 269
Chinese faces, 121
Chiti, 42

Darius, 359, 370; kings named Darius, 313n, 314; tombs of, 8, 312, 315n

Darius I: Bisitin rock relief, 11–12, 372n; founder of Persepolis, 298, 313n; Persepolis structures, 8, 307, 309*fig*, 311n, 312–16; tomb in Naqsh-i Rustam, 315n

Darius II, 315n

darugha, 339, 426

Darya Khan, 155

date palms, 136–37

Deccan, 204, 208, 224, 225, 233n

Deheq, 363–64

della Speranza, Father Francesco, 144

della Valle, Pietro, 1, 2, 7; 'Abbas I and, 327–28; Babylon, 118; Bembo source, 2, 14, 21, 118n; Cambay animal hospitals, 179; El-Mer, 401; Goa, 234; India choices, 6, 20; King's Plaza, 334; Kur river and Bendamir, 307; Melluha, 402n; Ogia, 319; Pelvaosuè, 315; Persepolis, 313; Persian sites not mentioned by, 372–73; *Viaggi*, 2, 3, 14; wife, 304–5

dervishes: Aleppo, 406–7; Baghdad, 117; Bembo staying with, 307, 315; guarding antiquities, 306; Isfahan clerics, 339; yogis like, 185

dever aga, 144, 426

Deyèmagarosi, 92

diamonds, 186–87, 233, 265, 269

Discalced Carmelites, 18, 36; Aleppo, 70, 219–20, 266; Basra, 133, 137; Father Anastasio, 301, 325; Father Angelo, 305, 325, 332; Father Aurelio, 305, 325; Father Celso, 219–20; Father Cornelio, 325; Father Feliciano of S. Rocco, 265, 271–72; Father Filippo, 356; Father Giovanni di S. Eliseo, 325; Father Giovanni Maria, 219–20; Father Martino, 325; Father Paolo di Jesus Maria of Genova, 325; Father Valerio, 36, 199, 219–20, 265, 266; Father Vladislao, 324; Goa, 219–20, 232, 239, 242–43, 265–66; Isfahan, 324–26, 360; Tripoli, 43

diseases, 32; Aleppo, 73; Bandar 'Abbas, 145, 147; *cerna*, 266–67, 426; cholera, 246–47; fevers, 46, 245–46, 331–32; Goa, 245–47; plague, 298n; prostitutes,

353; travelers visiting sick, 201, 296. *See also* medicine

Diu, 151–56, 158, 159n, 268, 269, 273

divorce, 80

Diyala River, 29, 127, 392–93, 393*fig*

Diyarbakır, 22, 93–103, 132, 341n

Doba, 269

dogs, Aleppo, 80

Dolfino, Giovanni, 422

Domgrim, 222

Dominicans, 18, 204–5; Bassein, 206; Daman, 160, 162, 194, 195; Father Antonio Velloso, 162, 196, 200, 201, 203, 209; Father Emmanuel of Santa Caterina, 207; Father Francesco Salema, 195; Father Giovanni of S. Michele, 204, 207; Goa, 232, 245; Mahim Quelme, 203–4; Tarapur, 202; Thane, 207

donkeys, 370–71

Dotti, Bartolomeo, 13

doves: kept by Turks, 80–81. *See also* pigeons

dragoman, 55n, 426

Drago Volante, 411, 418–19

dress and grooming: *aba*, 71, 331, 425; Aleppo, 57, 61–64, 62*fig*, 63*fig*, 64*fig*, 71, 78, 79, 403; Armenians of Isfahan, 357; Baghdad, 121; Bander, 142; Bembo, 12, 23, 29, 82, 85, 198, 290, 396, 421; Cyprus, 41, 42*fig*; Diyarbakır, 97; French styles, 162, 186, 233; *gibellini*, 63, 426; Goa, 233, 234; Grélot, 29; insults to, 64, 403; Jesuits, 71, 160; Persians, 299, 331, 344, 351–53, 352*fig*, 354, 359–60, 364; *qadi* in Aleppo, 57; Rustam sculptures, 316; Safavi soldiers, 344; shoes at mosque, 68; Surat, 172–75, 173*fig*, 186. *See also* men's dress and grooming; nudity; women's dress and grooming

Drusi (Druze), 43–44

du Mans, Father Raphaël, 19, 326; *Estat de la Perse en 1660*, 1–2, 10, 302n, 326n; Isfahan, 9–10, 326; Safavi history, 11; Shiraz glass, 302n

Dürer, Albrecht, 18, 31, 347n

Dutch, 17, 326; Aleppo, 50, 60; Anjidiv, 275; Basra, 136, 137; Cochin, 184, 261; French

Julfa, 327, 354–57; Armenians, 329, 330, 331, 345, 346, 349, 356–59
Junayd, Shaykh, 341
Justinus, Marcus Junianus, 352

kafir/cafro, 111, 164, 189, 211, 234, 304, 425
kalakgi, 103, 426
kalaks, 5, 103–17, 105*fig*, 398–99, 422, 426
kalantar, 356, 426
Kalutara, 268
Kanara, 221, 224, 234, 268, 269
Kangavar, 11, 368–70, 373
kanun, 39n, 426
Kapı, 50–52, 426
Karwar, 273, 277
Kassites, 122n, 396n
Kerbala, 22, 341n
Kermanshah, 376, 384, 389
Khalji, ʿAla al-Din, 223n
khan, 391, 426
Khan, Kamal, 228
Khan al-Gumruk, Aleppo, 60n
Khania, 415, 415*fig*
khanjar, 173–74, 174*fig*
Khawr Fakkan, 284
Khorasan, 351
Khusrau II, 375n, 376n, 377*fig*, 378n, 383
Kielle Minaret, 332–33
King's Plaza, Isfahan, 11, 334–37
Knights of Malta, 413
Kong, 7, 137n, 143–48, 215–16, 281, 286, 287–90, 298; Basra to, 6, 137, 138, 141–43, 422; baths, 24, 288; Carmelites, 22, 289; Portuguese, 20, 137n, 141, 143–44, 146–47, 287; travelers' expenses, 146, 285, 287, 288–89; wine, 8, 146–47, 302
kos, 171n, 426
Kurban Bayramı, 364, 404–5
Kurds, 94n; Cizre, 110; Diyarbakır, 94, 96; Iran, 362, 363, 364, 371, 374, 386, 387; Maraiana, 410; portable towns, 386; along Tigris journey, 106–9
Kuskh-i Zar, 320

La Bertecchia, M., 419
Lafoia river, 410
Lampicorno, 418

Langlès, M. A., 15–16
languages, 137; Arabic, 23, 102, 125, 313; Bembo studying, 23, 102; Bisitun, 372; Chaldean, 250, 407; Chardin's, 325; Goa, 227n; Grélot's, 27, 361; Kurd, 410; Persepolis, 313, 314*fig*; Persian, 23, 313, 347–48, 358, 359
Lannoy, Benjamin, 60n
Lar, 290n, 292–94, 300, 335
Larak, 269–70
Larnaca, 38, 39–40, 40*fig*
Layard, Sir Henry, 370n
Lazaretto Vecchio, 421
leagues, Dutch and Portuguese measures, 151
leather, 82, 269
Lebanon, Christians of, 43
Lent: Baghdad, 125, 127; Christians of St. Thomas, 260; Daman, 161; Goa, 220, 267–68; Indian fasts like, 181; on *St. Catherine*, 271, 278; Suda, 417
Libidia, 269
Limiso, 412, 413
lions, 397
Loe, Martin, 46
luigini/louis d'or, 97n
lunar eclipse, 103, 321

Macao, 268
Madonna d'Oliviera, 277, 278, 280, 281–82, 283, 286
Madonna of Remedy ship, 277
Madonna of Remedy temple, 204
Madras, 175, 207
Madura, 269
magic, 251, 259, 338. *See also* witchcraft
Magog, 169
Mahdi, 22, 368
Mahim, 158, 161, 203, 212, 273
Mahim Quelme, 203–4
Mahin, 317–19
mahmudi, 391, 393, 427
mahya, 403n, 427
Maidast, caravanserai, 29, 32, 385–86, 385*fig*
Malabar, 185n, 224, 247–61; Cananor, 229n, 268, 270; Christians of, 22, 223n,

money *(continued)*
  Christian communities' wealth, 7, 22, 23, 199, 207, 232, 243, 289, 327; elephant's worth, 191; Francesco da Venezia, 210–11; Goa imports, 269; Goa political figures, 244, 245; Isfahan prices, 330; marriage dowry, 79–80, 109, 184, 305; for pasha appointment, 55–56; for prayers, 67; rice as, 282; Sabaggio exploits, 224, 225; Shah Sulaiman, 339–40; Shiraz, 300; soldiers' pay, 153, 288; *waqf,* 407n, 428; winemaking permission, 72; wine prices, 302. *See also* coins; merchants; poverty; taxes; travel expenses
Monferé, Pierre, 296–97, 304
Monticelli, Ambrogio, 256
Mor, Captain, 274, 276, 280, 282, 283, 285, 287
Mora, Giovanni Battista, 422
Morelli, Iacopo, 14–15
Morosini, Girolamo, 422
Morosini family, 3, 4, 12, 33n, 34
mosques: Aleppo, 64–68, 67*fig,* 403; Baghdad, 120; Diyarbakır, 98, 99; Isfahan, 30, 338–39*fig,* 340*fig,* 342*fig;* jami', 30, 221n, 336n, 364n, 426; minarets, 64–67, 299, 332–33, 403; Shiraz, 299, 305; shoes, 68; Surat, 171
Mosul, 112n, 113–14, 132, 256
mourning, Portuguese customs, 287
mouz, 236, 427
Mozambique, 164n, 251, 256, 269
muassil, 54n, 427
mufti, 339, 427; Aleppo, 54, 57; Grand Mufti of Constantinople, 56, 57n
Mughal India, 27, 152–286; Ahmad Shahi dynasty, 152n, 156n, 159n; Bembo travel preparations, 5, 81–84; Delhi Sultanate, 20, 152, 154n; Emperor Akbar, 18, 20, 159n, 170n; Emperor Babur, 170n; Emperor Jahangir, 20, 170; Gujarat, 6, 152, 154n, 159n, 216n; religious communities, 6–7, 20, 22, 137n, 142n, 170n, 177, 192, 223, 299n; Seabra and, 22, 81–82, 83; Sind, 144n; Surat as most famous port in, 169. *See also* Goa; Great Mughal; Indians; Mumbai; Shivaji; Surat

Muhammad. *See* Islam; Prophet Muhammad
Muhammad II, 226n
Muhammad Shah III, Sultan, 225n
muhassil, Aleppo, 54, 57, 70, 407
mukarin, 82, 427
al-Mukha, 279
mules: chair on wheels with, 412; *mukarin,* 82n, 427; traveling with, 47, 86, 289, 305, 317–19
Mulla, 244, 246, 266
Mullasarai, 91
Mumbai, 7, 207–9, 211–18; English East India Company, 7, 17, 25, 209n, 211–18; Portuguese, 7, 157n, 158, 208, 212, 214, 216n, 217
Murad II, 226n
Murad IV, Sultan, 122n, 406
mural paintings, Isfahan, 349
Murat River, 88n
Murat Sui, 397
Murtaza 'Ali, 370
Musandam Peninsula, 150n, 284n
Muscat, 136, 143, 150n, 269, 282–83; Arabs of, 263, 270, 280–83
musk, 269
Muslims. *See* Islamic communities
müsellim, 54, 76, 427
Mussulapan, 269
Mustawfi, 398n, 399n

nabob, Surat, 172
Najaf, 367–68; 'Ali's tomb, 22, 340, 341n, 367
nakatkhuda, 283, 427
Naqsh-i Rustam, 9, 315–16
Narasimha, King, 247n
Nasr al-Din, Shah, 223–24
Navager, Bernardo, 419
Navarino, 419
navilii, 143, 427
navy: Venice, 4, 17, 34. *See also* boats/ships
Nealco, 370–71
Negapatam, 268, 270
Negombo, 268
Negri, Giacomo, 421
Neirab, 401n

tombs. *See* burials
Tower of Skulls, Isfahan, 332–33, 333*fig*
traghetti, 88, 428
transmigration of souls, belief in, 177,
178–80
travel expenses, 32, 422–24; Ana, 400, 423;
Baghdad, 394, 395, 423; Baghdad to
Basra, 125, 126–27, 130, 131, 422; Basra
to Kong, 137, 141, 422; Birecik, 89, 422;
Caffaro, 410; carts, 167, 201, 422; Cizre,
110, 422; Dahanu, 201; Diyarbakır to
Baghdad on *kalak*, 107, 114, 422; Fergu,
397; ferry over Diyala River, 393, 423;
Gary loan, 214; Goa, 83, 220, 242, 265–
66, 273, 423; guide (Hajji Osman), 395;
Hasankeyf, 107, 422; Hit, 398, 423; India
trip preparations, 5, 81–84; Isfahan departure, 346, 361; janissary on way to Baghdad, 367, 384; Khans paying expenses of
Europeans, 311; Kong, 146, 285, 287, 288–
89; Lar, 296; Mahin, 318; Mahyar, 321;
Maraiana, 410; money changing, 186, 265,
337, 424; Mosul, 114, 422; Mullasarai, 91,
422; Ogia, 319; in Ottoman vs. Persian
territory, 391; for *palanquins*, 163–64, 422,
423; river of Daman, 194; Scuerech, 92;
Surat, 186; Taiba, 401, 423; Velloso loan,
196. *See also* customs
Trincomalee, 187, 268
Tripoli, 5, 43–44, 62, 80, 236
Turcomans, 77
Turks, 23, 166; Aleppo, 46, 49, 52, 53, 57,
61–73, 77–82; Aq Quyunlu, 341n, 344n;
Baghdad, 121, 123–24, 393–94; Basra, 6;
burials, 71, 168, 189; and Capuchins, 112,
121, 124; Cyprus, 38, 41–42, 414; Diu,
154; Diyarbakır, 93, 97, 99, 102, 103;
dress, 57, 63–64, 79, 299, 351; eating
habits, 42, 73, 109, 111, 398; five curious
things, 61; food and wine prohibitions,
42, 44, 72, 82, 111; Hit, 398; insults by,
64, 79, 97, 102, 390–94; Isfahan, 329;
Iskenderun, 45; language, 313; Mandali,
391; Nineveh, 112, 113; Paliocastro, 414;
Persians hated by, 390; ruins destroyed
by, 41, 401; Sumbar, 389; Tabriz road,
348; and thieves along route, 86, 107,

108; traveling companions, 86, 88, 92–
93, 104–11, 117, 127, 130, 140, 396;
Tripoli, 43; year's length, 404. *See also*
dervishes; Ottoman Empire
turmeric, Goa, 239

'ulema, 57, 63–64, 428
'Umar, 340
University of Minnesota, James Ford Bell
Library, 16
Urfa, 90
Urum al-Sughra, 409
Usùbassi, 367
'Uthman, 341
Al-'Uzayr, 130
Uzun Hasan, 341, 344

Valerian, 315n
Velloso, Father Antonio, 162, 196, 200,
201, 203, 209
Vendramino, Vicenzo, 417
Venetian consuls, Aleppo, 46–50, 49*fig*, 59–
60, 67, 69; Marco Bembo, 3, 5, 12, 34,
47–49, 81, 402; Foscari, 4, 327, 405–9
Venezia, Fra Giacomo da, 84, 295, 362;
Aleppo, 71; Baghdad, 395; Chaul, 195–
96, 215; Daman, 168; Goa, 220, 221, 266;
Isfahan, 331, 360; Mumbai, 215–16
Venezia, Francesco da, 210–11, 215–16
Venice, 16–18, 240n; Aleppo's importance,
36n; Armenians, 356, 357–59; *bailo*, 40n;
Bembo's birth, 3; Bembo's departure, 4,
36; Bembo's manuscript, 14; Bembo's
pride in, 25–26, 239n; Bembo's return,
3, 12, 27, 30, 127n, 303n, 348, 395, 421;
Bembo's travel souvenirs, 8, 164, 288,
293–94, 304, 345, 351, 395; Bembo villa,
ii*fig*, 14, 27, 29; campanile of San Marco,
333, 421; Catholic, 21; Cyprus, 36n, 40,
41–42; dress, 41, 160; Francesco da
Venezia, 210–11, 215–16; Gary, 209, 210,
211; glass making, 302; Grand Council,
4, 12, 34; Isfahan news of, 19, 327; Jews,
171; navy, 4, 17, 34; Ottoman Empire/
War of Candia and, 4, 16, 17–18, 33,
36n, 213, 216; Patton, 84; Peloponnesian
campaign, 4, 16, 33n; representation

abroad, 32, 34; ships on trip, 414, 415, 417, 420; shop displays, 77, 334; *traghetti,* 88, 428; Zante, 37n; *zecchino,* 89n. *See also* Bembo family; Cornaro family; della Valle, Pietro; Morosini family; Polo, Marco; Venetian consuls, Aleppo; Venezia, Fra Giacomo da
Verecundia, 198
Verga, 159
Vijayanagar, 224–25, 247–48, 253, 270
Villa Barapocrana, 201–2
Villa Devier, 200–201
Villa Malvà, 402
Virupaksha II, 225n
voyvoda, 83n, 428

waqf, 407n, 428
War of Candia, 4, 16, 33, 213, 216
washing practices: *cerna* cure, 266–67; Daman, 161, 164; Goa, 244; Shiraz ruins, 306. *See also* baths
water: Aleppo, 68–69, 86; Baghdad, 117, 125; Bandar 'Abbas, 144–45; Basra, 136; Bassein, 206; Diyarbakır, 98–99; Euphrates River, 88, 132, 397–98; filtering, 125; healing, 132; Henkam Island, 284; Lafoia river, 410; Nineveh, 112; Ra'se Dastakan, 284; Shiraz, 301; Shiraz ruins, 305–6; spring water, 244; Surat, 189; Turkish canal, 409. *See also* cisterns; washing practices
weapons. *See* arms
wedding: Persian, 353–54. *See also* marriage
White Bridge, 410
wine: aga getting drunk, 102; Armenian toasts, 396; Basra, 136; Daman, 161; French ships, 419; Isfahan, 328–29, 330; Islamic/Turkish prohibition on, 44, 72, 111, 330; Kong, 8, 146–47, 302; palm, 201n, 202; Shiraz, 302, 304
winemaking: Aleppo, 72–73; Basra, 136; Julfa, 330; Nineveh not allowing, 114
"the Wise Men's" fortress, 222
witchcraft, 180, 236, 251, 262, 263. *See also* magic
women: Aleppo, 61–62, 62*fig,* 63*fig,* 72, 78–79; Bander, 142; burning on hus-

band's ashes, 182–83; *cassanairas,* 258, 425; Daman, 197–98; Diyarbakır, 97; Goa, 198, 231, 234–36, 242; Indian prostitutes, 180, 184; Indian religious men and, 180–81; Isfahan public courtesans, 353; Jedeideh, 408; Jews, 79; Julfa visits, 358; Kurds, 109; Muslims, 80; nudity superstitions, 185; *palanquin* traveling, 163, 198; Persian travelers, 362; punishment for violating, 103; saints, 145; Shah Sulaiman's harem, 339–40; Socotra, 250–51; Surat, 174–75, 176. *See also* marriage; women's dress and grooming
women's dress and grooming: Aleppo, 61–62, 62*fig,* 63*fig,* 78, 79; Bedouin, 62; Diyarbakır, 97; Goa, 234; pants, 352; Persia, 351–53, 352*fig,* 359–60; raqiya, 61–62, 97, 427; Shiraz, 299; Surat, 174–75; Tripoli, 62
worms, from Bandar 'Abbas water, 145, 147
writing shops, Isfahan, 345

Xerxes, 310n, 315n

yam, 238
Ya'rubid dynasty, 282n
Yazd-i Khvast, 9
Yazidi, Diyarbakır, 96
year's length, 404
yellow fever, 46
Yemen, 150n, 250n, 279n. *See also* Arabia Felix
yogis, 185

Zaga, King, 254
zago, 48, 428
Zamorin, 248
Zanganeh, Shaykh Ali Khan, 371, 384n
Zangiabad, 315, 317
Zante, 37–38, 37*fig,* 412, 419
Zanzibar, 268
Zapatu pagoda, Goa, 181
Zarqan, 307
zecchini, 83, 89n, 97, 126, 293, 428
Zina festivities, 77–79, 428
zoo, Isfahan, 30–31, 346–47
Zoroastrians, 192n, 313n, 329n, 360n

TEXT:
11.25/13.5 Adobe Garamond

DISPLAY:
Historical-Fell Type & Adobe Garamond

COMPOSITOR:
BookMatters, Berkeley

CARTOGRAPHER:
Bill Nelson

INDEXER:
Barbara Roos

PRINTER AND BINDER:
Maple-Vail Manufacturing Group